ACCLAIM FOR SHANE READ'S TEXTBOOKS

Shane Read has tried over 100 trials to verdict and is a bestselling and multiple award-winning author who also teaches highly acclaimed litigation courses throughout the United States. *Turning Points at Trial* is an award-winning and bestselling textbook, and the bestselling *Winning at Deposition* won the highest award from the Association of Continuing Legal Education for a legal textbook. He is the only author to win this prestigious award twice.

In Read's latest textbook, *Winning at Cross-Examination*, he brings you innovative strategies and skills to use at your next deposition or trial.

WINNING AT CROSS-EXAMINATION

"As Shakespeare said, 'If you can't run with the big dogs, stay on the porch.' Not only does Read's *Winning at Cross-Examination* give you the tips you need to run with the pack, he gives you real life examples of cross-examinations by the big dogs."

—Dicky Grigg, Past President, International Academy of Trial Lawyers

"Shane Read has done it again. Building on his model of teaching through great examples, he as has assembled the perfect 'how to' guide."

—Tracy W. McCormack, Director of Advocacy,
The University of Texas School of Law

"*Winning at Cross-Examination* is so full of so many wonderful things that it is almost impossible to do justice to it with simple descriptions. It should be an indispensable resource for young, aspiring trial lawyers, but trial lawyers of any age or experience would do well to refer to it regularly to achieve more focused and meaningful cross-examinations."

—Lewis Sifford, Past President, American Board of Trial Advocates

In this brilliant analysis of spectacular trial successes, Shane Read persuasively focuses on the pivotal role of a unifying theme, a carefully crafted bottom-line message, rooted in virtue and woven creatively into a compelling story. From that indispensable foundation, the trail lawyer's entire house—particularly the all-important role of effective cross-examination—is built. No courtroom "house builder" of our time is more skilled than Mark Lanier, the living embodiment of the author's "how to" guidance, who repeatedly strides across the pages of this eminently readable, extraordinarily practical book.

—Ken Starr, Former U.S. Solicitor General

TURNING POINTS AT TRIAL

"Required reading for trial lawyers, but also exceptionally informative for anyone interested in legal proceedings."

—*Kirkus Reviews*

"*Turning Points at Trial* showcases the work of outstanding trial attorneys using a combination of description, commentary, and transcripts. Through this layered approach, the author has created a superb modeling exemplar and how-to resource for trial and appellate attorneys of all experience levels."

—*The Colorado Lawyer*

"In *Turning Points at Trial*, a chamber of trial advocacy secrets and strategies is revealed. Read's mastery of writing in the narrative softens the edges to these academic and complex topics through storytelling, illustrative cases, and transcript excerpts. Great trial attorneys are masterful oral storytellers. Read does the same here, just on paper."

—*The Texas Bar Journal*

"*Turning Points at Trial* is a keeper. . . . This book is like going to an advanced seminar on litigation and listening to a prominent lawyer giving a presentation on a particular subject."

—*The Wisconsin Lawyer*

WINNING AT DEPOSITION

Winner of the Association of Continuing Legal Education's highest honor for a legal textbook.

"The book is a triumph.... [I]t makes for gripping reading, made all the better by Read's focus on the missteps of the famous lawyers and litigants he studies."

— *The Vermont Bar Journal*

"No matter how many depositions you have taken or defended, or how good you think you are, Shane Read's *Winning at Deposition* is a must read. It is the most informative and entertaining 'how to do it' book for trial lawyers I can ever remember reading."

—Robert G. Begam, Past President,
Association of Trial Lawyers of America (ATLA)

"*Winning at Deposition* is a cutting-edge litigation masterpiece."

—Jean Hoefer Toal, Chief Justice, Supreme Court of South Carolina

WINNING AT PERSUASION FOR LAWYERS

"A comprehensive, empowering set of strategies for improving public speaking."

—*Kirkus Reviews* (a starred review)

ACCLAIM FOR SHANE READ'S TRIAL CONSULTING AND TRAINING COURSES

"If you follow Shane's advice, he can turn you into a great trial lawyer and ensure you pick the best jury."

—Lisa Blue, Past President, The National Trial Lawyers and American Association of Justice, and National Trial Lawyer Hall of Fame Inductee (2015)

"Shane brings a career of studious dissection of what works in trial and what doesn't. Learn from Shane and kick your game way up!"

—Mark Lanier, recognized internationally as one of the top trial attorneys in the United States

"Shane Read is an immensely skilled teacher and storyteller. This is one of the best CLE programs of all time."

—Stacey Thomas, Program Manager, Pennsylvania Bar Institute

WINNING AT CROSS-EXAMINATION

A Modern Approach for Depositions and Trials

SHANE READ

Printed in the United States of America.

Cover design by George Foster
Interior design by Kevin Mellen

Library of Congress Cataloging-in-Publication Data

Read, Shane
Winning at Cross-Examination: A Modern Approach for Depositions and Trials / Shane Read
p. cm.
ISBN: 978-0-9850271-3-1

1. Cross-Examination—United States. 1. Read, Shane. II. Title

KF8900.R43 2020

Discounts are available for bulk orders.
Westway Publishing
4516 Lovers Lane, Suite 182
Dallas, TX 75225
support@westwaypublishing.com
(888) 992-9782

Shane Read is available for training and continuing legal education programs for organizations and law firms. For more information, go to www.shaneread.com or contact him at shane@shaneread.com.

For Linda

ENHANCE YOUR JOURNEY AS YOU READ THIS BOOK

You can enhance your learning experience in two important ways as you read this book. First, watch the videos that are referenced in the book. You will find them immensely helpful in learning the principles discussed in the text. Second, sign up for Shane Read's free bi-monthly newsletter which contains Shane's latest ideas, tips from other thought leaders, and bonus material not contained in this book.

Access the videos and newsletter at: www.shaneread.com/newsletter.

SHANE READ'S TRIAL CONSULTING AND IN-HOUSE BOOT CAMPS

Shane Read is a nationally recognized expert who has helped thousands of attorneys throughout the USA and Europe transform their deposition, trial, and oral advocacy skills through his consultations, in-house training programs, and keynote speeches. For more information, go to www.shaneread.com.

CONTENTS

INTRODUCTION

The purpose of this book is to expose the greatest myths of cross-examination and teach the correct techniques in a very engaging way. If you walk into any courtroom today, you are likely to see lawyers conducting very boring, long, and ineffective cross-examinations. The same is true of cross-examinations at depositions.

Instead, you should never be ineffective—much less boring—on cross-examination. Your job is to captivate, educate, and motivate jurors to believe the truth of what you are asking the witness and to discredit the witness's answer if he doesn't answer the way you want. It is that simple.

If you have read any of my other textbooks, you know that I am a passionate believer that the best way to learn trial skills is through the examination of famous trials and great lawyers. I believe if you cannot watch a live trial, the next best thing you can do is study videos or transcripts that are from interesting trials. After all, it is a lot easier to remember a principle or technique if it is taught in the context of a memorable event from a trial that grabs your attention. As Benjamin Franklin said, "Tell me and I forget. Teach me and I remember. Involve me and I learn."

Consequently, I hope you will find that this book engages, enlightens, and entertains you. The book is divided into three parts. Part I, "The Techniques," focuses on basic and advanced skills. In this regard, it does something unusual. Most cross-examination textbooks don't discuss how to develop an effective case strategy but focus solely on the mechanics of cross, or they don't treat it with the great importance it deserves. Not any more. This book begins with the most important part of any cross-examination: developing a case strategy that contains a bottom-line message that ensures victory.

Part II, "The Masters," analyzes how highly accomplished lawyers conduct cross-examination. It will be a chance to take what you have learned in Part I and examine two lawyers who use these skills in their most interesting trials.

Part III, "Famous Trials," examines videos of cross-examinations from the O.J. Simpson and George Zimmerman trials. Those trials were selected because of the compelling facts that caused the nation to follow them intensely. In addition, the trials were broadcast on television, providing a unique opportunity for you to learn from videos of famous cross-examinations on the book's website, www.winningatcross.com.

In addition, Part III analyzes the cross-examinations from the Proposition 8 trial where the plaintiffs challenged California's Proposition 8, which banned gay marriages. The trial was so important that it was performed as a one night stage reading on Broadway. It was directed by Rob Reiner and had an all-star cast, including George Clooney and Brad Pitt. (You can view it at www.winningatcross.com.)

I also believe that less is more. Let's get right to it.

PART I

The Principles

Part I teaches how to develop a case strategy so that your cross-examinations have a purpose. You will also learn basic and advanced techniques of cross-examination. Finally, you will learn the special skills to cross-examine an expert witness. After completing Part I, you will be ready to cross-examine anyone. We will then look at master cross-examiners in Part II and cross-examinations from famous trials in Part III. Let's begin this fascinating journey. As Nietzsche said, "He who would learn to fly one day must first learn to stand and walk. . . ."

CHAPTER ONE

Develop a Winning Case Strategy

"If I had eight hours to chop down a tree, I'd spend the first six of them sharpening my axe." —Abraham Lincoln

Do you know what your most important case is really all about? That is, can you boil down all the facts into one simple sentence—what I will refer to as a "bottom-line message"—that explains to a judge or jury why you should win? Most lawyers do not do this because it takes a lot of effort, and they don't realize that having a bottom-line message significantly affects outcomes. Having a winning bottom-line message affects your strategy for everything from discovery to trial preparation to the trial itself. For our purposes here, the simple truth is that you cannot begin to effectively cross-examine a witness at a deposition or trial if you have not first made the effort to develop a bottom-line message that ensures victory. In this chapter, you will learn how to answer important questions that will teach you how to create a bottom-line message and build a winning case strategy every time.

1.1 THREE QUESTIONS YOU MUST ANSWER TO DEVELOP A CASE STRATEGY

Developing a case strategy is not difficult, but it takes discipline. There are only three questions you need to answer:

1) What is the law that governs your case?
2) What is your bottom-line message?
3) How are you going to tell your story?

1.2 KNOW THE LAW

First, you must know the law that governs your case. A bottom-line message is nothing if its claim or defense is not supported by the law.

CHAPTER ROAD MAP

- Study the jury instructions at the beginning of your case.
- Create a persuasive bottom-line message.
- Create a story, using descriptive words, that tells the good, the bad, and the ugly.

People suffer wrongs every day, but that does not mean there is always a viable lawsuit.

Surprisingly, while many attorneys have a "pretty good" idea of what the law is that governs their claims or defenses, they do not know with certainty the details, and failure to have this knowledge can often prove devastating to their case. For example, a plaintiff's attorney may file a lawsuit, take ten depositions, and send out and respond to voluminous discovery requests, only to find out that what he thought was a breach of contract by the defendant was not a "material breach" as defined by the case law and that he cannot survive a defense motion for summary judgment.

There are myriad reasons why lawyers don't know the law as well as they should when a case begins. One reason is procrastination; it is easier to start a case and worry about the details later. Another may be an eagerness to take a case, believe your client, and hope the law can be massaged to fit the facts of the case. Whatever the reason, the failure to know the precise law that governs a case is a common mistake lawyers make, whether the case is small or large.

Let's look at one of the most famous cases of this century, *State v. Zimmerman*, and see how important it is to know the law. (We will also examine *State v. Zimmerman* in other parts of this book.) The following are the important facts from the case.

On Sunday, February 26, 2012, seventeen-year-old Trayvon Martin and his father, Tracy Martin, were visiting Tracy Martin's girlfriend (Brandy Green) and her twelve-year-old son (Chad Joseph), who lived in a townhouse in a gated complex known as "The Retreat at Twin Lakes" in Sanford, Florida. Around 6:00 p.m., Trayvon left the home and walked to a 7-Eleven store to buy some Skittles candy and an Arizona fruit drink. On his way back to Green's home, George Zimmerman, a neighborhood watch captain at The Retreat, saw Trayvon and called the police non-emergency number to report that Trayvon looked suspicious.

Zimmerman explained to the operator that there had been several recent break-ins in his neighborhood and said "there's a real suspicious guy. . . . This guy looks like he's up to no good, or he's on drugs or something." The operator replied that the police were on the way. Zimmerman responded, "These assholes, they always get away." Later in the phone call, Zimmerman said under his breath, "Fucking punks." Meanwhile, Trayvon Martin was talking on his cell phone to his friend, Rachel Jeantel.

What happened next that evening was hotly contested at trial. Both sides agreed that before the police arrived, Zimmerman had shot one bullet from his licensed handgun into Trayvon's chest. Trayvon was pronounced dead at the scene.

When police interviewed Zimmerman at the scene, he told them that he shot Trayvon because Trayvon had thrown him to the ground, gotten on top of him, and started hitting him in the face while he was flat on his back on the sidewalk. At trial, the prosecution argued that Zimmerman was a "wanna-be cop" who profiled Trayvon because he was black, and then followed him and shot him because he was so frustrated with the numerous burglaries that had occurred in his neighborhood. The prosecution charged Zimmerman with second degree murder; Zimmerman claimed he acted in self-defense.

Given what we have learned so far, the prosecutors had to develop a bottom-line message that was supported by the law. We will see that the prosecutors—for whatever reason—did not know the law well enough.

At the beginning of a case, you should go to your jurisdiction's court website to find the "pattern jury instructions" (the model set of instructions) for your type of case. Most state and federal appellate courts have pattern jury instructions that apply to the most common civil and criminal trials. Trial courts routinely use these instructions to provide uniformity and because the appellate court has approved their use.

In deciding whether to prosecute Zimmerman and what crime to charge him with, the prosecutors chose second-degree murder. It has three requirements under Florida law: 1) a person is dead, 2) the death was caused by the criminal act of another, and 3) the unlawful killing was done by an act imminently dangerous to another and demonstrated a depraved mind without regard for human life. Unlike first degree murder, premeditation is not required.

Next, it would also be crucial for the prosecutors to know how the Florida court would define the third element of second degree murder: an act that is "imminently dangerous to another and demonstrating a depraved mind." That definition has several components, but the most relevant one is that the act "is done from ill will, hatred, spite or evil intent." So, the key for the prosecutors was to prove that Zimmerman killed out of ill will or hatred.

Finally, the prosecutors would need to know whether there could be any legal defense for Zimmerman's actions, even if they proved these elements of second degree murder. A possible defense to second-degree murder includes self-defense. A person is justified in using deadly force "if he reasonably believes that such force is necessary to prevent imminent death or great bodily harm to himself."

Once you know the precise legal requirements that you will need to meet to win at trial, that knowledge will guide your investigation and preparation. Later, we will see that the prosecution made a critical error in charging Zimmerman with second degree murder. There were simply not enough facts for the prosecution to support the legal requirement of acting with ill will or hatred to prove that Zimmerman committed second degree murder when he decided to kill Trayvon.

Tellingly, the prosecutor's first sentence in opening statement at the Zimmerman trial was, "Good morning, 'Fucking punks, these assholes, they always get away.'" This bottom-line message was built on the theory that Zimmerman said those words—as recorded on a call he made to a police dispatcher—a few minutes before the murder and that was the only evidence of Zimmerman's ill will and hatred, which was necessary to prove second degree murder. The prosecutor's bottom-line message failed because he did not have enough evidence to back it up. He should get credit for taking the time to develop one, but he spent his time creating the wrong one.

The prosecutor mentioned this bottom-line message several times in his opening statement and closing argument. It was a refrain he would reuse repeatedly and each time follow with different facts. For example, "Those were the words in that man's chest when he got out of his car armed with a fully loaded semi-automatic pistol to follow on foot Trayvon Benjamin Martin, who was walking home from a 7-Eleven armed with 23 ounces of Arizona-brand fruit juice and a small bag of Skittles candies." But as the *New York Times* observed, the prosecution had a difficult case that was "weak on evidence and long on outrage." While the outrage was well founded, the problem was that the prosecution had very little evidence other than this one statement to prove ill will and hatred. The evidence at trial supported Zimmerman's self-defense claim that he was flat on his back on the sidewalk, getting repeatedly hit by Trayvon Martin just before he pulled his gun. An officer who arrived on the scene said he believed Zimmerman's account, and a forensic expert testified that the gunshots were consistent with Martin straddling Zimmerman while Zimmerman was lying on his back as the shooting took place. There was additional evidence from a neighbor who saw Martin punching Zimmerman in a mixed martial arts style while straddling Zimmerman, and that Zimmerman was crying for help.

Also, in contrast to the prosecutor's bottom-line message, Zimmerman's recorded call to the police revealed that Zimmerman was very calm and not angry. Furthermore, there were photographs of Zimmerman's head showing abrasions and bumps on the back of his head and a bloody nose.

1.3 WHAT IS YOUR BOTTOM-LINE MESSAGE?

After you have determined the law that governs your case, you must develop its bottom-line message. I did not create the idea of a bottom-line message—I found it when I was studying President Dwight D. Eisenhower. The concept is perfect for trial lawyers. One day, President Eisenhower became very frustrated with his speechwriters, who were submitting drafts for the upcoming State of the

Union address. He called them into the Oval Office and told them to throw away their drafts, and that before they wrote another word, they had to fit the speech's bottom-line message on the inside flap of a matchbook cover (Fig. 1).

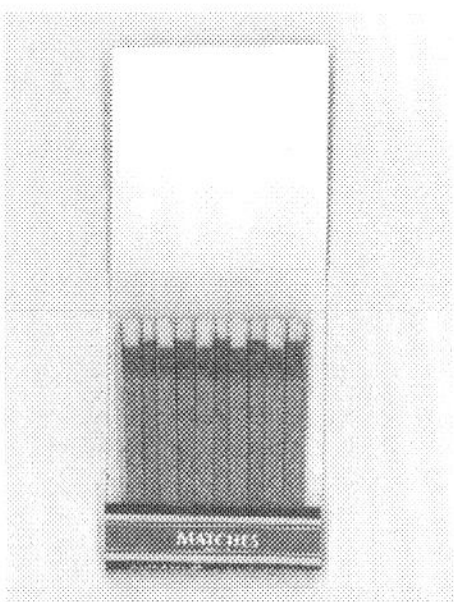

Figure 1. Inside flap of matchbook cover

Think of what that simple exercise teaches. Eisenhower knew that before writing a draft of a speech, contemplating its beginning and ending, or deciding on its order of topics, you must first decide what the message is. And then, not only must you decide on a message, but that message should be so clear and concise that you can write it on the inside flap of a matchbook cover. You can write about 12 words in this limited space. If President Eisenhower thought a bottom-line message was important enough to create in order to persuade the country with his State of the Union address, we should not be hesitant to try using one to persuade a jury in a courtroom. A modern take on this exercise is to fit your message into the original 140 character limit of a tweet.

Developing a bottom-line message long before deposition or trial forces you to focus on what is most important in developing your case. Your bottom-line message prevents you from following tempting rabbit trails that may be interesting but waste your resources, time, and energy. It also helps you to ask the right questions so that you get important information at deposition or trial. Without a clear bottom-line message, you may not realize what information is absolutely essential.

Almost every lawyer fails to find the bottom-line message for his or her case because our law schools and legal system teach us the wrong skills to accomplish this task. It is ironic, but law school is a terrible training ground for trial lawyers because it rewards students who focus on details at the expense of not rewarding those who focus on the main point. From the first day of law school, professors reward the highest grades to students who can spot the most issues in an exam question and write the longest answer with the most facts in it. In classroom discussions, the student who sees the complexities in a judicial ruling is rewarded instead of the student who clearly articulates the simple holding in the case.

After law school, the legal culture fosters even more emphasis on unnecessary details by encouraging lawyers to conduct vast amounts of discovery. Almost every lawsuit is now characterized by too many interrogatories, requests for production of documents, and depositions. All of this information overload makes it very easy to get lost in the trees and not see the forest.

If you correctly determine your bottom-line message, it does not matter what distractions you encounter or what obstacles the other side presents: you will always be on the right course.

> *It is the set of the sails, not the direction of the wind, that determines which way we will go.*
> —Jim Rohn, motivational speaker

As mentioned earlier, another reason why lawyers do not develop a bottom-line message is that it takes a lot of time to accomplish this task. Lawyers rationalize that it is hard to set aside the necessary time because there always seems to be more pressing matters. For example, at the beginning of a case, it is hard to focus on your bottom-line message because the trial is scheduled far off in the future. You are faced with what seem like more important deadlines: the need to send discovery to the opposing party, respond to discovery, and hand-hold your client through the beginnings of a lawsuit. Given these immediate problems, it is hard to get motivated to focus on the depositions and trial.

But these seemingly important pressing matters can undermine your case if you do not first set sail on the right course. Moreover, if you spend time at the beginning of a lawsuit determining your bottom-line message, you will be much more efficient in discovery because you will know the key legal issues and facts you must develop in order to win.

When lawyers tell me that they do not have enough time to focus on a bottom-line message because of other pressing matters, I respond, "You cannot afford not to." Whether you represent a plaintiff or defendant, it is the single most important task to accomplish. Let me repeat: there is nothing more important you can do to affect the outcome of the case. Even if your case does not go to trial, a bottom-line message will determine who wins on summary judgment or who can be the most persuasive at mediation or a settlement conference.

As we discuss actual cross-examinations throughout this book, you will see how incorrect bottom-line messages can have devastating consequences on the outcome of cases. Given its significance, you should develop your bottom-line message as soon as you get your case. It is safe to say that 99 percent of lawyers do not do this in the early stages of a case, and most never do it even when they get to trial.

All right, I already sense some resistance from you. Who has the time to spend brainstorming and developing a bottom-line message when you are overwhelmed with gathering all the information for an upcoming deposition or trial? Let me give you three examples at the outset to convince you to make the time, because it will affect the outcome of your case. The first example comes from U.S. history; the other two are from legendary trial lawyers.

Doris Kearns Goodwin's masterful biography of President Johnson revealed LBJ and his staff's failure to have a bottom-line message about the Vietnam War. Goodwin explains how LBJ would have lunch every Tuesday with leaders of his

Cabinet and national security advisors to plan the next steps for the Vietnam War. Goodwin faults LBJ for using these meetings as a tool for winning the war, because the attendees knew that LBJ wanted the meetings to focus on the operational rather than on strategic questions, and on logistics instead of structural considerations. For example, the meetings would discuss bombing targets, food rations, and new equipment that was available, but never once the nature of the war or its importance to national security. She wrote, "Someone once said as he watched Dean Rusk [Secretary of State] hurrying to the White House for a meeting of the Tuesday lunch, 'If you told him right now of a sure-fire way to defeat the Vietcong and to get out of Vietnam, he would groan that he was too busy to worry about that now; he had to discuss next week's bombing targets.'"

Trial lawyers need a bottom-line message to succeed too, as illustrated by Tom Girardi in our second example. Tom Girardi, a member of California's Trial Lawyer Hall of Fame, creates a bottom-line message for all his big cases, such as *Stow v. L.A. Dodgers*. In that case, Bryan Stow was a San Francisco Giants fan who was attending the opening day game at Dodger stadium while wearing a Giants jersey. He was brutally assaulted on the way to catch a taxi after the game as he walked through a Dodgers' parking lot that had no security. Girardi had the almost impossible task of suing the Dodgers in their hometown of Los Angeles and trying to find jurors who would rule against the beloved organization. But he learned through focus groups that while potential jurors loved the Dodgers and its current ownership, they did not like the former owner of the Dodgers, Frank McCourt, who was the owner when Stow was injured.

Girardi came up with his bottom-line message: "ABMD." That is, the Dodgers and their lawyers were going to blame the assault and lack of security on "Anyone But the McCourt Dodgers." Girardi wanted to constantly remind the jurors that he was suing the hated *McCourt* Dodgers. He also wanted to emphasize that the Dodgers were not going to take responsibility as they should. The bottom-line message helped Girardi provide a lens for the jurors to view the evidence in Stow's favor instead of the Dodgers'. For example, every time the Dodgers put on evidence that the Los Angeles Police Department, California Highway Patrol, or the FBI could have provided security, Girardi used his bottom-line message during the trial to show the jury that the McCourt Dodgers were shifting blame about the lack of security, instead of taking responsibility for the security they were legally responsible to provide. Developing that message was the key to winning the trial.

In our third example, Mark Lanier, a titan of the Plaintiffs' Bar, whom we will study in chapters 6–8, developed a winning bottom-line message that he had pared down as follows for the opening statement of his two-month trial, in which he represented plaintiffs who had defective hip replacement implants: "This is a case about six people who trusted a product, trusted a doctor, and got terrible results." Lanier then boldly told the jury, "I would be a fool to tell you these things if I couldn't prove them."

What makes Lanier's bottom-line message so powerful? First, it is succinct. Brevity speaks loudly. Second, it is memorable not only for the ideas it conveys, but also for its use of alliteration. Alliteration is where two or more adjacent or closely connected words in a sentence start with the same consonant or sound, which gives those words a certain ring and makes them easier to remember. Finally, Lanier uses the "Rule of Three," which will be discussed in more detail in chapter 3.

What Is the Human Value of the Bottom-Line Message?

For your bottom-line message to have any persuasive value, it has to stir the jurors' emotions. As we will discuss below, the best way to persuade an audience is through meaningful storytelling. For it to be meaningful, the audience has to care about what you are saying. It all begins with a bottom-line message that conveys a core human value. Lanier used "trust" as his human value, and Girardi used "blaming others" as his. Likewise, your bottom-line message and the story it is built on need to be important in order to motivate the jurors to vote for you and your side. Let's look at some sources for your bottom-line message that will inspire you to build your story and then develop the topics for your cross-examinations.

> *Think less about what you are doing and more about why you are doing it.*
> —Pharrell Williams

A great place to start is *The Book of Virtues* by William J. Bennett. Bennett's book is a collection of stories from the Bible, Greek mythology, American history, English poetry, and other sources that exemplify important character traits. Better yet, Bennett divides the stories in his book into ten traits that are essential to good character. Those traits are self-discipline, compassion, responsibility, friendship, work, courage, perseverance, honesty, loyalty, and faith. Do you have a breach of contract case that would be more interesting to the jury if you framed it around the human values of responsibility and honesty? If so, go to the specific chapter in Bennett's book and find a story that exemplifies that value, create a bottom-line message, and then expand on it for your opening statement and closing argument. By doing so, you can then ask questions on cross that tie into your bottom-line message.

On the other hand, you might want to characterize your opponent with the opposite of these good character traits. For example, your opponent in a breach of contract case may be irresponsible and dishonest. You can also frame your bottom-line message around your opponent's bad behavior using the seven deadly sins: wrath, greed, sloth, pride, lust, envy, and gluttony. Greed is an ugly trait that can describe many opponents' behavior.

Let's look at an example from a recent lawsuit involving a record $1.8 billion settlement agreement for insider trading. One of the top hedge fund companies in the country, SAC Capital Advisors (led by Steven Cohen, who is worth over $9 billion), settled criminal and civil charges of insider trading and agreed to unwind its business as an investment adviser. The FBI's special agent in charge, April Brooks, said, "Principles are just as important as profit. How your employees make their money is just as important as how much they make."

The special agent succinctly summarized her case with a perfect moral. She boiled down what she represented (principles) with what the defendant represented (profits). Her bottom-line message is effective because so few words are used. Her moral is also memorable because "principles" and "profits" is an alliteration, so there is a memorable ring to her word choice. If all else fails, any case can be boiled down to these purely moral terms that everyone understands: right versus wrong. Likewise, your cross-examinations should echo those themes.

Another source of inspiration is Aesop's fables. You have probably forgotten the details of these fables, but after each one, Aesop provides the moral of the story. What makes that helpful for the trial attorney is that you can skim through the morals at the bottom of each fable to find a moral that applies to your case. The website www.aesopfables.com has all the fables, as well as a table of contents that identifies the morals for each story. If the website is too overwhelming (there are 660 fables), go to www.read.gov/aesop001.html, which contains a selection of the more popular fables.

However, be forewarned that finding a moral that goes with an interesting fable can be challenging. For example, Aesop's *The Shipwrecked Impostor* has a good moral—"A liar deceives no one but himself"—that could apply to many cases, since almost every case involves a witness or party who is lying. But that fable tells the story of a dolphin who rescues a shipwrecked Chimpanzee, and its ending is not very interesting. On the other hand, many of us know *The Hare and the Tortoise*, but its moral of "slow but steady wins the race" has a more limited application to many legal disputes.

The Bottom-Line Message Cannot Be Bland

Many beginning lawyers will start their openings by saying, "This is a case about broken promises," or something to that effect. While such a tactic certainly frames the subject matter of the opening statement, it is not very creative. It would be similar to reading a headline on a website that said, "This is an article about the Yankees winning with their hitting." Instead, put some drama into it by writing something like, "Clutch Hit Shows Yankees' Grit."

> **Practice Tip**
>
> Capture the jury's attention. Instead of saying "This is a case about broken promises," declare that "The defendant promised gold and delivered mold."

Thelonious Monk, the great jazz pianist, once said that you should make your mistakes loud—don't hide them. The reason is that if you are cautious, you can never become great. Similarly, Steven Dietz, a playwright, said the most important thing he teaches students is "boldness. This is different from being 'interesting.' Boldness is action with purpose. I'd rather my students and their plays were strong and wrong than slight and right. Plays die of caution." Likewise, trials die from caution. Don't be boring. Juries will never reward you.

1.4 HOW ARE YOU GOING TO TELL YOUR STORY?

One of the biggest mistakes lawyers make is to overwhelm the jury with voluminous and boring information—a presentation method that is otherwise known as data dumping. The problem with the data dump is that it focuses the attention on the lawyer and all that the lawyer knows, instead of on the audience—jury or judge—and its needs.

The best way to convey information to a jury is with a story. Before you were able to read, your parents read you stories to entertain and convey information to you. As adults, we are informed and entertained by the news media, movies, books, and music predominantly through stories. So, we are most comfortable processing information when it is presented in the form of a story.

No less is true for jurors. They don't magically turn into robots that just compute data once they are in the jury box. A psychology study confirms this conclusion. The study revealed that "ease of story construction mediates perceptions of evidence strength, judgments of confidence, and the impact of information about witness credibility. . . .These results, combined with our previous research (Pennington & Hastie, 1988) support the claim that stories are the mediating mental structures that cause decisions in the juror's judgment task."

So, what is a story? Webster's dictionary defines a story as "an account of incidents or events." According to this definition, a story is nothing more than a recitation of facts. But your task as a trial lawyer is to meet a standard much higher than Webster's definition. You need to develop a meaningful story that will stir the jurors' emotions and motivate them to rule in your favor. A meaningful story relates a truth about an important human condition that captures the audience's attention and causes them to connect with your story. If your story does not make sense or does not connect with the emotions of jury, you will never persuade its members.

Professor Hannah B. Harvey is a professor in the storytelling program at East Tennessee State University and is an internationally recognized professional storyteller. She teaches that you need to answer the following questions in order to create your story. First, what happened? Second, what matters about what happened? That is, what truth does it convey? Third, think about all the characters in the story. Who are the main characters? What do they do? Explain how they relate to one another. Fourth, how can you, as narrator, link your audience to your story? Usually, the narrator sympathizes with the main character.

When answering these questions, make a list of all the important facts in your case. Put them in three columns: good facts, neutral facts, and bad facts. Analyze the bad facts and see if you can offer a legitimate explanation that could move them into the neutral category or good category. Mark Lanier, a master cross-examiner whom we will study in Part II, explained to me how he changes bad facts into good facts. Lanier tried several cases against Merck for selling a drug (Vioxx) that helped with pain but, if it was taken for too long, could cause heart failure. In the first Vioxx trial, Lanier won a national record-setting verdict representing plaintiff Bob Ernst, who was in excellent health when he died from taking Vioxx. But in another trial, Lanier represented John McDarby, who Lanier told me was "one pork chop away from a heart attack. He had every risk factor there was. He was very old, he was obese, he was diabetic, he had a family history, and he had high cholesterol." People asked Lanier how he could win with all those negatives. He replied, "I'm just going to turn them into positives."

He then demonstrated to me what he had explained to the jury at McDarby's trial:

> Look, we all live on a table or on flat land, but there's a table's edge or cliff, and that's the heart attack [Lanier points to the edge of a table in front of him]. It's the leading cause of death in America. Some of us live real close to the edge, and other people live far away. If you are a 17-year-old kid, you're far away from the edge, but as you get to be 75, you're closer. Male, closer; diabetic, closer; smoker, closer; and all of these things move you closer to the edge of the cliff. [As Lanier talks, he moves a Styrofoam cup, which represents the 17-year-old, from the center of the table closer and closer to its edge as he mentions the risk factors of "75, male, diabetic, and smoker," etc.]
>
> Now let me tell you about Vioxx. Vioxx is a shove toward the cliff. [Lanier pushes the cup that is now at the edge of the table and knocks it off.] If you're a 17-year-old guy—girl, it doesn't matter—you probably could take all the Vioxx you wanted. It's not going to bother you: You can take that

> stuff, you can take that shove, but you take someone who's right up against the edge of the cliff, and Vioxx is the last thing in the world that person needs to be taking. I'll prove that to you, and I'll prove that Mr. McDarby was right up at the edge of the cliff, and he had no business being on that drug.

Lanier's use of the cup and the table as a visual aid perfectly demonstrates how to turn bad facts into good facts. As hard as Merck argued that McDarby's heart attack was caused by his other risk factors, Merck could not overcome the powerful image of McDarby as the last person in the world who should have taken Vioxx, given how close to the edge he was.

After you have created your three columns of facts and answered the four questions above, create a storyboard. A storyboard is a series of pictures that explains your story. The first picture might explain what the conflict is. The second picture might show what happened; the third picture, how your opponent responded; the fourth picture, what happened to your client; and the fifth picture, why the story is important. A storyboard is important because it forces you to use the right side of your brain, its creative side, which responds to visual images.

You can create your storyboard on several pieces of paper or via a software program such as PowerPoint, Keynote (Mac users), or the online presentation service, Prezi. Whatever tool you use, the key to the storyboard is to create images. Even if you draw stick figures on paper, this process starts the important task of making your story come to life, and thus, it is much more powerful.

After you have created the storyboard, put the scenes in an order that is the most compelling for your story. How do the different scenes relate to one another? Does one scene propel action into another scene? Will your story be more powerful if you talk about a particular character first, or the ultimate conflict? It all depends on how you feel you can tell the most powerful story.

Begin with a Lightning Bolt

Although the creation of a winning opening statement is beyond the scope of this book, we need to briefly look at how a successful opening lays the groundwork for successful cross-examinations at trial. The one hard and fast rule for ordering the parts of your opening statement is that you must start strong. The first 30 seconds of your story are the most important and the hardest. Think of this first part of your opening statement as if it were a lightning bolt. Perhaps nothing is more dramatic and awe-inspiring in weather than a lightning bolt. It grabs everyone's attention. After seeing a lightning bolt, everyone waits to hear the thunder.

Sometimes, your bottom-line message will be the same as your lightning bolt. For instance, you may have an email or a statement from the other side in which they all but admit their wrongdoing, which not only sums up your case (your bottom-line message) but also becomes your best piece of evidence. Since it is your best piece of evidence, you should start out with it in your opening statement.

The first 30 seconds are important because that is when you have your best—and perhaps only—chance to grab your audience's attention. If you don't get it then, you will never get it. This principle is true whenever an audience is involved. News articles always lead with the attention-grabbing detail in order to entice the reader. Trailers for movies always start with an exciting scene. Musicians start their shows with one of their best songs. Art exhibitions put the most popular work of art on the brochure's cover.

Your story, which will become an opening statement, is no different. You must grab the jurors' attention and never let it go. The reason you cannot wait is that while every audience comes with an open mind, they quickly make snap judgments about you and your presentation. If you are bland and boring, the audience will quickly decide there are better ways to spend its time and will focus instead on something else.

People can't help but make these snap judgments. The reality and accuracy of snap judgments have received a lot of attention recently. Indeed, there is a new field of psychology that studies the part of our brain that makes these very quick judgments—and often accurate ones—using only minimal information. It is the study of the adaptive unconscious.

One psychologist conducted a study to measure the accuracy of students making snap judgments about a professor they did not know compared to the snap judgments of students who had taken a class with the professor for an entire semester. The study found that "a person watching a silent two-second video clip of a teacher he or she has never met will reach conclusions about how good that teacher is that are very similar to those of a student who has sat in the teacher's class for an entire semester." What is even more fascinating is that the students were watching a *silent* video clip. Other studies have shown that we start to make up our minds about other people within seven seconds of first meeting them.

To begin your opening, thank the jury sincerely for their sacrifice of serving on the jury. This creates an immediate connection between you and them. Then, start with your bottom-line message. Next, relate what your lightning bolt is, if it is different than your bottom-line message. Let's look at several ways you might start strong in an opening statement, which can be carried over to your themes in your cross-examinations.

1. Quote from Expected Witness Testimony

An excellent way to begin an opening is with an exact quote from your star witness's expected testimony. The quote should relate to an important part of the case. It needs to be dramatic, but you must be certain that the witness will testify exactly as you predict. You get this assurance from repeated witness preparation or knowing that the witness has made the statement previously in a deposition or a written document.

Likewise, you can capture the jury's attention by using a quote from a key witness for the opposing side that tears down their position and highlights the injustice of their position. When the devastating quote is from the opposing witness, you need to be certain that on cross-examination you can prove that the witness has made the statement in the past. Although lawyers are often fearful of boldly predicting testimony in opening statement, there is nothing to fear as long as the witness has made the statement prior to trial and you can prove it (i.e., through deposition testimony, e-mail, or written document).

2. Use a Dramatic Exhibit

Displaying an important trial exhibit such as a damaging admission in an email is a creative way to begin your opening. Oftentimes, the exhibits will be pre-admitted before the trial even starts by the agreement of counsel. Other times, you can argue to the judge that the exhibit will easily be admitted once the trial starts, so there is no harm in showing it.

Another tool to use is to create a persuasive aid such as a PowerPoint presentation. Such a presentation might display a picture of a road with signposts of the opposing side's mistakes to show the jury the journey you will embark on. Another idea is to show a photo of a jigsaw puzzle and explain to the jury that you are going to put the pieces of the puzzle together for the jury so that the picture on the puzzle is crystal clear.

3. Recite a Famous Quote

Consider starting your opening by using a famous quote that captures your bottom-line message. Quotations from famous people immediately create a bond between you and the jury. Everyone likes to be reminded of a quote on human behavior that captures their emotions. Even if the jury has not heard the quote before, it can grab their attention by ringing true to the human condition. There are several compilations of famous quotations available, including the excellent one on brainyquote.com's website. For a wealth of quotes that can be used at a trial, I am often drawn to those of Mark Twain.

4. Rely on a Familiar Saying

A familiar saying is a close cousin to a famous quote. While a quote is attributed to a famous person that gives it credibility (i.e., a quote from Mark Twain or Albert Einstein), a familiar saying is attributed to an anonymous source that has validity because it has survived the test of time. For example, "what goes around comes around" is not attributed to any particular person, but it is a saying that everyone has heard since childhood. Consider using the following when the defendant tries to absolve himself by pointing at others who should take responsibility: "When someone points a finger at someone else (gesture with your hand like a gun), there are three fingers always pointing right back." Finally, if you believe the prosecution's case is not thorough, you could argue that the prosecution rushed to judgment or that they were like a hunter with a gun who followed the sequence of "Ready, fire, aim!" instead of "Ready, aim, fire!"

5. Make a Comparison

A comparison can be a strong way to connect your case with something jurors are more familiar with. One type of comparison is an analogy. An analogy is a comparison that is made between two things to provide an explanation. For example, in a patent infringement case, which can be often quite technical and complicated, you could declare, "Like a student who looks over another student's shoulder and cheats on a test, Samsung stole Apple's ideas for its latest phone."

Metaphors and similes also draw comparisons. A metaphor makes comparisons by substituting one thing for another, while a simile makes specific use of the words "as" or "like." For example, a metaphor would be "Plaintiff's claim is a house of cards," and a simile would be "Plaintiff's claims are like a house of cards."

A comparison's importance is that it serves to create a strong image in the jurors' minds, capturing their attention and making them interested in what you have to say for the rest of your opening. The right image is extremely powerful, but if the image does not connect with the jurors, you will strike out and have little chance to recover. In the Apple and Samsung example, the image that Apple used could backfire if the facts do not support Apple. Samsung could respond in its opening, "Apple claims Samsung cheated. The exact opposite is true. Like the student taking the test, why would anyone try and get answers from someone who was failing the test. Samsung was the smartest one in the class. . . ."

Examples of Lightning Bolts from Speeches and Literature

Here are just a few famous and not-so-famous—but very effective—lightning bolts.

The human head is of the same approximate size and weight as a roaster chicken. I have never before had occasion to make the comparison, for never be-

Practice Tip

Hone your skill to create a lightning bolt by collecting articles that start strongly or very badly.

fore today have I seen a head in a roasting pan. . . . The heads have been put in roasting pans—which are of the disposable aluminum variety—for the same reason chickens are put in roasting pans: to catch the drippings. Surgery, even surgery upon the dead, is a tidy, orderly affair.

—*Stiff: The Curious Lives of Human Cadavers.* Mary Roach (Norton 2004)

In the normal course of events, Presidents come to this chamber to report on the state of the Union. Tonight, no such report is needed. It has already been delivered by the American people. . . . My fellow citizens, for the last nine days, the entire world has seen for itself the state of our Union—and it is strong.

—Address to Joint Session of Congress, President George W. Bush. September 20, 2001.

Mr. President, when the mariner has been tossed for many days, in thick weather, and on an unknown sea, he naturally avails himself of the first pause in the storm, the earliest glance of the sun, to take his latitude and ascertain how far the elements have driven him from his true course. Let us imitate this prudence, and, before we float farther on the waves of this debate, refer to the point from which we departed, that we may at least be able to conjecture where we now are. I ask for the reading of the resolution before the Senate.

—Second Reply to Senator Hayne, Daniel Webster[1]

I speak to you for the first time as Prime Minister in a solemn hour for the life of our country, of our Empire, of our allies, and, above all, for the cause of freedom.

—Address to British Parliament, Winston Churchill, May 1940.

If you really want to hear about it, the first thing you'll probably want to know is where I was born, and what my lousy childhood was like, and how my parents were occupied and all before they had me, and all that David Copperfield kind of crap, but I don't feel like going into it, if you want to know the truth. In the first place, that stuff bores me, and in the second place, my parents would have about two hemorrhages apiece if I told anything pretty personal about them. They're quite touchy about anything like that, especially my father.

—*The Catcher in the Rye*, J.D. Salinger.

Use Descriptive Language

Use descriptive language to make your story more meaningful. Let's take a lesson from a master. Billy Collins was the U.S. Poet Laureate (the nation's official poet) from 2001 to 2003 and winner of the Mark Twain Prize for humor in poetry. He has won nearly every imaginable honor for poetry. He believes that imagery is crucial for making big ideas understandable. One of his most famous poems is "The Lanyard." (See Collins Clip One at www.winningatcross.com.) He uses the image of a lanyard that he made at summer camp to illustrate how his mother's unselfish love for him contrasts with his inability to appreciate its magnitude. It is well worth spending a few minutes to watch Collins's live reading of the poem on the book's website. Below is an excerpt.[2] Pay attention to the descriptive language that makes the images come alive.

> The other day I was ricocheting slowly
> off the blue walls of this room,
> moving as if underwater from typewriter to piano,
> from bookshelf to an envelope lying on the floor,
> when I found myself in the L section of the dictionary
> where my eyes fell upon the word lanyard.
>
> No cookie nibbled by a French novelist
> could send one into the past more suddenly—
> a past where I sat at a workbench at a camp
> by a deep Adirondack lake
> learning how to braid long thin plastic strips
> into a lanyard, a gift for my mother. . . .

There are no wasted words here. The rich descriptions draw the reader in, much more so than if he had told a simple story that just related the facts. Instead of describing himself as a writer just sitting in a room when he suddenly remembers being at camp when he was younger, he is instead "ricocheting slowly off the blue walls of this room, moving as if underwater from typewriter to piano" when he remembers sitting "at a workbench at a camp by a deep Adirondack lake."

So, when you are developing your story, use all the tools great writers rely on: metaphors, similes, descriptive words, and sensory images. Your goal is to awaken the senses of the jury, and the more senses that you can involve, the more connected the jury will be to the story—and to you.

Make your characters three-dimensional, not just two-dimensional. If you represent a company, the manager has more than a name and a title. Describe the manager's personality. What was the manager's tone of voice? Did the manager have a common saying that people knew him or her by?

> *The difference between the almost right word and the right word is really a large matter—it's the difference between the lightning bug and the lightning.*
>
> —Mark Twain

Use images and descriptive words in your story so that jurors can see, touch, taste, hear, and even smell what is going on in each scene. For example, don't say the plaintiff was taken to the emergency room, but instead that the plaintiff was "rushed to the emergency room in an ambulance. Strapped tightly to the gurney, the plaintiff could hear the wailing sirens outside and the life support monitors beeping inside."

> *When poets write about a large topic, they use imagery as a point of entry.*
> —Billy Collins, former U.S. Poet Laureate

Mark Lanier, during the trial we are going to study in chapter 6, told his story about Johnson & Johnson's allegedly defective hip implant in just this way. He explained to the jury that the devastation from Hurricane Harvey in his hometown, Houston, caused him to think about home inspections. He told the jurors to consider themselves to be like home inspectors—that their job was to examine the house that Johnson & Johnson had built and that his job was to show them everything they needed to file a report. He then began his story by describing the bad foundation that Johnson & Johnson's house was built on, in terms of the design, marketing, and sale of its metal-on-metal hip implant.

Be Skeptical of Your Client's Story

When you create your story, avoid the big mistake of buying into your client's story hook, line, and sinker. It is not that clients always lie, but it is certainly true that they are often mistaken about details and frequently exaggerate the wrong that the other side committed. More important, clients are almost always in denial to some extent about their own wrongdoing. Clients typically will claim that they have done nothing wrong when facts later prove otherwise. You need to learn every important fact about your case as soon as possible so you can develop a theory and theme for the case that will ring true to the jury.

Almost everyone has an agenda that affects how truthful he or she will be. For example, in an ideal world, the most respected judges in the country—those on the Supreme Court—would be counted on to be 100 percent forthcoming and honest. However, even these judges have been documented to be less than straightforward when it served their agenda. A recent study found that nominees to the Supreme Court answer only "between 60 and 70 percent of their questions [at their confirmation hearings] in a fully forthcoming manner."

Determine Your Opponent's Story

Equally as important as determining your bottom-line message and story is your discerning what your opponent's bottom-line message and story are. It is very rare that an attorney takes the time to determine how their opponent is going to try and win their case. As explained in the earlier section, one reason for this failure is that attorneys and their clients are in denial about the bad facts in the case. It is ingrained in every client's DNA. By the time a lawsuit is filed, both sides are very self-righteous.

But the attorney who can find out what the truth is has a distinct advantage, because that is what will be revealed at trial. You must be objective enough to see the weaknesses in your case, or your witnesses will be surprised at the deposition and then the trial, when asked about bad facts that you have not recognized. When you uncover your opponent's theory, you can prepare your witnesses for the hard questions they will be asked.

The best way to make sure your bottom-line message is solid is to prepare a closing argument as if you were the opposing counsel. By assuming the role of your opponent, you will see facts in a whole new light. Facts that you previously thought were helpful will become neutralized, and facts that hurt your case will become magnified. The reason is that when you start arguing the other side of your case, you will naturally give facts a different context and a different meaning. Once you draft your opponent's closing, you will see more clearly the weaknesses in your case and be able to take corrective action by finding evidence to bolster those weaknesses.

The hardest thing about this exercise is forcing yourself to do it early in your case. But it bears repeating because it is so important. Set aside a few hours of uninterrupted time one morning early in the case. Prepare a mock closing for the other side. It obviously does not have to be perfectly organized. Practice delivering it with emotion. Really get into it with some passion. Again, your delivery does not need to be perfect. After doing this exercise, I guarantee that you will see weaknesses you had not seen before.

> **Practice Tip**
>
> For every hour you spend preparing your case, spend 20 minutes looking for its weaknesses as if you represented your opponent.

1.5 CREATE A TRIAL PLAYBOOK

After determining the law, creating a bottom-line message, and deciding how you are going to tell your story, make a "trial playbook" that will govern your case. The trial playbook should not be more than one page. Less is more. This trial guide should contain only the most important facts, themes, and so on of the case and nothing more.

Keep the trial playbook with you at all times. If you do not keep it on your iPad or laptop, put it in a three-ring binder and put two other sections behind it. One section will have a one- or two-paragraph summary of the key witnesses in the case. The other section will have the key documents in the case. The following table shows what the trial playbook should look like.

TRIAL PLAYBOOK	
A. Bottom-line message	A. Opponent's bottom-line message
B. Your lightning bolt (attention grabber)	B. Opponent's lightning bolt
C. Most important facts 1. 2. 3. 4. 5. *Reference the source of each fact (i.e., does it come from a witness or a document?)	C. Most important facts 1. 2. 3. 4. 5.
D. Most important exhibits (limit 5)	D. Most important exhibits (limit 5)
E. Legal elements of claims/defenses	E. Legal elements of claims/defenses

Now you know how to develop a winning case strategy. In chapter 2, we will turn our focus to learning the techniques for conducting a successful cross-examination.

1.6 CHAPTER CHECKLIST

1. Two main complaints of jurors are "Why did the trial take so long?" and "Why do lawyers repeat everything—do the lawyers really think we are that dumb?"
2. To win at trial, you must answer three questions: 1) What is the law?; 2) What is your bottom-line message?; and 3) How are you going to tell your story?
3. Most lawyers only have a pretty good idea of what the law is that governs their case instead of the precise legal requirements necessary to win.
4. Your explanation for why you should win at a trial—your bottom-line message—must fit on the inside of a matchbook cover. Remember Tom Girardi's

bottom-line message? He predicted the defendant would assert the "ABMD" defense at trial: "Anyone But the McCourt Dodgers" was responsible for the brutal assault on the plaintiff.

5. For your bottom-line message to be persuasive, it must embody an important human value that captures the jury's interest.
6. Mark Lanier's bottom-line message: "This is a case about six people who trusted a product, trusted a doctor, and got terrible results."
7. Sources for human condition stories with ethical morals are *The Book of Virtues* and Aesop's fables.
8. Tell your story by using descriptive language, and remember that less is more.
9. A story answers four questions: 1) What happened?; 2) What matters about what happened?; 3) Who are the main characters and how do they relate to each other?; and 4) How can you link your audience to your story?
10. Make your characters three-dimensional, not just two-dimensional.
11. You need a lightning bolt to grab the jurors' attention. Sources include: quote from expected testimony, important piece of evidence, demonstrative exhibit, and famous quote.
12. Hone your skill to develop a good lightning bolt by noticing whether articles you read or TV shows that you watch capture your attention in the very beginning.
13. Mark Lanier linked the jurors to his story by telling them that they were home inspectors whose job was to examine the house that Johnson & Johnson had built and to file a report.
14. Be skeptical of your client's story. Don't get burned at trial by accepting your client's version at face value.
15. For every hour you spend preparing your case, spend 20 minutes looking for its weaknesses as if you represented your opponent.
16. Create a "trial playbook" that contains on one page your bottom-line message, your lightning bolt, and the most important facts, exhibits, and legal claims and defenses.

CHAPTER TWO

Essential Techniques of Cross-Examination

"More cross-examinations are suicidal than homicidal."

—*Emory R. Buckner*

2.1 Deposition v. Trial

When I teach at seminars, I start by asking the lawyers to raise their hands if they are definitely going to trial in the next twelve months. Almost no hands go up. But the truth is, anyone who has an upcoming *deposition* is, in a sense, going to trial, because depositions have replaced trials for determining the ultimate outcome of most cases.

For example, in contrast to a few decades ago when trials were common, studies now show that over 90 percent of all lawsuits are settled before trial. For those cases that settle, the deposition is very often *the* event that becomes the turning point. It is the time when you either get the opposing witness to collapse or your witness irreparably falters. Consequently, the deposition becomes the moment when one side realizes it cannot recover and the case needs to be settled. In short, for all intents and purposes, deposition testimony is trial testimony. A bad deposition can't be fixed, and it can ruin a case.

Despite the statistics, lawyers still do not treat their cross-examination of the witness at a deposition like they would at a trial. They spend little time learning what law is relevant to the matter or reviewing documents before questioning the witness. Whether it is procrastination, a lack of a sense of urgency, or a denial of statistics, attorneys mistakenly believe that they can get prepared and correct any mistakes made at the deposition by the time the trial arrives—an achievement that rarely happens.

CHAPTER ROAD MAP

- Learn why the conventional wisdom is wrong; instead of being subtle, be bold.
- Learn the keys to a successful outline and how to form your questions.
- Limit your cross to your three most important points.

Consequently, all the skills and strategies presented in this book for cross-examinations at trial apply equally to cross-examinations at deposition. The only caveat is if you think your case will likely go to trial. In that case, save your ammunition for court.

2.2 MOST CROSS-EXAMINATIONS ARE SUICIDAL AND NOT HOMICIDAL

Buckner's observation (quoted under this chapter's heading) is true for several reasons. First, attorneys have unrealistic expectations as to what a successful cross-examination should be. Perhaps because Hollywood has focused on cross-examinations as the turning points in a trial, the attorney's prowess in TV shows and movies has been exaggerated for dramatic effect. There is nothing more entertaining than watching a TV show or movie where a witness on the stand confesses to wrongdoing, even if that almost never happens in a real courtroom. Second, there is a lot of bad scholarly advice on how to conduct cross-examinations. Many attorneys who don't know better follow this advice and consequently think they have prepared a homicidal examination, when instead they have prepared what will become a suicidal examination.

The misconceptions that Hollywood promotes and the decades of incorrect teachings in textbooks and law schools have resulted in creating what I call the four myths of cross-examination. Before we learn how to cross-examine the correct way—whether in a deposition or at trial—we need to examine these myths and learn why they are not true.

2.3 FOUR MYTHS ABOUT CROSS-EXAMINATION

The first myth was created by Hollywood and made famous in the *Perry Mason* television shows (1957–1966) and then somewhat more recently in *Law & Order* (1990–2010) and classic movies such as *A Few Good Men* (1992). Hollywood has created an expectation among its viewers that a good lawyer will be able to get a witness to confess to wrongdoing on the witness stand. This expectation creates a needless fear in real attorneys who think they should be able to accomplish what actors can. Hollywood's portrayal of courtroom scenes could not be further from the truth.

Let's look at one example from *A Few Good Men*, when Jack Nicholson delivered one of the most famous lines in movie history. In that movie, Tom Cruise plays an inexperienced military defense attorney, Lt. Daniel Kaffee, who is representing two Marines (Dawson and Downey) who are charged with killing a fellow Marine (Santiago) at Guantanamo Bay Naval Base in Cuba.

The prosecution presented a simple case of murder that was based on the theory that Dawson and Downey assaulted Santiago and stuffed a rag in Santiago's mouth, which led to his suffocation, as revenge for Santiago reporting to authorities that Dawson had illegally fired his rifle at a Cuban guard. But one of the defendants' attorneys, Lt. Cdr. JoAnne Galloway (portrayed by actress Demi Moore) suspects it is more complicated than that.

The defense learned that Santiago was a complainer, a slacker, and that he sent a request for a transfer because he felt he was being ostracized for speaking out about problems at Guantanamo. In addition, Colonel Jessup (Jack Nicholson) is a very demanding base commander who did not like Santiago's complaints or his work ethic.

Galloway believes that Jessup issued a Code Red (an order to bully a marine who was not toeing the line) because he did not like Santiago's complaints. The Code Red had a tragic outcome when Santiago unexpectedly died from suffocation because of a respiratory condition he had.

The night before the trial resumes, Kaffee is discouraged (and drunk) as he discusses trial strategies with his co-counsel, Galloway and Lt. Sam Weinberg (Kevin Pollack). Galloway comes up with the idea to call Jessup to the stand and "end this thing" by proving that Jessup told Kendrick (Santiago's commanding officer) to order Dawson and Downey to carry out a Code Red on Santiago. When Kaffee incredulously asks Galloway how they can prove this, she replies, "You put him on the stand, and you get it from him!" Kaffee asks rhetorically how he can just put him on the stand and "get it from him" without any proof. Kaffee calls her "galactically stupid," and Galloway storms out of the apartment and into a rainstorm. Kaffee chases her and calls her name, but she doesn't turn around. Kaffee then screams, "I'm going to put Jessup on the stand." Galloway turns to face him to show her respect that he has finally come to his senses. In reality, it would be ridiculous, but on the screen, it is compelling drama.

This ridiculousness continues when there is another planning meeting the next day. Kaffee explains that now he thinks Jessup is dying to tell the court he ordered the Code Red because he doesn't like anyone, particularly, Kaffee, telling him how to run his base. Kaffee explains, "I am going to shake him, put him on the defensive, and lead him right where he is dying to go." Weinberg replies skeptically, "That's it. That's the plan? How are you going to do it?" Kaffee responds, "I have no idea." Again, if this were the real world, the movie would have stopped there and the credits would have begun to roll. Not so. Instead, Kaffee is next in a courtroom with the climax of the movie about to unfold.

Kaffee begins to execute his plan in which he does the unthinkable for a defense attorney in military courts—accuse a superior officer of lying without any proof to back it up. Despite the lack of proof, Kaffee's instincts tell him that the power of his questions will force Jessup to admit that he gave the Code Red. However, Kaffee knows that if he fails, he will be punished for falsely accusing a superior officer of a crime.

In this famous scene, Kaffee builds his cross-examination and then accuses Jessup of signing a phony transfer order for Santiago and doctoring the logbooks, and then he finally screams, "Did you order the Code Red?" Before Jessup responds, the court advises the witness that he does not need to answer the question. But only in Hollywood would a witness answer a question that incriminates himself despite a judge's warning. "I'll answer the question. You want answers?" Kaffee responds, "I want the truth." Then Jessup begins his famous soliloquy with, "You can't handle the truth," and ultimately confesses to ordering the Code Red.

The reality is, however, that the confessions we see in the movies and on TV almost never occur in the courtroom because a person's self-preservation instinct is so strong that it prevents him from confessing when he knows it will hurt him. Unfortunately, attorneys continue to conduct suicidal cross-examinations by trying to get the witness to confess when there is no legitimate hope of accomplishing this. As a result, the witness wins and the attorney loses.

Another myth is that the witness has the power to hurt you. At first glance, cross-examination *seems* difficult because the attorney does not know what the witness is going to say, so it would appear the witness has all the leverage. However, the reality is that you get to choose which topics to question the witness on and then which questions to ask. Think about what a shift of power that is. You are in control, not the witness. You can question the witness on topics that give you the leverage, not him. It has been said that 95 percent of getting the right answer is asking the right question. I would tweak that quote as follows: 100 percent of getting the right answer is asking the right question.

Nonetheless, attorneys are concerned that even if they ask the right questions, the witness will give an answer that is detrimental to the case. But it does not matter what the witness says; it only matters whether or not the witness will be believed. With an effective cross-examination, the witness will either not be believed or will give you the answer you want. Either way, you win.

Practice Tip

The most important principle of cross-examination is that it does not matter what the witness says—it only matters whether the witness will be believed.

The third myth is fostered by many attorneys, but its most influential promoters might be Irving Younger (discussed in the following section) and Thomas A. Mauet, the author of several editions of a law school textbook called *Trial Techniques*. Mauet instructs that you "ask only enough questions on cross-examination to establish the points you intend to make during your closing argument." Under this theory, "you avoid asking the last question that explicitly drives home your point. Instead, your cross will merely suggest the point. During the closing argument you will rhetorically pose that last question and answer it the way you want it answered, when the witness is not around to give you a bad answer."

He claims that this is the modern way to cross-examine a witness: prioritizing subtlety over a direct approach. The test to determine if you are being subtle is to decide on the point you want to make in closing argument and "make sure you don't ask it as a question during the cross-examination."

The problem with Mauet's advice is that it assumes that opposing counsel is not smart enough to ask the witness on redirect examination the ultimate question you have failed to ask on cross-examination (redirect examination occurs after cross-examination and gives the attorney who conducted the direct examination the chance to address topics raised on cross-examination).

Why would any competent opposing counsel remain silent—oblivious to your line of questioning—and not elicit the bad answer you have avoided on cross? Mauet's advice is a recipe for failure as soon as redirect begins.

Now, let's look at the fourth myth in the next section.

2.4 IRVING YOUNGER'S TEN COMMANDMENTS ARE WRONG

The fourth myth is that Irving Younger's Ten Commandments of Cross-Examination are gospel. Irving Younger had a distinguished career as a professor of trial techniques at Cornell Law School, attorney at a large New York law firm, and judge on the Civil, Criminal, and Supreme Courts of New York City. Before his death in 1988, he was also the author of books on evidence and trial advocacy. Part of his legacy includes an article he wrote for the American Bar Association, "The Art of Cross-Examination," in which he created the "Ten Commandments of Cross-Examination." Younger lectured around the country, and many law professors continue to teach his Ten Commandments of Cross-Examination without exploring whether they really make sense. YouTube has a collection of some of Younger's presentations on the Ten Commandments (see Younger clip one at www.winningatcross.com at chapter 2), and his influence continues, as evidenced by 225,000-plus views of the clip.

Younger was a strong believer in his commandments. He wrote, "I cannot tell you how powerfully I want to preach these Ten Commandments. You should never violate them; if you do, you will want the ground to open up beneath your feet, so that you will sink in and be devoured forever. Every time you violate these commandments, your case will blow up in your face. . . . They come from on high; they must be obeyed."

I disagree. If we revisit them, you will see that some should have never been included in his list and are flat-out wrong.

Below are Younger's Ten Commandments. I have highlighted in bold the ones that are wrong:

1. Be brief.
2. Use plain words.
3. **Use only leading questions.**

4. Be prepared.
5. Listen.
6. **Do not quarrel.**
7. Avoid repetition.
8. **Disallow witness explanation.**
9. **Limit questioning.**
10. **Save for summation.**

While some of Younger's commandments are very good (indeed, five of them), the ones that he got wrong are so incorrect that they undercut his whole list. In fact, if you follow his advice, your case will blow up in your face. Let's look at the bad commandments in the order of worst to least worst.

In number 10, Younger proclaims that "you should save the ultimate point for summation." This idea is similar to Mauet's, but Younger approaches the idea from a different angle. Mauet incorrectly argues that you should not ask the ultimate question on cross but make your point rhetorically in closing when the witness is no longer there to answer. As we just learned, such a strategy assumes that opposing counsel is so incompetent that he won't let the witness explain the answer to the ultimate question on redirect examination.

On the other hand, Younger argues that during your cross you should ask "the one question" that the jury will not understand why you asked—but you ask it anyway, because you know that you can explain it in closing argument. Your question will be so intriguing that the jury will think about it for the rest of the trial and wonder why you asked it; then you can give them the prize in your closing argument. Younger advises, "The temptation, however, is to explain it all on the cross-examination. How do you explain it? By asking the witness a question that permits the witness to explain. That will always be the one question too many, and the force of the impeachment will disappear. You must save it."

Younger then gives an example to support this commandment. He asks you to imagine that you are the prosecutor in the Watergate trial. Your task is to cross-examine John Mitchell (he was Nixon's Attorney General and then director of the Committee to Re-Elect the President), a defendant who has testified on direct examination for several days that he knew nothing about the criminal activities at the White House. To impeach him, Younger teaches that you should just ask one question: "John Mitchell, you were born, weren't you, on March 10, 1920?" When Mitchell answers, "Yes," you should stop and sit down.

Younger says, "Leave it that way. You must not explain it. The trial can go on for another six months, and the jury will think of nothing but your questions. In your closing argument, you ask, 'Do you remember my cross-examination of

John Mitchell? Do you remember the one question I asked him? Did you understand what I was driving at? Then let me tell you what I was driving at.' Now, you give them the whole story." Younger believes, with this technique, the jury would go into deliberations talking only about your one question during cross-examination and come back in 30 seconds with a conviction.

One problem with this commandment is that professors and teachers at continuing legal education (CLE) courses repeat it and other commandments without ever examining the foundations for them. If they had, they would have realized that Younger's example makes no sense. I suppose Younger's point is that Mitchell's claim not to know anything could not be true, since he at least admitted on cross to knowing the day he was born. But that is only my speculation, and Younger doesn't explain it in his article. Do you understand what Younger was trying to accomplish? If you hesitated, you can be certain that jurors who do not study cross-examinations like you are now would struggle to find the point in Younger's cross-examination.

Second, even if we did not examine the underlying reasoning for the commandment, the tenth commandment is wrong on its face. The admonition to "save it for summation" assumes that jurors are not human but rather data banks that you can just pour information into that will somehow sort out the important information from the unimportant. The jurors would certainly notice the attorney's one-question cross-examination because such a short cross-examination would be unusual in a trial, but they are not going to spend any time thinking about the "clever" question after you asked it. They are not going to be "intrigued" about it for the remainder of trial and wait excitedly for the prize you will give them in your explanation at closing argument.

Instead, jurors make up their minds quickly. Their conclusion would be that your cross did not make any sense.

In chapter 1, we learned that people can't help but make snap judgments. The reality and accuracy of snap judgments have received a lot of attention recently. Remember the study that found that "a person watching a silent two-second video clip of a teacher he or she has never met will reach very similar conclusions about how good that teacher is as those of students who have sat in the teacher's class for an entire semester."

In contrast to Younger's claim, jurors make snap judgments about the effectiveness of your cross-examination as soon as you conduct it. A cross-examination is a battle between your credibility and that of the witness. Jurors quickly decide who won. If the reason for your asking only one question is not abundantly clear to the jury

> **Practice Tip**
>
> Start strong. Studies have shown that people make up their minds about other people within seven seconds of first meeting them.

when you ask it on cross-examination, you are foolish to think they are going to remember—or care about—why you asked it and what your clever reasons were for asking it back then.

Younger proclaimed that if you did not follow his commandments, your cross-examination would "blow up in your face." I could not disagree more. If you follow commandment number 10, you will have failed completely. Never try to tie up the reasons for asking your questions on cross-examination in closing argument. Younger's tenth commandment should be replaced with, "Never save it for summation. Make your points on cross now." The jury is quickly deciding who won the battle of cross-examination, and you need to make clear who has won.

Younger's tenth commandment is so wrong but followed so often that it merits further analysis, especially for any attorneys who are not completely convinced by the above argument. Let's look at what one of the greatest civil attorneys in the country does on cross-examination. Mark Lanier, who I interviewed for *Turning Points at Trial*, is a legend in the courtroom. In 2015, *The National Trial Lawyers* named Mark Lanier the Trial Lawyer of the Year. In 2010, *The National Law Journal* declared that Mark Lanier was "one of the decade's most influential lawyers." His trial verdicts for plaintiffs have set records. For example, in a recent trial, he obtained for one family a $9 billion verdict (including punitive damages) against a pharmaceutical company.

Lanier ignores Younger's tenth commandment. But he doesn't just ignore it; he does the exact opposite of it, and he does it on all his cross-examinations. In a recent trial, he was suing Johnson & Johnson and DePuy on behalf of plaintiffs who had hip replacement surgeries with DePuy hip implants that allegedly were designed defectively.

Lanier was cross-examining the president of DePuy (see chapter 7). His cross-examination took an entire day. Do you think he snuck in some subtle questions hoping to wrap it all together in closing as Younger commands? No. Do you think he saved the ultimate question for closing to rhetorically ask the witness in closing as Mauet advises? No.

Instead, for the entire day, he had three themes. That's it. And just so it was crystal clear for the jury and the witness what the ultimate questions were and that he was not saving anything for closing, he wrote each theme on the top of a sheet of paper that he displayed on an ELMO (document projector) to the jury. Throughout the cross, he would return to the theme at the top of the page and remind the jury about what his main point was. Lanier's three themes were expressed by him as: 1) "I want the jury to hear from you how marketing/sales run the company, not science;" 2) the wording used in advertising DePuy hip implants provided confusion instead of clarity; and 3) Johnson & Johnson and

DePuy are companies that are intertwined (Johnson & Johnson was denying responsibility for what DePuy did).

> **Practice Tip**
>
> Your themes on cross should be so clear that if someone walked into the courtroom and knew nothing about your case, they would be able to easily follow and be convinced by the points you are making.

Now, let's examine Younger's ninth commandment, which is closely related to the tenth. Younger relates that the "ninth commandment is to avoid asking the one question too many." He recites a classic trial story to support his commandment. The case involves the prosecution of a defendant for assault. The defendant is accused of getting into a vicious brawl and biting off the victim's nose. The prosecution relies on a single eyewitness—other than the victim—who claims that the defendant committed the assault. Younger uses the following cross-examination to prove his point that you should not ask the "one question too many."

Q. *Where were the defendant and the victim when the fight broke out?*
A. In the middle of a field.

Q. *Where were you?*
A. On the edge of the field.

Q. *What were you doing?*
A. Bird watching.

Q. *Where were the trees?*
A. On the edge of the field.

Q. *Were you looking at the birds?*
A. Yes.

Q. *So your back was to the people fighting?*
A. Yes.

Younger instructs that after getting this helpful answer, "You stop and sit down. And what will you argue in the summation? He could not have seen it. His back was to them. You have challenged perception. Instead, you ask the one question too many:

> Question: 'Well, if your back was to them, how can you say that the defendant bit off the victim's nose?'
>
> And the answer: 'Well, I saw him spit it out.'

That is the kind of answer you will get every time you ask the one question too many."

While Younger's example is clever, funny, and memorable, it is not good. Before I tell you why, think for a moment, and ask yourself why this is a bad commandment and terrible example.

If you follow Younger's advice, imagine the scene if you had conducted the cross-examination as Younger teaches, emphatically ended your cross-examination where he instructs, and then walked back to your counsel table with a confident sense of accomplishment. Your credibility has been on the line, you think you have won, and you will now argue in your closing argument that your client should be acquitted because your debilitating cross-examination of the prosecution's star witness proves the eyewitness could not have seen the assault.

The reason Younger's commandment is wrong is that if you don't ask the last question, the prosecutor will on redirect examination. It is the same problem with Mauet's advice (discussed earlier) to save the ultimate question for your closing argument. Your momentary victory on cross-examination will be immediately taken away when the prosecution asks the "one question too many" that you so cleverly avoided asking. When the prosecutor does this, you will look like a fool, and the jury will be disappointed in you, not the prosecution.

The truth is that the example is flawed to begin with. Younger uses it with the assumption that all the prosecutor elicited from the witness on direct examination was that the witness saw the defendant bite the victim's nose off. But, the reality is that the prosecutor certainly would have elicited the dramatic fact that the witness also saw the defendant spit the victim's nose out of his mouth. Younger's example only works if the prosecutor did not know this last fact. But it is not possible that a witness during his interview prior to trial—even the very briefest one—would not tell the prosecutor about this memorable sight when relating what happened. This commandment should be changed to "Be the truth-teller in the courtroom."

Commandment eight should also be disregarded. It is closely related to number nine but states: "Disallow witness explanation." Younger declares that a "trial lawyer must never permit the witness to explain anything on cross-examination." While you should not ask a witness to explain his inconsistent answers because he will generally have an answer that helps his case, Younger's commandment is wrong because he intends something different.

The example Younger uses to support his eighth commandment shows how closely related the eighth commandment is to the ninth. Indeed, Younger even admitted "the number [of commandments] is really less than ten" but that ten "has a certain literary ring. . . ."

The example Younger uses does not prove his point, but instead undermines it completely. Younger sets forth a famous cross-examination Lincoln conducted.

Although Younger admits that Lincoln was a virtuoso, he uses the example to show where mere mortals should stop their cross-examination rather than continuing on as Lincoln did.

Long before Lincoln became President, in *People v. Armstrong*, he represented a defendant who was charged with first-degree murder. The prosecution's case relied on a single eyewitness who claimed to have seen Armstrong use an unloaded revolver to hit the victim repeatedly in the head until he died. Lincoln's cross-examination of the star witness was as follows:

Q. Did you actually see the fight?
A. Yes.

Q. And you stood near them?
A. No, it was about a 150 feet or more.

Q. In the open field?
A. No, in the timber.

Q. What kind of timber?
A. Beech.

Q. Leaves on it rather thick in August?
A. Yes.

Q. What time did all this occur?
A. Eleven o'clock at night.

Q. Did you have a candle?
A. No, what would I want a candle for?

Younger writes that unless you are a genius like Lincoln, you should "stop and sit down. The witness has been impeached. He could not have perceived the murder." By sitting down, you would be in compliance with the eighth commandment to "disallow witness explanation." As the example shows, the witness asks Lincoln why he would need a candle, and instead of responding, you abruptly stop and sit.

Let's assume you followed Younger's eighth amendment. Think about the consequences before you read the answers that follow.

First, are you being the truth-teller in the courtroom? No, in fact, you are not being forthright because the witness has asked a legitimate question and you have decided not to answer it and cut off any further exchange. Is that the impression you want to leave with the jury?

Second, on redirect examination, the prosecution is going to phrase a question this way:

Q. Let me start where Lincoln so abruptly stopped. Do you remember asking him why you would need a candle before he abruptly sat down?
A. Yes.

Q. Let me ask you the question he refused to. Is there a reason you did not need a candle?
A. Yes. I could see because there was a full moon.

Younger fails to take into account that the prosecutor is going to protect his witness on redirect. If the defense had made any headway on cross-examination that the prosecutor can correct, he will, particularly when the witness explicitly asks the defense attorney a question.

Third, Younger's example does not prove his point because the last two questions about the time of night and whether the witness had a candle to see by would only be successful if there had not been a bright moon. Consequently, if you could prove that there was no moonlight, you would not need to be a virtuoso like Lincoln to continue the cross-examination as he did. Here is the remainder of Lincoln's cross-examination, which almost any lawyer could have accomplished.

Q. How could you see from a distance of a 150 feet or more without a candle at eleven o'clock at night?
A. The moon was shining real bright.

Q. A full moon?
A. Yes, a full moon.

Lincoln then presented the witness with an almanac, and asked:

Q. Does the almanac not say that on August 29 [the night of the murder], the moon had disappeared; the moon was barely past the first quarter instead of being full?
A. [Witness does not answer.]

Q. Does not the almanac also say that the moon had disappeared by eleven o'clock?
A. [Witness does not answer.]

Q. Is it not a fact that it was too dark to see anything from 50 feet, let alone 150 feet?
A. [Again, witness does not answer.]

Lincoln did not ask any more questions and won the trial. Contrary to Younger's analysis, anyone could have conducted this cross-examination. It did not take any super human skill to impeach the witness with scientific proof that there was no moonlight at the time of the murder.

Lincoln's genius actually comes from the legend that Lincoln did not use a real almanac, but tricked the witness with a fake one that showed no moonlight. If that is true, Lincoln was either brilliant or lucky. If the prosecutor had a real almanac, he could use it on redirect examination to show that Lincoln had tried to trick the witness and the jury. If the prosecutor did not have an almanac, he could call a witness later in the trial who had time to review the almanac and determine that the moon was out.

Younger's sixth commandment, "Do not quarrel," would be correct if he meant "do not argue with the witness." But Younger means something different. He explains that if during your cross-examination you get an answer that is "contradictory, absurd, patently false, irrational, crazy, or lunatic," you should end your cross. Don't follow Younger's advice. Instead of sitting down, highlight the irrational answer for the jury.

Younger goes on to give an anecdote from the Nuremberg trials to allegedly prove his point that you should not argue. After World War II, some German officials were prosecuted for the war crimes that they had committed against the Jews. The Russian prosecutor kept arguing through his questions that the witness was a fascist beast. The witness denied being so each time he was asked. Younger criticized the Russian prosecutor for violating the sixth commandment by quarrelling with the witness. Younger said that such quarrelling must be avoided.

> **Practice Tip**
>
> Write down a witness's absurd answer so the jury can see it on an ELMO or easel. The time to win is now. Disregard Younger's advice, and instead make sure the witness and jury know why you are sitting down before you do so.

But there are many times that you should use cross-examination to argue your case to the jury, even though you know the witness will give negative answers to your questions. We will study how to do this later, but suffice it for now to say that if the defendant were to take the stand, there is nothing wrong with asking him several questions that are consistent with your closing argument—even though you know the witness will not answer yes.

Example

Q. You were at the intersection of Rheims and Preston Road at 11:00 p.m. on August 6?
A. No.

Q. You had a black gun in your right hand?
A. No.

Q. You approached Ms. Smith, pointed your gun at her, and demanded her purse?
A. No.

I am not going to reproduce the entire line of questioning here, but the point is that you are arguing the facts of your case for two reasons. First, you want to remind the jury of the facts. Second, you want the jury to contrast the truth of your questions with the lies of the defendant's answers. If you have credibility with the jury, each of the witness's denials will be a further nail in his coffin.

Finally, in his third commandment, Younger sets forth that you should "use only leading questions." He adds that "you should never ask anything but leading questions on cross-examination." Such an admonition makes for a boring cross-examination and can undermine it. Wouldn't it be better if the commandment read, "Only ask leading questions unless the answer to a non-leading question cannot hurt you"? This principle is discussed more fully in Section 2.9 and its example of O.J. Simpson explaining what he meant when he answered, "Not so physical." But for now, know that it is perfectly fine to ask the witness to explain something if you know that whatever the explanation will be, the answer will not hurt the point you are trying to make on cross-examination.

Now that we have looked at the four greatest myths of cross-examination, let's examine some principles that will work every time.

2.5 HOW TO CHOOSE YOUR TOPICS FOR CROSS

Many attorneys find that direct examination is the most difficult part of the trial because they are trying to have a conversation with a witness who, like most people, is probably scared to death to speak in public and, unlike in a normal conversation, is prohibited by the rules from asking them questions.

On the other hand, there are legal treatises that make cross-examination so complicated and scary that one can't imagine ever even attempting one. But it is really not that hard. The first step to conducting a successful cross is choosing your topics. An easy acronym to remember to help you select the right topics is "CROSS." If you will learn what this acronym stands for and use it, you will be guaranteed success the next time you conduct a cross-examination.

The "C" in CROSS stands for *credibility*. Almost any witness can be cross-examined on his credibility. The reason for this is that most witnesses at a trial are associated in one way or another with one side in the trial. Ask yourself if the witness has a reason to favor one side or the other. For example, if you are cross-examining a defense witness, the witness may be an employee of the defendant company and his livelihood depends on the defendant's success. Or the witness may be a colleague who is a friend of the defendant who is accused of wrongdoing. A party that calls a family member to testify presents an obvious target for a credibility attack on cross-examination. So, ask yourself if the witness has a financial or emotional relationship with the side for which he is testifying.

In addition to bias or favoritism toward one side, another credibility attack concerns the witness's trustworthiness. Is there a way to attack a witness's truthfulness? Shortly, we will discuss how you can do this using the witness's prior inconsistent statements. The areas of credibility attacks that fall under the "C" umbrella are not statements, but rather the witness's prior acts that would undercut the witness's credibility or challenge the accuracy of his or her perceptions.

Such prior bad acts might include a felony conviction within the past ten years. Other bad acts may be admissible if they are probative of truthfulness, such as a false statement on a loan application. Not all of these bad acts will be admissible, and they are subject to the discretion of the judge. In federal court their admissibility in evidence is governed by Rules 608-609 of the Federal Rules of Evidence.

Another way to attack a witness's trustworthiness is to challenge his perception of what he saw or heard. For example, determine whether the witness really could have seen an accident as well as he claims. Perhaps the lighting was not very good. Or, it could be that the witness did not see the accident from beginning to end but only a part of it.

Finally, you can challenge the witness's recollection of events. Is the witness credible when he recalls with seemingly perfect memory the precise details of what he observed several years ago? On the other hand, if the witness does not recall simple things that he certainly should remember, you can challenge his credibility, too.

The "R" of CROSS stands for *restrict*. That is, your goal on cross is to restrain or limit the witness's damaging testimony. One way to do this at trial is to show the jury the witness's lack of knowledge about important matters. For example, assume you represent a plaintiff in an employment discrimination case. A supervisor has testified for the defendant employer that last year, he oversaw the plaintiff's work and noticed it was sloppy, and that the plaintiff did not interact well with the witness. On cross, you could challenge the witness—restrict his testimony by showing that in previous years, the supervisor did not oversee the plaintiff's work. Moreover, the supervisor did not know that the plaintiff did excellent work for a previous supervisor and that the previous supervisor never complained about the plaintiff.

> **Practice Tip**
>
> Challenge a witness's credibility by showing:
>
> 1. Favoritism for one side.
> 2. Past criminal convictions or evidence of untruthfulness.
> 3. Perceptions of what happened are not as clear as direct testimony suggests.
> 4. Memory of past events is too good.
> 5. Lack of memory of basic facts.

The "O" in CROSS stands for *outrageous statements* the witness has made prior to trial or on the stand. Outrageous statements are those that exceed the limits of what jurors will believe as true. President Bill Clinton made several such statements, including: 1) "It depends on the meaning of what the word 'is' is" and 2) "I smoked, but I never inhaled." Clinton gave the first answer in his sworn grand jury testimony when he was asked by the prosecutor if his attorney had been correct in stating at a deposition that there was no sexual relationship between Clinton and Monica Lewinsky. Clinton gave the second answer to a question on *60 Minutes* where he was asked if he ever had smoked marijuana.

The outrageous statement is the gold mine of cross-examination material. Sometimes witnesses will just give them to you when they know that they have been caught, as Clinton did above. Other times you will need to build up to the ultimate question with a series of preliminary questions that get admissions for each answer. This technique of using several common-sense questions to build to an ultimate question that elicits an unbelievable answer is discussed in Section 3.11.

Either way, if you get an outrageous answer, you have won your cross. Why? Because if the jury decides that what the witness says on an important point is outrageous, then that witness has lost all credibility. In your closing argument, you can submit the famous quote attributed to both Albert Einstein and the Bible (Luke 16:10): "Whoever is careless with the truth in small matters cannot be trusted with important matters."

The first "S" in CROSS represents *statements* made by the witness prior to trial that are inconsistent with his trial testimony. The ideal letter in an acronym for this category would be "P" for prior inconsistent statements. But if that letter were used, the acronym would be CROPS, which has nothing to do with cross-examination. Consequently, you will have to humor me and try a little harder on this component of the acronym to remember that "S" doesn't only mean *statements*, but rather *prior inconsistent statements*.

Once you can remember what the first "S" stands for, consider how you can cross-examine the witness with prior inconsistent statements, which can be sworn or unsworn written and oral statements that contradict the trial testimony. This can also include omissions in prior statements that hurt the witness's credibility. We will look at omissions later in this chapter, but for now, all you need to know is that you can impeach a witness's trial testimony by showing a failure to include information in a prior statement that he should have included. For example, assume a witness testifies at trial that his back hurt after a car accident. You could impeach him with his deposition testimony, where he was asked what hurt after the accident and he did not mention his back. Such an omission would prove that he was exaggerating his injuries at trial.

Cast a wide net when looking for these statements to use for your cross. Check the obvious places such as emails and letters. But also check the witness's Facebook page and other social media platforms. Don't forget oral statements the witness has made to other people. Oftentimes, the witness

> *No man has a good enough memory to be a successful liar.*
> —Abraham Lincoln

has had conversations with other people that are inconsistent with his trial testimony.

The second "S" stands for *support your case*. This is one of the most neglected tools in an attorney's arsenal. Even though a witness has hurt you on direct, there are many ways to ask questions that will support your case. There are two ways to do this. First, you can elicit testimony that will support your case. For example, in the Casey Anthony trial, where Casey was accused of killing her very young daughter, Caylee, the defense had to figure out a way to cross-examine the prosecution witnesses that were providing very damaging testimony. Many prosecution witnesses testified how Casey partied at bars, hung out with friends, and did not show sadness during the time that Caylee was missing and before she was found dead.

But, the defense picked an excellent strategy on cross. The defense focused on the second "S" of CROSS. The defense asked most of the witnesses—after the jury had heard some devastating testimony—the following question: "Isn't it true that when you saw Casey with Caylee, Casey loved Caylee?" "Isn't it true that Casey cared for Caylee?" The witnesses answered, "Yes," which supported the defense's BLM (bottom-line message) that a mother could not kill a daughter she loved.

The second way to support your case is to ask questions that argue your case—like those you might include in a closing argument—even though you know the witness will answer no to them. Using this technique, you don't care what the witness says; all you care about is the jury hearing your argument and the witness's denial. For example, if the defendant were on the stand claiming he was in the house just to buy drugs, you could argue your case by asking the defendant (but really arguing) the following questions about a prosecution for selling drugs:

Q. *You were* ***alone*** *in the house when the police came because you were in charge of selling drugs in the house?*
A. No.

Q. *You saw the three guns and an automatic rifle on the kitchen counter?*
A. No.

Q. *You knew they were loaded?*
A. No.

Q. *You saw the ziplock baggies next to the stove?*
A. No.

Q. *You saw the bags of cocaine, razor blade, and Pyrex bowl used to make crack cocaine on the small table in the middle of the kitchen?*
A. No.

2.6 DO YOU NEED TO CROSS?

> **Practice Tip**
>
> Remember to use the acronym CROSS when you determine your topics for cross:
>
> **C**redibility
> **R**estrict damaging testimony
> **O**utrageous statements
> **S**tatements (prior statements)
> **S**upport your case

Ninety-five percent of the time, you will need to cross-examine the witness. But there may be circumstances where you go through CROSS and decide that the witness's direct testimony did not hurt you. If so, there is no point in cross-examining. Second, it may be that the witness's testimony hurt you, but if you cross-examine the witness, you will give the witness a second chance to repeat his or her story and tell it in an even better way the second time around. Let's look at two examples.

The first example is that of a criminal defendant's mother testifying for her son who is charged with the federal offense of being a convicted felon in possession of a firearm. Assume that her son was arrested after he pointed a gun at someone in a parking lot who called 911 after the confrontation. When the police arrived, they found the defendant sitting in a car with a gun underneath his seat. The defendant claims at trial that he never pointed a gun, that it was his girlfriend's car, and that he did not know there was a gun in it.

Assume the defendant's mother takes the stand and testifies that a few hours before the alleged assault, she saw her son leave her house and he did not have a gun. She is a very nice person who is clearly uncomfortable testifying and does not want to be there. It is also obvious that her testimony does not hurt your case because she was not in the parking lot at the time of the assault or her son's arrest. Some prosecutors would cross-examine her with these typical questions: 1) You care about your son? 2) You love your son? 3) Throughout his life, you have helped him when he needed it? 4) You would do anything for him? 5) You were not in the parking lot when the assault occurred? and 5) You were not there when the police found a gun underneath the car seat he was sitting in?

While the first three questions show the witness's bias and the last two questions allow you to argue your case to the jury, the cross is frankly not very good, because the witness's bias is so obvious and the questions that argue your case to the jury are not earth-shattering. Indeed, the wiser choice is not to cross-examine her. You do not want to be seen by the jury as beating up on a witness. You always want to be fair. Is it fair for you to make the defendant's mother defensive and uncomfortable when it is obvious to everyone that a mother is going to protect her son? Second, why do this if the testimony, even if it is believed, will not hurt you?

In the following second example, your cross may have the unintended consequence of giving the witness a chance to repeat his story. Let's look at the California Proposition 8 trial, which we will examine in detail in chapter 9. For now, all you need to know is that the plaintiffs (two gay couples) were alleging that California's Proposition 8, which banned same-sex marriages, violated their Constitutional rights.

One plaintiff, Paul Katami, had testified how the passage of Proposition 8 had discriminated against his desire to marry his partner. On cross, the defense attorney was trying to get the plaintiff to agree that a reason for passing Prop 8 was so that children would not be taught about gay sexuality in first and second grade. However, the cross simply allowed the plaintiff to repeat his direct testimony. The following is an excerpt[1] from the direct and the cross.

David Boies, one of the plaintiffs' attorneys, asked Katami on direct why he and his partner needed to get married instead of registering in California as domestic partners. Katami concluded his direct examination testimony with the following:

> A. We hear a lot of, "What's the big deal? [You] get most of the same rights, virtually all of the same rights." The big deal is—and we've discussed this. The big deal is, it's creating a separate category for us. And that's a major deal because it makes you into a second, third, and, as Mr. Olson [plaintiffs' co-counsel] said today, a fourth-class citizen now that we actually recognize marriages from other states. . . . "Oh, but you have the same rights." Yeah, but what am I supposed to do, go have a domestic partner ceremony and then a reception? It's not what you do. None of our friends have ever said, "Hey, this is my domestic partner." By allowing us full access to those rights, not even the rights as much as it is the identity of being married, the full access to being a full participant as a citizen of our country and our state, that's denied. And when your state sanctions something that segregates you, it fortifies people's biases, in my opinion. It gives them an excuse to say, "It's not right. You don't deserve it because the state tells us that." . . . We're not a country about us and them. We're supposed to be a country about us, all of us, working in concert, doing things together. That's why we have these protections. My state is supposed to protect me. It's not supposed to discriminate against me.
>
> MR. BOIES: Your Honor, I have no more questions.

What possible good could come from cross-examining this witness? Are you going to prove that Katami should be satisfied with being able to register as having a domestic partner? Are you going to try and prove that he should not feel like a second-class citizen? Are you going to prove that he is mistaken about his feelings that Proposition 8 infringes on his rights? Instead, ask yourself whether anything good can come from your cross-examination. The answer is no. This case is going to be won or lost on the expert witnesses. That is, will the judge believe the defense's expert witness that same-sex marriage will harm the institution of heterosexual marriages? That was the reason Californians voted for Prop 8.

Here is an excerpt of defense counsel's cross-examination. Defense counsel tried to show that the intent of Prop 8 was not to discriminate against gays, but one of its goals was to protect children from learning about gays and sex in the first and second grades. Read the excerpt below and see if you agree with me that defense counsel makes very little headway and instead allows the plaintiff to repeat his direct testimony.

Q. *Do you think that first and second graders should be taught about sex in the public schools?*
A. I'm not part of any unified school district or school district at all, so I can't speak to what is taught, what is not taught. And you would have to define what you mean by "sex" exactly and how that's taught.

Q. *My question is to you. In your opinion, do you think kids as young as first and second grade should be taught about sex? In other words, traditional sex education, should that start in first and second grade? You don't think that, do you?*
A. No, I haven't thought about it.

Q. *You don't think that kids as young as first and second grade should be taught a traditional sex-ed curriculum, taught about the particulars of sex between individuals, do you?*
A. Again, [I'm] not a parent. I can't answer that question with any surety. I don't know. It depends on the curriculum. It depends on what's being taught and how it's taught.

Q. *Do you think kids that are in first and second grade have the capability to process issues of sex? Do you think that, Mr. Katami?*
A. I am not an expert on child development.

***

Q. *Now, Mr. Katami, you testified on your direct examination that you had a particular problem with part of this exhibit, which is the official argument in favor of Prop 8, that voting yes would protect our children. You had a problem with that, didn't you?*
A. I have an issue, that—

Q. *Particularly—*
A. I'm sorry.

Q. *Particularly you took issue with being associated with something that was bad; that somehow you had to be protected from children. You had a problem with that, is that correct?*

A. I have an issue with the verbiage saying "protect your children," because to me that insinuates that you have to protect from something that is going to harm you.

* * *

Q. *Is it your opinion that there was nothing that kids needed to be protected against?*
A. It was my opinion—

MR. BOIES: Objection, Your Honor.
COURT: Maybe you can rephrase it. That is a little far afield [**Even the judge is becoming frustrated with the cross.**]
DEFENSE COUNSEL: I'm sorry.

Q. *You testified that you had a problem with the part of what's in evidence as Plaintiffs' Exhibit 1 that says that we need to protect our children. You testified to that today, correct?*
A. I did.

Q. *OK. And the fact is, you don't think kids need to be protected from exposure to same-sex relationships, correct?*
A. My opinion, same-sex relationships are not something to be protected from.

Q. *There is nothing wrong with it in your opinion, correct?*
A. Same-sex relationships?

Q. *Yes.*
A. Nothing wrong with it.

In these last few questions above, defense counsel—hopefully—could not have thought that the witness was going to dramatically confess (à la Jack Nicholson in *A Few Good Men*) that there was something wrong with same-sex relationships. If so, then he was just arguing his point to the judge; however, the consequence was that the judge may have felt he was unfairly beating up on a witness. You do not ever want to create more sympathy for a witness you are cross-examining by asking unfair or unduly harsh questions.

On redirect that only lasted for two questions, plaintiffs' counsel quickly reversed any headway that defense counsel might have possibly made.

Q. *As you understood it, was there anything in Proposition 8 about what was going to be taught in schools?*
A. No.

Q. *Was there anything in Proposition 8 that talked about whether kids would be taught about sex in second grade as opposed to sixth grade or eighth grade?*
A. To my understanding, not at all.

MR. BOIES: No more questions, Your Honor.
COURT: Very well. Then, Mr. Katami, you may step down, sir.

2.7 THE 10 PERCENT VERSUS 65 PERCENT PRINCIPLE

Let's assume you cross-examine a witness and succeed in accomplishing your goal. You have won, or so you think you have. But just because you won the cross-examination, it does not follow that the jury will remember your win during deliberations. The reason is the "10 percent versus 65 percent" principle. Studies have shown that if you hear information only, you will only remember 10 percent of it three days later. But if that information is conveyed with a picture in addition to the spoken word, your chances of recalling that information three days later increases to 65 percent, or more than six times.

Camine Gallo, a communications expert, analyzed the effectiveness of TED Talks in his book, *Talk Like Ted.* He summarized the science of communicating through words and pictures. Neuroscience has a term for this 10 percent versus 65 percent principle. It is called the "Picture Superiority Effect" (PSE). Other researchers refer to it as the multimedia principle. Scientists have found that our brains process information from sound and pictures differently. While sound is processed by one brain channel, pictures are processed by several, giving them more chances to be remembered. Gallo instructs his readers to view the TED Talk given by Brene Brown to illustrate the powerful use of pictures and words. You can view the TedTalk at www.winningatcross.com. Gallo uses the following example to explain the science. If you were asked to remember the word "dog," your brain would register it as a verbal code. But if you were shown a picture of a dog and asked to remember it, the picture would be recorded in your brain visually among several different channels and your chances of recall would grow. This example is even more important if you are asking someone to remember a topic that is new to them.

> **Practice Tip**
>
> The conclusion among scientists is that people (and therefore jurors) are much more likely to remember information and concepts if they are presented information in words and pictures instead of words alone.

While Gallo declares that this new research has enormous implications for presentations, think of the impact it has for cross-examination. Armed with this information, why would you ever just ask a bunch of questions on cross? Your questions on cross need to be asked in the context of demonstrative exhibits or real exhibits.

Real exhibits are the evidence admitted at trial, such as emails, letters, company policies, and photographs. These exhibits will go back with the jury during deliberations. Demonstrative exhibits are tangible items created after the event in question and are used at trial to explain relevant facts to the jury. For example, a photo of the intersection taken a month after a car wreck used to cross a witness on what she was able to see would be a demonstrative exhibit. You would offer the exhibit to the court specifically as a demonstrative exhibit. By using the words "demonstrative exhibit," you are signaling that you do not intend it to go back with the jury during deliberations. Other items, such as your drawings on a sheet of paper shown on an ELMO, are understood by the court and opposing counsel to be demonstrative exhibits, so they do not need to be offered into evidence as such in order to get the court's permission to use them. You might show the witnesses objects such as a dictionary or baseball cap (see chapter 8) that are also considered demonstrative exhibits, even though you do not formally offer them as such.

Consequently, on cross-examination, make sure you have real and demonstrative exhibits displayed somewhere in front of the jury during most of your questions. Otherwise, the jury is only going to remember about 10 percent of what you are communicating.

2.8 HOW TO PREPARE A CROSS-EXAMINATION

Having looked at the five main areas where a witness can be cross-examined, let's see how to prepare a cross-examination.

1. Determine Weaknesses

As shown previously, most witnesses have a weakness, or at least they can provide testimony that will support part of your case. Prior to trial, decide where to attack each witness. Remember the acronym CROSS. Think through each of the topics of CROSS and determine your best lines of attack.

> **Practice Tip**
>
> To succeed, you must know the facts better than the witness does. It is as simple as that.

A first step in answering these questions is to summarize all the prior oral and written statements of the witness. Many lawyers make the mistake of summarizing everything. Instead, you only need to look for and summarize the major points. In a 200-page deposition, it would be reasonable for you to have a three or four page single-spaced summary that cites to the page numbers of the essence of the witness's testimony. Once you have summarized the statements, organize them by topic on your computer.

By doing this, you can determine which categories of CROSS to use. In addition to looking at written statements, another way to determine a witness's weaknesses is to interview people who know the witness. They may provide invaluable insights for cross-examination topics.

2. Make Only Three Major Points

Just as you do for your opening statement and direct examination, decide on the themes you want the jury to understand after you have completed your cross-examination. After you decide what the possible themes of cross-examination are, limit them to three (see the Rule of Three in chapter 3 for a more detailed discussion). Not only do you tax the jury's attention span by having more than three themes, but each additional theme you present diminishes the emphasis and importance of the others. Once you pick a theme, each question under that theme must directly relate to it; otherwise, you should not ask it.

Earlier, we examined how Lanier ignores Younger's tenth commandment, which instructs lawyers to make subtle points on cross and then to make their point in closing when the witness isn't there. In that example, Lanier spent an entire day with a witness on cross but had only three major themes.

In chapter 1, we looked at the importance of developing a story for your case. Likewise, in cross-examination, your themes should tie into the themes you used in the story you told in your opening statement. In essence, cross-examination is your chance to argue your winning opening statement themes again through your questions of the witness. In the Lanier example just discussed, one of his themes on cross was that DePuy put marketing ahead of research. Lanier was using the "C" of CROSS to undermine the witness's credibility by showing that DePuy put profits ahead of safety. It was one of the same themes that he used during his opening. By using the same theme, the jury knew exactly why Lanier was asking the questions he did. Consequently, you need to spend a lot of time deciding on what themes you will use in your opening statement, because they will dictate what themes you should use on cross-examination.

3. Begin Powerfully and End Memorably

Whatever your order of topics is, start and end with the most important questions. Cross-examination is no time to forget the power of primacy and recency effects on the jury. That is, people are more likely to remember what is presented first (primacy) and last (recency) in a presentation. Once you have written an outline, divide the outline so that each major point is on a separate sheet of paper. By doing this, you will achieve flexibility in the order you conduct cross-examination, depending of course on what happens during direct examination.

> **Practice Tip**
>
> One of the biggest mistakes attorneys make is trying to cover too many points. Don't water down your best points for the sake of having a lot of points.

For example, during direct examination, if the testimony provides fruitful material for cross-examination on a topic you have already prepared, write the key words from that testimony down on the corresponding topic page in your cross-examination outline. If the testimony involves a new line of inquiry for cross-examination, write it down on a separate sheet of paper. As the direct examination concludes, put your topic sheets in the order you want to proceed, given how the direct examination has developed.

The key to successful cross-examination is flexibility. If the direct examination ends with testimony that is helpful to you, use it to support your case immediately on cross-examination.

Likewise, it is absolutely paramount to end your cross-examination with a confrontation you know that you can win. Don't ruin a successful cross-examination by letting the witness leave the jury with the impression that he won the last battle.

Example: Starting Powerfully—Cross-Examination (Stephen Jones) from *U.S. v. McVeigh*

This example comes from the Oklahoma City bombing trial. On April 19, 1995, Timothy McVeigh detonated explosives contained in a Ryder truck that was parked outside the Murrah Federal Building. The explosion killed 168 people including 19 children and injured more than 650 others and damaged over 300 buildings.

Defense counsel Stephen Jones had the right idea to start his cross-examination of Lori Fortier on a powerful point. Fortier, a key government witness, had told one story to the FBI when she was first interviewed and a different story to the jury. The government contended that she had denied her knowledge about Timothy McVeigh's planning of the attack when she was first interviewed by the FBI because she was fearful of the consequences, and that she was now telling the truth at trial about her detailed knowledge of McVeigh's plan.

COURT: The jury will recall that we heard testimony—direct testimony from witness Lori Fortier—and now we're ready for cross-examination.
JONES: Ms. Fortier, would you agree with me that you either made false statements to agents of the Federal Bureau of Investigation . . . or you're making false statements to this jury of strangers yesterday?

Example: Ending Memorably—Cross-Examination (Stephen Jones) from *U.S. v. McVeigh*

Here, Jones ends his cross-examination by showing the jury that because Fortier had detailed knowledge about the making of the bomb and could face prosecution, she had an incentive to make things up to help the prosecution's case against McVeigh so that she would not get prosecuted.

Q. Well, in any event, no charges have been filed against you by Arizona or Oklahoma, have they?
A. No.

Q. Or anywhere else.
A. No.

Q. And your husband has not been charged as a participant in this crime; is that correct?
A. That's correct.

Q. And his sentencing [is still pending]?
A. Yes.

Q. And you have avoided any jail sentence.
A. Yes.

Q. You have avoided any forfeiture of your home or car; is that correct?
A. Yes.

Q. And when this is over with, you will leave the stand and return home to your children; is that correct?
A. Yes.

JONES: No further questions.

4. Create an Outline

As a general rule, it is better to start your cross-examination of a witness by eliciting facts from him that will support your case before you attack him on credibility or some other weakness. By doing this at the start of cross, before you suggest to the jury that the witness is not trustworthy through an attack, the witness will be more likely to answer those questions freely. However, the key is to be flexible and to use an order—based on what happens during direct examination—that is memorable and easy for the jury to understand.

Below is a sample reference outline, much like the one that you will create after you have decided on the topics for your cross using the CROSS acronym (see section 2.5). Next to each topic in your outline, reference the item (e.g., a deposition transcript or an email) that you can challenge the witness with if he does not answer the way you want. For example, if you are cross-examining a witness to support a part of your case, note the page and line of the deposition where the witness has said what you need. That way, if the witness does not answer correctly, you will have the page cited and can refer to it quickly. Also, tab the relevant page in the deposition.

The following is a sample outline. In this situation, the defense will cross-examine the plaintiff, who was in a car wreck. The plaintiff claims—for the first time—at trial that he has a shooting pain in his back that has been constant since the accident a year ago. He also says that it is an excruciatingly painful condition.

Outline

I. Injuries

A. Important to tell doctors about injuries

[This line of questioning uses common sense reasoning as the leverage to get the answers you want (see section 3.11.)]

—Went to doctor to get help

—Important to tell doctor about pain

—Doctor can't help with pain unless you tell him about it

B. Exaggerating injuries at trial

—Did not go to emergency room on night of accident (deposition p. 9, lines 4–7)

—First time went to doctor was one week after accident (deposition p. 15, lines 10–11)

—Never complained to doctor about pain in lower back (medical records exhibit 10, p. 117)

—Complained only about pain in upper neck (medical records exhibit 10, p. 117)

—Went to doctor again two months after accident (medical records exhibit 10, p. 210)

—Told doctor "95 percent better" (medical records exhibit 10, p. 212)

—On second visit, did not complain of lower back pain (medical records exhibit 10, p. 212)

—Never missed a day of work after accident (deposition p. 20, lines 3–8)

II. Very little damage to car

—Only damage to plaintiff's car was small dent in rear bumper (exhibit 21: photo of rear bumper)

—No damage to any other part of plaintiff's car (exhibits 22–25: photos of plaintiff's entire car)

—Cost of repairs was $600 (exhibit 17: receipt from service center)

—Absolutely no damage to defendant's car (exhibits 26–29: photos of defendant's entire car)

> *Three things cannot be long hidden: the sun, the moon, and the truth.*
> —Buddha

Once you have created your detailed reference outline, you'll need a version that you can use at the deposition or trial. This will be a very simplified topic outline that guides you but prevents you from getting bogged down in the details. Leave your reference outline with your co-counsel at the counsel table so that she can refer you to a particular part of the outline, in case the witness gives you a surprise answer. If you are trying the case by yourself, just leave it on the counsel table near a cup of water so that you can look at it while you get a sip of water during your cross. The jury will never know you are looking at your outline. As we will learn from master cross-examiner Tom Girardi in chapter 5, his trial outline only has the phrases for each topic and no more than ten words on a page.

5. Make Eye Contact

As suggested by the preceding section, whether in your conference room for the deposition or the courtroom, you need to know your cross cold. Avoid looking at your outline except when absolutely necessary. Limit doing so to only once or twice during each cross; ideally, not at all. The reason is that you need to keep eye contact with the jury. You need to listen intently to the witness's answers so you can pounce on any opening he gives you.

Instead of looking at a bunch of notes all the time, keep things informative and entertaining for the jury. Always have something for them to see while you are talking. For example, it could be an exhibit on the ELMO projector that you are marking up as you read it to the witness to impeach his testimony (discussed in the next section). Or, perhaps you have an easel with charts to show the witness and jury. Or, you have boards where you write the witness's answers or check off boxes, depending on what the chart shows.

> **Practice Tip**
>
> You must listen intently to the answer to make sure the witness has not dodged the question. You must also look for any defensive body language. If your head is buried in your outline, you won't have a chance of noticing—or winning.

The trick to not looking at your notes is to have a set of exhibits in the order you want to ask the witness about them. That is really your outline anyway, and it will remind you of your topics. The charts, diagrams, and drawings you are going to show the jury will also help you remember your questions.

2.9 HOW TO ASK QUESTIONS

1. Use Leading Questions

A leading question suggests the answer. The majority—but by no means all—of your questions in cross-examination should be leading. The reason for using leading questions is that you are in a battle and want to force the witness to answer the precise question you are asking. Leading him to answer only "yes" or "no" achieves this result. If you don't ask a leading question, you give the witness the chance to take control and explain his side of the story. That is what the witness does on direct examination with his attorney. Don't let him repeat his direct examination during cross.

There are two techniques to master: structure of the question you ask and proper tone of voice. First, the structure of the question should be simple. A good rule of thumb is to have only one new fact or proposition per question. That way, it is clear to the witness and jury which fact you are asserting as true. Although this sounds simple, it is often difficult because in normal conversation, we rarely speak in sentences that contain only one proposition. Second, your tone of voice must be authoritative, so that the jurors will understand exactly what the expected answer should be, and that what you believe to be true is true.

One of the most common mistakes on cross-examination is to ask vague, argumentative, or compound questions. By using only one main proposition per question, you will have concise sentences that will force your witness to give you the answer you want.

Example: Asking Concise Questions (Daniel Petrocelli) from *Goldman v. Simpson*

Below is a short exchange by Daniel Petrocelli, the attorney for Fred Goldman, during his questioning of O. J. Simpson in the civil trial brought against Simpson for wrongful death after his acquittal in the criminal trial. Petrocelli asks Simpson about a violent confrontation on New Year's Day in 1989 that resulted in Nicole Brown having a bruised and beaten face. See how you would improve the examination.

Q. Let's talk about 1989, OK? That was an angry, intense, physical confrontation, true?
A. Correct.

Q. You're what, at the time, six-two, 215 pounds?
A. Yes.

Q. Nicole, five-eight, 135 pounds?
A. Yes.

Although these questions are perfectly fine because they are simple enough, they serve as a good teaching tool because they technically would have been better if they had only contained one fact. Why? Although Simpson did not deny any of Petrocelli's statements, if he had, it would have been unclear what fact he was denying since there is more than one fact in each question. More important, if Petrocelli had put only one fact in each question, the theme of physical domination would have been before the jury for a longer period of time. The following would have been a better way to ask the questions:

Q. Let's talk about 1989, OK? It was a physical confrontation?
A. Yes.

Q. It was an angry confrontation?
A. Yes.

Q. It was intense?
A. Yes.

Q. Now, let me ask you some questions about your size. You are 6 feet, 2 inches tall?
A. Yes.

Q. You weigh 215 pounds?
A. Yes.

Q. Now, in contrast, Nicole was 5 feet, 8 inches?
A. Yes.

Q. She was 135 pounds?
A. Yes.

Q. So, at the time of this confrontation, you weighed about 80 more pounds than she did?
A. Yes.

Q. And you were half a foot taller?
A. Yes.

2. Signal to the Witness and the Jury What Answer You Want

Another tool in asking leading questions is to use certain phrases to signal to the witness and the jury that you want a certain answer, such as yes or no. Some of these phrases are in boldface in the following example where the defense attorney wants a yes answer from the victim.

Example: Using leading questions to get a witness to say yes

*Q. **Isn't it true** that the robbery happened on January 12?*
A. Yes.

*Q. You were near the city park, **right**?*
A. Yes.

*Q. **Isn't it a fact** that you were walking?*
A. Yes.

*Q. **The truth is**, the robber approached you from behind?*
A. Yes.

Notice how the words in boldface train the witness to answer "yes." But don't ask all your questions this way or they will become predictable and therefore boring. Instead, simply ask the question authoritatively; the witness will realize that the jury is expecting him to answer yes. The best way to ask a question is to use a very authoritative tone so that the jury knows what answer you are expecting. In the preceding example, you could instead just declare, with a strong, yet non-threatening, voice: "You were walking," and "The robber approached from behind."

Of course, using a leading question doesn't mean that the witness has to answer yes. A leading question simply "leads" or prompts the witness to answer the question in a particular way. Sometimes having the witness say no is also effective. This is particularly true when you are trying to establish the witness's lack of knowledge. Notice in the following example that the question is worded in the form of a negative question, and that the phrases at the end of the first few questions train the witness to say no. Then, near the end of the questioning, there is no longer the need for such training.

> **Practice Tip**
>
> To guarantee that you ask a leading question, begin it with 1) "isn't it a fact," 2) "isn't it true," and 3) "the truth is," each of which alerts the witness and jury that you expect yes as the answer.

Example: Using leading questions to get witness to say no

Q. You weren't at the intersection of Main and Commerce, were you?
A. No.

Q. You did not see what happened there on the night of January 12, did you?
A. No.

Q. You did not see a robbery that night, right?
A. No.

Q. You don't know if there were one or two robbers? **[Said with an authoritative tone]**
A. No.

Whether you are leading the witness to answer yes or leading the witness to answer no, the power you have to make him answer the way you want is based on all the facts of the case. The facts of the case include physical evidence, the witness's prior statements, and the testimony that has come out at trial. With this information, you can lead the witness to provide the answers you want. If the witness fails to answer correctly, you can impeach him (discussed in chapter 3), and if he gives an outrageous answer, the jury won't believe it, so the incorrect answer doesn't matter.

3. Avoid the Danger of Failing to Use Leading Questions

Let's look at an example that shows both the success of using leading questions and the failure when you don't. The transcript below is from the O.J. Simpson criminal trial. (The video, "Shipp clip 1," can be seen at www.winningatcross.com

under chapter 2.) The witness in the trial is Ron Shipp, who was a Los Angeles Police Department officer from 1974 to 1989. He had met O.J. earlier through Shipp's brother, who had played football against O.J. in high school. While an officer, he formed a close friendship with O.J. He visited his home sometimes as often as twice a week from 1978 to 1982, when he patrolled West Los Angeles, where O.J.'s home was located.

When he was transferred to patrol a different section of Los Angeles in 1982, he saw O.J. less but still maintained a friendship with him. He also became Nicole's friend. She asked him for help after she was beaten by O.J. on January 1, 1989. At her request, Shipp spoke to O.J. about the profile for a batterer in order to see if he would admit to having a problem. O.J. denied that he was a batterer and, instead, asked Shipp to "take care" of the potential charges. Shipp attempted to do so by talking to the detective handling the case.

Shipp was also with O.J. Simpson on the night of June 13, 1994, the evening after the murders, when O.J. returned from Chicago. At his home that night, O.J. told Shipp that he had had dreams of killing Nicole.

The prosecution called Shipp as a witness for the sole purpose of telling the jury that O.J. had told him about his dream of killing Nicole. Why the prosecution thought this would be proof that O.J. actually killed Nicole is beyond this book's realm, but suffice it to say that if your case has been reduced to relying on a dream to prove a murder, you are in real trouble.

As you read the following first set of questions, ask yourself if Carl Douglas, the defense attorney, has a clear theme on cross.

Q. O.J. Simpson is a football fan, isn't he? [**A good simple leading question with one fact**]
A. Yeah, he loves football. Yes, he does.

Q. He goes to games a lot, doesn't he? [**same**]
A. Yes, he does.

Q. You and O.J. Simpson have never attended a football game together? [**same**]
A. Never.

Q. In 26 years that he's been your supposed friend, have you? [**same**]
A. Not one.

Q. You and your wife have never gone on a double date with Nicole and O.J. Simpson in the entire time that you've known them, have you? [**same**]
A. You're absolutely correct.

Douglas attacks Shipp's credibility (the "C" of CROSS) and Shipp's allegedly outrageous statement ("O") that he is O.J.'s friend. He points out that O.J. and Shipp never really socialized in public. But watch what happens next when

Douglas asks a leading question, and Shipp does not answer the question directly and instead adds on facts that help the prosecution.

Q. *You and your wife and he and his ex-wife never went to a movie or a play or a concert together, the four of you, have you?*
A. My wife and I were invited shortly after he beat up Nicole, and that's—

We will look at this in detail in chapter 3, but when a witness does not answer your question, simply repeat it. Don't ask the judge for help because the judge is probably not listening to the testimony and might give you an incorrect ruling as Judge Ito does next. The ruling below is wrong because the question asked if Shipp and his wife had ever gone to a movie, play, or concert with O.J. and his ex-wife. Shipp does not answer the question about whether he and his wife had gone to an event with them but instead volunteers that he was invited to an event with them in order to add that he was invited shortly after Nicole's beating.

Q. *Move to strike that, Your Honor. Non-responsive.*
COURT: Overruled.

Q. *Your wife and you were invited, but you never went, did you?*
A. Never went. **[Douglas repeats the question in substance and gets the answer he needs.]**

Q. *All the times that you claim that you were over his house playing tennis, you have never in your entire life played tennis on the same court with O.J. Simpson, have you?*
A. Never.

Q. *You're not really this man's friend, are you, sir?*
A. Well, OK, if you want me to really explain it, I guess you can say I was like everybody else, one of his servants. I did police stuff for him all the time. I ran license plates. That's what it was. OK, like I said, I loved the guy.

Q. *You weren't the kind of friend that he would share some private secret with, were you, sir?*
A. Nothing except for the 1989 beating where he needed me.

Douglas builds momentum to the dramatic moment of the last question, but he makes a mistake that is common on cross-examination: he tries to get the witness to confess (i.e., that Shipp is not O.J.'s friend). Here, he gets burned when he asks, "You weren't the kind of friend that he would share some private secret with, were you, sir? (A. Nothing except for the 1989 beating [of Nicole] where he needed me.)"

Shipp's answer is credible and not outrageous. As a result, it undercuts the entire preceding line of questions. The last question does not have the power of common-sense reasoning (see discussion at 3.11) behind it because Douglas knows before he asks the last question that Shipp had helped O.J. with a very personal problem he had when he hit Nicole in 1989. Consequently, Shipp's answer is believable: although they might not have done a lot of things socially together, Shipp was a friend O.J. could count on in a personal crisis. Shipp's sincerity really comes through when you watch the video. On the other hand, if Shipp had not helped O.J. with the aftermath of the 1989 beating, Douglas's last question would have had the power of common sense to force Shipp to answer that he was not the type of friend with whom O.J. would share a private secret. The last question should not have been asked because it cannot force the answer wanted.

In this next section, Douglas tries to show the jury that if O.J. had told Shipp about his dream of killing Nicole, then Shipp would have told people who interviewed him after the murder.

Q1. Because sometime after meeting with Phil and Bill and Marcia [the prosecution team], you met with Mr. Douglas, didn't you? **[It's very odd that Douglas refers to prosecution team by their first names and then refers to himself by his last name. Anyhow, Douglas asks a leading question with one simple fact.]**
A. That's correct.

Q2. Remember that?
A. Oh, yes, I do.

Q3. And you and I met in your attorney's office, didn't you? **[a good leading question with one simple fact]**
A. That's correct.

Q4. Remember that?
A. Yes, I do.

Q5. During any part of the 45 minutes that you and I spoke, did you ever mention anything about this conversation with Mr. Simpson? **[same]**
A. No, sir.

Q6. Didn't I ask you during that conversation to tell me the worst things that you knew about O.J. Simpson? **[same]**
A. Yes, you did.

Q7. And wouldn't you agree that this statement about this supposed dream is a pretty bad thing about Mr. Simpson? **[same]**
A. Yes, it is.

Q8. So did you lie when you didn't tell me about that dream? **[same]**
A. I sure did.

Q9. You did. OK. You've lied a few times, haven't you, sir? **[same]**
A. Never in court.

When you are cross-examining, you need to make sure the jury is absolutely certain by your questions as to what you believe the truth to be. In Q7, Douglas admits to the jury that the "dream is a pretty bad thing about Mr. Simpson." Douglas makes this admission in order to prove that Shipp is making up the story in court since he did not tell investigators on either side about the "bad thing" after the murders.

But, by revealing his concern about the dream, Douglas admits to the jury that if they believe O.J. in fact had a dream about killing Nicole, then it is damaging evidence against O.J. It is a big and unnecessary risk to take. Consequently, Douglas should not have asked this line of questions.

* * *

Q. *OK. So let me get this straight. You met for 90 minutes with Phil and Marcia and Bill and never mentioned this conversation, correct?*
A. Never did. **[a good simple leading question with one main proposition]**

Q. *You met for 25 minutes with Joe Brown and never discussed this conversation, correct?* **[same]**
A. Did not.

Q. *You met with me in your attorney's office for 45 minutes and never talked about this conversation, correct?* **[same]**
A. Correct.

Q. *And you are Mr. Simpson's friend as far you think, correct?* **[same]**
A. Yes.

Q. *Now, you said that the reason why you didn't tell Phil about the conversation was because of what?* **[Non-leading question. It uses the word "what."]**
A. I said I didn't tell Phil because at the time I really did not want to be really involved in all this, and I didn't want to be going down as being the person to nail O.J.

Q. *Let me ask you this. You're not, so don't worry about that. But let me ask you this—*
MARCIA CLARK: Objection to that editorial.

JUDGE ITO: Sustained. Counsel, you know better.

Q. *Sorry, Your Honor.*
CLARK: Motion to strike.

JUDGE ITO: Jury is to disregard the counsel's remark.

This is a great illustration of the danger in asking non-leading questions on cross-examination: "Now, you said that the reason why you didn't tell Phil about the conversation was because of what?" ("Phil" refers to Detective Phil Vannatter, who interviewed Shipp after the murders.) By asking the non-leading question, Douglas gives the witness the freedom to answer in a way that devastates Douglas: "I didn't want to be going down as a person to nail O.J." The answer's effect is revealed by Douglas's reaction and the court's scolding.

Q. *So the promise of anonymity was the reason or the motivation for you to share intimate secrets with your friend to a total stranger?* **[leading question with one simple fact]**
A. Correct.

Q. *Have you in the past shared intimate secrets about a friend to somebody writing a book?* **[same]**
A. Never.

Q. *Never before. Have you in the past lied to police officers about a murder investigation?* **[same]**
A. Never.

Q. ***Never before.***

Douglas asks simple leading questions with one fact in them.

Q. *Isn't it true, sir, that you were hopeful that you would be able to garner some publicity by making up false allegations about Mr. Simpson?*
A. No, it's not true at all.

Q. *Didn't you think, sir, that by concocting this story about Mr. Simpson, it might enhance your own person profile?*
A. Mr. Douglas, I put all my faith in God, and my conscience since Nicole's been dead, I've felt nothing but guilt, my own personal guilt, that I didn't do as much as I probably should've.

This part shows the importance of sizing up your witness on cross-examination. By now, Shipp's demeanor and sincerity should have told Douglas that he was not going to get anywhere with Shipp by continually asking ultimate questions. In the video clip, notice the following: Douglas goes to his notes and checks off questions. This is a terrible practice. The only thing ever to check off is your themes of cross-examination, not an individual question unless it is the most important question you have to ask. Even so, don't check off the question after you ask it but at a time that is less noticeable and distracting.

Note that Douglas does not vary his tone of voice throughout the entire clip. Every question sounds like the ultimate question. The problem with his style is that by continuing to do it, the jurors become desensitized to the point that they do not know what the truly important questions are.

4. Mix in Open-Ended Questions

Open-ended questions—the opposite of leading questions—begin with words such as who, what, when, where, why, or how. Many professors and attorneys believe that these questions should never be used on cross and for the most part, they are right. The rationale is that it gives the witness a chance to explain, which is exactly what Shipp did. He could not wait to tell the jury that the reason he did not tell the police about O.J.'s dream was because he did not want to "nail O.J."

But, on cross-examination these questions can be freely used if you know what the witness must answer based on a prior statement he has made or the evidence in the case. Such questions provide variety and show the jury that you are not being unduly unfair to the witness by always making her answer yes or no to leading questions.

For instance, assume the witness gave a prior statement that she was twenty feet from the intersection when she saw a car wreck. For variety, instead of asking the leading question, "You were 20 feet away from the intersection when you saw the accident, weren't you?" You could ask the open-ended question, "How far away from the intersection were you?" Even though it is an open-ended question, the witness has to answer "20 feet" or else you can impeach her with her prior statement.

5. Usually Avoid Asking Questions Where the Answer is Unknown

If you don't know what the witness must answer, asking an open-ended question can prove dangerous. A variation of the following well-known example has been taught in law school for years. It is the hypothetical that Irving Younger uses to proclaim his ninth commandment, which prohibits you from asking the one question too many. Professors also use it to teach the principle that you should never ask a question to which you do not know the answer.

Q. *You admit that your head was turned when the large brawl took place?*
A. Yes.

Q. *Then, how can you claim my client bit a part of Mr. Smith's nose off since you didn't see the fight take place?*
A. I saw your client spit it out of his mouth after the brawl.

On the contrary, it is perfectly acceptable, and even advisable, to ask a witness an open-ended question when you do not know how the witness will answer—*but* only when the answer simply does not matter. Obviously, in the previous example, the answer is detrimental.

So, the rule for most situations, then, is that you should never ask a question unless you know the answer the witness must give or the answer does not matter. In the next example, the answer does not hurt the attorney.

Example of open-ended questions where answer does not matter (Daniel Petrocelli) from *Goldman v. Simpson*

Just prior to the example, Petrocelli asks Simpson about beating Nicole over the years. The one physical altercation O.J. refers to in the next passage concerns

New Year's Day 1989, when Nicole called 911 after O.J. struck her several times. For context, the passage begins with his answer:

A. There was one very physical altercation, and there were other times when they were not so physical.

Q. *What do you mean by "not so physical," Mr. Simpson?*
A. Well, Nicole hit me a few times, and I didn't consider that too physical.

Petrocelli asks an open-ended question because there is not an answer that can hurt him. The answer O.J. gives undercuts his prior claim—not shown here—that Nicole could be very physical and that is why he had to fight back when she attacked. It hurts his credibility to now say that when she hit him, he did not consider it "too physical." That answer would not have been elicited if an open-ended question had not been asked.

There is an important exception to this rule that is often overlooked. Mauet declares, "Play it safe. Many witnesses will seize every opportunity to hurt you. Cross-examination is not a discovery deposition. . . . Accordingly, your cross-examination should tread on safe ground." In some criminal trials, however, many defense attorneys would never win if they always treaded on safe ground. Defense attorneys are sometimes forced to ask questions where the answer is not absolutely certain because of their inability (through lack of cooperation by the witnesses) to interview police officers and other government witnesses prior to trial. Necessity dictates taking calculated risks. These questions are critical for developing information with which to cross-examine other witnesses or to use later in the cross-examination of the same witness.

6. Make Your Points Clear

Your points on cross must be crystal clear. From the first words of the opening statement through the last words of the closing argument, you should aggressively convince the jury of your client's position. As we saw earlier in this chapter, the third myth of cross, to be subtle, could not be more wrong. Furthermore, as we will see in Part II, all the master cross-examiners that we study will ask questions that contain an unmistakable theme in them.

7. Use Visual Aids

Don't forget the study discussed earlier in section 2.7 that people will only remember 10 percent of your cross-examination if you don't use visual aids. Always have something to show the jury during your questioning. For example, if the witness's testimony does not make sense in light of photographs taken, show the photographs to the witness and jury during your cross-examination. Moreover, don't be afraid to use an easel or ELMO. You can have the witness draw a diagram that will reveal how implausible the testimony is. Or, if the witness makes some outrageous statements, write them on an easel so the jury both sees and hears the words. Be creative and keep the jury's attention.

> *I hear and I forget. I see and I remember. . . .*
> —Confucius,
> ancient Chinese philosopher

2.10 HOW TO AVOID OBJECTIONS

Below are the most common and important objections you will see at trial. Your guiding principle should be to only ask questions for which you have a good faith basis. That means that your questions are supported by relevant and admissible facts in the case or reasonable inferences that can be drawn from the evidence in the trial. This principle is grounded in several rules of evidence and the case law. If you stick to this principle, you can avoid objections such as "misstates the evidence" and "relevance" (meaning the question is irrelevant to the issue being litigated at trial).

Another objection is that the question is "argumentative." Under Federal Rule of Evidence 611, the judge must exercise reasonable control over the witness and protect the witness from harassment and undue embarrassment. This is hardly a clear line. The best way to determine whether your question will avoid this objection is to know your judge's opinion on cross-examination. Most judges will err on the side of allowing a wide-ranging cross-examination because of a party's right to confront witnesses at trial. What appears as harassing to one side is seen by the other side as a necessary confrontation of that witness's testimony. In any event, if a judge sustains—that is, upholds—an objection that the question is argumentative, simply rephrase the question and omit the argumentative language within it.

A fourth objection is "beyond the scope." This objection means that the question is beyond the scope of testimony of the direct examination. That is, your question on cross asks about a topic that was not raised on direct examination. This objection is based on Federal Rule of Evidence 611. But that rule also provides that the court may use its discretion to permit questions into additional matters. The rule also allows you to cross-examine the witness on matters that affect the witness's credibility, which can encompass a wide range of topics that were not brought out on direct testimony. Finally, the common law and many state rules of evidence allow for a wide-ranging cross-examination that does not have the limitations of the federal rule. In short, know your jurisdiction and your judge.

A fifth objection is "asked and answered." This objection means that your current question had already been asked by you previously and that the witness has answered it. Generally, the objection will be overruled, because although you may have asked the question previously, the witness has not answered it. That explains why you have to ask it again.

2.11 CHAPTER CHECKLIST

1. Don't underestimate the importance of cross-examination at a deposition. Because almost all cases settle instead of going to trial, deposition testimony is essentially trial testimony.
2. There are four myths of cross-examination: 1) you can get the witness to confess, 2) the witness has the power to hurt you, 3) you need to be subtle on cross and make your point during closing argument, and 4) the advice in many of Irving Younger's Ten Commandments is correct.
3. The most important principle of cross is that it does not matter what the witness says, only whether the witness is believed.
4. To succeed, you must know the facts better than the witness does. It is as simple as that.
5. Start strong. Studies have shown that people make up their minds about other people within seven seconds of first meeting them.
6. Write down a witness's absurd answer so the jury can see it on an ELMO or easel. The time to win is now. Disregard Younger's advice and, instead, make sure the witness and jury know why you are ending your cross.
7. Choose your topics for cross by using the acronym CROSS: **C**redibility, **R**estrict damaging testimony, **O**utrageous statements, **S**tatements that are inconsistent, and **S**upport your case.
8. Challenge a witness's credibility by showing: 1) his favoritism for one side, 2) his past criminal convictions or bad acts demonstrating a lack of trustworthiness, 3) his perceptions of what happened are not as clear as his direct testimony, 4) his too-good-to-be-true memory of past events, and 5) his poor memory of basic facts.
9. Your themes on cross should be so clear that if someone walked into the courtroom and knew nothing about your case, he would be able to easily follow your cross.
10. Limit your themes to three. Don't dilute your best points by trying to cover everything.
11. Remember that sometimes it is better not to cross at all (e.g., when the plaintiff in Prop 8 trial testifies on direct why he feels it puts gays in a lessor category than heterosexuals).
12. Use visual aids on cross. Studies have shown that if you hear information only, you will only remember 10 percent of it three days later. But if that information is conveyed with a picture in addition to the spoken words, your chances of recalling that information three days later increases to 65 percent.
13. The five steps to creating an outline are: 1) determine the witness's weaknesses, 2) make only three major points, 3) begin powerfully and end mem-

orably, 4) elicit favorable facts first before you attack the witness, and 5) put a citation for the exhibit number, deposition page, or other reference next to each critical fact in your outline, in case the witness does not answer your question the way you want.

14. After creating a reference outline, create a second outline for the trial or deposition that only includes the topics of your cross. This will prevent you from getting lost in your notes.
15. Do not look at your outline during cross unless, on very rare occasions, it is absolutely necessary to do so.
16. You must listen intently to the witness's answer to make sure the witness has not dodged the question.
17. You must also look for any defensive body language; if your head is buried in your outline, you won't have a chance to win.
18. Always have something for the jury to see while you conduct the cross.
19. You should primarily use leading questions. A leading question contains one fact or proposition that suggests the answer to the witness.
20. To get a witness to say yes, end your question with the word "right" or start your question with the phrases "isn't it true," "isn't it a fact," or "the truth is."
21. Never ask a question that you do not know the answer to, unless the answer does not matter. The only other exception to this rule is if you are a criminal defense attorney and you need to take the calculated risk that the question might provide an answer that will help you defeat the current witness or others.
22. Your guiding principle should be to only ask questions for which you have a good faith basis. That means that your questions are supported by relevant and admissible facts in the case or reasonable inferences that can be drawn from the evidence in the trial.

CHAPTER THREE

Advanced Techniques

"Be yourself, everyone else is already taken."—*Oscar Wilde*

Now that you have learned the essentials of cross-examination, let's explore how to become a master cross-examiner. Do not wait until your second deposition or trial to employ these techniques. They are easily learned and should be used at your first opportunity. The techniques are described here as "advanced" simply because they build upon the easier-to-understand skills that you learned in chapter 2. As you implement the following techniques, apply them in a way that is consistent with your personality and courtroom demeanor (note the Oscar Wilde quote that kicked off this chapter). Your identity as a lawyer is uniquely yours.

3.1 LESS IS MORE

"Less is more" is an aphorism that should guide everything in your trial preparation and cross-examination. It is the opposite of the data dump discussed in chapter 1. The aphorism is attributed to Ludwig Mies, who was a pioneering master of modern architecture. He believed that the "long road from the material through function to form has only one goal: to create order out of the unholy confusion of today."

The saying is no less true for cross-examinations at depositions and trials. Are you unsure whether a line of questioning on cross is very important? When in doubt, leave it out.

Perhaps the best example of less is more comes from Abraham Lincoln, one of the greatest orators and lawyers this country has ever known. He practiced this principle long before Mies coined the phrase. Let's take a quick

> **CHAPTER ROAD MAP**
>
> - How to make cross-examinations clear, concise, and creative.
> - How to use a new technique to ensure successful impeachment with prior inconsistent statements.
> - How to use fail-safe tricks to handle the evasive witness.

look at the Gettysburg Address; then I will explain how you can improve your cross-examination skills by learning from Lincoln's techniques.

In an epic Civil War battle, Union and Confederate troops had fought for three days (July 1–3, 1863). At the end of the battle, there were more than 50,000 dead and wounded. Four months later, Lincoln came to the dedication of the national cemetery where 3,500 troops were buried.

Prior to the creation of United States national cemeteries in 1862, soldiers in the Civil War were typically buried at the battlefields where they died. When Andrew Curtin, the governor of Pennsylvania, toured the Gettysburg battlefield and saw the makeshift graves marked by boards and cracker boxes, he decided to create a national cemetery there—even though farmers had already resumed farming in the area, albeit around the buried bodies. Seventeen acres were acquired for the Gettysburg National Cemetery.

Edward Everett, a former U.S. Senator who was widely considered the most popular orator in the country and a protege of Daniel Webster, was invited to give the keynote address at the dedication of the cemetery.

The dedication was on November 19, 1863, before 15,000–20,000 people. Edward Everett delivered a speech that lasted over two hours. President Lincoln spoke for two minutes using only 272 words—a great example of how less is more.

The next day, Everett wrote Lincoln a note saying, "I should be glad if I could flatter myself that I came as near to the central idea of the occasion, in two hours, as you did in two minutes."

Lincoln saw the occasion as a chance to define what war was about and who we are. In the address, he defines what soldiers died for, and he did it in two minutes.

Are you still resisting the idea that less is more? Remember the two main complaints from jurors: "Why do trials take so long?" and "Why do the lawyers think we are dumb?"

Practice Tip

Ernest Hemingway's friends challenged him to write a story in six words or less. His response: "For sale: baby shoes never worn."

3.2 RULE OF THREE

When your cross-examination is complex and hard to follow, your audience will fight you. Instead of winning them over to your side, the jury will become irritated with you and stop listening. Instead, you want them to say "yes" to the ideas you are presenting. Make it easy and interesting for them. The "rule of three" is a perfect framework for cross-examination because it ensures that you apply the principle of less is more. Never try to convey more than three points, unless you have thought long and hard about it and you have a really good reason.

The rule of three is a tried-and-true rule that is widely used in literature, movies, music, and advertising, because it provides a powerful way for conveying information to audiences. Almost every song is built around a three-chord progression. Painters rely on three primary colors. Our day is built around three meals. Stories have a beginning, middle, and an end. Our country was founded on three inalienable rights: "Life, liberty, and the pursuit of happiness." The Christian religion is grounded in the Holy Trinity. The examples go on and on.

The point is that groups of three have a familiar rhythm to them that are easy for audiences to understand and remember. For example, in the Gettysburg Address, Lincoln crafted his address on the past, present, and future. In addition, the climax of his speech incorporates this powerful rule. As the address crescendos to a climax, Lincoln urges the audience to not let the soldiers' deaths be in vain but to resolve that the nation will "have a new birth of freedom—and that the government *of the people, by the people, for the people* shall not perish from the earth." This definition of democracy, using a list of three qualities, is one of Lincoln's—or for that matter, any other president's—most memorable phrases. Lincoln's economic word choice is so much more memorable than if he would have listed ten qualities of a democracy or droned on and on as Edward Everett did in his two-hour speech before Lincoln's powerful address.

In Mark Lanier's opening, which we discussed in chapter 1, he told the jury there were three things that were wrong with Johnson & Johnson's house (beside each following item, I have put in brackets a description of the photo he showed the jury). He told the jury: 1) Johnson & Johnson's house was built on a poor foundation [photo of cracked foundation], 2) Johnson & Johnson used shoddy equipment [photo of exposed wires], and 3) Johnson & Johnson's product caused bad damage [photo of dead and damaged hip tissue]. Notice that he did not overwhelm the jury and ask them to find ten or 20 things wrong with the house, but he followed the rule of three and simplified it for the jury. He would then use and expand on those themes in his cross-examinations, which are analyzed in chapters 6, 7, and 8.

3.3 USE INSIGHTS FROM BEHAVIORAL SCIENCE TO PERSUADE JURORS

Throughout the past several decades, advances in behavioral science research have shed enormous light on how people make decisions. That research provides insights for trial lawyers to use so that their cross-examinations persuade jurors to reach a favorable decision.

Much of the ground-breaking research was done by Daniel Kahneman, the only psychologist to win the Nobel Prize in Economics, and his colleague Amos Tversky. Before their breakthrough research, the prevailing view was that humans were rational decision makers who made financial choices on an unemotional assessment of costs and benefits. But in Kahneman's book, *Thinking, Fast and Slow* (New York: Farrar, Straus and Giroux, 2013), he summarized his life's research, which proved how wrong this assumption was. Instead, he proved that humans—whether making an economic decision or any other type of decision—make decisions that they think are based on reason when they often really make them based on emotions, usually without realizing it.

Two other books that also brought these new developments in behavioral science research to mainstream audiences are *Pre-Suasion: A Revolutionary Way to Influence and Persuade* by Robert Cialdini (New York: Simon & Schuster, 2016), and *Nudge: Improving Decisions About Health, Wealth, and Happiness,* by Richard H. Thaler (winner of the Nobel Prize in Economics) and Cass Sunstein (New York: Penguin, 2009). Below are the principles from the books that can be applied to cross-examinations.

Cross-examiners Are Choice Architects

Much of the recent research in behavioral science confirms what you might already believe, but it should give you more confidence to execute cross-examinations using these principles. For example, all three books explain the research that sheds light on how the human brain makes imperfect decisions. One of the causes of imperfect decisions is a brain dysfunction called confirmation bias. That is, the brain forms a belief and will sift through subsequently conflicting information to find only the evidence that supports the initial belief.

Although there was no research regarding confirmation bias hundreds of years ago, the principle existed. In 1620, Francis Bacon said, "Once a human intellect has adopted an opinion (either as something it likes or as something generally accepted) it draws everything else in to confirm and support it. Even if there are more and stronger instances against it than there are in its favor, the intellect either overlooks these or treats them as negligible or does some line-drawing that lets it shift them out of the way and reject them."

Cialdini explains that the research shows that "the best persuaders become the best through pre-suasion—the process of arranging for recipients to be receptive to a message before they encounter it. . . . The answer lies partly in a poorly appreciated tenet of all communication: What we present first changes the way people experience what we present to them next" (Cialdini 2016, 4).

Similarly, the authors of *Nudge* relate a study were schools were able to increase the consumption of healthy food items—and decrease the consumption of unhealthy food items—by as much as 25 percent simply by arranging them at eye level or changing their position or order in the line of food items or by putting them in a separate line. "There is no such thing as a neutral design." We are all choice architects. "A choice architect has the responsibility for organizing the context in which people make decisions." "A good rule of thumb is to assume that 'everything matters'" (Thaler and Sunstein 2009, 3).

You need to give a lot of thought to the order of your questions on cross-examination. What topic you discuss first will have a binding impact on the topics you should address next because jurors will view the subsequent points through the conclusions they have made about your first topic. As a result, a chronological cross-examination may be the worst structure because it means you have given no thought to the order of your topics other than the path of least resistance: "I'll start at the beginning and finish at the end." Instead, after reading this section, you will realize that you should start your cross-examination with your counterthemes and then present your themes.

The Importance of Counterthemes

In addition to using themes on your cross-examination that are the same or build on those from your opening statement, you need to push yourself to find counterthemes—or counterarguments—to use in your cross-examination. That is, your opponent—if he is any good—will have themes for his opening that will tie into his themes on direct examination. In addition to structuring your questions on cross around the themes of your opening statement, create themes that counter your opponent's themes that are used on direct examination.

Cialdini, discussed in the previous section, advises:

> "[I]n contests of persuasion, counterarguments are typically more powerful than arguments. This superiority emerges especially when a counterclaim does more than refute a rival's claim by showing it to be mistaken or misdirected in the particular instance, but does so instead by showing the rival communicator to be an untrustworthy source of information" (Cialdini 2016, 92).

Cialdini adds the following:

> "Issuing a counterargument demonstrating that an opponent's argument is not to be believed because its maker is misinformed on the topic will usually succeed on that singular issue. But a counterargument that undermines an opponent's argument by showing him or her to be dishonest in

the matter will normally win that battle *plus* future battles with the opponent" (Cialdini 2016, 92).

Cross-examiners should take his advice to heart. Our whole goal is to prove that the witness is incorrect, but if we can also show that the witness–and by implication the attorney who sponsored him on direct examination–is not trustworthy, it is game, set, and match.

Consequently, your counterthemes are more important to winning your case than your themes. Lead with your counterthemes on cross-examination once you have developed them. Cialdini gives the following example. In the late 1960s, Big Tobacco was surprised by a three-year slide in cigarette consumption despite its very powerful advertising campaigns which were consistent with previous years. Big Tobacco soon realized that the cause of the decline was the power of counterarguments. In 1967, the US Federal Communications Commission (FCC) ruled that the "fairness doctrine" permitted opponents of tobacco use to have free equal time on radio and television to counter Big Tobacco's advertising. For example, if "a tobacco ad featured healthy, attractive, independent characters, the opposing ads would counterargue that, in fact, tobacco use led to diseased health, damaged attractiveness, and slavish dependence" (Cialdini 2016, 94). The counterarguments were so powerful that Big Tobacco learned that it could *increase* sales by *not* advertising on radio and TV so that consumers would not be exposed to the counterarguments of its opponents. Instead, Big Tobacco focused its advertising in the print media and billboards where the fairness doctrine did not apply, and its opponents could not use free advertising to counter its arguments.

The lesson here is that you need to anticipate your opponent's themes on direct examination and have a countertheme and counterargument that annihilates the direct examination. For example, in a products liability case, if on direct the witness brags about his company's emphasis on safety and the studies it conducted before marketing its product, use counterthemes of "putting profits over safety" and "rigged tests" to discredit that testimony and prove how the theme that was presented on direct is untrustworthy.

Elevated Attention Affects Outcomes

Cialdini points to a study that found that if a person with a clipboard approached a person and asked if they would spend a few minutes answering a survey, only 29 percent consented. But if the researcher first asked, "Do you consider yourself a helpful person?" Nearly everyone said, "yes." In that privileged moment—after subjects had confirmed privately and affirmed publicly their helpful natures—the researchers pounced, requesting help with their survey. As a result, 77.3 percent then volunteered (Cialdini 2016, 25).

Unlike the study above, cross-examination does not allow lawyers to persuade jurors by asking them an initial question that will make them more receptive to their cross-examination (Although this can and should be done in voir dire.) Nonetheless, lawyers can elevate the themes and counterthemes (for simplicity, I refer to both of these as themes for the remainder of this section) in their case on cross-examination so that jurors see those things that you believe are most important to your case. Cialdini uses the study above to argue that "Frequently the factor that is most likely to determine a person's choice in a situation is not the one that counsels most wisely there; it is one that has been elevated in attention (and, thereby, in privilege) at the time of the decision" (Cialdini 2016, 25).

Highlighting your themes and important facts has another effect. Cialdini explains that your ruthless channeling of attention "not only promotes the now-focal aspect of the situation but also suppresses all competing aspects of it—even critically important ones" (Cialdini 2016, 26-8).

The Primacy of Associations: Words and Metaphors

The reknowned psycholinguist Gun Semin said that the main purpose of speech is to direct listeners' attention to a selected sector of reality. Once that is accomplished, the listeners' existing associations to the now-spotlighted sector will take over to determine the reaction. Cialdini thinks that "no longer should we think of language as primarily a mechanism of conveyance but of influence." He then cites the famous writer Joseph Campbell, who wrote *The Power of Myth* and is credited for inspiring the movie *Star Wars*. Campbell said, "If you want to change the world, change the metaphor" (Cialdini 2016, 100).

Cialdini also cites Joseph Conrad, the great novelist, who said, "He who wants to persuade should put his trust not in the right argument, but in the right word." Cialdini then cites several studies and examples where the proper word choice and/or metaphor made a big difference in persuasion. In one anecdote, he tells of a life insurance salesman, Ben Feldman, who single-handedly sold more policies in the 1980s than 1,500 *agencies* in the U.S. Obviously, he had tremendous drive, but he also had a way with words. Instead of talking about death with potential customers, he talked instead about how you would "walk out of life," and how there would then be a breach in your family responsibilities that would need to be filled. Feldman would pitch, "When you walk out, your insurance money walks in." This metaphoric lesson on moral responsibility would seal the deal. Other examples include companies that don't tell customers the "cost" or "price" of their offerings, words which imply a loss of resources, but instead use words like "purchase" or "investment"—terms that connote gain (Cialdini 2016, 107-109).

Consequently, the words that we use in our cross-examination questions are outcome determinative. Assume you are a prosecutor in a typical case where the IRS has been defrauded through the submission of fake tax returns that resulted in erroneous refunds. The traditional and non-persuasive way to summarize your theme in opening and build on it in cross would be: "This is a case about a defendant who submitted false tax returns to the IRS and then got refunds that he was not entitled to and deposited those monies in bank accounts which he controlled." You would then build your cross-examination questions around the technical words you used, such as "false tax returns," "deposited monies," and "control of bank accounts."

But there is a much better way to build your cross-examination: use descriptive words, such as, "The defendant is an accountant who *stole* innocent *people's identities* in order to steal from the IRS and then hid the money in *falsified* bank accounts he *alone secretly controlled*." In this better version, you would frame your questions using "stolen identities," "falsified bank accounts," and "secretly controlled accounts," words that are much easier for the jurors to understand and relate to.

The authors of *Nudge* come at this idea of word choice from a different angle than Cialdini, but they arrive at the same result. They call the technique "framing." How you frame information matters. Imagine that you need heart surgery. If the doctor told you that after five years, ninety people out of one hundred were still alive, you would probably agree to the surgery. But if you were instead told that ten people out of one hundred died after five years, your decision would be different. Specialists are not immune from framing. In a study, doctors were more likely to recommend surgery when told that ninety out of one hundred were alive after five years than when they were told that ten out of one hundred were dead after five years. "Framing works because people tend to be somewhat mindless, passive decision makers" (Tahler and Sunstein 2009, 37).

As a result, be aware that jurors are passive decision makers. This is why your themes for trial are so important.

Building Trust Persuades Jurors

In *Pre-suasion,* Cialdini cites how a company's best fire-alarm salesman succeeded. His goal was to build trust in order to get the sale. He would knock on the door and ask to come inside. Once inside and after the conversation had started, he would interrupt and pretend that he had forgotten his notebook, which he had purposefully left in his car. The potential customer would let him leave the room, walk to his car, and then return with the notebook. This process gained the trust of the potential customer who let him walk through the house unaccompanied to get the notebook and return without watching him (Cialdini 2016, 7).

The same is true for cross-examination. You must build trust with the jurors and never lose it. Always back up your claims with proof. Never ask a question where you lose credibility and the witness gains it by his answer.

In addition, you cannot be afraid of the weaknesses in your case. You must admit to them on cross-examination. There is only one story for the trial, and you are going to tell it—the good, the bad, and the ugly. Cialdini relates:

> When a legitimate expert on a topic speaks, people are usually persuaded . . . . This is especially true when the recipient is uncertain of what to do. . . . Rather than succumbing to the tendency to describe all of the most favorable features of an offer or idea up front and reserving mention of any drawbacks until the end of the presentation (or never), a communicator who references a weakness early on is immediately seen as more honest. The advantage of this sequence is that, with perceived truthfulness already in place, when the major strengths of the case are advanced, the audience is more likely to believe them." (Cialdini 2016, 164-5.)

In court, we must be *the* best expert in the room. Obviously, we must be seen as trustworthy. We all know that to be seen as trustworthy, we need to admit to the jury the weaknesses in our case in opening statement, on direct examination, etc. But I disagree with Cialdini that we should admit our weaknesses up front on cross-examination. That idea is inconsistent with the theme of his book that pre-suasion is important and that once an audience hears your positive theme, it is more likely to link later facts to that positive theme. I have also never seen great trial lawyers—who have the benefit of trial consultants' expertise—front-load their cross-examinations with weaknesses. Nonetheless, you must deal with your weaknesses on cross to maintain credibility.

The Fallacy of Multi-tasking

Never bore the jury on cross-examination and let them think about something other than your cross. Research shows that when we pay attention to something, the cost is that we don't pay attention to something else. The same is true for jurors. Multi-tasking simply doesn't work. Even though there are two channels of information available, we consciously select only the one we want to register at that moment. Cialdini explains that "the best we can do to handle multiple channels of information is to switch back and forth among them, opening and closing the door of mindfulness to each in turn" (Cialdini 2016, 28).

For example, multi-tasking gives you the apparent ability to focus on several activities in the same time frame—perhaps talking on the phone while reading an email message, or if you are a juror, trying to pay attention to a cross or thinking about what you are missing at work. Although it might seem that we are concentrating on more than one thing simultaneously, that's an illusion. We are just rapidly alternating our focus. However, just as there is a price for paying attention, there is a charge for switching it. For about a half second during a shift of focus, we experience a mental dead spot, called an attentional blink, when we can't register the newly highlighted information consciously (Cialdini 2016, 30).

To counteract multi-tasking, renowned psychotherapist Milton Erickson would lower the volume of his voice at a crucial point when talking to patients. Patients had to lean forward. This non-verbal communication—the leaning in posture of the patients—indicated that he was successful in getting them to pay attention to his most important point.

You can do the same thing on cross-examination. Pause before a big question. Slow down the tempo of your question to highlight important words. Emphasize through the volume of your voice the key word in your question. All these techniques grab and keep a jury's attention. Finally, use the techniques in this book so that the jury is never tempted to multi-task and turn its focus away from your cross-examination to something else.

3.4 YOUR DEMEANOR

Don't make it personal. This is the trap everyone falls into. Remember the greatest myth of cross-examination is that a lawyer can get a witness to confess. Making it personal is exactly what Tom Cruise's character did in *A Few Good Men*. That clash of egos between the lawyer and the witness is what makes it such a memorable scene. Unfortunately, that is not reality. If you follow his example in a courtroom, the jury will see that you are too emotional and not a truth-finder, because you are biased and not rational. Instead, your goal is to be the reasonable truth-teller in the courtroom at all costs.

> **Practice Tip**
>
> A cross-examination should be: 1) **clear** (uses questions that have only one fact or proposition), 2) **concise** (contains no more than three themes), and 3) **creative** (employs visual aids that are displayed throughout the cross).

Instead of making it personal, focus on the facts, and ask your questions in a calm and confident manner. There is no reason to be nervous, because you are asking only those questions that can force the witness to answer in the manner you want, as discussed in chapter 2, sections 2.3 and 2.5. On the other hand, you should not be overly aggressive or antagonistic. When the jury feels sorry for the witness because you are seen as being mean, unfair, or just unlikeable, a good cross becomes a bad cross. Likewise, your tone of voice should always make it clear to the jury that what you believe is the truth, and that you expect the witness to answer the way you want him to.

3.5 HIGHLIGHT WHAT WAS NOT ASKED ON DIRECT

What should you be doing during direct? Listen, listen, and listen. Your goal is to find something important to add to the outline you have already created for cross. There will almost always be something you can add. The gold mine you are looking for can be found by learning what the other lawyer was afraid to ask on direct. Finding gold is easier than you think. Most lawyers are afraid to bring out the weaknesses of their witness's testimony on direct. The reasons are twofold: witnesses don't like to admit mistakes in front of a jury, and lawyers are not confident they can discuss those weaknesses effectively, so they punt the responsibility, and that gives you the opportunity to cash in.

When this happens, add the topic that was left out to the first part of your cross where it will make the biggest impact. Such a cross could go like this: "Ms. Witness, I was listening intently to your direct examination, and I noticed your lawyer asked you a lot of different questions, but the one question he did not ask you was, 'How many beers did you drink before you got into your car?'"

Even if weaknesses are brought out on direct and there is no need to emphasize them, you still need to be flexible with your cross-examination. Assuming opposing counsel is good and ends his direct examination on a strong point, perhaps you should alter the order of topics in your outline so that you start your cross on the topic that the direct examination ended on. That way, you immediately challenge one of your opponent's strongest points.

3.6 IMPEACHMENT WITH PRIOR INCONSISTENT STATEMENTS

Impeachment means to challenge the truth of a witness's testimony with contradictory proof. One way is to use prior statements (the first "S" of CROSS: *prior inconsistent statements*) that are inconsistent with the witness's trial testimony. In addition, the prior statement—whether oral or written—might have failed to include critical information that should have reasonably been included. This is known as a prior inconsistent omission. This omission can be used to contradict testimony if the witness testifies to new facts that should have been included in a prior statement but were left out. While this section focuses on impeachment at trial, the same techniques apply to depositions.

There are seven common mistakes that attorneys make when impeaching a witness:

1) Attorneys try to impeach a witness with a prior statement that is not precisely contradictory. Close enough is not good enough. Obviously, if the current testimony is that the traffic light was red, a prior statement that

it was green is contradictory. But if the current testimony is that Paul was a bad employee who could not handle simple assignments, a prior statement that he was never late to work is not inconsistent enough to prove that the plaintiff was a good worker.

2) Attorneys try to impeach witnesses with multiple inconsistencies instead of just one at a time. For example, an attorney might ask, "On direct examination, you said that you had interviewed four witnesses, visited the accident scene, and conducted three tests, but in your deposition, you said you had not done all those things." Instead, if all these inconsistencies are important, take one at a time. This will allow you to emphasize each inconsistent statement more effectively and keep the theme of inconsistency before the jury for a longer period of time.
3) Attorneys do not make it clear to the jury that the witness has been untruthful at trial by testifying inconsistently; instead, they will attempt to refresh the witness's memory with his prior inconsistent statement. Of course, if the witness makes an innocent mistake and forgets something, refreshing his memory is appropriate. The point is that you need to make clear to the jury what you are doing: are you helping the witness remember or challenging his truthfulness? For example, when confronted with a significant inconsistent statement, attorneys will not follow the steps discussed below (the ABCs) but will instead say, "Didn't you say in your deposition . . . ?" When the question is phrased in that manner, it lessens the impact of the impeachment and gives the jury the impression that the witness has made an innocent mistake, and that you are just trying to help him remember.
4) Attorneys mistakenly let the witness read the inconsistent statement. The attorney should always maintain control of the prior inconsistent statement. That way, you can highlight what needs to be emphasized from the deposition by reading it aloud, which prevents the witness from reading the transcript aloud ineffectively or adding commentary to it, either of which could minimizing what he said in the deposition.
5) The fifth mistake—which will be discussed further in section 3.8—is that after successfully impeaching the witness, attorneys will ask the witness to compare and contrast the answer given in the prior statement with the answer given at trial. The problem with this is that the witness always has a good answer.
6) Lawyers tend to impeach on a minor point. Lawyers simply cannot help themselves to avoid this mistake. They have studied the deposition for so long and prepared for cross so much that they want to prove to the jury every little error the witness has made in her testimony. Perhaps the

witness has testified to incorrect dates, times of the meetings, and precisely who was there, as well as several other minor details. It may not matter at all. But the lawyer believes that if he can catch the witness in ten little mistakes, then he can make something big out of it. In truth, the lawyer just winds up playing a gotcha game, and instead of winning the battle, the lawyer looks petty, and the jurors wind up sympathizing with the witness who is getting unfairly beaten up.

Consequently, only impeach a witness on very important points. You are challenging the witness's truthfulness. You are making a big accusation. No one wants to be accused of being a liar. Here is a test that ensures success: put yourself in the jurors' shoes. Would a juror want to be challenged for not testifying correctly about dates and unimportant details that happened long ago? Of course not. Then why would you do that to the witness? You never want the jurors to sympathize with the witness during your cross-examination.

7) The seventh mistake is that lawyers do not know the proper technique for impeachment. I won't list the many overly complicated ways that it has been taught, but instead, I will cut right to the chase and teach you a new way that works every time.

3.7 THE ABCs OF IMPEACHMENT

Here is an acronym for impeachment that is easy to remember. It is the ABCs of impeachment.

This new technique reduces the number of impeachment steps to only three and is more powerful and memorable than other techniques.

First, **accuse** the witness of making a false statement at trial (the "A" of ABC). Next, **build up** the prior statement ("B"). Build up means to show the jury the trustworthiness of the prior statement with which you intend to impeach the witness. Finally, **confront** the witness with the prior inconsistent statement or omission ("C").

Example: Impeaching with Prior Inconsistent Statement

In the following example, assume that the witness testifies at trial that the traffic light was red at the time of the accident, but at her deposition, she testified that the light was green. You believe the truth is that the light was green.

Step 1: Accuse

Q1. Your testimony in court here today is that the traffic light was red? **[Your tone should be one of disbelief.]**

A. Yes.

Q2. Isn't it a fact that the light was green? **[This is the ultimate question. Your tone should be authoritative. You want to make it clear to the jury what you believe the truth is.]**
A. No. **[You don't care that she says no because you will prove she is lying.]**

Step 1 should take no more than two or three questions. Your goal here is simple: make it clear to the jury that there is an important inconsistency and that you believe the prior statement is the truthful one. The way to achieve Step 1 is to ask simple questions and use your tone of voice to indicate to the jury which of the two statements should be believed. This tactic is better than saying, "You're lying in court, aren't you?" because that question might be ruled by some judges as being too argumentative.

For Q2 in this example, it is crucial to emphatically tell the jury what you believe the truth is. Otherwise, the jury will have no idea why you are impeaching the witness or what your point is. For example, the truth in this example could be any number of facts, depending on what the deposition says. Although you have studied the deposition for days, the jury has no idea what is in it or why you are about to go through all these steps. Leave no doubt in the jury's mind by using the right tone of voice and by setting up what is in the deposition.

Depending on what is in the deposition and the point you are trying to make, Q2 could be any of the following: 1) Isn't it a fact the light was yellow? 2) Isn't it a fact you have no idea what color the light was? or 3) Isn't it a fact that you have testified in the past inconsistently about what the color of the light is?

Step 2: Build Up

Q. Do you recall giving a deposition in this case?
A. Yes.

Q. The deposition took place at your attorney's office?
A. Yes.

Q. She was present when I asked you questions?
A. Yes.

Q. A court reporter was present, just like the one here in court, who took down every word you said? **[Many attorneys ask this question to show that the witness knew her statement was important enough to be recorded. I usually don't ask it to save time, but I don't have a strong opinion about whether you should ask it or not.]**
A. Yes.

Q. You were under oath?
A. Yes.

Q. You swore to tell the truth, and nothing but the truth?
A. Yes.

Q. In fact, it was the same oath that you took today?
A. Yes.

This step is essential. Obviously, the courtroom is a formal and important setting. Build up the prior statement to show the jury that the witness knew—or should have known—the importance of the circumstances under which the prior statement was made. For example, if it is a statement the witness gave to a doctor for his treatment, you could point out that it is important to tell the truth to a doctor so that you can get the correct treatment. Or, the prior inconsistent statement might be what an officer wrote on his police report. You could emphasize that it is important for a police officer to write an accurate report because other officers and even judges will rely on it.

If it is a deposition, emphasizing that the prior statement was given under the same oath as the one taken at trial is persuasive. Also, showing that the witness had an attorney present enhances the reliability of the prior statement. In short, the prior statement was not made on a whim but under very formal circumstances and under oath.

Step 3: Confront

Q1. Your Honor, may I approach the witness? **[In federal court and many state courts, you must ask permission from the judge to approach the witness.]**
Court: Yes.

Q2. This is your deposition, isn't it? **[Show witness the deposition.]**
A. Yes.

Q3. You signed it at the end?
A. Yes.

Q4. And you were given an opportunity to review it for any mistakes before you signed it?
A. Yes.

Q5. Let me direct your attention to page 30, line 4. **[Point to the relevant lines on the page.]** *Isn't it a fact that you were asked the following question and gave the following answer: "Question: What was the color of the traffic light? Answer: Green."*
A. Yes.

Q6. Did I read that correctly? **[Use authoritative tone]**
A. Yes.

The beauty of Q6 is that it gives you the opportunity to emphasize the contradictory statement. Of course you read it correctly, but why not ask the witness to confirm that and highlight your proof?

Q3 and Q4 are good questions to ask if the witness has signed the deposition. Witnesses are not required to do this but are given the opportunity to review a deposition and make changes within 30 days of its preparation under Fed. Rule

30(e). By asking these questions, you build up the prior statements' reliability by showing the jury that the witness had the opportunity to review the deposition to correct it for any mistakes.

Also, never let the witness read aloud the prior inconsistent statement during the "confrontation." It is essential that you maintain control of the questioning and use the appropriate tone you want the jury to hear.

> **Practice Tip**
>
> When you give witnesses the opportunity to read their prior statement, they often will speak softly or try and explain away their answer. Instead, you should read the statement to stay in control.

An even more powerful way to execute Step 3 is to use visual aids. Instead of asking the court for permission to approach the witness and then reading the deposition to the witness, use your ELMO to display the deposition to the jury.

By using this technique, the jury not only gets to hear you read the inconsistent statement, but it gets to see it in black and white as you read it.

An even better technique is to play the inconsistent statement from the video deposition. Nothing is more persuasive than showing a video clip of a witness saying something in a deposition that is completely different from their trial testimony. Not only will the jury remember the impeachment better, but the witness will be more scared of your questions for the remainder of your cross. Here is the key to success: prior to trial, you must pick only the very best parts to use for impeachment. For a typical witness, this would be three or four video clips at most (one for each of your themes). In contrast, if you had 20 video clips, you would be spending an inordinate amount of time trying to edit the deposition prior to trial.

Moreover, once in the courtroom, your assistant needs to quickly find the relevant video clip. Having fewer to choose from will make the process easier, quicker, and less stressful. After direct examination is over, tell your assistant to get ready to find a particular clip or clips so that when the time comes, the video will be ready to play as soon as you give the signal. The steps for impeachment using the deposition video clip are the same as those for reading the transcript to the witness, except that you play the video for the witness and the jury. Here is an example:

> **Practice Tip**
>
> Make sure that the impeaching video can be quickly shown to the jury. You don't want to accuse the witness of lying and then fumble around trying to prove your point.

Step 3: Confront (using ELMO or video clip)

If you only have the transcript of the deposition, ask the following question:

Q. *Isn't it a fact that you were asked the following question and gave the following answer: "Question: What was the color of the traffic light? Answer: Green."*
A. Yes.
[As you ask the question and read the answer, underline or highlight the important words or the entire question and answer for dramatic effect.]

If you have a video of the deposition, ask the following question:

Q. *Isn't it a fact that you were asked the following question and gave the following answer:* **[play the video clip for the jury].**

3.8 THE BIGGEST MISTAKE LAWYERS MAKE DURING IMPEACHMENT

The biggest and most common mistake lawyers make during impeachment is that after they confront the witness, they ask the witness to explain the inconsistent statement. The lawyer cannot resist asking the witness some variant of this question: "Were you telling the truth in the deposition, or are you telling the truth now, at trial?" or "How can you say today the light was red when you said in your deposition that the light was green?" This type of question is irresistible to many lawyers, but it is fatal. Remember: the greatest myth of cross is that you can get the witness to confess to being a liar. Your goal with impeachment is a much simpler and realistic one: to *prove* that the witness is a liar. Also, by asking such a question, you give control of the flow of information back to the witness, and you weaken the dramatic effect of the impeachment.

Lawyers often ask me, "What do I do if after the confrontation, the witness starts explaining to the jury why there is an inconsistency, even though I never asked for an explanation?" Lawyers ask this because they are scared that if the witness does this, it will undercut their entire effort. Instead of being scared and defeated, take control and use the situation as an opportunity to show the jury that the witness is biased and afraid because she cannot answer a simple question. Here's what you should do:

Q. *Let me direct your attention to page 30, line 4.* **[Point to the relevant lines on the page.]** *Isn't it a fact that you were asked the following question and gave the following answer: "Question: What was the color of the traffic light? Answer: Green."*
A. Yes.

Q. *Did I read that correctly?* **[Your tone should be very authoritative.]**
Yes, but I said that in my deposition because I was nervous. I've had more time to think about what happened, and now I am certain the light was red.

If that happens, take control and walk right back up to the witness stand and repeat these two questions. The only allowable answer is "yes" to your very simple questions. The beauty of doing this is that the jury now gets to hear your impeachment a second time. It also has the added bonus of showing the jury that the witness cannot answer a simple question because she is biased in that she feels the need to offer excuses and explanations when you did not ask for any. Here's how the exchange would look if you followed this advice:

Q. *Let me direct your attention to page 30, line 4.* [**Point to the relevant lines on the page.**] *Isn't it a fact that you were asked the following question and gave the following answer: "Question: What was the color of the traffic light? Answer: Green."*
A. Yes.

Q. *Did I read that correctly?* [**Your tone should be very authoritative.**]
A. Yes, but I said that in my deposition because I was nervous. I've had more time to think about what happened, and now I am certain the light was red.

Q. *Ms. Smith, it is a very simple question* [**said with emphasis**]. *Let me show you your deposition again. Isn't it a fact that you were asked, "What was the color of the traffic light?" And you answered, "Green." Did I read that correctly?*
A. Yes.

Q. *And your sworn testimony in your deposition is that the light was green?*
A. Yes.

> **Practice Tip**
>
> After you have used the ABCs at least once, you can abbreviate Steps 2 and 3 as you see fit since the jury will understand the point you are making.

After you complete your cross-examination, it is likely that on redirect examination, opposing counsel will ask the witness to explain the inconsistency between her trial testimony and the statement with which you impeached her. But if your impeachment was clear, important, and dramatic, the witness' effort to wiggle out of the impeachment on redirect with her own attorney trying to help her will only look weak.

3.9 IMPEACHMENT WITH PRIOR INCONSISTENT OMISSION

Another way to impeach a witness with his prior statement is to prove that he left out something (omitted) in the statement that he should have reasonably included (omission impeachment). This is a must-use tool for when a witness exaggerates, embellishes, or does anything to make his testimony stronger by adding facts that were not included in a prior statement. The ABCs technique for this situation is exactly the same as above: accuse, build up, and confront.

Example: Police Officer Accused of Using Excessive Force (Cross-Examination of Officer)

Step 1: Accuse

Q. *Your testimony in court here today is that Mr. Smith reached for your gun during his arrest?* **[Use an incredulous tone.]**
A. Yes.

Q. *In fact, the truth is Mr. Smith never reached for your gun?* **[Confident and declaratory tone]**
A. No, that's not true.

Step 2: Build Up

Q. *Do you recall giving a deposition in this case?*
A. Yes.

Q. *The deposition took place at your attorney's office?*
A. Yes.

Q. *She was present when I asked you questions?*
A. Yes.

Q. *You were under oath?*
A. Yes.

Q. *You swore to tell the truth, and nothing but the truth?*
A. Yes.

Q. *In fact, it was the same oath as if you were in a courtroom?*
A. Yes.

Step 3: Confront

Q. *Your Honor, may I approach the witness?*
Court: Yes.

Q. *This is your deposition, isn't it?* **[Show deposition to the witness.]**
A. Yes.

Q. *You signed it at the end?*
A. Yes.

Q. *And you were given an opportunity to review it for any mistakes before you signed it?*
A. Yes.

Q. *Let me direct your attention to page 30, line 4.* **[Point to the relevant lines on the page.]** *Isn't it a fact that you were asked the following question and gave the following answer: "Question: What did Mr. Smith do to threaten you during his arrest? Answer: He would not put his hands behind his back and tried to get away from me."*

Q. Did I read that correctly? [**Your tone should be very authoritative.**]
A. Yes.

Q. Nowhere in that answer did you say that Mr. Smith reached for your gun?
A. No.

Q. Or tried to grab for your gun?
A. No.

Q. Or made any attempt to get your gun?
A. No.

Q. In fact, not just in this question, but nowhere in your entire deposition did you ever say that Mr. Smith tried to reach for your gun? [**Your tone has conviction.**]
A. No.

3.10 PROVING UP IMPEACHMENT

> **Practice Tip**
>
> Your tone of voice is critical for success. From your inflection, volume, and pitch, the jury should have no doubt that you disbelieve the current testimony and that the truth is contained in the prior statement or its omission.

On the rarest of occasions, a witness may deny that the deposition or grand jury statement you are impeaching him with is correct. If he denies the proof you have, you are entitled to corroborate its veracity by calling a witness. In this case, you would call the court reporter who took the deposition or grand jury testimony and have him testify to its accuracy.

On the other hand, a witness may deny having made a previous oral statement that undercuts his credibility. Let's use the example below to learn what to do.

Example: Witness Denial of Prior Oral Statement

Q. Isn't it a fact that you told your roommate that you were not raped?
A. No.

If this happens, you are allowed to "prove up" the impeachment. In this case, all you have to do is call the roommate to the stand to ask her about the statement to prove that the witness is lying.

3.11 USE COMMON SENSE TO BUILD YOUR QUESTIONS

In chapter 2, we learned the importance of the "O" in CROSS: getting an outrageous answer—that does not have the ring of truth to it—from the witness. Who decides whether an answer has the ring of truth? Obviously, the jury. Webster's dictionary defines common sense as "sound and prudent judgment based on a simple perception of the situation or facts." Indeed, before they deliberate, jurors are instructed by the judge as follows: "While you should consider only the evidence in the case, you are permitted to draw such reasonable inferences from the testimony and exhibits as you feel are justified in the light of common experience. In other words, you may make deductions and reach conclusions that reason and common sense lead you to draw from the facts."

Consequently, if your question to the witness makes sense to the jury, you win. On the other hand, if you get an answer that you don't want and the answer makes sense, you lose. It is that simple.

Sometimes the answer your question seeks is so obvious that you do not need any setup from other questions to win on the ultimate question. For example, "Officer, to know the exact words my client used to allegedly confess, it would have been better if you had recorded the interview, true?" The officer will probably deflect, avoid answering the question, and respond with something like, "There was no need to record it because I was taking careful notes." We all know, using our common sense, that an audio or video recording is going to be more accurate than handwritten notes.

Other times, you cannot win on the ultimate question without asking a series of questions to prove your point. There are two ways to do this. The traditional way is to imagine that you are building a staircase that leads to the ultimate question. Each step on the staircase is a question you ask the witness that builds on the witness's admission to the previous question. Each admission makes it more likely that the witness will admit the answer to your next question, because you have built momentum and the admission to one question logically leads to another.

Once you get several admissions, you will have reached the final step of the staircase, and you will win on the ultimate question you finally ask. Why? Because when the witness denies the ultimate question, his answer will defy common sense based on the previous admissions you have gotten. In other words, the jury will credit your question and discredit the witness's answer. Prosecutors and defense attorneys frequently rely on this strategy in criminal trials because there are often no depositions and a lack of written statements. However, all attorneys, regardless of whether they have such evidence, should know how to use this technique.

A more creative way to implement this strategy is used by Mark Lanier, as we will see in chapters 6 through 8. In short, you start with the ultimate question instead of ending with it. That is, have the witness deny the ultimate question at the outset, and then build your staircase one step at a time. By the end, you have so undermined the first answer you got that there is no need to ask the ultimate question at the end. This alternative method has the distinct advantage of signaling to the jury what your ultimate point is at the beginning of your questioning so that they understand why you are asking the questions that follow. Let's look at an example that will explain everything.

Example: Using Common Sense to Win on the Ultimate Question

Assume that the defendant, Mr. Jones, is charged with being a felon in possession of a firearm. He lives in a state where you can possess a gun if you are 18 years or older, but he is facing a federal trial because of the federal law that prohibits convicted felons from possessing guns. On February 2 of last year, he was driving home in his fiancée's car when he was stopped by the police for running a stop sign just before he pulled into the parking lot of his apartment building.

When the police approached the car, they saw the handle of a gun protruding from underneath the driver's seat. The defendant denied that he knew the gun was there.

At trial, Ms. Coleman, the defendant's fiancée, testifies as follows. The night before her fiancée's arrest, she was driving her nephew who is 19 years old to a McDonald's. She noticed a bulge in his waistband and found out that it was a pistol. She took the gun from him and put it under her seat. When she got back home, she did not take the gun inside because she knew her fiancée, with whom she lived, would be there and that he could not be around guns because of his prior felony conviction.

At first glance, it appears that Ms. Coleman has provided a solid excuse for her fiancée's possession of the gun. The only way to achieve any success on cross is to use common sense questions to undercut her credibility. Here is one way to do it.

Q. Ms. Coleman, the truth is that the gun is Mr. Jones's. **[Here is the ultimate question that is traditionally asked at the end, but that I like to ask at the beginning.]**
A. No.

Q. Ms. Coleman, you can legally possess a handgun, right?
A. Yes.

Q. You are older than 18?
A. Yes.

Q. You have never been convicted of a felony?
A. True.

Q. There is nothing wrong in any way with you having the gun found in the car your fiancée was driving?
A. Correct.

Q. Let me turn to your nephew for a moment. I know you don't want him to have guns, but there is nothing illegal about him having a gun?
A. True.

Q. He's 19 years old?
A. Yes.

Q. He's never been convicted of a felony?
A. Yes.

Q. In short, both of you could possess that gun without any fear of being charged with a crime?
A. Yes.

The above series of questions shows that Ms. Coleman risked no harm in claiming at trial the gun was hers or her nephew's. Next, you would need to show she is lying in order to protect her fiancée. First, you could ask the obvious questions about her bias for testifying.

Q. Ms. Coleman, you have been engaged for six months to Mr. Jones?
A. Yes.

Q. It goes without saying that you love him?
A. Yes.

Q. You count on him for both emotional and financial support?
A. Yes.

Then, you could challenge the reasonableness of her actions.

Q. Ms. Coleman, you claim that you took the gun from your nephew on the way to McDonald's. You could have thrown the gun away at the dumpster outside of McDonald's?
A. Yes.

Q. You could have thrown away the gun at the dumpster at the parking lot at your apartment complex?
A. Yes.

Q. In fact, you could have thrown away that gun at any number of trash cans on the way from McDonald's to your home?
A. Yes.

Q. Let me turn your attention to the car. It is the only car you and your fiancée have?
A. Yes.

Q. So, you share it for everything?
A. Yes.

Q. You claimed on direct that you left the gun in the car because you didn't want to bring it into your apartment where your fiancée was because he could not be near guns?
A. Yes.

Q. Yet, you left the gun in a car that you both share all the time?
A. Yes.

Q. You could have locked the gun in the trunk of your car where he would not be near it when he was in the car?
A. Yes.

Q. But you did not, did you?
A. True.

Q. Let me ask a few more questions on what you could have done if you had really found the gun. When the police arrested your fiancée at your apartment's parking lot, you ran out to see what was going on?
A. Yes.

Q. You saw four officers there?
A. Yes.

Q. When you saw them arrest your fiancée, you heard your fiancée yell, "Tell them it's not my gun."
A. Yes.

Q. You never told any officer on the scene that you had found the gun the night before?
A. True.

Q. After the arrest, you did not go to the police station to tell the police that the gun was yours?
A. Correct.

Q. At no point from the day of his arrest until this trial, have you tried to tell any officer that you had found the gun?
A. True.

Since the ultimate question, "The truth is, the gun is Mr. Jones's?", was asked at the beginning, there is no need to ask it again here. If you wanted to, you could sarcastically ask, "Are you still telling this jury that the gun is not Mr. Jones's?" However, if you followed the traditional method, you would not ask it at the beginning of your cross, but rather only at the end. Decide which way you prefer. In any event, each of these questions succeeds because they are built on a common-sense proposition that forces Coleman to either answer "yes" or "no" at the risk of being disbelieved. If the witness does not give an answer that common sense requires, she will have given an even more outrageous answer.

3.12 MASTER THE WITNESS WHO EVADES THE QUESTION

It is human nature to avoid answering questions that make you look bad or undercut your beliefs. Not surprisingly, the pressure cooker of a courtroom fosters this reaction in spades. Consequently, as soon as you start to make a point on your cross-examination, you will often find that the witness will stand his ground and refuse to directly answer your question. Instead, he will give an explanation, answer a different question, give you a canned response that is only somewhat related to the question, or try to distract you in any way he can. Even if you have never tried a case, you know this is true if you have watched a political news program. Do the politicians and talking heads answer a difficult question directly, or do they evade?

These tactics strike fear in a new attorney, and for good reason. What do you do when you are at deposition or in court with a jury watching, and the witness won't answer your question?

There are two techniques that guarantee victory and are easy to learn. As mentioned in chapter 2, your question must be simple and contain one fact or proposition that forces the witness to answer "yes" or "no." If it is not simple, then the witness has every right to give you an explanation that you do not want.

One technique is to repeat the question until the witness answers or the judge intervenes and directs the witness to answer. At trial, here is how it plays out.

While you are cross-examining the witness, the judge may be listening to you, but there is just as much of a chance that he is working on other legal matters on his computer. After all, he is not the fact finder; the jury is. So, he does not have to pay close attention to the trial—only enough to rule on objections. As a result, if you ask the court to instruct the witness to answer the question the first time you ask it, he probably will not have heard your question and will be reluctant to rule and just ask you to repeat the question.

Instead of asking the judge for help, repeat the question, and that repetition will get his attention. If the witness does not answer and you need to repeat the question a third time, the judge will grow impatient. He wants to move the trial along quickly, and witnesses who don't answer questions can really impede a trial's progress. Consequently, after your third attempt, the judge will almost always admonish the witness, "Answer the question." Now, instead of getting one victory, you get two. The witness is forced to answer the question, and the jury sees that the judge is on your side and not the witness's.

> **Practice Tip**
>
> When the witness does not answer a question, repeat the question until the witness does. That is *all* you have to do. However, most attorneys do not do this. Instead, they get emotional, argue with the witness, and forget the original question they asked.

Not only do you get your question answered, but another process takes place at the same time. Every instance where you have to repeat a simple question, the jury grows impatient with the witness's evasion and views you as reasonable and the witness as unreasonable. You are winning the credibility contest with the witness, which is the most important battle of cross-examination.

Example: Witness Who Argues

Here, a police officer is cross-examined by the defense counsel about his police report. In his report, he left the box blank where it asks for a description of where the drugs were found.

Q. *Officer, the heroin you found does not belong to Mr. Smith, does it?* **[Cross-examiner's theme]**
A. Yes, it does.

Q. *Let me ask you a few questions about that. When you arrested Mr. Smith at his home, you will agree there were several adults in the living room?*
A. Yes.

Q. *In fact, a party was going on?*
A. Yes.

Q. *The apartment is a three-bedroom apartment?*
A. Yes.

Q. *Here's my point: I know that you testified on direct that you found the heroin in Mr. Smith's bedroom,* ***but based on your police report, there is no way to know in what room the drugs were found?*** **[simple question asked for the first time.]**
A. They were found in his bedroom.

Q. *My question is,* ***based on your police report*** **[said with emphasis]**, *there is no way to know where the drugs were found?*
A. My memory is clear. They were found in his bedroom.

Q. *My question is,* ***based on your police report*** **[said with emphasis again]**, *there is no way to know where the drugs were found?*
A. It does not matter what my police report said; I know they were found in the bedroom.

[Repeat the question slower this time for emphasis.]

Q. *You will agree, officer, based on your police report, there is no way to know where the drugs were found?*
Court: Officer, answer the question.
A. Yes.

Another reason to avoid asking the court to rule that the witness's answer is non-responsive and to instruct the witness to answer the question is that you may not get the ruling you deserve. As mentioned above, the main reason for this is that judges are not paying very much attention to your questions in a jury trial. When you object that the answer is non-responsive, the judge is not going to say, "I wasn't listening." Instead, he may ask you to repeat the question or possibly make a quick decision based on an absence of information. By the way, in the judge's defense, he knows his ruling is not going to affect the outcome of the trial, he hates objections, and most trials are boring, so judges are accustomed to not paying attention.

We briefly looked at an example of where this happened in chapter 2, but let's take a closer look here. In the O.J. Simpson criminal trial, the defense attorney, Carl Douglas, tries to undermine Detective Ron Shipp's claim that O.J. was his friend.

Q. You and your wife have never gone on a double date with Nicole and O.J. Simpson in the entire time that you've known them, have you?
A. You're absolutely correct.

Q. You and your wife and he and his ex-wife never ***went*** *to a movie or a play or a concert together, the four of you, have you?*
A. My wife and I were **invited** shortly after he beat up Nicole, and that's-
Attorney: Move to strike that, Your Honor. Non-responsive.
Court: Overruled.

Douglas's objection is entirely appropriate. The question is not whether Shipp was *invited* but whether Shipp *went* to a movie. Instead of answering the question of whether he went to a movie, Shipp argues with the attorney and explains that he was invited so he can squeeze in the bad fact—from the defense's point of view—that O.J. had beaten Nicole in the past.

Who knows what Judge Ito was doing before the objection. But when he makes the wrong ruling, Douglas loses credibility in front of the jury because the judge has now blessed an answer that is argumentative instead of one that answers the question. Instead of objecting, Douglas should have just repeated his question again. By doing this, the jury would have seen that it was a simple question and that the witness was getting defensive and arguing instead of answering a legitimate question.

Another problem with asking the judge to instruct the witness to answer the question or to strike the non-responsive answer is that attorneys often make this request out of fear of the answer. Let's look an example from a domestic violence trial:

Q. When the police arrived at your house, you told the police, "I'm sorry, I'm sorry."
A. I also told them, "She was drunk and attacked me—
Attorney: Objection! Non-responsive. Your Honor, I ask the court to instruct the jury to disregard the last answer.
Court: The jury will disregard the last answer.

In the example just cited, the attorney hurriedly objects to try and interrupt a harmful answer because he is afraid if that if the witness makes the statement—which this witness had time to blurt out—the jury will believe it. On the contrary, by showing fear, the attorney confirms the truth of the bad answer.

> **Practice Tip**
>
> Instead of fearing a bad answer, just calmly ask the question again. If you do that, the jury will see your question as truthful and view the witness's desperate attempt to evade the question as an unbelievable embellishment.

I don't like caveats, but I feel compelled to alert you to one here. Two of the great lawyers profiled in this book, Tom Girardi and Mark Lanier, will sometimes repeat the question as has been taught in this section. But they also use an alternative technique; they will make a non-responsive objection and calmly ask the judge to instruct the witness to answer the question. When Girardi and Lanier make this request to a judge, it is a powerful moment. The judge will then turn to the witness and say in a stern voice, "Answer the question." Such a command from a judge would make any witness squirm. It also confirms to the jury that the lawyer is asking simple and fair questions and the witness is being evasive.

This technique works for these famous lawyers for a couple of reasons. First, they command a lot of respect when they walk into a courtroom. Judges are going to pay attention to Girardi and Lanier's questions the first time they ask them. Second, Girardi and Lanier are exciting to watch and listen to in a courtroom. Consequently, judges are less likely to be doing other work while they are on the bench during their trials. As a result, know your judge and decide how much attention he is paying to your cross when you decide how to handle an evasive witness.

Example from the Media

One of the best examples of how to handle a witness who does not answer a question comes not from a lawyer but a well-known British journalist. The technique is exactly the same: when an interviewee or witness does not answer a question, repeat it until he does.

Jeremy Paxman was a famous late-night interviewer on BBC television from 1985–2014. He was known for his hard-hitting interviews. In the interview below, he is questioning Michael Howard, the United Kingdom's Home Secretary. The interview led to the downfall of Howard as leader of the Conservative Party. (See video Paxman Clip One at www.winningatcross.com.)

In 1997, Home Secretary Howard (the interviewee) was being criticized over how he handled Her Majesty's Prison Service during a time that saw several escapes. Derek Lewis, the director of the prison service, had fired a warden during that time. Paxman was trying to find out if Howard had threatened to overrule Lewis's decision to fire the warden. Paxman asked the same question 12 times. Ask yourself if Paxman, by repeating his questions, proves that Howard threatened to overrule Lewis.

Q. *Mr. Howard, have you ever lied in any public statement?*
A. Certainly not. I gave a very full account of the dismissal of Derek Lewis to the House of Commons Select Committee, and to the House of Commons itself in a debate that took place. There can have been few decisions that have been subjected to more close and minute scrutiny in recent years than that decision. It was a decision that it was necessary for me to take after terrorists had escaped from Whitemoor, other dangerous prisoners had escaped from Parkhurst, and an independent report had found that there were serious weaknesses in the management of the Prison Service from top to bottom.

Q. *Derek Lewis says, "Howard had certainly told me that the Governor of Parkhurst should be suspended, and* ***had threatened to overrule me****." Are you saying Mr. Lewis is lying?*
A. I have given a full account of this, and the position is what I told the House of Commons, and let me tell you what the position is.

Q. *So you are saying that Mr. Lewis lied.* ***Did you threaten to overrule him?*** **[First time question is asked.]**
A. I was not entitled to **instruct** Derek Lewis, and I did not instruct him. And the truth of—

Q. *Did you* ***threaten*** *to overrule him?*
A. **The truth of the matter** is that Mr. Marriott was not suspended. I did not—

Q. *Did you* ***threaten*** *to overrule him?*
A. I did not **overrule** Derek Lewis.

Q. *Did you* ***threaten*** *to overrule him?*
A. **I took advice** on what I could or could not do—

Q. *Did you* ***threaten*** *to overrule him Mr. Howard?*
A. And I acted scrupulously in accordance with that advice. **I did not overrule Derek Lewis.**

Q. *Did you* ***threaten*** *to overrule him?*
A. Mr. Marriott was **not suspended.**

Q. *Did you* ***threaten*** *to overrule him?*
A. **I have accounted** for my decision to dismiss Derek Lewis—

Q. *Did you* ***threaten*** *to overrule him?*
A. —in great detail before the House of Commons.

Q. *I note you're not answering the question, whether you* ***threatened*** *to overrule him?*
A. **The important aspect of this**, which is very clear to bear in mind—

Q. *I'm sorry, I'm going to be frightfully rude but, I'm sorry, it's a straight yes or no question. It's a straight yes or no answer.*
A. You can put the question, and I will give you an answer.

Q. *Did you **threaten** to overrule him?*
A. **I discussed** this matter with Derek Lewis. I gave him the benefit of my opinion. I gave him the benefit of my opinion in strong language but I did not instruct him, because I was not entitled to instruct him. I was entitled to express my opinion and that is what I did.

Q. *With respect, that is not answering the question of whether you **threatened** to overrule him.*
A. It's dealing with the relevant point, which is what **I was entitled to do** and what I was not entitled to do. I have dealt with this in detail before the House of Commons and before the Select Committee.

Q. *With respect, you haven't answered the question of whether you **threatened** to overrule him.*
A. Well, you see, **the question is what was I entitled to do** and what was I not entitled to do? I was not entitled to instruct him and I did not do that.

Q. *Right. We'll leave that aspect there and move onto this question of your bid for the leadership of the party. Wouldn't a reasonable . . . .*

Why is this technique so successful? First, Paxman structures a very simple question with one proposition in it: "Did you threaten to overrule him?" If you have a complicated question with a lot of facts, it makes it very easy for the witness to evade a direct answer. On the other hand, when you ask a simple question, the only answer is a simple one: "yes," "no," or "I don't know."

Second, the technique works because when the witness fails to answer a simple question with a direct answer, the witness loses credibility with the jury (the "C" of CROSS). Every time you repeat the simple question and the witness fails to answer, you win again. By the end of this interview, is there any doubt in your mind that Secretary Howard threatened to overrule Lewis? In response to the simple question, the witness evaded with the following answers (there are too many to list all of them): 1) …the question is what I was entitled to do…; 2) I instructed him . . . ; 3) I advised him . . . ; 4) I did not overrule . . . ; 5) I have accounted . . . ; and 6) I gave him the benefit of my opinion in strong language.

The only difference between this interview and a trial is that after the third or fourth time of repeating the question at trial, the judge would have interrupted you and sternly instructed the witness, "Just answer the question." If it were a deposition, the witness's attorney might instruct his client to answer or risk having the opposing attorney file a motion with the court after the deposition, one that asks the court to compel the witness to answer the question that was asked at the deposition.

We can also learn from David Bernick, one of the leading defense attorneys in the country, who is featured in my trial advocacy textbook, *Turning Points at Trial.* He had several phrases he always used with a difficult witness. When a witness answers that you are implying something, fire back, "I'm asking you for a fact." When a witness gives an outrageous answer, respond sarcastically in the first part of your next question to highlight the unresponsive answer. For example, a key government witness in a criminal prosecution admitted to destroying personal calendars that a judge had ordered him to turn over a month before trial. When the witness explained, "I was just cleaning out, that's all." Bernick sarcastically responded, "Just cleaning out, that's all?" Other phrases Bernick used when a witness did not answer a question include: 1) "I didn't ask you that," 2) "Please answer the question," 3) "It's a simple question," 4) "I'm not asking you to speculate," and, 5) "Answer yes or no."

3.13 THE "I DON'T REMEMBER" WITNESS

One of the most frustrating witnesses is the one who claims not to remember events that he should. However, remember the "O" in the CROSS acronym from chapter 2: your goal on cross is not to get the witness to admit he is lying; just prove that he is by getting him to make an outrageous statement. Consequently, when you get him to make outrageous statements such as "I don't know" when the jury knows that he should, you have won. Here's an example:

The defendant is on trial for selling heroin out of a trap house. "Trap" is slang for a house that is used to sell drugs. The defendant was caught in the back bedroom as a SWAT team executed a search warrant after several purchases had been made by undercover police officers. None of the purchases had been made from the defendant, but the defendant was the only one in the house when the SWAT team arrived. In addition to finding the defendant in a bedroom, the police found several loaded handguns on tables throughout the house and on the kitchen counter. In addition, there were drugs, drug packaging, scales, and cash on the kitchen counter.

The defendant testified at trial that he had been at the house just to buy drugs and that he was allowed inside because he knew the sellers. The defendant had given several different versions before trial of exactly how he had entered the house and bought drugs on the day of the search warrant. On direct examination, the defendant claimed to not remember a lot of details of what he had done before the police arrived.

Q. *Tell the jury exactly what you were doing before the police arrived?* **[Prosecutor knows from direct examination that the defendant will claim he doesn't know.]**

A. I don't remember. All I know is that I was there to buy drugs.

Q. Tell the jury how long you had been at the house before the police arrived?
A. I don't remember.

Q. Did you go in the front door or the side door?
A. I'm not sure.

Q. Did you drive or walk to the house?
A. I don't remember. It happened six months ago.

Q. Are you telling this jury that you don't remember what you were doing the moments before 20 armed police officers busted down the doors of the house you were in?
A. Yes.

With this line of questioning, you have made your point crystal clear to the jury. Everyone on the jury has probably been pulled over by the police for a simple traffic violation. Everyone remembers exactly where they were when that happened and what they were doing before it. The defendant's outrageous statement that he doesn't know when he was arrested by a swarm of SWAT officers is all the victory you need.

In another example, Alberto Gonzales, the U.S. Attorney General in 2007, was asked to testify at a Congressional hearing on the handling of the Department of Justice's firing of eight U.S. Attorneys. The question was whether the firings were politically motivated or not.

In the four-hour testimony, Gonzales answered, "I don't recall," or similarly, with such statements as "I don't remember," 64 times. For example, Gonzales was asked about a recent meeting that was reflected in his calendar. He said that he had "searched my memory . . . but I have no recollection of that meeting." One senator said that he was "concerned about his recollection," and a journalist commented that it was so bad that if you had asked Gonzales where he had parked his car, he would have answered, "I don't remember."

3.14 THE CHARACTER WITNESS

On the rare occasion, a character witness may be called under Federal Rules of Evidence 404, 405, and 608 (or similar state rules). If this happens, it usually occurs when a criminal defendant calls a character witness to testify to a defendant's character for peacefulness and truthfulness and that the defendant could not have committed the crime. This is rarely done, because such a strategy is fraught with danger. First, you can easily restrict the damage of the direct testimony (the "R" of CROSS) by questioning him about his lack of knowledge regarding the alleged crime and where the defendant was (see the following example).

In this example, a defense witness, the preacher at the defendant's church, testified on direct that the defendant was known as a peaceful person. The prosecution uses the "R" in CROSS to restrict that damaging testimony:

Q. Reverend, you preside over a large church, correct?
A. Yes.

Q. It has over a thousand members and several hundred that attend each Sunday?
A. Yes.

Q. You saw the defendant only at services?
A. Yes.

Q. My point is, you never saw him on a church retreat, or at summer camp?
A. Well, yes, that's true.

Q. Let me turn your attention to the afternoon of January 6th of this year when a violent bank robbery occurred. You weren't anywhere near the Chase Bank on Cole Avenue, were you?
A. No.

Q. You don't know whether or not the defendant, wearing a red sweatshirt and blue jeans, went up to the teller, pointed a gun at her, and demanded all her money?
A. No.

Q. In fact, you have no idea about the peacefulness and truthfulness of the defendant on that afternoon because you never saw him that Monday afternoon, did you?
A. No.

Q. If it was proven beyond a doubt that the defendant was guilty of a bank robbery, that would change your opinion of him, wouldn't it?
A. Of course it would.

Remember, whenever a character witness testifies, he is an easy target for the "R" in CROSS. The witness does not know much about the crime or where the defendant was during it.

3.15 THE WITNESS WHO QUIBBLES

Perhaps the most frustrating thing in a deposition or trial occurs when a witness quibbles with the way you have phrased your question. There are four steps to solve this problem. The problem gets solved because the witness is either forced to answer the question or loses credibility for failing to do so.

David Boies, whom we will study in chapter 9, provides the perfect demonstration of how to solve this problem, and he had to do it quite often with Bill Gates. Boies was the attorney for the Department of Justice, which sued Microsoft for Antitrust violations in the late 1990s. The Department of Justice claimed that Microsoft bundled its web browser Internet Explorer software with its Microsoft Windows operating system. This bundling resulted in Microsoft's stifling competition, since Windows users had free access to Internet Explorer as opposed to other browsers such as Netscape that had to be purchased at a store (browsers were not free at that time nor could you download them). Below, Boies asks Gates about an e-mail he wrote in January 1996:

Q. *What were the non-Microsoft browsers that you were concerned about in January of 1996?*
A. What's the question? You're trying to get me to recall what other browsers I was thinking about when I wrote that sentence [in an email]?

Q. *No, because you've told me that you don't know what you were thinking about when you wrote that sentence. Right? What I'm trying to do is get you to tell me what non-Microsoft browsers you were concerned about in January of 1996.*
A. If it had been only one, I probably would have used the name of it. Instead, I seem to be using the term non-Microsoft browsers. **[Boise did not ask Gates "how many," but Gates tries to avoid the question by not answering it, so Boies repeats the question.]**

Q. *My question is what non-Microsoft browsers were you concerned about in January of 1996?*
A. I'm sure—what's the question? Is it—are you asking me about when I wrote this e-mail or what are you asking me about?

Q. *I'm asking you about January of 1996.*
A. That month?

Q. *Yes, sir.*
A. And what about it? **[Gates is in full dodging mode.]**

Q. *What non-Microsoft browsers were you concerned about in January of 1996?* **[This is the third time Boies has asked the exact same question. Look how Gates dodges the question a third time.]**
A. I don't know what you mean "concerned." **[Witness quibbles with the word "concerned."]**

Q. *What is it about the word "concerned" that you don't understand?* **[This is Step One, which you should take when a witness claims he does not understand a word.]**
A. I'm not sure what you mean by it. Is there a document where I use that term?

Q. *Is the term "concerned" a term that you're familiar with in the English language?* **[Step Two]**
A. Yes.

Q. *Does it have a meaning that you're familiar with?* **[Step Three]**
A. Yes.

Q. *Using the word "concerned" consistent with the normal meaning that it has in the English language, what Microsoft—or what non-Microsoft browsers were you concerned about in January of 1996?* **[Step Four (Repeat the question). This is also the fourth time the question is asked.]**
A. Well, I think I would have been concerned about Internet Explorer, what was going on with it. We would have been looking at other browsers that were in use at the time. Certainly [Netscape] Navigator was one of those. And I don't know which browser AOL was using at the time, but it was another browser.

Steps to Take When the Witness Quibbles

1. Ask the witness what he does not understand about the word (e.g., the word "concerned").
2. Ask if the witness is familiar with that word as it is used in the English language.
3. Ask the witness if he is familiar with the meaning of that word.
4. Ask the witness your original question again but begin by saying: "*Using the word* [insert relevant word] *consistent with the normal meaning that it has in the English language*". For example, "Using the word 'concerned' consistent with the normal meaning that it has in the English language, what non-Microsoft browsers were you concerned about?

Above, Boies gets his answer because Gates finally implies that he was concerned about Netscape Navigator and other browsers. But Boies notices (see following excerpt) that Gates inserts the phrase that he was "looking at" Netscape Navigator and others. It can be maddening when a witness doesn't answer a question directly, particularly a witness like Gates, who failed to do so throughout the deposition. You need to choose your battles carefully. Calculate how much time you can afford to pursue a line of questioning to get a direct answer at the risk of not having enough time to ask another line of questions. It is a calculation you constantly need to make with a witness who quibbles.

Here, Boies continues to battle. Even though he never gets the perfect answer that he wants from Gates, he still wins the war of credibility, as you'll see in the following excerpt.

Q. *What I'm asking, Mr. Gates, is what other browsers or what non Microsoft browsers were you concerned about in January of 1996?* ***I'm not asking what you were looking at****, although that may be part of the answer, and I don't mean to exclude it, but what non-Microsoft browsers were you concerned about in January of 1996?* **[The fifth time the question is asked.]**

A. Well, our concern was to provide the best Internet support, among other things, in Windows. And in dealing with that concern, I'm sure we looked at **competitive products**, including the ones I mentioned.

Q. *Let me try to use your words and see if we can move this along. What competitive products did you look at in January of 1996 in terms of browsers?* **[A variant of the original question that has been asked six times.]**

A. I don't remember looking at any specific products during that month.

Q. *Were there specific competitive products that in January of 1996 you wanted to increase Microsoft's share with respect to those products?* **[The seventh time]**

Gates' Attorney: Objection.

Q. *Do you understand the question, Mr. Gates?*
A. I'm pausing to see if I can understand it.

Q. *If you don't understand it, I'd be happy to rephrase it.*
A. Go ahead and rephrase it. I probably could have understood it if I thought about it, but go ahead.

Q. *In January 1996, you were aware that there were non-Microsoft browsers that were being marketed; is that correct?* [**Boies is now backtracking and losing ground on the concession he got earlier. Gates probably enjoys trying to frustrate Boies. Watch what happens a few questions later.**]
A. I can't really confine it to that month, but I'm sure in that time period I was aware of other browsers being out.

Q. *And were those non-Microsoft browsers, or at least some of them, being marketed in competition with Microsoft's browser?*
A. Users were making choices about which browser to select. [**Gates does not answer the question but starts to talk about "users."**]

Q. *Is the term "competition" a term that you're familiar with, Mr. Gates?*
A. Yes.

Q. *And does it have a meaning in the English language that you're familiar with?*
A. Any lack of understanding of the question doesn't stem from the use of that word.

Q. *And you understand what is meant by non-Microsoft browsers, do you not, sir?*
A. No.

Q. *You don't? Is that what you're telling me? You don't understand what that means?* [**Boies is incredulous.**]
A. You'll have to be more specific. [**Boies and Gates argue for another five minutes over terminology before the following and final question on this topic is asked.**]

Q. *Let's focus on January of 1996. What were the non-Microsoft browsers that, in your view, were competing with Internet Explorer in January of 1996?*
A. Well, users could choose from a number of browsers, including the original Mosaic browser, the Netscape Navigator, and I don't know what version they had out at the time. The AOL browser. And some others that were in the market.

The Mosaic browser mentioned in the last answer was really considered a part of the Netscape Navigator, so this last answer was really no more complete than the one given much earlier where Gates implied that he was concerned with Netscape Navigator. Boies could have stopped when he got the partial admission in response to the fifth time he asked the question (see previous example) and been no worse off regarding the substance of Gates's answers. When a witness does not answer the question, decide how important it is that you get the exact answer you want since you will have to expend time and energy pursuing the answer you want.

Another lesson is that if a witness does not answer a simple question, you may not get the admission you want, but the jury will discredit the witness for failing to answer simple questions that the jury expects a witness to answer. Gates's continuing efforts to duck questions, redirect questions by pretending not to understand the question, and his failure to understand words such as "concerned" and "non-Microsoft browsers" give Boies all the ammunition he would ever need to prove Gates was disingenuous.

This deposition excerpt was played at the trial, and it had just the effect Boies wanted. Microsoft was so worried about how Gates came across that it hired an expert to try and explain to the media why he was not more forthcoming. In essence, the hired expert declared that depositions are often messy and that Gates did not want Boies to put words in his mouth.

3.16 THE THREE CAMERA DEPOSITION

As previously stated (see chapter 2), you should prepare for and conduct the deposition as if you were at trial. Along those lines, Mark Lanier, who was briefly mentioned in earlier chapters and will be discussed in depth in later chapters, created the "three camera deposition." His goal was to design a deposition video that mimicked as much as possible the live testimony in a courtroom. Before we look at it, let's examine the current state of affairs of using deposition testimony during a trial.

The deposition testimony of a witness is substituted at trial for live testimony for a number of reasons. Since many state rules are modeled after the federal rules, let's look at Rule 32 of the Federal Rules of Civil Procedure. It provides that a party may use a deposition at trial if the witness is unavailable. Under this rule, a witness, whether a party or not, is unavailable if the court finds that the witness is dead, that the witness is more than 100 miles from the trial (unless the witness's absence was procured by the party offering the deposition), that the witness cannot attend because of "age, illness, infirmity, or imprisonment," or that there are exceptional circumstances.

When a witness is unavailable, the party may call the witness by deposition at trial. A couple of different scenarios follow. All of them are bad because the presentation of the deposition is beyond boring, and the jury will not remember any of the questions and answers. In addition, the jury will take its wrath out on the attorney who makes them sit through such a painful presentation.

If the deposition was not videoed, all that exists is a transcript of the testimony. Consequently, an attorney will read the questions and answers from the deposition to the jury. That is a sure fire way to put the jury to sleep. A slightly better way is for the attorney to have an assistant take the witness stand. Then the attorney reads the questions from the deposition and the assistant reads the answers. Even in this situation, it will not take long for the jury to lose interest. One reason is that there is no way for the assistant to recreate the emotions of the deposition or channel the witness who actually testified at the deposition.

A third way, but almost equally ineffective, is to play a video of the deposition if it was videoed. Attorneys rarely take the time needed to edit these videos so that only the most important testimony is played for the jury. In any event, all the jury sees at trial is a video of the witness because only one camera has been used at the deposition; it is focused on the witness and never moves. The jury hears the attorney ask questions, but he or she is never on camera. Another problem is that when the attorney shows the witness a document, the jury cannot see it because the camera at the deposition doesn't focus on it. Again, the camera is only on the witness. This creates the obvious problem that the jury cannot see the important document that the attorney shows the witness.

Enter Mark Lanier. He knows that if you don't present evidence that is interesting and memorable, all you are presenting are boring facts that the jury will forget. Although more expensive, here is how his three camera deposition works. (A video of a deposition that Lanier recreated for a seminar can be found at www.winningatcross.com under the title, "The Three Camera Deposition.") One camera is trained on the witness, and another camera is focused on the attorney asking questions. A third camera captures the documents that Lanier displays for the witness on the ELMO (document camera). When the deposition is played at trial, Lanier edits it carefully so that it appears as if the jury were watching the witness in person. For example, the jury sees Lanier ask a question, then the video switches to the camera that shows the witness answering the question. While the use of two camera angles instead of one is unique, Lanier makes it even better when he shows the witness a document.

At this point, the video shows the document with a small insert of the camera that is focused on the witness. (see 1:45 and 3:50 of the video clip). This arrangement focuses the jury on the important exhibit that Lanier asks the witness about, but it also allows the jury to see the witness's reaction to the exhibit. When Lanier wants the jury to focus more on the witness's answer than the exhibit, he edits the video so that all the jury sees is the witness's answer. Likewise, when Lanier asks a question but is really arguing his case to the jury, the camera is focused entirely on him (see 4:44). The point is that the video provides a lot to keep the jury's attention. It switches seamlessly between a view of Lanier, the witness, and the document depending on what Lanier wants to emphasize.

There is a lot more to learn in this video regarding Lanier's questioning style and use of visual aids, but those skills will be analyzed in chapters 6–8.

3.17 EXAMPLES FROM THE O.J. SIMPSON CIVIL CASE

The following excerpt is from the O.J. Simpson civil trial, and it has many examples related to the topics discussed in this chapter, as well as a few examples related to topics in the previous chapter. While we will examine cross-examination transcripts in more depth in later chapters, this a good starting point for seeing how the techniques taught in this book are used in actual trials.

Dan Petrocelli is the attorney for plaintiff Fred Goldman, the father of Ron Goldman, who was murdered along with Nicole Brown Simpson. He has called O.J. as an adverse (or hostile) witness in his case-in-chief. That means that instead of conducting a direct examination as you would with a neutral or friendly witness, the court allows you to cross-examine a witness that is expected to help the other side or be adverse to your position at trial.

Beginning

Here is the beginning of the cross-examination. Decide if you can understand Petrocelli's theme and if it needs any improvement. Also, notice how simple the questions are that force a "yes" answer from O.J.

Q. *Mr. Simpson, you first met Nicole when she was eighteen years old; is that true?* **[one main fact]**
A. That's correct.

Q. *She was a waitress, just having graduated from high school?*
A. A waitress, but I think she graduated when she was sixteen.

Q. *And you were a football player in the NFL at the time?* **[same]**
A. That's correct.

Q. *Almost 30 years old, right?* **[same]**
A. Twenty-nine.

Q. *And a month away from 30, right?* **[Immediately, Petrocelli shows O.J. that if he doesn't answer the question, he will force him to.]**
A. Yes.

Q. *And you were married at the time to your then wife?* **[one fact]**
A. Yes.

Q. *And [you had] two children?* **[one fact]**
A. Yes.

Q. *And living together, right?* **[one fact]**
A. Yes.

Q. *And when you met Nicole, you struck up, immediately, a romantic relationship with her, right?* **[one fact]**
A. Immediately, yes.

Q. And then in a short time, you got her a place to live, and the two of you began your relationship together, right?
A. Yes. I helped her get a place to live, yes.

The theme is fairly clear, but the line of questioning could be improved by declaring the theme in the first question: "Mr. Simpson, when you became romantically involved with Nicole, you had all the power, and she had none." Simpson would have denied this statement and answered, "no," which would have been perfect because the proposition would then have been proved with the facts that were revealed when Petrocelli asked Simpson about the leverage he had over Nicole due to his age, wealth, and celebrity status.

Impeachment with Prior Inconsistent Oral Statement

Below is an example of using the first "S" of CROSS, impeachment with a prior inconsistent statement. After showing that O.J. had the power, Petrocelli proves that O.J.'s relationship with Nicole was rocky. Ask yourself what you would have done if O.J. had not provided an admission such as the one he gives at the end of the excerpt. The answer will be provided below the excerpt.

Q. And it was a problem relationship for you throughout much of the time, true?
A. Not true. **[Petrocelli will now impeach this answer.]**

*Q. Did you not tell the Los Angeles police detectives who interviewed you on June 13, 1994, hours after Nicole's death, that you had **always had problems** with your relationship with Nicole; it was a problem relationship?*
A. Yes. We had problems in our relationship, but I don't think it was mostly a problem. **[O. J. does not admit that he "always" had problems.]**

***

*Q. Petrocelli: Did you not say to Detectives Lange and Vannatter, on June 13, 1994, concerning your relationship with Nicole, "I have **always** had problems with her, you know—that's our relationship, has been a problem relationship." Did you say that?*
A. Yes.

If O.J. had continued his denial, Petrocelli could have played for the jury a recording of the interview the detectives made. If O.J. had denied it was his voice on the recording, Petrocelli could have called one of the detectives to authenticate the accuracy of the tape.

Impeachment with Deposition Transcripts

As we learned earlier, you can use statements made at a deposition to impeach a witness.

Q. Let's talk about 1989, OK? That was an angry, intense, physical confrontation, true?
A. Correct.

Q. You're what, at the time, six-two, 215 pounds?
A. Yes.

Q. Nicole, five-eight, 135 pounds?
A. Yes.

Q. And you hit her that day, didn't you, sir?
A. No.

Q. Did your hand make contact with her face at all to cause injuries on her face? Yes or no?
A. I don't know.

Q. Didn't you testify—you remember testifying in this deposition, sir?
A. Yes.

Q. Remember I took your deposition over a number of days, and Mr. Kelly, Mr. Brewer also asked you questions?
A. Yes.

Q. Let me read from that deposition. By the way, you understand and you understood then, you were under oath and subject to the same penalty of perjury, just as you are today?
A. Yes.
Petrocelli: Line—page 1,032, Mr. Baker, line 21. . .
[**Petrocelli reading:**]

"Q. You were in such a rage that you don't remember what you did; is that right?"
A. I remember exactly what I did."

Petrocelli's impeachment would have been stronger if he had followed the ABCs of Impeachment. In fairness, since I had not created the technique at the time of this trial, that would have been hard for him to do. But, let's assume that time travel was possible and he had the benefit of seeing into the future. Here is what he could have done.

Hypothetical Cross-Examination

Step 1: Accuse the Witness

Q. Let's talk about 1989, OK? That was an angry, intense, physical confrontation, true? [**Clear theme is presented.**]
A. Correct.

Q. You're what, at the time, six-two, 215 pounds?
A. Yes.

Q. *Nicole, five-eight, 135 pounds?*
A. Yes.

Q. *And you hit her that day, didn't you, sir?*
A. No.

Q. *Your hand made contact with her face and caused injuries to her face? Yes or no?*
A. I don't know.

Q. *The truth is you know exactly what you did in that fight?* **[This is the "A" of ABC. Accuse the witness of the inaccurate statement and tell the jury what the truth is.]**
A. No.

Now, build up the prior inconsistent statement. This is the "B" of the ABCs.

Step 2: Build Up

Q. *Do you recall giving a deposition in this case?*
A. Yes.

Q. *The deposition took place at your attorney's office?*
A. Yes.

Q. *He was present when I asked you questions?*
A. Yes.

Q. *You were under oath?*
A. Yes.

Q. *You swore to tell the truth, and nothing but the truth?*
A. Yes.

Q. *In fact, it was the same oath as if you were in a courtroom?* **[The most important question in step two because it shows the oath at deposition is exactly the same as the one in court.]**
A. Yes.

Now, confront the witness. This is the "C" of the ABCs.

Step 3: Confront the Witness

Q. *Your Honor, may I approach the witness?*
Court: Yes.

Q. *This is your deposition, isn't it?* **[Show Simpson the deposition.]**
A. Yes.

Q. *You signed it at the end?*
A. Yes.

Q. *And you were given an opportunity to review it for any mistakes before you signed it?*
A. Yes.

Q. Let me direct your attention to page 1,032, line 21.
[Attorney reading:]

"Q. You were in such a rage that you don't remember what you did; is that right?"
A. I remember exactly what I did."

Q. Did I read that correctly? **[Your tone should be very authoritative.]**
A. Yes.

The advantage of using the ABCs is that it proves a stronger point than the one Petrocelli actually proved. Petrocelli merely showed that Simpson forgot what he had said in his deposition. He made the classic mistake of refreshing the witness's memory instead of impeaching him to attack his credibility. By using the ABCs, you make the stronger point that the witness is not simply forgetful but rather an untrustworthy witness.

Impeachment with Exhibits

Another powerful technique is to use emails, documents, or photographs to impeach a witness's testimony. In the following excerpt, Petrocelli shows the jury photos of Nicole's beaten face as he questions O.J.

Petrocelli: Let's put some photos up. And I apologize to the jury for having to show those photos. Exhibit 3. [**Plaintiffs' Exhibit 3 is displayed.**]

Q. You've seen those photos before, Mr. Simpson?
A. Yes.

Q. OK. Tell us how she got the welt over the right eye.
A. I don't know specifically how.

Q. You did hit her there?
A. No.

Q. And it's your testimony, before this jury, that you never touched her face with your hand, true?
A. I don't know, as I told you in the deposition, in wrestling her, maybe my hand hit—hit or was on her face. I certainly didn't punch her or slap her.

Q. You say your hand was on her face. Did you strike her at any time?
A. As I told you, I had her in a head lock at one point, in trying to get her out of the door, so I would assume that my hand was somewhere around her—her face.

Q. When you say "head lock," you said in the deposition that you had her head in kind of a head lock to get her out of the room, true?
A. At one point, yes.

Q. Are you saying that that's when that injury to her eye occurred?
A. I don't know when it occurred. But I'm assuming it occurred during the altercation or when she fell outside and—

Q. I would ask—
A. —I was a cause of all of that.

Q. I would ask that you not assume anything. Either tell us what happened or—
Baker: I would ask Mr. Petrocelli not to give my client legal advice.
Court: Overruled.

Q. Petrocelli: I just want to know what your recollection, sir, is; that's all. Just tell us what you remember.
A. I don't—I don't remember specifically when any single mark or injury came on her face, any of them. But I'm assuming they all happened during this altercation.

Q. I would ask that you not assume anything. Just tell us what you—
Baker: Again I ask that Mr. Petrocelli—
Court: Overruled. He may frame the question as he wishes.

Q. Petrocelli: Are you saying now that it's possible that you might have struck her with your hand, delivered a blow to her right eye to cause that mark? Yes or no?
A. No.

Q. It's not possible?
A. I did not punch her or slap her. That didn't happen.

Q. Did you strike her with your hand?
A. No.

Given what O.J. has said in his deposition, Petrocelli does not expect that O.J. will admit at trial that he hit Nicole in the face. But his goal is to win this line of questioning by getting an outrageous answer from O.J. in light of the photographs of Nicole's bruised and swollen face that proved she had been punched. Every time that O.J. claims in some form that he did not strike her or cause the injuries, his unbelievable answers are gold, and Petrocelli gets the "O" (outrageous statement) from CROSS.

Using Open-Ended Questions

It is a good idea to ask some non-leading questions for variety, but only do this when it does not matter how the witness answers. For example, in Q5 through Q13 below, it does not matter that O.J. answers "never," because that answer is not believable in light of the photos. The jury had also seen Nicole's diary where Nicole had written that O.J. had beaten her. In addition, Q2 is fine because it does not matter how O.J. defines "not so physical."

Q1. Well, there was more than one physical altercation, true?
A. I think you'd have to define that. There was one very physical altercation, and there were other times when they were not so physical.

Q2. What do you mean by "not so physical," Mr. Simpson? **[non-leading]**
A. Well, Nicole hit me a few times, and I didn't consider that too physical.

Q3. So the ones that were not so physical are the times when you say Nicole hit you, true?
A. Yes. And one time I grabbed her at a door and pushed her outside the door. That—if you call that physical, that's physical, yes.

Q4. And how many times did Nicole hit you, as you say?
A. Numerous times.

Q5. OK. And how many times, Mr. Simpson, in the course of these physical alterations, did you hit Nicole? **[A non-leading question followed by several others.]**
A. Never.

Q6. How many times did you strike Nicole?
A. Never.

Q7. How many times did you slap Nicole?
A. Never.

Q8. How many times did you kick her?
A. Never.

Q9. How many times did you beat her, sir?
A. Never.

Q10. And if Nicole said you hit her, she would be lying; is that true?
Baker: I object, Your Honor.
Court: Sustained. . . .

Q11. And you are aware that Nicole has written down in writings that you hit her, true?
A. Yes.

Q12. And you are aware that her writings describe numerous incidents when you hit her, true?
Baker: I object to this again.
Court: Overruled.
Baker: I think we need to approach.
Court: No. Overruled.
Petrocelli: Please answer the question.
A. Yes.

Q13. And your view is all that is false, true?
A. True, yes.

Keeping Eye Contact with Witness

Most attorneys ask a question and while the witness answers it, they look at their notes to see their next question, so that they can be ready to ask it when the witness finishes. When you do this, you miss everything, including the jurors' reactions and the witness's body language.

This next excerpt continues from the one just cited. Watch what a difference it makes when Petrocelli keeps his eye on the witness during the answers.

Q. *And you said Nicole is one of the most physically conditioned women you've ever known, right?*
A. Yes.

Q. *You said, at least that night, she was quite a match for you, right?*
A. It's tough—it was tough to get her out of the room, yes.

Q. *So what you did is, you started to sort of try to, from behind her, put your arms around her and get her out of the room, right?*
A. I don't know if that's necessarily true.

Q. *At some point, you think, in the process of trying to get her out the 15 feet or so to the door so you could close your door, you got her in a head lock; is that right?*
A. I don't think that's necessarily true.

Q. *Is that a fair description?*
A. No.

Q. *Well, tell us, then.*
A. She jumped on me, on the bed, and with her knees and arms—and then I kind of grabbed her, and we kind of fell over on the floor. And then I was trying to get her—to get her out of the door, and she was grabbing things and hitting. And eventually, I got her out of the door.

Q. *OK. And when you said you grabbed her, you put your right hand into a fist—*
A. Yes.

Q. *—just now.* **[Petrocelli notices a telling body motion O.J. makes.]** *Is that what you did that night when you grabbed her?*
A. Quite possibly when I grabbed her arm, quite possibly I did.

Q. *When you did—***now, you just put both hands in a fist**. *When you did it that night, did you punch her in the face with your hands?*
A. No. No.

O.J. has really dug himself into a hole. In the previous excerpts, he denies beating Nicole despite photos and a diary to the contrary. Now, he puts both hands in a fist as he explains their fight. If Petrocelli had been looking at his notes instead of O.J., he would have missed this important detail.

The "O" of CROSS

Here, Petrocelli questions O.J. about a photograph that revealed red marks on Nicole's neck that are in the shape of a hand. See if you agree with O.J.'s implication in this exchange that he could have touched her neck but it was not his hand that caused the red marks and bruising.

Q. *Did you put your fingers and hands on her throat and leave marks on her throat, sir?*
A. I don't recall doing that at all, no.

Q. *You are aware she had marks on her throat, are you not?*
A. I'm aware that someone said she did, yes.

Q. *You believe that's false?*
A. I never saw them. And the next day, she showed me all her bruises. . . .

Q. *It's your testimony that you never touched her throat, right?*
A. I don't know. When you say "touched her throat," I was wrestling her; I could have touched her throat, yes.

End Strong

Your last line of questioning must be powerful and winning, because the jury will remember who won the exchange, based on the theory that jurors remember what they hear first and last the most (primacy and recency). In the questions preceding this excerpt, O.J. discussed the famous Bronco chase and his conversations on the phone with the police during it. Simpson admitted that he had written a suicide note prior to the police chase.

One way to end your cross is to ask a series of questions that summarize the main points in your case. Even though the witness will not answer "yes," you can concisely remind the jury of the main facts in your case and let the jury decide the meaning of the witness's demeanor when he denies your claims.

Q. *Please. And the question—you never accused the person on the telephone from the police department when you were talking* **[during the Bronco chase]** *of planting evidence against you, correct?*
A. Correct.

Q. *Or framing you for a murder that you did not commit?*
Correct?
A. That's correct.

Q. *And the reason you didn't do so, Mr. Simpson, is because you knew you committed those murders, correct?*
A. That's incorrect.

Q. *And that is why you were going to kill yourself, because you knew you were going to spend the rest of your life in jail, correct?*
A. That's incorrect.

Q. *And you knew that you dropped the blood at Bundy, correct?*
A. That's incorrect.

Q. *And knew, sir, that you went there that night and you confronted Nicole and you killed her—*
BAKER: Your Honor, I'm going to object.

Q. —correct?
Baker: This has been asked and a speech is already—

Q. Correct?
Baker: It's already been asked and answered.
Court: Overruled. You may answer.
A. No, Mr. Petrocelli. That's totally, absolutely incorrect.

Q. And Ronald Goldman came upon you when you were there with Nicole, and you did not expect him that night, correct?
Baker: I'm going to object.
A. I don't know Ron Goldman.
Court: Overruled.

Q. And Ronald Goldman got into a fight with you as he tried to stop you, and you cut him and you slashed him until he died, collapsed in your arms. True or untrue?
A. Untrue.

Q. And you left him there to die, Mr. Simpson, with his eyes open, looking right at you. True or untrue?
A. That's untrue.
Petrocelli: I have no further questions.

The defense attorney's objections highlight Petrocelli's success and the damage he did to O.J. by asking the questions.

3.18 CHAPTER CHECKLIST

1. Less is more. If you have any doubt about the importance of a line of questioning, leave it out.
2. Follow the Rule of Three and limit your major points to three. Mark Lanier told the jury in his opening that he would show Johnson & Johnson's house was 1) built on a poor foundation, 2) was built with shoddy equipment, and 3) caused bad damage. His cross-examinations were built on these three points.
3. While your credibility is at stake throughout a trial, perhaps there is no greater moment when you risk losing it than on cross, since there is a witness who can immediately damage you if your claim is wrong.
4. Robert Cialdini explains, "The best persuaders become the best through pre-suasion—the process of arranging for recipients to be receptive to a message before they encounter it . . . . The answer lies partly in a poorly appreciated tenet of all communication: 'What we present first changes the way people experience what we present to them next'" (Cialdini 2016, 4).
5. The authors of *Nudge* relate a study where the sale of food items could be increased or decreased by their positioning in a cafeteria line. "There is no

such thing as a neutral design. . . . A choice architect has the responsibility for organizing the context in which people make decisions. . . . A good rule of thumb is to assume that 'everything matters' " (Thaler and Sunstein 2009, 3).

6. Elevate the themes in your cross-examination so that jurors see what you believe is important in your case. Cialdini uses a study to argue that "Frequently the factor that is most likely to determine a person's choice in a situation is not the one that counsels most wisely there; it is one that has been elevated in attention (and, thereby, in privilege) at the time of the decision" (Cialdini 2016, 25).
7. The ruthless channeling of attention to your themes on cross promotes your positive message but also suppresses all competing aspects of it—even critically important ones.
8. Joseph Campbell, who wrote *The Power of Myth* and is credited for inspiring the movie *Star Wars*, said, "If you want to change the world, change the metaphor."
9. Cialdini cites several studies and examples where the proper word choice and/or metaphor made a big difference in persuasion. In one anecdote, he tells of a life insurance salesman, Ben Feldman, who, instead of talking about death with potential customers, he talked instead about how you would "Walk out of life." There would then be a breach in your family responsibilities that would need to be filled. Feldman would pitch, "When you walk out, your insurance money walks in." This metaphoric lesson of moral responsibility would seal the deal (Cialdini 2016, 107–109).
10. The words you use to frame your questions are important. Remember the heart surgery study from *Nudge*. In a study, doctors were more likely to recommend surgery when told that 90 out of 100 were alive after five years than when they were told that 10 out of 100 were dead after five years. "Framing works because people tend to be somewhat mindless, passive decision makers" (Thaler and Sunstein 2009, 37).
11. You must build trust with the jurors and never lose it. Always back up your claims with proof. Never ask a question where you lose credibility and the witness gains it by his answer.
12. Never bore the jury on cross-examination. Research shows that when we pay attention to something, the cost is that we don't pay attention to something else. The same is true for jurors. When jurors switch their attention from your cross-examination to something else, there is a price that is paid. For about a half second during a shift of focus, we experience a mental dead spot, called an attentional blink, when we can't register the newly highlight information consciously.
13. To counteract multi-tasking, you can do several things: pause before a big question, slow down the tempo of your question to highlight important words, and emphasize through volume the key word in your question.

14. Robert Cialdini, an expert on persuasion explains: "[I]n contests of persuasion, counterarguments are typically more powerful than arguments. This superiority emerges especially when a counterclaim does more than refute a rival's claim by showing it to be mistaken or misdirected in the particular instance, but does so instead by showing the rival communicator to be an untrustworthy source of information" (Cialdini 2016, 92).
15. Your demeanor is important. Instead of making it personal, focus on the facts, and ask your questions in a calm and confident manner.
16. A successful cross-examination is: 1) clear (questioning that has one fact or proposition only), 2) concise (no more than three themes), and 3) creative (uses visual aids throughout).
17. Highlight what was not asked on direct. If appropriate, get the witness to admit he left out important facts during direct testimony or that his lawyer failed to ask important questions.
18. Be flexible with the order of your topics. If opposing counsel ends direct on a strong point, consider altering the order of topics in your outline so that you start your cross on the topic that direct examination ended on. By doing so, you immediately challenge one of your opponent's strongest points.
19. The seven common impeachment mistakes are: 1) trying to impeach with a prior statement that is not precisely contradictory, 2) trying to impeach with multiple inconsistencies instead of just one at a time, 3) refreshing the witness's memory instead of impeaching, 4) letting the witness read the inconsistent statement, 5) letting the witness compare prior statement with current statement, 6) impeaching on a minor point that the juror does not care about, and 7) not knowing the proper technique.
20. The three steps for the ABCs of impeachment are: 1) *accuse* the witness of making a false statement at trial (the "A" of ABC.), 2) *build up* the prior statement (the "B" of ABC), and 3) *confront* the witness with the prior inconsistent statement or omission (the "C" of ABC).
21. When confronting the witness, don't allow her to read the prior statement since she will use the opportunity to put her spin on it. Maintain control and read it yourself.
22. If you use a video clip from a deposition for impeachment, make sure that the impeaching video can be quickly shown to the jury. You don't want to accuse the witness of lying and then fumble around trying to prove your point.
23. The biggest and most common mistake lawyers make during impeachment is that after they confront the witness, they ask the witness to explain the inconsistent statements. Don't give control back to the witness.
24. Another way to impeach a witness with her prior statement is to prove that she left out something that she should have reasonably included (omission

impeachment). This is a must-use tool when a witness exaggerates, embellishes, or does anything to make her testimony stronger by adding facts that were not included in a prior statement.

25. Your tone of voice is critical for success. By your inflection, volume, and pitch, the jury should have no doubt that you disbelieve the current testimony and that the truth is contained in the prior statement or its omission. From your tone, the jury should never be confused about which statement you believe to be true.
26. When the witness does not answer a question, whether you are in court or at a deposition, repeat the question until the witness answers it. That is *all* you have to do. But most attorneys do not do this. Instead, they get emotional, argue with the witness, and forget the original question they asked.
27. If you object that the answer is non-responsive, you need to make sure the judge has been paying attention to your question in order to get a favorable ruling (sometimes judges are not listening carefully and will err on the witness's behalf).
28. Instead of fearing a bad answer, just calmly ask the question again. If you do that, the jury will see your question as containing truthful facts, and they will view the witness's desperate attempt to evade the question as an embellishment that should not be believed.
29. Other techniques to use when the witness does not answer the question include saying the following before repeating your question: 1) "I didn't ask you that," 2) "Please answer the question," 3) "It's a simple question," and 4) "I'm not asking you to speculate. Answer yes or no."
30. The three camera deposition is the best way to present the deposition testimony of an unavailable witness. Have one camera trained on the witness, one on yourself, and the third on the documents you are showing the witness on the ELMO. Then, edit the video to show one camera angle or two (a screen with an insert of the other camera) where appropriate to make it interesting for the jury.

CHAPTER FOUR

The Expert Witness

"Truth is ever to be found in the simplicity, and not in the multiplicity and confusion of things."—*Isaac Newton*

At first glance, taking an expert witness's deposition or cross-examining her at trial can appear very challenging. The two main reasons are that you will almost certainly have less expertise than the expert, and the expert is usually a professional witness who has learned how to defend her positions from having been cross-examined by other attorneys. Don't be overwhelmed. There are a few easy tricks to master that will guarantee success. However, before we learn these secrets, let's look at one preliminary issue: How does a witness get accepted by the court to give expert testimony?

4.1 REQUIREMENTS OF THE DAUBERT STANDARD

In order to testify at trial, an expert must meet the criteria set forth in the Daubert standard, which is a rule of evidence regarding the admissibility of an expert witness's scientific testimony; it is based in part on the U.S. Supreme Court case *Daubert v. Merrell Dow Pharmaceuticals, Inc.*, 509 U.S. 579 (1993). Federal judges and many state judges use this determination to decide whether an expert's opinion is trustworthy. A judge uses the following criteria: whether a theory or technique can be (and has been) tested, whether it has been subjected to peer review and publication, the known or potential rate of error, and whether the theory or technique is generally accepted.

There is no need to get caught up in the *Daubert* criteria since most experts will satisfy them. But, if you believe that an expert does not meet the criteria, you must make an objection (usually before trial), and then the court will hold a hearing before trial or outside the presence of the jury during trial (known as a

CHAPTER ROAD MAP

- Learn unique topics to cross an expert on.
- Learn from a famous trial example how to cross an expert on his lack of qualifications.
- Learn from the Zimmerman trial how to undermine an expert's credibility by pointing out what he has failed to do.

Daubert hearing). Attorney David Boies made just such a challenge in the Proposition 8 trial, which we will analyze in Chapter Nine.

4.2 DISCOVERY QUESTIONS TO ASK AT A DEPOSITION

You can win at trial by asking a series of specific questions at deposition—not cross-examination questions, but rather discovery questions that will help you develop a successful cross-examination for trial.

First, ask the expert to explain the methodology she used in formulating her opinion. An expert's report will discuss in summary fashion her opinion and the reasons for it. However, a deposition is critical in helping to understand the details behind the reasons for the opinion. You need the details for two reasons: 1) when she tries to explain the reasons for her opinion in detail, you might find that the expert used flawed reasoning; 2) the explanations will help your side's expert develop better counterarguments for her deposition or trial testimony.

A simple way to do this is to show the expert her report at the deposition and have her go through each paragraph and explain her conclusions.

> **Practice Tip**
>
> Every expert has to make assumptions, and when they do, you can show that if the assumptions were different, the conclusions would be different.

In order to ensure that the expert does not add important details later, pin her down on her opinions. Ask the following to ensure there are no surprises at trial: 1) "Have you stated all the reasons for your opinion in your report and in this deposition?" and 2) "Have you relied on any authorities other than those mentioned in your report and in this deposition?" This way, if the witness tries to give additional reasons or authorities at trial that support her opinion, she will look disingenuous.

Second, ask the expert witness, "Why do you disagree with [name of your expert]?" One of the most important things you can accomplish at the deposition is to find out exactly which points the expert disagrees with and the reasons why. Show the witness your expert's report. Go through the important paragraphs and ask the witness why she agrees or disagrees with your expert's findings. This question will prevent any surprises at trial.

Third, ask the expert how frequently she has been hired by plaintiffs or defendants. Usually, the expert will say that she testifies about 60–40 for one side over the other. Upon closer investigation, the facts often show that the expert clearly is hired much more often by one side than the other. For that same reason, don't take your own expert's word for it that she testifies similarly. You will be unpleasantly surprised when she testifies differently at her deposition.

Fourth, near the end of the deposition, ask the expert the following: "Are you going to testify at trial to any opinions you have not given here today? Are there any assumptions or reasons that support your opinions that you are going to testify at trial that you have not stated here today?" If she answers yes, explore what those opinions are and what the reasons are. These questions will help you nail down the extent of the expert's opinions.

> **Practice Tip**
>
> Ask the adverse expert what percentage of her income is derived from being a paid expert. Often, a majority of an expert's livelihood is dependent on being hired as an expert and this reveals her bias.

Experts are always trying to add to their opinions at trial. For example, they may come up with additional reasons to support their conclusion or give an alternative conclusion for the first time at trial. Since most judges will not allow an expert to go beyond her opinions set forth in her expert report, you need to make sure in the deposition that the expert states clearly all the opinions she is rendering and her reasons for them.

Sometimes the expert will hedge and say that she may change her opinion depending on other depositions or facts that come to light. That is why you should generally take an expert's deposition at the end of the discovery. That way, she can't hedge her conclusions and you can be certain she won't have a good reason to change her opinion.

4.3 PREPARING FOR CROSS-EXAMINATION

The most efficient way to prepare for cross is to ask *your* expert to tell you what questions you need to ask the *opposing* expert. After all, the subject area will be difficult to grasp and only by talking to your expert can you make the deposition or trial a level playing field. Have your expert teach you what you need to know so that you can ask intelligent questions and understand the opposing expert's answers. Specifically, ask your expert to go through the opposing expert's written report with you and explain its strengths and weaknesses, sentence by sentence. Then, have your expert review the opposing expert's curriculum vitae and again review its strengths and weaknesses with you.

Gather all the key information you can about the opposing expert. A good place to start is Westlaw or LexisNexis. For example, LexisNexis has "Expert Research on Demand," formerly known as IDEX, which provides information regarding Daubert challenges, deposition transcripts, trial testimony, verdicts, settlements, and other valuable information.

Scour the Internet for information about the opposing expert. Is there anything on Facebook or LinkedIn that reveals he belongs to groups that might undercut his credibility? Has the board his specialty is certified by taken any adverse action against him? For many kinds of doctors, there are various websites that have patient reviews.

Look into specialized litigation groups that have their own databases, such as the Defense Research Institute (DRI), a large international organization of defense attorneys and in-house counsel, and the American Association for Justice (AAJ), an organization of plaintiff's trial attorneys. Finally, a lot of experts have their own websites, and it is shocking to see the kinds of proclamations they put on them. You can use these proclamations to undercut their credibility.

Also, collect an expert's previous depositions and trial testimonies. Under Federal Rule 26(a)(2)(B), an expert must disclose in his report a list of all cases in which he has testified during the previous four years, either at deposition or trial. Contact the attorneys who took the expert's deposition in the cases listed. The attorneys often respond by sending you trial or deposition transcripts in which they were involved. This step is important because it can help you determine if the expert has testified significantly differently before on the same issue that is in your current trial case. Don't forget to ask the attorney what he thought of the expert. He may gladly turn over his entire investigative file to help you out.

The opposing expert must also provide a list of his own publications. Have your expert review those publications to determine how good they are. Those publications are often not directly on point to the subject matter of the expert's opinion. Such information can be used to undercut his authority for arriving at opinions that hurt your case. In addition, check the sources the expert refers to in his report. Many times the articles or treatises the expert refers to are not credible.

Finally, when you send out your notice of deposition, use a subpoena *duces tecum* to request that the expert bring to the deposition the articles he has relied on. Simply state in your notice to the expert that the notice includes a subpoena *duces tecum* and list on a separate page in the notice the documents you wish the expert to bring. The reason to do this is that some of the articles in the opponent's report that *your* expert needs to review may be difficult for him to find.

> *An expert is a person hired to divorce yourself from your common sense.*
>
> —Mark Twain

Experts Are Hard to Pin Down

The first thing you will learn about an expert is that he can be very hard to pin down. Indeed, it can be very difficult to get him to commit to anything other than his ultimate (final) conclusion. For example, if you ask him if today is Monday, he will probably say, "It depends what part of the world you are in." An expert will emphatically declare his final opinion but less strongly how he got there. The reason is that an expert never wants to get boxed in by assumptions that—if later changed—would force him to alter his opinion. The expert is getting paid a lot of money to help the other side, and he will do everything he can to come through on his commitment.

Let's look at an example from the Microsoft antitrust trial where an expert admitted to an assumption only after being confronted with his own sworn testimony in a prior lawsuit. In the trial where this cross took place, the Department of Justice and several states sued Microsoft for antitrust violations, alleging that Microsoft bundled its web browsing software, Internet Explorer, with its Windows operating system. The plaintiffs claimed that this bundling resulted in Microsoft's stifling competition and suppressing innovation, since Windows users had free access to Internet Explorer as opposed to other browsers, such as Netscape, that had to be purchased at a store. Microsoft stated that the bundling of Microsoft Windows and Internet Explorer was the result of innovation that met consumers' needs.

The trial started on May 18, 1998, in Washington, D.C. A witness for the plaintiffs claimed that a Microsoft vice-president declared that it was Microsoft's goal to extinguish Netscape (a rival browser) by giving away Internet Explorer with Windows. Judge Jackson issued his findings on November 5, 1999, stating that Microsoft had a monopoly of the personal computer operating systems market and that Microsoft had smothered the competition, including Apple, Java, and Netscape. The case was settled after an appeal.

Example: Cross-examination of Dean Schmalensee (*U.S. v. Microsoft*)

In this example, David Boies tries to get Microsoft's expert, Dean Schmalensee, to admit to a simple type of methodology that even a layperson would understand and agree with. However, the expert—as is true with most experts—does not want to give an inch in the deposition for fear of letting down his client by making any concessions at all.

Q. *Now, would you also agree that* ***the standard way*** *of approaching that question, that is, the question as to whether a firm has monopoly power, is to first define a relevant market and then look at what the share of that market is, and then if the share is sufficiently high, to look at conditions of entry?*

A. That is, as Professor Fisher [a government expert] indicated in his testimony, one approach. It provides some information. Market share, particularly in areas where market boundaries are difficult to draw or fluid, is not terribly informative. That is **an approach**. It is useful in some circumstances. [**The expert will only concede that it is "an approach," not that it is the standard way**.]

Q. Well, more than being an approach, would you agree that that is the traditional and most common approach?

A. I haven't done a survey. I have, of course, written on its utility for the last 20 years or so, and there are some circumstances in which it is not particularly informative, as Professor Fisher has said, and some where it is. It is **an approach** that has been used for a long time. **[Again, the expert will only admit that it is "an approach."]**

Q. Let me put before you and offer in evidence plaintiffs' exhibit 1526, which are excerpts from testimony that you gave in the Bristol case [another lawsuit] that you referred to. . . . Let me direct your attention, Dean Schmalensee to page 541 and lines 11 through 19, and the question and answer there, which I will read . . . [reading]: "Question: how does an economist such as yourself go about determining whether a seller of a product has monopoly power in a given product market?
Answer: There are a number of approaches depending on the availability of data. The ***traditional and most common approach*** *in an instance where one can define a relevant market in the antitrust sense, is to first look at shares of that market and then if shares are large, to move on to consider conditions of entry."*

Now, recognizing that there may be cases in which you want to take a different approach, ***would you agree that the traditional and most common approach*** *is the approach that you have identified here?*

A. When, as that indicates, one can define a relevant market in an antitrust sense, **yes**.

In the example, only after being confronted with his prior sworn statement does the witness admit the obvious: the starting point for determining if there is a monopoly is to first determine the relevant market. This expert would not have admitted this fact if he had not been confronted with his prior sworn statement. Why would the expert not admit such a simple fact, particularly if he had said so under oath in the past?

Experts often won't give up an inch of ground in certain areas, even if the inch doesn't really matter. As seen below in the section on "confirm favorable facts," an expert will sometimes have to concede the truth of certain favorable facts to your side or else he will look foolish. Your job at a deposition is to determine which facts the expert will concede so that you can use those facts to support your case at settlement or later at trial.

Style of Questioning at a Deposition

Many experts are arrogant. They also enjoy spouting off their opinions. This combination works perfectly for the examiner who is respectful and sincerely interested in the opinion the expert is so proud of. The examiner should also mix in a dose of feigned ignorance if necessary. The more respect you show and the more you encourage him to explain his reasoning to you, the more you will get him to talk. Time after time, questions such as "I don't understand, will you explain this to me?" are met with a free-flowing response from the expert.

If you have ammunition to use against the witness, use it after you have gained all the favorable information you need. On the other hand, you might want to start off attacking the witness if he is clearly unqualified or has made a key mistake in his report. You can put the expert on the defensive early. Such an attack may cause him to back away from some of his conclusions before he is able to regain his footing later in the deposition.

4.4 KEYS TO ATTACKING AN EXPERT EFFECTIVELY

Now that we have seen how difficult it can be to get experts to answer simple questions, let's look at some techniques that you can use to be successful at a deposition (and at trial). First, you must choose your style of confrontation. Are you going to try and battle wits with the expert? I recommend that you don't but with two caveats that I will get to in a moment.

> *Assume that an expert called against you has come prepared to do all the harm he can, and will avail himself of every opportunity to do so which you may inadvertently give him.*
> —Francis L. Wellman, *The Art of Cross-Examination*

The Irish playwright George Bernard Shaw once said, "I learned long ago, never to wrestle with a pig. You get dirty, and besides, the pig likes it." This is the perfect analogy for trying to match wits with an expert witness. By definition, he has expertise in an area that you probably do not. In addition, he likely has post-graduate degrees and may have published articles or even books on his specialty. Why in the world would you want to pretend that you could wrestle with him in court on his turf and win?

For example, if you are cross-examining an expert who is a surgeon, there is likely no way you can carry on a scientific discussion with her about the intricate details of a surgery. As soon as the surgeon saw that you were gaining ground, she could defend herself by using medical terms or discussing procedures you were unfamiliar with. Then, you would be lost and the jury would see the witness as the truth-teller.

If you need convincing from someone other than George Bernard Shaw, you can find guidance from Isaac Newton in the quote at the beginning of this chapter. To get to the truth, your goal should be to simplify ideas on cross, not make them more confusing. There is a great danger that you and the jury will get lost in the details. Instead, make the expert battle you on your turf by choosing simple topics that you know you can win on. I call this the Shaw approach.

Here are the two caveats I mentioned earlier. First, if you are regularly involved in the same type of cases, such as defective product cases, you could certainly gain the knowledge required to become a competent expert who could challenge the expert witness on his turf. The second caveat is that you may just be unusually smart and able to learn the subject matter well enough to become an expert no matter what type of case you are trying. However, those kinds of attorneys are few and far between.

Using the Shaw approach, go through your CROSS analysis to determine the expert's weaknesses. Credibility rarely fails to be a productive line of attack. Questioning the opposing expert about his education, experience, and the number of times he has testified for plaintiffs or defendants should be fruitful. Since your expert, just like the other side's, is getting paid, there is no point in cross-examining the expert on the issue that he "is being paid for his testimony."

Let's return to the Microsoft trial to examine the trial testimony of one of the Department of Justice's technical experts, Glenn Weadock, and see how Microsoft's attorney, Rick Pepperman, attacks his testimony.

1. Support Your Case (the Second S of CROSS)

Like with other witnesses, it is best to get the cross-examination witness to confirm favorable facts before you challenge him. In the questions below, Pepperman tries to get the government's expert to admit that Microsoft was not trying to create a monopoly by having its Internet Explorer accessible through Windows 98, but rather that it tried to provide convenience for its customers by linking the browser to its Windows 98 operating system. The Department of Justice contended that Microsoft should not have put its browser, Internet Explorer, on computers with the Windows 98 operating system, or it should have given consumers a choice of other Internet browsers to use. Microsoft contended it was easier for customers to browse the Internet or Intranet (a private network accessible only to an organization's members) by having Internet Explorer imbedded in Windows.

By taking a focused deposition, Pepperman was able to ask questions at trial with the comfort of knowing that he already knew the answers because they had been provided at the deposition.

Q. *And I think you agree with me that the number of organizations that want no Internet access and intranet access is decreasing?*

A. Yeah, I think that's probably a fair statement.

Q. *At the bottom of page 16 [of direct testimony][1], you list as one of the reasons why an organization might want to have no web-browsing software on its computer is to, quote, make it more difficult for certain employees to access the public Internet in order to reduce the amount of unproductive time employees spend surfing the net on subjects unrelated to their jobs. Do you see that, sir?*

A. OK, I see it.

Q. Again, sir, web-browsing software might be needed so that employees can access a private intranet; is that correct?
A. Yeah, that's correct. . . .

Q. So, there are companies, sir, you would agree, that don't want their employees accessing the public Internet but still may want web-browsing software [such as Internet Explorer] on their computers so that their employees can access a private intranet?
A. Yes.

* * *

Q. And would you also consider as another potential advantage that a user who has experience with the public Internet can use a private intranet without learning an entirely new user interface?
A. Yes, I would agree with that.

Q. And that is because he or she could use the same user interface to browse an intranet that is used to browse the Internet; correct?
A. Supposing for the sake of this discussion that they used the same web browser in both cases, yes, that would be a benefit.

Q. And you agree, don't you, sir, that the number of users who have experience with the Internet is growing rapidly over time?
A. I do.

Q. And isn't it also true, sir, that organizations that want to make it difficult—make it more difficult for certain employees to access the Internet can do so by a variety of means other than by not installing web-browsing software on those employees' computers?
A. Yes, they have several choices.

At the deposition, get the expert to confirm as many of your favorable facts as possible. This tactic succeeds because an expert has to admit the truth of at least some undisputed facts or he will look like a fool. However, he will fight you to the death on the interpretation of the facts. So, ask about facts, but don't ask about his interpretation of the facts or go too far and try to get the expert to admit to facts that are in dispute.

> **Practice Tip**
>
> You will always succeed at trial by cross-examining an expert on facts that are helpful to your case that he must agree with or else look foolish.

Q1. Does Microsoft, to your knowledge, prohibit those end users from removing the Internet Explorer icon from the Windows desktop?
A. Generally, no, no, they don't . . . .

Q2. And Microsoft also doesn't prohibit end users from removing the entry for Internet Explorer on the start menu, correct?
A. That's correct.

Q3. And Microsoft does not prohibit end users from removing the Internet Explorer option on the quick launch menu, correct?
A. That is also correct.

Q4. And in fact, ***you're not aware of anything*** *that Microsoft does to restrict organizations' ability to remove the most commonly used means of accessing Internet Explorer, correct?*
A. **Absolutely not correct. Absolutely not.**

In Q4, Pepperman goes too far. There is no way the expert is going to admit that Microsoft does not do "anything" to restrict a customer's ability to remove its web browser, Internet Explorer. That was a central issue in the case. If one could have easily removed Internet Explorer with the click of a button, it certainly would have weakened the government's case that Microsoft was trying to monopolize the browser market by bundling its Windows operating system with a web browser.

2. Credibility (Lack of Expertise)

There is almost always room to attack an expert's credibility (the C of CROSS) through his lack of qualifications. Oftentimes, the expert has exaggerated accomplishments on his curriculum vitae (resume). Other times, he has simply listed accomplishments that look better on paper than they really are. Or he may have been more proficient in the past but has no recent experience.

Q. And the plaintiffs have identified you in court papers as one of their technical experts, correct?
A. I believe that that's the case, although I am not sure I can recall a particular document that uses those terms. But I think that is true.

Q. You do not, however, consider yourself, sir, to be an expert in the ***design*** *of operating system software, do you?*
A. No, I do not.

Q. And you have never worked on the ***development*** *of an operating system, have you?*
A. No. That is correct.

Based on his deposition, the attorney highlights for the judge that the expert lacks expertise in areas that are central to two issues at trial: the design and development of Microsoft's Windows operating system.

Pepperman continues to hammer the theme of inexperience:

Q. If you could turn to your direct testimony on the second page, paragraph 2, you write, "I am a seminar developer, seminar instructor, author of computer books and videos, and computer consultant." do you see that, sir?
A. I do.

Q. *You have, however, never provided consulting services to a software company concerning the* ***design or development*** *of operating software, have you, sir?*
A. No. That's correct. There's lots of different kinds of computer consulting.

Q. *And the subject of which features should or should not be included in an operating system has never been the primary focus of any of the books, articles, or videos you have written, correct?*
A. That is correct.

Q. *And, similarly, that subject has never been the primary focus of any of the seminars you have developed or taught, correct, sir?*
A. It has never been the primary focus. The issue of what operating systems look like and what vendors, with particular respect to Windows, include with their operating systems is a subject that comes up in my seminars, but it's not a primary focus, I think was your question.

Q. *That was my question, sir.*

Q. *And it's true, isn't it, sir, that you have never written anything about Windows 98 that has been published in a peer-review journal or publication?*
A. In a peer-review—no, that is certainly correct . . . .

Notice how Pepperman dissects the expert's qualifications. While on paper, it may look impressive that the expert is a consultant, lectures at seminars, and has written books—even some that have been widely read—such "expertise" is really not relevant to the issue at hand regarding operating systems.

> **Practice Tip**
>
> Don't be intimidated by an expert's publications. Many times, the articles are either not focused on the topic in dispute or have not been subject to peer review (i.e., scientific journals).

Pepperman continues to humble this expert:

Q. *You also state, sir, in paragraph 2 on page 2 of your direct testimony, the last sentence of that paragraph, that you are the, quote, "president of Independent Software, Inc." Do you see that, sir?*
A. There are no quotes. You added that.

Q. *I was quoting from it, sir. Do you see where I am referring?*
A. Yes, I do.

Q. *You are also the one and only employee of Independent Software, aren't you, sir?*
A. That's correct.

In a few series of questions, Pepperman has established that this "expert" is not an expert in the design of operating software systems, has never written anything on this topic subject to peer review, and is the president of a company that employs one person—himself.

3. Credibility (Meaningless Memberships and Organizations)

Always question the expert about the organizations he brags about in his curriculum vitae (CV). Without fail, experts throw in the kitchen sink and list everything they belong to in order to bolster their perceived expertise. However, many of the organizations do nothing to establish expertise—but they look good on paper.

Q. *The last sentence of that paragraph reads, "My current professional memberships include the American Society for training and development and the association for computing machinery." Do you see that, sir?*
A. I do.

Q. *I notice that you use the verb "include" in that sentence. Those two organizations are, in fact, the only organizations to which you currently belong, correct?*
A. The only professional organizations—

Q. *Yes, sir.*
A. —or organization of any kind?

Q. *Professional associations.*
A. That's right.

* * *

Q. *Now, isn't it true that there are no specific requirements or certification procedures for joining either of the two organizations that you've listed in your direct testimony?*
A. Yes, that is true.

Q. *And leaving aside the general presumption that applicants for these organizations are probably people who work in the industry, all that someone needs to do to join these two organizations is send in a check, correct, sir?*
A. That is true.

4. Credibility (Irrelevant Education)

In addition to an expert's memberships, his training often is an area of weakness to explore. For example, an expert's educational background may be impressive but not relevant to his claimed expertise.

Q. *And you received from Stanford a bachelor's of science degree in general engineering; is that correct?*
A. That is correct.

Q. *And since graduating from Stanford, you have not received any graduate degrees from any formal universities; is that correct, sir?*
A. That is correct.

Q. No master's degrees?
A. I think that was encompassed in your earlier question. [**Expert gets defensive.**]

Q. And no doctorate degrees, correct, sir?
A. Again, same answer.

* * *

Q. Isn't it true, sir, that you took only two computer science courses at Stanford?
A. I think that's correct.

Q. And one of those two courses was a basic introductory course, something like programming 101?
A. That is correct.

5. Lack of Preparation for Deposition or Trial

An expert's opinion can also be affected by how much or how little work he put into preparing his expert report, preparing himself for the deposition, and preparing himself for trial. This lack of preparation is something you should attack at trial, but be careful about exploring it at a deposition, because if you point out omissions the expert has made at the deposition, he may be able to correct them prior to trial and thus be better prepared when it counts.

Let's look at another example from the Weadock cross at the Microsoft trial. Below, the expert's failure to read only one deposition undercuts his credibility.

*Q. The next to last bullet point [of his expert report] reads, "**my review of documents and deposition testimony** [of Microsoft employees and other witnesses] in the months prior to this trial." Do you see that?*
A. I do.

*Q. Now, at the time you submitted your expert report in this case on September 3, 1998, isn't it true that you had at that time **read only one of the 98 depositions** that had been taken in this case?*

* * *

A. I think that may be true.

Q. And that one deposition was the deposition of Jim Allchin, a Microsoft employee?
A. Right.

6. Biased Investigation

You should also determine what tests and kinds of investigations the expert conducted in formulating his opinions and attack them if there is any bias. In the example we have been looking at, Weadock interviewed several companies. Pepperman wanted to find out if the expert's opinion was completely objective or if it had been influenced by the companies he had interviewed because the companies did not like Microsoft. The following is an exchange where

Pepperman showed that one such interviewed company was, indeed, biased against Microsoft:

Q. *You also interviewed the Sabre Group, correct?*
A. Yes, that's correct.

Q. *Now, the Sabre Group offers an online reservation service called Travelocity; is that right?*
A. That is correct, yes.

Q. *And that online service competes with Microsoft's Expedia service, correct?*
A. That's my understanding.

Q. *And the Sabre group is also an* ***outspoken critic of Microsoft****; isn't that right?*
A. I don't know if they are outspoken or not.

Q. *Were you aware that the Sabre group* ***is a member of Procomp, an anti-Microsoft lobbying group*** *here in Washington, D.C.?*
A. No, I wasn't.

Q. *Were you—were you aware that the CEO of the Sabre group,* ***Mr. Michael Durham, publicly criticized Microsoft*** *on April 30, 1998 in testimony before the House Commerce Committee?*
A. Gosh, Mr. Pepperman. Lots and lots of people publicly criticize Microsoft. I am not aware of all of them.

Q. *A lot of them made up your focus group, didn't they, sir?*
A. I wouldn't call it a focus group. These are illustrative examples—companies that I had conversation with—one of 10 areas that I relied upon in my testimony.

Q. *Well, it's true, isn't it, that one of the representatives of the Sabre group, whom you interviewed, told you that, as a matter of company policy, if there is a product available that is comparable to a Microsoft product,* ***the Sabre group always uses the non-Microsoft product****, correct?*
A. That is correct.

7. Two Areas Not Worth Exploring

Finally, let's look at two areas that are a waste of time to explore with an expert. Although questions about an expert's compensation should be asked at a deposition if it is not already known through a discovery disclosure, there is no point in bringing it out at trial since your expert likely will also be compensated. That is, since your expert is also getting paid, you are not going to get much mileage out of the fact that the fact finder should not believe the opposing party's expert because he is getting paid. However, this is a mistake that many attorneys make at trial.

Q. *The Department of Justice is compensating you for your services at the rate of $100 per hour, correct?*
A. That's correct.

Q. And that is your normal consulting rate, correct?
A. Yes, sir.

Another mistake at trial is trying to get the expert to admit that he would slant his opinion in favor of the side that hired him. No expert is ever going to admit this (remember Myth 1 discussed at the beginning of chapter 2). In the next exchange, notice how well the expert handles such questions:

Q. Mr. Weadock, do you know who Michael Wilson is?
A. Yes, I do.

Q. Who is Mr. Wilson?
A. He's one of the people who works with the Department of Justice. . . .

Q. Have you had discussions with Mr. Wilson?
A. Yes.

Q. Do you know who "wanpt" [the initials on an email] is?
A. I would guess it's Pauline Wan.

Q. Have you ever had discussions with Ms. Wan?
A. Yes.

*Q. About midway through the e-mail, Mr. Wilson includes a parenthetical that reads, "I also think he wants to teach b/c he hinted that the teaching course is more prompt at paying his invoices. He hasn't received payment for his February bill for January work—**we need to keep Glenn happy because he's the most efficient, articulate, and flexible expert we have.**"*

Q. The "Glenn" referred to in that parenthetical is you, Mr. Weadock?
A. I am pleased to say that it appears to be.

Q. And has Mr. Wilson ever described you in your presence as the Department of Justice's most flexible expert?
A. Not in my presence. And I think if you look at the context of this memo, he is talking about scheduling.

Q. But Mr. Wilson is—
A. **I would hope that Mr. Wilson doesn't mean that I'm flexible in my opinions. Anybody who knows me very well knows that my opinions are generally my own and not easily influenced.**

Q. Mr. Wilson notes in this e-mail that you actually have a scheduling conflict for a meeting that was being scheduled, correct? [**The attorney tries to backpedal from accusing the witness of slanting his opinion for monetary gain to soften the failure of his attack.**]
A. Yeah, I think so.

Q. So in the context of saying you have a scheduling conflict, he's saying that you have the most flexible schedule, correct? That's your understanding? [**The attorney has now completely backpedalled.**]
A. I mean, we'd have to ask him exactly what he means, but that's the way I take his memo.

Most important, notice that the attorney made the mistake of not asking such questions at the deposition. If he had, he would have known that the witness had a good explanation for the e-mail. By doing so, the attorney would have avoided the embarrassment of trying to make the witness look overreaching and then having that backfire on him because it was the attorney who was overreaching.

Instead of trying to get the witness to confess that he is biased (see Myth 1 of "The Four Myths about Cross-Examination" in chapter 2), your goal should be to undermine his credibility (the C of CROSS). The correct way to conduct such a cross is illustrated below in this hypothetical example:

Example: Cross-Examination Regarding Bias of Plaintiff's Expert Doctor

Q. Doctor, you were hired by the plaintiff in this case?
A. Yes.

Q. How many times have you testified in court?
A. Fifteen times.

Q. Of those 15 times, how many have been for a plaintiff?
A. Fourteen times.

Q. So, out of all the times you have ever testified in court, only once have you testified for the defense?
A. Yes.

Q. In truth, when you have testified in court, almost 95 percent of the time it has been for a plaintiff?
A. Yes.

This cross-examination clearly establishes that the witness must have some bias—although he will never admit it on the stand—since he testifies so often for a plaintiff. Given that this is often a good line of cross-examination, make sure your expert has a history of testifying for both sides, or that he is very well qualified but has only rarely testified in court.

8. Attack the Expert's Assumptions

Another tactic for successfully cross-examining an expert witness is to challenge his assumptions. By virtue of being an expert—and not an eyewitness—the expert has necessarily made assumptions. Experts have a marked tendency to slant their argument to the side that hired them and to discount the value of alternative assumptions that might help the other side. Show the jury that the expert is unwilling to consider reasonable alternatives. Would the expert's opinion change if he had different assumptions? The expert won't admit he used the wrong assumptions, but by showing his unwillingness to consider reasonable assumptions that are different, the jury will see his bias.

Example: Cross-Examination of Plaintiff's Economist

In this example, the plaintiff has called an economist to calculate his damages. Like all experts, he has necessarily made assumptions.

Q. *Let's show the jury the assumptions you have made in this case. In order to calculate the damages for the plaintiff, you had to make certain assumptions, true?*
A. Yes. But they were all reasonable assumptions that anyone would make.

Q. *Well, let's see if that is correct or if I can convince you differently. You made assumptions about the plaintiff's life expectancy?*
A. Yes.

Q. *One assumption I disagree with you on is your calculation that the plaintiff will live 11 years longer than the average male?*
A. His health is fine.

Q. *I understand that is your claim, but my question is, you assume that the plaintiff will live 11 years longer than the average?*
A. Yes.

Q. *You would certainly agree that if you based your assumption on the average life expectancy, you would have calculated a significantly lower damages number?*
A. My calculations are accurate.

Q. *It is a simple question. If you based your assumptions on average life expectancy, your number would have been significantly lower?*
A. Yes.

Q. *Another assumption you made is that the plaintiff would continue to work seven years longer than the average male?*
A. Yes.

Q. *You also make some assumptions about inflation?*
A. Yes.

Q. *For example, the rate you assume is much higher. . . .*

Instead of making his calculations based on averages, the expert has increased his damages calculations by making assumptions that favor the plaintiff. He also reveals his bias by not answering simple questions.

9. Restrict the Expert's Damaging Testimony

Another successful tactic is to restrict (the R of the CROSS acronym) the damaging testimony of the expert, because there is always something the expert has not done. This line of attack is even more powerful against an expert witness than a lay witness because the expert witness claims to be the ultimate authority. Consequently, when you can show the jury that the other side's expert has failed to do something, it not only undercuts that witness, but it undercuts their entire case.

Restricting the testimony always works because no human can possibly have done everything to prepare for trial. More important, experts often are overly confident and will prepare less for trial because they think jurors will just be wowed by their qualifications.

Here are some examples of areas where you can attack an expert for things he has not done, which will undercut the effect of his ultimate opinion in the minds of the jury.

First, you can find reputable treatises, articles, or textbooks that the expert has not read that support your own expert's conclusion. There is no way anyone can read everything.

Second, you can attack the limits of the investigation. There is not enough time or money to conduct every test or review every document before trial. For example, an expert accident reconstructionist often forms her opinions from data obtained from an accident, but she may not have taken the time to actually visit the scene where the accident occurred. On cross, the expert may try to explain that there was no need to visit the scene of the accident, but if your expert has, the opposing expert will be hard-pressed to explain to the jury why she hasn't.

> **Practice Tip**
> Have an objective that is reasonable and attainable.

In medical malpractice cases, a successful line of questioning for a plaintiff's attorney might center on the defense expert's failure to see the patient during the questioned treatment. By necessity, all the defense expert can do is review medical records. He wasn't in the operating room and did not have to make the tough choices in the heat of the moment. A "hindsight is 20-20" theme on cross is a theme to which the jury can relate.

4.5 CROSS OF AN EXPERT IN ZIMMERMAN TRIAL

Several examples of cross-examinations of expert witnesses are presented throughout this book, including Tom Girardi's cross of William Squires in chapter 5 and David Boies' cross of David Blankenhorn in chapter 9. But for now, let's look at a cross-examination from the State v. Zimmerman trial, which was also discussed in chapter 1. Zimmerman's defense to the charge that he murdered Trayvon Martin was that Martin had pushed him down and was straddling him and violently punching him in the head when Zimmerman pulled his gun and shot him in self-defense. The defense called Dennis Root, who was a self-defense expert. One of the prosecutors, John Guy, conducted a cross-examination that nicely illustrates use of the R of the CROSS acronym ("Restrict the damaging testimony"). See if you think he is successful in conveying to the jury that the "expert" failed to do a lot of things he should have done, thereby undercutting his conclusion that Zimmerman acted in self-defense.

Q. But you would agree with me that the only person that you interviewed who had first-hand information on this event from the start to the finish was the defendant, right?
A. Yes sir. He was the only one that I actually spoke to in person outside of Mr. Pollock. I did interview Mr. Pollock, but unfortunately our schedules were such that I had to do it over the phone. I called him and spoke to him over the phone.

Right off the bat, the prosecutor shows the jury that the expert's source of information is limited to the defendant and one other person, effectively tainting his entire testimony. There were several neighbors who saw and heard the fight. If Root were trying to present an unbiased opinion, he should have interviewed all the people who had knowledge about the fight. His failure to do so immediately undercuts the strength of his opinion.

***

Q. And your conversation with the defendant, he described this whole event to you, right?
A. Yes, sir.

Q. OK, but you didn't have him mark on a diagram where he claimed, or an aerial photograph where he claimed the confrontation began?
A. No sir.

Q. And you didn't have him mark how it progressed from where he claimed it started to where it ended?
A. I didn't require Mr. Zimmerman to create any kind of drawings or mark on any kind of pictures or anything.

The prosecutor points out that the expert's failed to have the defendant explain, by using a diagram or drawing a picture, what happened. By doing this, the jury can infer that his failure to take this step would negatively affect his ability to understand what happened.

***

Q. You didn't ask the defendant what hand Trayvon Martin used to punch him, right?
A. No, sir.

Q. You didn't ask him how long it was between the time he had got punched, as he claims, and the time he went to the ground?
A. I didn't ask him for specific times, and again I—... asked him to tell me what took place.

Q. And you didn't ask the defendant whether or not he tried to strike Trayvon Martin.
A. No, again, **I didn't spend a lot of time asking him a lot of things.**

This last statement is golden. The prosecutor has used the theme of "what you did not do" to get the witness to become very defensive and then admit, "I didn't spend a lot of time asking him a lot of things."

Q. *The defendant never told you, did he, what he was doing with his hands once it was going on.*
A. No, sir. I don't recall him saying anything.

Q. *So you went to the scene to try to get an idea of the lighting, and the sun had not gone down?*
A. Correct, it was not completely set.

Q. *Right. So you didn't wait until it had set?*
A. No sir.

Q. *And you didn't go back?*
A. No.

Q. *When it was dark some other day?*
A. No.

The prosecutor ends with the fact that the expert went to the scene of the fight during the daytime, rather than at nighttime, which is when the fight took place. If he had gone at night, he could have given a better opinion about where the fight occurred according to what Zimmerman and the neighbors said. He also would have been in a better position to corroborate or dispute what Zimmerman claimed to have seen in the dark before and during the fight. Zimmerman's perceptions are obviously crucial to determining his belief of whether he was in imminent danger of serious bodily injury or death when he shot Trayvon.

This good cross could have been made even better with a list showing the jury what the expert did not do in his investigation. The way to execute it would be to start by telling the jury: "Mr. Root, I want to talk to you first about the things you did not do." As you tell the jury this, write at the top of a sheet of paper on an ELMO, "Things Expert Did Not Do." Then, after each helpful answer you get, write that information in a list.

Here is what it would look like:

THINGS EXPERT DID NOT DO

1. No interviews of eyewitness other than Zimmerman and Pollack
2. No diagram of scene
3. No questions about what hand Trayvon used to punch Zimmerman
4. No questions about whether Zimmerman struck Trayvon
5. No questions about timing of sequence of events
6. "I did not spend a lot of time asking him a lot of things."
7. Did not visit scene at night, which is when fight took place.

To emphasize how damaging the admission is in number six, you should underline it after you write it.

4.6 MARK LANIER CROSS-EXAMINES AN EXPERT

In chapter 6, we will examine Mark Lanier's skills in-depth, but for now, let's take a quick look at his cross-examination of an expert witness in the Johnson & Johnson (J&J) baby powder litigation. In the video clip that can be found at winningatcross.com under the title "J&J Needle in a Hay Stack," Lanier explains how he cross-examined an expert for J&J who told the jury that J&J's baby powder did not contain asbestos and therefore could not have caused ovarian cancer in the plaintiffs that Lanier represented. In 2018, Lanier would win a $4.69 billion verdict for 22 women and their families in this trial. Before you watch the video, read the rest of this section.

Here was Lanier's problem. Johnson & Johnson had hundreds of tests that showed that its baby powder did not have asbestos. These tests had used polarized light microscopy to test for the presence of asbestos. However, the technique could only find the presence of asbestos if it was present in a quantity of greater than .01 percent. Lanier had the challenge of explaining why the tests his expert conducted found asbestos in contrast to the ones J&J conducted. Before you look at the video, ask yourself how you could visually explain to the jury that J&J equipment's was not sensitive enough to detect asbestos while the equipment that Lanier's expert used was.

There could be any number of ways to demonstrate the different sensitivities of the tests: graphs, charts, or tables. But Lanier found the best one. As he explains in the video, the testing procedure J&J used and the science behind it is very complicated. It was a near certainty that very few on the jury would understand the process. Instead of using graphs or charts, Lanier used a bathroom scale, a jeweler's scale, some needles, and a bale of hay to prove his point. After you watch the video, read the next paragraphs.

There are so many things that make Lanier's points clear and memorable. First, he could have put anything on the bathroom scale to demonstrate whether it was sensitive enough to find asbestos. But, Lanier uses a needle because asbestos is shaped in the form of a needle. It is the perfect metaphor. After he puts onto a scale many needles and other objects that that scale is not sensitive enough to weigh, he then tells the witness that it is a "rigged test," which is one of his themes for cross-examination.

Lanier then uses a jeweler's scale, which is able to measure the weight of the first needle he puts on it. He makes his point that J&J did not find asbestos because it did not use the right equipment.

J&J's response to this argument was that it had also used transmission electron microscopy, which was a very sensitive technique, and it had not found any asbestos either. The science behind the transmission electron microscopy was complex and would also be nearly impossible to explain to a jury. To rebut this technique, Lanier had to show that J&J had not used a big enough sample size to determine if there was asbestos.

So, he brought out a bale of hay from underneath his counsel table at trial and suggested to the witness that the technique of using transmission electron microscopy to detect asbestos was literally like looking for a needle in a haystack. To make his point crystal clear, Lanier stuck a needle in the haystack on counsel table.

He then tore a piece of hay from the haystack and suggested to the witness that J&J had only tested an "itsy, bitsy" sample. When the witness denied that it was too small of a sample, Lanier showed how well prepared he can be for his cross-examinations. He had done the math and proved to the jury that based on J&J's protocol for testing, it would take 600,000 years to test an entire bottle of baby powder. His point? J&J tested such a small sample of powder that the company was never going to have a chance of finding asbestos.

Lanier then argued to the witness that the proper testing procedure was the pre-concentration method. He then went back to the bale of hay to explain how that test worked. First, a piece of the bale of hay would be broken off and put it in a tub a water. Then, all the hay would float to the top, and if there were any needles, they would sink to the bottom. Then, you would scrape the bottom of the tub and put the residue under a microscope to reveal any asbestos needles.

That is the test that Lanier's expert used, and he found asbestos in 70 percent of the baby powder bottles. Then, Lanier combined this demonstration with a damaging document that he showed to the jury. That document stated that in 1973, the Colorado School of Mines had told J&J that the pre-concentration test was the only way to find the proverbial "needle in a haystack"—that is, determine if asbestos was present. J&J decided not to use that test.

4.7 CHAPTER CHECKLIST

1. For an expert witness to be able to testify, the Supreme Court in *Daubert* required courts to inquire as follows: whether a theory or technique can be (and has been) tested, whether it has been subjected to peer review and publication, the known or potential rate of error, and whether the theory or technique is generally accepted.
2. Do the following to prepare for cross: 1) have your expert review the opposing expert's report and curriculum vitae (CV) so he can suggest questions for you, 2) collect information about the opposing expert from LexisNexis expert databases, 3) scour the internet for damaging information,

4) collect prior deposition and trial testimony to find inconsistent opinions, and 5) determine what assumptions the opposing expert has made and how his opinions might change if different assumptions were made.

3. So you won't be surprised at trial, ask the following discovery questions at deposition: 1) ask the opposing expert to explain the reasons that support his opinion, 2) confirm that he has stated all his reasons, 3) ask why the opposing expert disagrees with your expert, 4) ask how frequently he has testified for plaintiffs and then also for defendants, and 5) ask what assumptions he has made.
4. Every expert has to make assumptions, and when they do, you can show that if their assumptions were different, their conclusions would be different as well.
5. The Irish playwright George Bernard Shaw once said, "I learned long ago, never to wrestle with a pig. You get dirty, and besides, the pig likes it." This is the perfect analogy for trying to match wits with an expert witness. Don't do it.
6. You will always have success at trial by cross-examining an expert on facts that he must agree with—or else look foolish—that are helpful to your case.
7. Don't be intimidated by an expert's publications. Many times, the articles are either not directly on the topic in dispute or have not been subject to peer review (i.e., scientific journals).
8. Always question the expert about the organizations he brags about in his CV. Without fail, experts throw in the kitchen sink and list every organization to which they belong in order to bolster their perceived expertise. However, many of the organizations do nothing to establish expertise—they just look good on paper.
9. In addition to exploring an expert's memberships, his training is often an area of weakness to explore. For example, an expert's educational background may be impressive but not relevant to his claimed expertise.
10. An expert's opinion can also be affected by how much or how little work he has done in preparing his expert report, preparing for the deposition, or preparing for trial. This is an area that you should attack at trial, but be careful about exploring it at a deposition, because if you point out omissions the expert has made at the deposition, he may be able to correct them prior to trial and be better prepared when it counts.
11. You should also determine what investigation the expert has conducted in formulating his opinions and attack them if there is any bias.
12. There is no point in bringing out at trial that the expert is being paid, since your expert will also be compensated.
13. Another successful topic is using the "R" of the CROSS acronym to "restrict" the damaging testimony of the expert because there is always something the expert has not done. Consequently, when you can show the jury that

the other side's expert has failed to do something, it not only undercuts that witness, but it undercuts their entire case.

14. In the Zimmerman case, the prosecution was able to show the jury that the self-defense expert: 1) did not conduct interviews of eyewitnesses other than Zimmerman and Pollack, 2) did not create a diagram of scene, 3) did not ask questions about what hand Trayvon used to punch Zimmerman, 4) did not ask questions about whether Zimmerman struck Trayvon, 5) did not ask questions about timing of sequence of events, 6) stated, "I did not spend a lot of time asking him a lot of things," and 7) did not visit scene at night, which is when the fight took place.
15. Think creatively about how you can transform the complicated into the simple. Lanier uses a bathroom scale, a jeweler's scale, needles, and a bale of hay to explain to jurors the complex science of testing a product to see if it contains asbestos.

PART II

The Masters

Now that we have examined the principles of cross-examination and challenged the conventional wisdom, let's look at two masters as they conduct cross-examinations: Tom Girardi and Mark Lanier. You will find that each attorney follows the principles discussed in the previous chapters but that they also have a unique style. We cannot forget that cross-examination is also an art form. Once you see what works for each attorney, decide if the way they apply the principles would fit your personality and natural skill set. If you like what you see and the results, do your best to imitate these attorneys. Or, perhaps you will need to make adjustments to what you see so that the technique fits your personality. The aim of Part II is to reinforce what you have already learned and inspire you to be creative in order to have even more success.

CHAPTER FIVE

Tom Girardi Cross-Examines in *Stow v. Dodgers*

"On cross-examination, you want to be pinpointed, focused, and then sit down."—*Tom Girardi*

5.1 TOM GIRARDI

Tom Girardi is a partner of the law firm Girardi Keese and has been practicing law since 1965. His distinguished career includes many firsts. He was the first lawyer in California to win a million-dollar verdict in a medical malpractice case. He was the youngest member ever to be admitted to the International Academy of Trial Lawyers, an organization limited to 500 lawyers in the world. In addition, he is a member of the Inner Circle of Advocates, an organization limited to 100 lawyers who have obtained the largest verdicts in the United States.

Girardi was inducted into the Trial Lawyer Hall of Fame by the California State Bar in 2003. In a recent survey of 65,000 lawyers to determine the finest lawyer in California, he received the most votes. He was the 2015 president of the Litigation Counsel of America and president of the American Board of Trial Advocates. In April 2014, he was inducted into the American Trial Lawyer Hall of Fame.

He has had many record-setting verdicts but is most famous for *Anderson v. Pacific Gas & Electric*, which involved two trials that lasted over seven months and resulted in $131,000,000 for 40 plaintiffs. These verdicts caused an eventual settlement of the entire litigation for $333,000,000. The litigation became immortalized in the movie Erin Brockovich. In addition to his unrivaled legal career, he

CHAPTER ROAD MAP

- Be focused like a laser on your cross.
- Set up the ultimate question you want a "yes" to by getting the witness to answer "yes" to several set-up questions.
- Ask questions that have the power of undisputed facts and common sense on your side.

is a Trustee of the Library of Congress and the host of the weekly radio show, "Champions of Justice," which is broadcast on both coasts.

5.2 GIRARDI'S STRATEGIES FOR CROSS-EXAMINATION

Girardi believes the trick to successful cross-examination is to be "limited and pinpoint," because as soon as you get too far afield, you let that witness argue for the other side. You want to focus on those points "where you really have them and forget about the other stuff. Don't give them the opportunity to get up there and start explaining a good part of the defense case. You want to be pinpointed, focused, and then sit down." Another reason that it is important to conduct a focused cross-examination is that the jury is a lot more likely to follow and remember your cross if it isn't diluted within a three-hour session.

Most attorneys err on the side of very long crosses because they want to make sure they cover every possible point. So I asked Girardi if it takes a lot of experience and confidence to conduct an efficient short cross. Girardi provided the following analogy:

> Well, if you've ever argued with your wife, you know how to get your points across; it isn't with some long speech. It's just, "Hey honey I was sorry I got in late last night. I was with these lawyers, and it was hard to get away." And end it.
>
> We're in the persuasion business. How do you get somebody to say I'll marry you? Is it with a 20-paragraph thing, or is it "I love you" and she comes back and says "I'll marry you"? So I think we forget sometimes, as trial lawyers, we're in the persuasion business, and how we persuade in other times [involves] the same things we should be using when we persuade a jury. And that is to be concise, hit the point, don't be overbearing, don't be overreaching, be a nice guy—all that really is much better at selling [and being persuasive].

Girardi used a boxing analogy to describe the kind of demeanor an attorney should have on cross-examination. He explained that you do not want to be too argumentative, except on the rare occasion when you have a "real jerk on the stand, [then] you can't be too docile." But in a typical cross, he thinks that "three left jabs and a right [punch] is probably the best way you cross. And you set 'em up."

Girardi gave the following example:

> The left jabs would be, "Now you're employed by the defendant in this case, are you not?" "Yes." "And matter of fact, the reason that you're in the case is because the very fine defense lawyer hired you to come in and give

> opinions, right? And that very fine defense lawyer told you the reason that this case is there, isn't it?" And they say yes to all those. And then you say, "Isn't it a fact that the document that you didn't see says this? You didn't see it did you?" So then the jab, jab, jab and then, you know, the one good punch you got, then put it on there.
>
> That's much more effective than [being] high pitched, with every question trying to be a knockout punch on stuff that doesn't matter. The other thing is this: the witness starts to feel at ease when you ask the softball questions. And then the witness thinks that, "OK, I got this," and then you come in with the thing that you got in your briefcase that really massacres him.

Not only does this strategy work for getting the answer you need, but you also maintain your credibility with the jury. Girardi gave another example. "Suppose that you have a medical malpractice case and you are cross-examining a doctor who speaks in soft tones and says, 'That's a good question counsel, but I think this.' Well, you better not be laying into that guy, baby, because that jury loves him. And if you start being an asshole in front of him, you've lost everything."

In such a situation, limit yourself to your best points and be content. Girardi shared how this might play out:

> "But doctor, you know, you never reviewed the medical records from Cedars Sinai, did you? And doctor, wouldn't you think as a man of your profession, a man who wants to come here and guide this jury, it would be important to know all the facts and not just some of 'em? You'd agree with me on that, right?" So that's your play there, OK?

I followed up with Girardi on this point because I believe so many lawyers fall into the trap of arguing with the witness. Girardi agreed. He put it this way:

> You have to have gone through this a bunch of times, and having gone through it a bunch of times, it becomes much easier to know how to do it. Because there's a huge . . . , the problem is, you wanna say, "You rotten, lying SOB, this is what you said here and now look at you." That isn't near as effective as saying, "Doctor, did you violate the very oath you took in this courtroom in any way?" Now that's much more effective, isn't it, than calling the guy a dirty bastard son of a bitch.

> *Here's the thing that you gotta remember. I don't wanna call this witness an ass, a liar, a cheat, or a thief. I wanna lay it out, and I want the jury to go into the jury room and say, 'That guy was a liar.' You want them to say it, not you.*
>
> —Tom Girardi

In chapters 2 and 3, we looked at how to get the witness to give an outrageous answer, one that does not have the ring of truth to it. I asked Girardi about his technique for doing this. He instructs that you need three or four yeses in a row before you ask the ultimate question. Then when the witness says no, he looks bad. For example, you might ask an expert witness the following: "Doctor, in this case, it was important for you to know the history, wasn't it? It was important for you to know that he'd had a prior heart attack. Wasn't that important? It was important for you to know that if you have a prior heart attack, that one better be very careful of the drugs that are to be given? And doctor in this case, you saw that they were somewhat careful about the first three issues, but doctor, they weren't careful about the fourth, were they?"

Based on the previous admissions, when the doctor denies there was any wrong doing in the last question, the jury won't believe him because it is not a reasonable position to take.

Girardi believes that while other lawyers can help you get ready for some parts of the trial, "when it comes time to the cross-examination of key witness, it's all up to you, baby. And you're the person that has to dig it out because you gotta have those facts." This preparation results not only in a focused cross as discussed above, but it allows you to have a commanding presence during cross. He explains that you don't want to refer to a bunch of notes in the courtroom because that will put the jury to sleep. "The last thing you want to do is walk up there with your notes and read them. On the other hand, you don't want to forget certain issues. So I'll have a little piece of paper and I'll have ten words on it just to make sure I cover each of those ten subjects. And that's all you need and then you never read it. As you're finishing one thing, you kind of glance down and remember what the next thing is and then you talk about that. So it never looks like you're reading anything."

When a witness answers differently than Girardi expects, he has the deposition transcript or exhibit ready, so that he can confront the witness with it. He explains how he takes the the witness's deposition answers and builds them up to confront the witness during cross:

> Doctor, you know, I suppose the most important thing about a trial is the fact that the people who come in, people like you, testify under penalty of perjury, right? Doctor, in this case, when you took the stand, this wonderful court attendant, Margie, asked you to raise your right hand. And she asked you, do you declare under penalty of perjury the testimony you're about to give is the truth, the whole truth, and nothing but the truth. You were here for that right, doc? And doctor, if you violated that in front of this jury, that would be bad, wouldn't it? Because if you violated on one

issue, I suppose maybe they're gonna not necessarily believe you on the next issue. Do you agree with me or not? And Doctor, in this case, let me read from your deposition. Doctor, that was also under penalty of perjury too, wasn't it? The person there, the court reporter also said to you that your answers are under penalty of perjury, and here's your answer, yes. And here's the question you were asked, and here's the answer you gave. It's pretty bad, isn't it, Doc?

As noted before, there are two schools of thought on whether you should show your hand in a cross-examination at a deposition. Here is Girardi's viewpoint:

> In a deposition, you save it, that's what you do. You got the knockout punch. You keep that in your pocket. All you do in the deposition is set him up and let him say a few more times the lies that you can impeach him on. And you don't go further than that because then at trial, you've really got something to work with. If you try to do the knockout punch, they're gonna do everything they can to clear the ice. For example, "Doctor, didn't you make a mistake when you said such and such, and was it really such and such?" They clean it up. It's hard, especially for young lawyers, to keep things in their pocket. You know, you get so excited. You got this guy nailed, baby. You wanna go for it.

I asked Girardi how he would respond to the argument that since so many cases settle, if you save the knockout punch for trial, you're really saving it for nothing. He quickly responded:

> No, you're not at all. So, if the case is going to settle, one of the reasons that it settled is because they know you got the ammo, and if the case is gonna settle, the large cases, it's always gonna be settled in conference in front of the judge. So even if you want five million bucks and they offer three, at that settlement conference, you're gonna start to reveal some of the good shit you have. And that settlement judge is gonna say, "Holy Toledo," and bring them in and say, "Hey you guys, you could be toast." You know what I mean? So saving it even though the case settles, doesn't mean you save it.
>
> And then sometimes you can tell the other side, "Hey listen, I want you to look at page 34 of the depo." This is now when they're pretty serious about settling it. "Look at page 34 of the depo. Do you think that's gonna be a problem for you? Let's see if we can resolve this."

Girardi discussed the importance of starting your cross strong. He explained that you want the witness to start to wiggle a bit. Not only does it get the witness on the defensive after a good direct examination, but the jury sees this change in confidence. "So if you have a pretty good punch right at the beginning, we fire that, and it's not the entire case but it's just a pretty good punch. And then you go through the cross and then you end up with something pretty good too. Because you want that guy up there uncomfortable, and if the first punch keeps him on edge, you gain a lot. And then hold the final punch till the end."

I asked Girardi if he agreed with Irving Younger's commandment (see chapter 2) that you should be subtle on cross and tie everything up in closing. Girardi believes you need to be clear enough that the jury will understand your points. If you save it for closing, it is too late because jurors make up their minds very quickly. He told me of an experiment he conducted, with the agreement of the opposing attorney and the judge, in three of his cases. The jurors were given a short questionnaire after voir dire, after opening statement, and at the close of the case on how they voted.

Eighty-five percent of the jurors voted the same way after opening statement as they did on the final verdict at the end of the trial. Girardi was quick to point out that the experiment is not scientific because you are talking about 36 and not 3600 people, but "that's a little hint that these guys are making up their minds early."

> **Practice Tip**
>
> Since the opposing party can gather a lot of ammunition on your expert if he has testified a great deal, one strategy is to get a fresh expert and not use the usual crowd.

For expert witnesses, you have to be prepared. Girardi pointed out that the other side has the ability to get the testimony in every single case that that your expert has testified in. And indeed, that could be a ton of great stuff, and it's going to hurt you in your case. So, you need to not only prepare your expert, but you also need to be doing the same when you cross-examine the opposing expert, whether it is in a deposition or a trial.

5.3 BACKGROUND OF *STOW V. LOS ANGELES DODGERS*

Before we look at Girardi's cross-examination transcripts, let's familiarize ourselves with the main facts in the case, because doing so will help to put the cross's argument in context.

On March 31, 2011, Bryan Stow and his friends went to Dodger Stadium for the opening-day game of the 2011 season. He and his friends were San Francisco Giants' fans and were wearing Giants clothing. As Stow was leaving the game, he was assaulted in the parking lot by Louis Sanchez and Marvin Norwood. The attack caused massive brain damage that would leave Stow wheelchair-bound and prevent him from ever working or living independently again.

At trial, Girardi had to prove that the Dodgers failed to use reasonable care in protecting their customers. Girardi contended that the Dodgers tried to blame everyone but themselves for Stow's beating. This included blaming the LAPD, the fans in Sanchez and Norwood's section who failed to report the duo's conduct to ballpark security, and, of course, Bryan and his friends.

Amazingly, for all the security for opening day, there was none in Parking Lot 2 after the game where the assault took place. Also, there were no officers in the Loge section where Louis Sanchez was visibly intoxicated, verbally assaulting others, throwing things at Giants fans, and starting fights in clear violation of the Dodgers' own policies and procedures. For example, no security guard or usher was assigned to work in the section where Sanchez and Norwood were sitting throughout the game. Moreover, while two security guards were deployed to Lot 2 after the game, they arrived approximately 20 minutes after the end of the game and after Bryan was attacked. The Dodgers attempted to paint the picture of a drunken Bryan Stow who shared blame for the fate he met on that evening.

Upon arriving at the Dodgers game, Bryan and his friends came across a Dodgers security guard who said, "Look at these fucking idiots," while looking directly at them. This was the Stow groups' first interaction with anyone at Dodger Stadium.

Others continued the heckling. While some fans were engaging in good-natured fun, others were out to harass, intimidate, and make Giants fans feel as uncomfortable as possible. Unfortunately for the Stow group, the Dodger fans they ran into fell into the latter category. Even though they did encounter some rough fans, the Stow group made it through the game without any major incidents. That is because Norwood and Sanchez were on the other side of the stadium.

Marvin Norwood and Louis Sanchez arrived at the game with Dorene Sanchez (Louis's sister and Marvin's fiancée), and Louis's son, Louie. Upon arriving at Dodger Stadium, Marvin and Louis drank beer in the parking lot. This violated Dodger policy prohibiting alcohol consumption in the parking lot and was grounds for ejection from the premises. Marvin and Louis purchased beers shortly after entering the stadium. Soon Louis began heckling Giants fans in their area, Loge 149. The heckling progressed to vulgarity. Louis began yelling, "Fuck the Giants" at the top of his lungs. Louis was directing his statements at the two Giants fans, Griffith McDaniel and Katie Gillespie, seated in his section. The Dodger Fan Code of Conduct explicitly prohibits "foul/abusive language or obscene gestures." Sanchez's actions also violated another code which provides that "our fans experience will not be disrupted by unruly actions or behavior."

Louis and Marvin consumed approximately six to ten 16-ounce beers during the game. One fan seated in section Loge 149 stated that Louis "was so drunk, he couldn't even walk…he was like wobbly." The Dodger Fan Code of Conduct provides "fans will consume alcoholic beverages in a responsible manner. Intervention with impaired, intoxicated, or underage guests will be handled in a prompt and safe manner. Those appearing intoxicated will be denied entry or will be subject to ejection from the stadium."

Soon thereafter, Louis began throwing food at the same Giants fans. He even hollered "You're next" to Griffith McDaniel after a fight broke out in the Loge area. Because there was no security to report his behavior to, Grif McDaniel and Katie Gillespie hoped it would defuse on its own. Because Louis did not have his own sunflower seeds, he began taking them out of another fan's purse without her permission. Again, when throwing food was not causing enough of a ruckus, Louis switched to even more outrageous behavior.

Louis then decided to throw a soda at the two Giants fans he had been harassing all day, Katie Gillespie and Grif McDaniel. Louis took a soda, shook it, and released the cap causing liquid to squirt all over the two Giants fans. In shock, Katie and Grif stood up immediately. Then, Louis stood as if to provoke a fight. Grif, Katie's boyfriend, stood there staring at Louis; the two men were engaged in a standoff, and a crowd gathered. Then, Marvin intervened, pulling Louis back. Security never responded to the altercation. Throughout the entire game, Katie and Grif looked for security or an usher that they could report Louis's behavior to, but they never saw any Dodger personnel. Following the altercation, the Sanchez group then went toward the exit of the stadium; Katie and Grif went the other direction.

Upon reaching the parking lot, Louis and Marvin decided to smoke marijuana, a violation of Dodger policy, as well as a violation of the law at that time. But, again security did not respond to their behavior.

Prior to encountering Bryan Stow and his friends in Lot 2, Louis and Marvin encountered a group of young Giants fans as they were leaving the stadium. Louis ran toward the teenagers, began punching them, and said, "Fuck the Giants." The young men were stunned by the behavior. The young men just kept walking away, and Louis and Marvin retreated. Louis and Marvin began yelling slurs and profanity at the other Giants fans that would walk by their vehicle. They were saying, "Fuck the Giants," "Giants Suck," and other profanity.

Following the game, Bryan and his friends arrived at Lot 2. Since they had arrived by taxi, they planned to leave the same way. Due to the length of the cab line and the heavy traffic, the Stow group decided to try to catch a cab that was about to enter the stadium, rather than one already stuck in stadium traffic. It was during this process that Bryan encountered Louis and Marvin.

Louis and Marvin were in the parking lot getting high. When Bryan walked by Louis and Marvin, Louis began yelling "Fuck the Giants," "Fucking faggots," and started harassing him. In response to Louis's harassment, Bryan said something to the effect of "It's not that serious. It's not like a heart attack. You know what a heart attack is?" Bryan and his friends continued to walk away. Upon hearing Bryan's statement, Dorene Sanchez told Louis that Bryan was "talking shit." In response, Louis took off looking for Bryan. Marvin followed after Louis.

Louis yelled, "What the fuck did you say, homey?" Then he pushed Bryan, causing Bryan to fall into his friends' arms. Bryan and his friends continued walking through the parking lot away from Louis and Marvin. A few minutes passed. Then Bryan was punched from behind by Louis, and Bryan fell to the ground unconscious. Then Sanchez and Norwood began kicking Bryan in the head repeatedly. Corey, Bryan's friend, ran over to Bryan, threw his body on top of Bryan's, and yelled, "You've already knocked him out. Leave him alone!" Then, Louis and Marvin ran off.

Louis and Marvin ran back to Dorene Sanchez's vehicle yelling "Drive, drive, drive," and "Get in the fucking car, drive." The group then drove off. As Louis and Marvin fled, Bryan lay unconscious in Lot 2 waiting for help. Approximately eight minutes after Bryan was knocked unconscious, an ambulance still had not arrived at the scene.

Bryan suffered a traumatic brain injury and now has heterotopic ossification (a common but very painful complication where bone grows in abnormal places such as soft tissue), as well as severe cognitive defects. Bryan requires 24-hour attendant care. He cannot walk more than a few feet even when aided by a walker. He has difficulty engaging in everyday activities and requires assistance in most basic activities, such as bathing.

At trial, Girardi presented evidence that there were previous incidents of fan violence at Dodger Stadium. For example, on September 19, 2003, during a Giants-Dodgers game, there was a shooting in the parking lot at Dodger Stadium that resulted in a fatality. On July 17, 2005, during another Giants game at Dodger Stadium, there was a brutal assault on Maria Helenius that left her with three facial fractures and the permanent loss of sight in one eye. It was also known that there was a higher incidence of violence when the Dodgers were playing the Giants, especially on opening day. In addition, in 2009, uniformed LAPD officers were no longer allowed inside the stadium.

One of the Dodgers' primary defenses was that they had plenty of security on opening day. The Dodgers claimed that 223 Dodger personnel were on duty, with 67 of them in the 27 parking lots. There were also FBI agents and 195 LAPD officers on duty during the game.

At trial, Girardi pointed out that the FBI was deployed to prevent terrorism, and of the 195 LAPD officers, more than half were patrolling areas outside of Dodger property, such as the exterior streets and Elysian Park. In fact, only the Parking Lot Group, which was comprised of 54 officers, was dedicated solely to monitoring the parking lots at Dodger Stadium. Based on these figures, there was approximately one LAPD or security guard for every 455 fans. Each of the 121 LAPD/ LAD security personnel was responsible for several acres of parking lot, as the Dodger Stadium property is comprised of 330 acres.

In particular, the two Los Angeles Dodgers employees assigned to patrol Lot 2 following the game, Bryan Hill and Bryan Hines, made it to their designated post well after the beating of Bryan Stow and at least 20 minutes after the game had ended. According to the eyewitnesses who were present at the scene of the incident, there was no security in sight when Sanchez and Norwood were stalking Bryan Stow and his friends through the parking lots. There also was no security in sight when Stow was attacked and repeatedly kicked in the head, and no security was present when Sanchez and Norwood fled the scene.

5.4 CROSS-EXAMINATION OF DEFENDANT'S EXPERT

As you will see, what stands out most about Girardi's cross is how efficient it is. Most attorneys get bogged down in the details with an expert and consequently spend way too much time examining them. Girardi's cross-examination only fills up 25 transcript pages. It is difficult to translate that into minutes, but by any standard, it is a very quick cross-examination.

Girardi conducts an efficient and very effective cross-examination because he focuses only on the most important points that he wants to make. As discussed in chapter 3, less is more. Let's look at the topics he addresses and then examine some excerpts.

The topics Girardi wants to discuss (and the points he wants to make) really fall under these three categories: 1) the law the Dodgers had to follow to protect their fans, 2) the expert's lack of qualifications, and 3) an expert's opinion that defies common sense. Applying the acronym of CROSS that we learned about in chapter 2, let's see which topics Girardi will use in his cross-examination. Repeat this exercise as you read the transcripts in this chapter and the remainder of the book. If you do, you will quickly master the skills and be able to identify successful areas to cross-examine in every case.

The first topic Girardi wants to discuss corresponds to the second "S" of CROSS: *support your case.* Girardi will use this expert to admit to the jury the standard of care the Dodgers had to provide to its fans at the game. Girardi knows he will get the answer he wants to this question because if he doesn't, he can show the expert what the law is. This is an important topic for Girardi to discuss because the law helps the plaintiff. The law requires the Dodgers to protect its fans, and it is a responsibility that it cannot delegate to other police or security forces.

The second topic he wants to discuss at cross is the "O" of CROSS: *outrageous statement*. It is the hardest topic for attorneys to succeed on, because the lawyer's questions must be so well-crafted that as soon as the jurors hear them, they will answer them the way Girardi wants them to, in spite of the opposite answers that the expert gives.

The third topic is the "C" of CROSS: *credibility*. As with any expert, you want to poke holes in his claimed expertise by establishing his lack of experience, education, or some other failing. Girardi knows that the expert will have to admit certain facts that undercut his expertise.

Finally, you will see that Girardi uses the themes on his cross that he will weave into his closing argument. Those themes are related to his bottom line message that framed his entire case that we analyzed in chapter 1. Girardi wanted the jury to hear throughout the trial that the McCourt Dodgers would shift the blame for the lack of protection of its fans to other police agencies even though the law required them to be solely responsible for fan safety. Girardi called such a tactic the "ABMD" defense: the Dodgers would try and shift responsibility to "Anyone But the McCourt Dodgers." This bottom line message also reminded the jury that the plaintiff was not suing the current owners of the Dodgers, who were very popular, but instead the former owner (McCourt), who was not.

Start Strong

William Squire was the defendant's expert who was called to testify that the Dodgers provided a safe environment for their fans at the game. Girardi does not waste any time getting to the bottom line message of his case, which, as we learned in chapter 1, is Anyone But the McCourt Dodgers (ABMD). He forms his first question from the words that will be used to instruct the jury on a landowner's responsibility.

> **Practice Tip**
>
> Always start your cross-examination on a strong point that you know will win. It is the most important point in a cross. The jury wants to immediately know if it should accept or reject the witness's testimony on direct examination.

Q1. You understand, don't you, that it's the obligation of the owner of the property to make sure the place is safe for the people? **[He knows the witness has to answer yes because the question is based on what the law is.]**

A. Yes.

Q2. Absolutely, positively, without a doubt, right? **[If your point is important, find a way to repeat the question so the jury will be certain not to miss it. Asking a witness how certain he is of his answer is one way to do it.]**
A. Yes.

Q3. Now, then, you gave the opinion that even if Hines and Hill [Dodger security personnel] were in Lot 2, that all the assaults would have happened, right?
A. Yes.

Q4. So the Dodger policy was to have Hines and Hill there, and they weren't there. And you are of the opinion that it would have happened anyway?
A. Well, yes.

***

*Q5. So your whole idea here is that the Dodgers' policy, where they had two people assigned to Lot 2, would not have prevented the five assaults that took place in Lot 2 from the time the game ended up **until the time Bryan Stow got massacred**?*
A. That's my opinion.
Mr. Fox: **It's argumentative, the end of it**.
Court: **Objection overruled**.

Q6. So there can be assaults going on for about 25 minutes, I guess, in Lot 2, five of them, and no security there, and it doesn't matter as far as you're concerned, that the Dodgers were doing the right thing, right? **[said sarcastically]**
Mr. Fox: Asked and answered.
Court: Overruled.
Witness: Well, I believe there was security out there.

The expert is forced to take a difficult position at trial based on the facts. He asserts that the Dodgers were correct when they *scheduled* two security personnel for Lot 2 but were not negligent when the two security personnel *failed to show up* for their scheduled duty. Such an opinion defies common sense, but it is really the only position the expert can take. It is Girardi's task to phrase his questions in such a way that the expert's inconsistent positions are highlighted for the jury. This culminates in Q6, where Girardi sarcastically asks how the expert can suggest the Dodgers were doing the right thing if five assaults occurred in Lot 2. The defense attorney tries to protect his witness from the answer the question calls for, and when he fails, the witness dodges the question and explains that there was other security out there.

One important technique to remember on cross is to listen carefully to make sure the witness answers your question. Unlike most lawyers, Girardi's head is not buried in notes that he is carrying; instead, he is focused intently on the witness. When the witness does not answer his last question, he breaks the question down (shown below) into a few simple questions to effectively ask it again. Girardi knows that the witness will not confess that the Dodgers were negligent, but he benefits by letting the jury hear the witness's answers again, thus letting it can decide whether the answers are outrageous or not.

Q7. ***No. Just a minute. The obligation for security is the Dodgers', right?***
A. Yes.

Q8. And they had two people assigned to that?
A. Yes.

Q9. And they weren't there?
A. Correct.

Q10. And there were five assaults?
A. I don't know if there were five, but correct.

Q11. So, it's your position that the Dodgers were doing the proper thing to take care of the fans in Lot 2?
A. Is this a yes or no answer?

Q12. Yes.
A. Yes.

This exchange perfectly demonstrate the technique of how to ask the ultimate question, which Girardi discusses at the beginning of this chapter. Q11 is what the entire battle at trial is about. So, Girardi needs to set it up in a way where the jury will disagree with the witness's answer. To use Girardi's boxing analogy, he asks several questions where the witness must answer yes. These are the left jabs. After the left jabs set the witness up, he comes in with the right punch, which is Q11. It does not matter that the witness does not admit that the Dodgers were negligent—and Girardi does not expect him to—it only matters whether the jury believes this answer after having heard the witness's previous answers.

Using the CROSS acronym, which topic for cross-examination does this fall under? It's the second "S" of CROSS, since Girardi is using this section to *support* his case. He wants to get as many admissions as possible from the expert that are consistent with what his own expert will say. In addition, through the witness's answer to Q11, he gets the *outrageous statement*, the "O" of CROSS.

Witness's Expertise

Girardi then switches to the witness's expertise. He asks how many times George Steinbrenner, then-owner of the New York Yankees, fired him, and then he quickly uses that answer to undermine the witness's claimed expertise regarding his opinion that the Dodgers acted appropriately.

Q. Did you get fired by Steinbrenner five times?
A. Four.

Q. Four times.
A. Yeah. Yes.

Q. So I guess, as I understand it, we wouldn't have to have any security in any of those lots to prevent assaults on people after the game, right?
A. Is this still a yes or no answer?

Q. Yes.
A. Yes.

Q. That's your opinion?
A. Yes.

Q. So, that would discharge an owner's responsibility, in your view, to keep the area safe when the Dodgers don't have any security people in that whole parking lot, right?
A. Still a yes or no answer?

Q. Yes.
A. Yes

Q. Gee. The Dodgers were wasting a heck of a lot of money by hiring the few guys they had?
MR. FOX: Argumentative, Your Honor.
COURT: Sustained.
MR. GIRARDI: I'll withdraw it.

Whether a question is argumentative or not depends on its context and the judge. Not every judge would have sustained—that is, upheld—this objection, and you will see that a different judge overruled similar objections in the trial discussed in chapter 6. If you lose the objection, simply move on as Girardi does next or you can rephrase the question that cures the problem. In the above example, it would be hard to rephrase the question. Girardi knows he has made his point, the jury has heard it despite the objection, and he wisely moves on.

Applying the CROSS acronym, Girardi first attacks the witness's credibility, the "C" of CROSS, and then gets an outrageous statement, the "O" of CROSS. For each section below, continue this exercise of deciding what topic of CROSS the section falls under and you will soon develop the skills to organize your questions for the desired effect based on the acronym.

Expert's Opinion

Q. We know they scheduled it, and the reason they scheduled it is because they knew they better have somebody in Lot 2, right?
A. That was the best practice to have people in the parking lots at the game, yes.

Q. And you know that, although it's the best practice to have people in the parking lot, security in the parking lot after the game, you knew that the Lot 2 people didn't get there for 25 or 35 minutes? **[Girardi frames the question perfectly. If the jury silently**

believes that security should have arrived sooner than 25 minutes after the game, Girardi wins no matter what the witness answers.]

MR. FOX: It's been asked and answered. Cumulative.
COURT: Overruled.

Q. *Right?*
A. Not correct, no.

Q. *How long did it take them to get there?*
A. Well, it took them 25 minutes to get to the scene and didn't take them 25 minutes to get to Lot 2.

Here, the expert does his best to defend the Dodgers, but the distinction he makes—that security got to Lot 2 sooner than the scene of Stow's assault in Lot 2—does not matter, as Girardi will quickly point out to the jury.

Q. *Well, this thing happened in Lot 2?*
A. It did, in the back of Lot 2, yes.

Q. *Matter of fact, they were told by other fans, as they were coming, that there was a terrible assault that took place, and they went* ***directly*** *to that assault, didn't they?*
A. That's correct.

Q. *And it took them 25 minutes from after the game to get there?*
A. I think about 25, yeah.

Girardi has now forced the expert to implicitly admit that there really is no difference between arriving at Lot 2 and at the scene of Stow's assault, since the security personnel went directly to the Stow assault when they arrived at Lot 2. The expert has to admit that it took 25 minutes to get to Lot 2 because that is what the facts showed.

Q. *And it's your opinion that an owner who has the responsibility to keep the place safe for the fans* ***didn't have to have somebody on point [in the parking lots] when those 55,000 people were coming out of those doors?***
A. Well, the 55,070 people that was paid attendance that night or were in the building. Those officers had a **responsibility until the game was over** to make sure they were safe inside the building.

Practice Tip

You have two options when a witness does not answer the question. Repeat it until he does or object that the answer is non-responsive and move to strike the answer, and then, if you want, ask the court to instruct the witness to answer.

MR. GIRARDI: We will make a motion to strike.
COURT: It's nonresponsive. Objection sustained.

Q. *Sir, the owner of the property has the only responsibility for the safety of the fans, true or false?*
A. I think I've answered that. Yes.

Q. Would it surprise you that other teams, when it gets to the end of the game, that people will be deployed two innings ahead, two and a half innings ahead so they could be in the parking lot to make sure the fans are properly taken care of?
A. Would I be surprised by that?

Q. Yes.
A. No.

Q. Matter of fact, do you know of any stadium in trying to protect the people that are going into the parking lot and has the obligation to protect the people that would not have the security people deployed before the end of the game?
A. I can't answer that. I'm sure that there are. I'm sure that there's some that don't.

Q. You don't know of any. You can't give us any, right?
A. Yes.

In the second-to-last answer, the witness tries to help the Dodgers as best he can given the facts of what other stadiums do. Unfortunately, there is nothing he can do because he cannot name another team that does not deploy its security to protect its fans outside the stadium.

*Q. Now, the Dodgers staff was in **total disarray** with respect to important security decisions, weren't they?* **[Girardi turns to a new theme: total disarray.]**

MR. FOX: It's vague, your honor. It's argumentative.
COURT: Do you understand the question?
WITNESS: I certainly don't, no. **[It does not matter that the witness does not agree that the staff was in total disarray or that he states that he does not understand the question. Girardi has alerted the jury to the theme he is going to pursue.]**
COURT: Alright. Rephrase.

Q. You read, I think, the testimony of Shahram Ariane, right?
A. Yes.

Q. As a matter of fact, one of the reasons he quit, as he testified to here, is because they were getting rid of uniformed police officers. Do you know that?

MR. FOX: Misstates his testimony, your honor.
COURT: Well, he's asking for his knowledge. Objection overruled.
WITNESS: I believe that was one of the reasons, yes.

Q. Ray Maytorena, you read his testimony, did you not?
A. Yes.

Q. Did you read his testimony that Francine Hughes wouldn't know security if her life depended on it, and he was going to quit because she was incompetent?

MR. FOX: Objection, your honor. Misstates evidence.
COURT: Well, it's asking again, I have no way of knowing that, but if you—
WITNESS: I read that he was not happy having to report to Francine. I remember that, yes. **[The witness minimizes the damaging fact and suggests that Maytorena was simply not happy.]**

Q. Well, you recall that he didn't like Francine because she didn't know anything about security?

MR. FOX: It's argumentative, your honor.
COURT: Objection overruled.
WITNESS: I think he didn't want to report to a woman, to be honest with you.

Q. Did he say that? **[This question gives the witness the chance to either say yes or no. It does not matter what the witness says because whatever the answer is, Girardi can show the witness the deposition that proves Maytorena never made the statement the witness claims.]**
A. No. I don't believe he did, but I—

Q. But the truth of the matter, she did have zero security training, right?
A. As I did when I took over, yeah. **[The witness does not answer the question. Girardi listens and sarcastically responds with the question below.]**

Q. OK. Fine. She had zero security training?
A. Well, she—training, yes. But she had some experience with security in a real estate environment in her life. Yep.

Q. And Ray Maytorena indicated that he was going to quit because he could not stand to operate under somebody who had no security experience, right?
A. That's what he said, but I think he was going to be let go before he decided to quit.

The witness finally answers the original question in response to the last question, but he still feels compelled to add an opinion that Maytorena was going to be fired. Girardi has achieved two goals by carefully listening to the answers and being persistent. Whenever he notices that the witness does not answer a question, Girardi then repeats the question, and each time the witness does not answer a simple question from Girardi, the jury sees Girardi as being more credible and the witness as being biased.

Expert's Qualifications Continued

Q. You do not claim to be an expert in stadium management, do you?
A. I certainly do.

Q. What courses have you taken in stadium management?
A. What courses have I taken?

Q. Yeah.
A. I actually teach a course there. **[The witness does not answer the question. Girardi will repeat it next.]**

Q. No. Which ones have you taken?
A. Mr. Steinbrenner's theory on running a stadium for three years. I got my master's and PhD., I think, there. Working at—being recruited to work at Giants stadium, being recruited to work at Walt Disney World, being recruited to work at Cleveland Browns stadium, being recruited to work at Giants stadium, hired on by other stadiums to

consult. Whether I passed any actual courses, no, but I think I've got the experience to consider myself an expert in stadium management, yes. [**The witness has not answered the simple question. Girardi could have asked it again, but sometimes moving on is fine, especially if the witness's answer is so clearly self-serving and you think there are bigger battles to fight.**]

> **Practice Tip**
>
> Make sure your expert is better qualified than your opponent's expert. If he is, then it is very effective to highlight the differences for the jury.

Q. Have you ever written a book like Gil Fried, "Managing Sports Facilities"? [**Gil Fried is the plaintiff's expert.**]
A. No, I do that work. I don't write.

Q. ***Once again, sir,*** *have you ever written any book like Gil Fried, "Managing Sports Facilities"?* [**Using the phrase "once again" to begin a question that the witness has previously dodged is a great way to signal to the jury that the witness has not answered a simple question.**]
A. Not written a book, but I actually did the intro to chapter 3 of his book, yes.

Q. That wasn't really your intro?
A. I wrote that.

Q. No. That was somebody else?
A. No. I wrote that, sir. Well written, too, I thought.

Q. Yeah. We'll see. Do you have an opinion that a uniformed police presence is a larger deterrent than a guy with a t-shirt?
A. Not necessarily, no.

In the last question, Girardi pivots to another topic: the fact that the Dodgers replaced many uniformed officers with employees wearing security t-shirts. Girardi is confident that the jury will use its common sense to answer the last question differently than the witness did. If common sense tells the jury that uniformed police officers provide more deterrence than personnel wearing t-shirts provide, Girardi wins the battle.

The last question's effectiveness is increased dramatically because Girardi asks it after a series of simple questions about the expert's qualifications are not answered as directly as they should have been. The witness appears defensive. At that moment, Girardi asks the last question, for which common sense dictates only one answer.

Girardi then questions the witness about the failure of Dodger security to observe the altercations in section 149 where Sanchez was sitting. This next excerpt provides a good view of the tug of war between an attorney and a witness. Notice Girardi's response when the witness does not directly answer the question. Also, see if you would make the same objections as defense counsel does, or if the objections sometimes highlight a damaging answer that follows the overruled objection.

Dodger Security Fails to See Fights in Stands

Q. *Then you recall the testimony, do you not, that through this whole two and a half hours, this guy Sanchez was jumping up and down in a drunken stupor yelling, "F the Giants," right?*

MR. FOX: Misstates the evidence, jumping up and down. **[The objection to correct the fact that the witness was standing instead of jumping up and down when he yelled, "F the Giants," is not worth the damage done when Girardi gets to repeat the question a second time for the jury.]**

COURT: The question of whether or not this gentleman remembers it that way, the question—

WITNESS: No.

Q. *BY MR. GIRARDI: You didn't read anything that this person was standing and yelling, "F the giants"?*

A. Not for two and a half hours, no. OK.

Q. *How many hours was he doing it?* **[This is a non-leading question, which is usually not a good to ask on cross unless you can force the witness to answer differently if he gives you a bad answer or if any answer he gives cannot hurt you. The former exception applies here. Girardi knows that the testimony of other witnesses reveals that the bad behavior did not just quickly appear and vanish but persisted for a long time.]**

A. I don't know. I think Ms. Burge—it was about the sixth inning where he started getting louder. So that wouldn't be two and a half hours.

Q. *All right. Then you know about the fact that he threw the coke at the two young people, right?*

A. I understand he shook the coke, and he sprayed her. I don't recall throwing the coke. That's semantics. **[Since it really doesn't make a difference, the witness should have just directly answered the question.]**

Q. *And then you recall he gets out of his seat and he goes walking over to the two young people where he's going to cuss the guy off. You saw that?*

A. Yes, I read that. I didn't see it.

Q. *And he was pulled away?*

A. Yes.

Q. *Now, all this was going on under the careful watch of the security people and ushers at Dodger stadium, right?* **[Girardi sarcastically points out how all of this could have happened if security was in place to protect the fans.]**

A. Well, once again, as I stated earlier, when everybody is standing up, it's a pretty tough thing to see. It was the end of the game, correct?

Q. *It's OK to assault people at the end of the game if you have the responsibility to keep things safe?* **[Girardi pounces on the excuse that the witness gives. Always carefully listen to an answer. If the witness gives you a disingenuous answer, use it as part of your next question as Girardi did here.]**

A. I didn't say—I'm just saying it's more difficult to see everything when everybody is standing up and leaving. [**The witness makes a good point but look at Girardi's response.**]

Q. *Especially if you're [security] in 161 and these people are in 149, right?*
A. Well, especially when people are leaving the aisles and walking on the concourses, yeah.

Q. *You saw the video of the fight. You said that, right?*
A. Yes.

Q. *And it took place for quite some time, didn't it?*
A. Define "quite some time."

Q. *OK. It wasn't one guy pushing another guy, like this was it?*
A. No.

Q. *It went—we saw it. They were going hammer and toe to each other, right?*
A. Yeah. Well, from what I saw, yes.

Q. *Was it a little surprising to hear in Dodger stadium where the owner has the responsibility to secure safety for the fans that you had something like this and not one safety person would come up?* [**Girardi reminds the jury in this question that the Dodgers had the legal responsibility to keep fans safe.**]
A. I don't know what they were doing at the time. It could have been, you know, handling some issues on the concourse, giving directions. I don't know, but it was surprising it was not addressed, yes.

Q. *So your opinion that if we had somebody in the stands who was behaving the way Sanchez was behaving that that would not be a basis to throw him out?*
A. If it was observed or reported, yes.

Q. *Well, there's an obligation to observe in these ushers and security people. They're not there to watch the game. They're there to observe stuff like this, aren't they?*
A. Whose to say they weren't observing the section.

Q. *I beg your pardon?* [**Girardi has the power of facts and common sense on his side. If Sanchez was acting badly since at least the sixth inning as the witness admits, then someone in security should have seen it.**]
A. Who's to say they were not observing the seating section.

Q. *Well, if they were observing, don't you think they should have done something about it?*
A. Had they seen something, yes.

Q. *And then the mere fact that the outrageous behavior took place at the end of the game, isn't it just as important that we protect the fans at the end of the game than in the eighth inning of the game?*
A. Protect the fans at all times.

Q. *At all times. And that's why we have the two people in security in Lot 2?*
A. They were scheduled to be in Lot 2, yes. That's where they had them scheduled, yep.

Q. *Just so we're clear, absolutely, positively, without a doubt for the Dodgers to have nobody in Lot 2 at the end of the game, did not violate any policy, and they still were meeting their standard to take care of the fans leaving the game, right?*

MR. FOX: Asked and answered. And argumentative.
COURT: Overruled.
WITNESS: I believe they would have been negligent had they not scheduled somebody to be in Lot 2.

Q. *I take it, though, scheduling somebody in Lot 2 doesn't mean a darn thing to a fan if when he gets to Lot 2 and there ain't nobody there?*

MR. Fox: Speculation.
COURT: Overruled.
WITNESS: As I mentioned yesterday, had they been in Lot 2, it's not guaranteed that they would have seen the incident.

Q. *Well, for the 25 minutes the two guys are in Lot 2, they're not guaranteed they would see the incident, right?* [**said sarcastically**]
A. That's correct.

Q. *So it wasn't guaranteed they would see the incident. Do you think maybe we needed some more people in Lot 2 to make sure we took care of the fans?*
A. I think that's — LAPD was in Lot 2. Should have been out there.

Q. *The Dodgers have the responsibility, not LAPD. Did the Dodgers, therefore, need more people to be able to pick up this five-person assault?*
A. Once again, I think the Dodgers met with the LAPD. They saw the event action plan, and they thought there would be LAPD out there.

Q. *There's no evidence of any LAPD person being in Lot 2, is there?*
A. There's no evidence they weren't either.

Q. *No. No. There's no evidence they were, yes or no.* [**Again, Girardi listens carefully to the answer and repeats his question when necessary.**]
A. No.

> **Practice Tip**
>
> When the witness gives an answer that is inconsistent with common sense, Girardi will repeat the answer sarcastically to highlight it for the jury.

Girardi then concluded his cross by pointing out that although there was a police watchtower in Lot 2, it was unoccupied.

Redirect

Let's fast-forward to the end of the redirect examination conducted by defense counsel (redirect occurs after cross-examination and gives the opposing lawyer the opportunity to clear up any points he wants to that were made on cross).

Q. Have any of the questions asked you by Mr. Girardi changed your opinion that the Dodgers acted within industry standards in terms of the operation of their stadium on March 31, 2011?
A. No.

Q. One other area. We talked about the Dodgers doing the right thing and whether they—Mr. Girardi asked if they acted perfectly. You said, "I don't think they acted perfectly," right?
A. Yes.

Q. But here's the question: on March 31, 2011, did the Dodgers organization act reasonably?
A. Yes.

Q. Nothing further.

Defense counsel has ended strong. Girardi does not let his good finish last long and immediately attacks on recross (some judges, as this one did, allow attorneys to conduct a recross examination after redirect).

Recross

Q. So they acted reasonably, even if they violated their own rules of who to put in Lot 2? That's reasonable, isn't it? [**said sarcastically**]
A. They scheduled somebody for Lot 2. They had done that for games previous to this.

Q. Right. We're talking about acting reasonably. They didn't act reasonably if they didn't even put the people in Lot 2 that they knew they had to get to Lot 2, right?
A. I stated they scheduled those two people for Lot 2.

Q. No. No. I understand they scheduled them. But deployment is just as important as putting it on the list, isn't it?
A. Yes.

This last answer is a huge admission. The reason Girardi gets it is because common sense requires it. It would make no sense if the the witness said that the Dodgers were required to schedule security for Lot 2 but then not be required to deploy security there.

Use Your Theme from Cross-Examination in Your Closing Argument

Girardi knows how important it is to tie the themes you make in cross to the points you are going to make in closing argument. Here is an excerpt from his closing argument that was built in part on the cross-examination of this witness.

Hines testified under oath that the only way to provide proper security was to have more security in Lot 2. That was the guy that couldn't get there because they had him over in the stands someplace, and he was trying to get back. . . .

Security is not just numbers. It's having the people doing the right job [**a powerful theme**]. *That's important, too. It doesn't matter if there were a hundred security people if they are all sitting in one corner. You have to have the security people in the right places. . . .*

Our best expert, I think, was their guy Squires. *Squires said that it met protocol to assign these two people to Lot 2, but apparently you didn't actually have to have the people there* [**said with sarcasm**]. *You just had to assign them there, and then that's all you had to do, and then we've done what we should do.*

You see, assigning people to Lot 2 doesn't do anybody in Lot 2 too much protection unless you actually go to Lot 2.

I want to talk about the uniformed police issue. As you know, there was an issue about uniformed police officers being there on security.

And there was a cost item. So I think they're five-hour shifts. And if you have a T-shirt on, you only get 30 bucks [per hour]. If you have the full uniform on, you get 50 bucks [per hour]. There's a 20-buck difference. That would be a hundred bucks per police officer.

So if you had a hundred police officers as opposed to polo shirts but in uniform, that would be a substantial amount of money. That would cost about $10,000 per game. If you had 80 games, that would be about $800,000.

Well, the total budget they had was 2 million. . . . So this would bring up the budget to almost 3 million bucks.

And the evidence was pretty clear, especially when you have gang problems, just maybe the appearance of the man in blue would stop some of the nonsense.

Do you think Sanchez would have been yelling those obscenities for five innings if, in fact, a few rows up was a person in blue watching it?

Do you think he would have been thrown out of the game immediately when he was doing those sorts of things, throwing beer, charging for a fight, et cetera?

5.5 CROSS-EXAMINATION OF THE HEAD OF OPERATIONS OF DODGER STADIUM

Francine Hughes was in charge of operations at Dodger Stadium.

Unlike Irving Younger's commandment to be subtle on cross, Girardi gets right the to the point. He wants to show the jury who was in charge and what was done.

Q. Ms. Hughes, you were in charge of security on the opening day of March 2011; is that correct?

A. I was responsible for the oversight of security, yes.

***

Q. Now, then, when the last pitch was thrown on opening day 2011, you expected ***your security people*** *assigned to Lot 2 to be in Lot 2; is that correct?*
A. My expectation is that we had **some type of security** in Lot 2. Whether it was our security or LAPD, that was my expectation. [**The witness does not answer the question**.]

Q. No. Ma'am, you expected your security people to be in Lot 2 when the last pitch was thrown?
A. We expected security to be out there, but we also had LAPD, sir.

Q. LAPD had no actual responsibility for this private property; the Dodgers did, didn't they?
Mr. Fox: Calls for a legal conclusion, your Honor.
Court: You're asking for her understanding, counsel?
Mr. Girardi: Yes, your Honor.
Court: All right. He's asking for your understanding. The objection is overruled.
Witness: Sir, my understanding was that LAPD was to be in the parking lots, and they were to assist us with the parking lot security.

Remember, the witness is never going to confess that the Dodgers were negligent. You are just trying to weaken the witness's credibility. Here, the witness shifts the blame to the LAPD, which she was expecting to be there. But, that reasoning is inconsistent with the law that states that the Dodgers cannot delegate the responsibility of protection to anyone else. It is a theme Girardi used in his opening statement and with other witnesses. Let's watch how Girardi emphasizes this Dodger attitude in his closing argument.

Girardi Discusses Jury Instructions in Closing Argument

Now then, I'll tell you this. This is really great. ***You know what the biggest help to us in this case is? It's the law. I think when they wrote the law, I think they were thinking in terms of Bryan in this case****. . . .*

So what did we hear in this case? ***There is a huge defense in this case, and it's the ABMD defense, anybody but McCourt Dodgers—right?—the LAPD, the CHP, the FBI, fans, et cetera.***

However, jury instruction 1, just a couple of sentences, "One who owns, controls, and/or manages property has an affirmative duty to exercise reasonable care for the protection of the individuals coming onto the property. The duty is non-delegable. A landowner cannot avoid that duty by designating it to another party." OK?. . .

The FBI had a presence there. That was because Major League Baseball was concerned about terrorism. They weren't concerned about assaults in the parking lot and drunken people yelling obscenities and so forth.

Practice Tip

Every question on cross should be important and have a purpose. Otherwise, don't waste time with it. A good test is to determine if you are likely going to refer to your point in closing argument.

The CHP [California Highway Patrol], they didn't get inside the parking lot. They were outside.

LAPD was there, 65 of them across the street in the park, but they had no—they were just backup. And the law says that you have to follow—no kidding on this one. ***He can't delegate—the owner of this property can't delegate it to anybody else. It's his ballgame. He has to keep that property safe.***

And we'll see exactly what they did with that, and, of course, they didn't. So that's a pretty good help.

Cross cont'd: Security Assignments for Lot 2

Q. *Didn't you assign people to Lot 2?*
A. I did not assign people, sir. The assignment was done by our security director.

Q. *I'd like to show you exhibit number 12 in evidence. We've put here in yellow Brian Hill and Brian Hines, patrol Lot 2. Do you see that?*
A. Yes.

Q. *And right above that, it says location until the second inning.*
A. Yes, sir.

Q. *So those two people were supposed to be there until the second inning?*
A. Correct.

Q. *All right. Then if we look across, location end of game, patrol Lot 2, those are the same two people, right?*
A. Yes, sir.

Q. *And they didn't get there until there were five assaults in Lot 2; isn't that correct?*

MR. FOX: Foundation.
COURT: Objection sustained.

Q. *Well, you know—as the security person, you knew that there were five assaults in Lot 2 before Hill and Hines got there?*

MR. FOX: Objection. Vague, your Honor. Misstates her testimony.
COURT: You may answer the question.
WITNESS: I'm sorry. I was not aware of five assaults in the parking lot, and I wasn't sure when Hill and Hines arrived at the parking lot.

The defense attorney objects to a lack of foundation because he does not concede that five assaults occurred in Lot 2. Thus, the question lacks foundation because it assumes a fact that has not been proven or it has a fact the witness has no basis for knowing. For the judge, it is a judgment call; some judges would sustain this objection, and others would overrule it. When it is sustained above, Girardi simply rephrases the question so that it asks about the witness's personal knowledge of the five fights.

The objection actually highlights a problem for the witness: she should know by the time of trial how many assaults took place in Lot 2. For whatever reason, she was not prepared to answer this question, and her lack of preparation fits in with Girardi's theme that the Dodgers were not prepared for opening day when the assault occurred. Girardi followed with this exchange.

Q. *So you're in charge of stadium operations, and you have—certainly this was a very serious matter that took place in Lot 2. Would you agree with me on that?*
A. Very serious, sir, yes.

Q. *And you never got any feedback if your people were there or not there?*
A. I never received notification until the incident had already occurred . . . .

The witness does not answer the question and simply deflects by saying she never received an alert about the assault until after it had occurred. Girardi has made his point and moves on to her qualifications.

Witness's Qualifications

Q. *Now, ma'am, you had no security training whatsoever, did you?*
A. Correct.

Q. *You'd never been involved in security for a stadium; is that correct?*
A. Correct.

Q. *Or a concert or anything?*
A. Correct.

Q. *But you were the person that oversaw the security budgets, right?*
A. Yes. To a certain degree.

Girardi's theme is clear, and each question has one main fact in it. His leading questions are textbook examples of how to prove a point. Next, Girardi will ask the witness about the organizations she should know about and belong to if she had a lot of experience in security.

Q. *Do you know what the ASIS is?*
A. I'm not aware of what the acronym stands for, sir, but I know that it's a security organization that does some training.

Q. *That's a security organization that does training for security people?*
A. That's correct from my understanding.

Q. *Do you know what IAVM is?*
A. That's the International Association for Venue Management.

Q. *Are you a member of that?*
A. I was at one time, yes, sir.

Q. *Were you on that night of March 31, 2011?*
A. No, sir.

Security Problems on Opening Day

Girardi next contrasts her lack of experience in security with the voluminous security problems on the day that Stow was assaulted. Girardi has boxes of field incident cards that were used by the Dodgers to document incidents during the game.

Q. There were literally hundreds of unruly incidents that happened before and during this game, right?
A. Not to my knowledge.

Q. Well, did you see those cards that were filled out for that night?
A. I didn't review the [field incident] cards, no, sir.

Q. Would it come as a surprise to you that there were 1,700 incidents that took place of fan misbehavior?

MR. FOX: Relevance, your Honor, and there is no evidence, no foundation.
COURT: Overruled.
WITNESS: Seventeen hundred incidents occurred on that day, sir?
MR. GIRARDI: Yes.

Girardi then pivots to the security briefing that Hughes attended before the game.

Security Briefing

Q. And at that briefing, the security people were there?
A. Yes, sir.

Q. And during that briefing, were the security people told that there isn't enough security?
A. Never, sir.

Q. Were you familiar with Mr. Heavens?
A. I'm familiar with the name, but I couldn't actually identify him. No, sir.

Q. I'll represent to you he was one of your security people who has testified in this case.
A. OK.

Q. Was there a warning given that night of not to get involved in any fights but to call security?
A. Not to my recollection, sir.

Q. Was there a warning that said we're short on security, we don't want anybody hurt, so you have to call a supervisor if there's a fight?
A. No, sir.

Q. So if Mr. Heavens testified to that, he was being mistaken; is that right?
A. I'm not sure what he heard, sir, but that's not based on my recollection.

Watchtower Was Unoccupied

Q. There used to be a watchtower that was for the purpose of security of parking Lot 2?
A. There are watchtowers in the parking lot. Yes.

Q. And there was a watchtower in 2009 in parking Lot 2?
A. I couldn't tell you the exact location, no.

> **Practice Tip**
>
> When the witness cannot answer a question because she does not remember or answers it differently than you expect, you need to have the documents immediately available to show the jury so that you can prove your point.

For an inexperienced lawyer, this last answer would be a problem. You will see that Girardi is trying to show the jury that the watchtower was not only located in Lot 2, but that it had been occupied in previous years but was unoccupied when Stow was assaulted. Watch what Girardi does.

Q. All right. We'll just let you take a look at it [exhibits 169-1 and 169-2]. That is the deployment sheet, is it not?
A. Yes, sir.

Q. And this assigns various people, various security people to various locations in the stadium, is that correct?
A. Yes, sir

Q. And what is the date of this particular deployment sheet?
A. April 13, 2009.

Q. And this is part of the business records of the Dodgers?
A. Yes, sir.

MR. GIRARDI: We would introduce this at this time.
COURT: Let me see it, please. Any objection?
MR. FOX: No objection.
COURT: Received.
(Exhibits 169-1 and 169-2 received in evidence.)

Q. Now, then, can we show here any area with respect to the watchtower. If they would blow that up so the ladies and gentlemen can see. You see there where it says watchtower, Lot 1 and 2?
A. Yes, sir.

Q. And then who's the person in charge of watchtower 1 and 2?
A. The person assigned to the watchtower would be Bobby Sonora.

Q. And what year is this?
A. 2009.

Q. OK. Cool. What is the purpose of the watchtower?
A. Based on my understanding, the watchtower is so you can have a bird's-eye view of the particular parking lot.

Q. It's security?
A. Yes, sir.

***

Q. This is 2010 now. And here do we have a watchtower Lot 1 and 2?
A. Yes, sir.

Q. And who's in charge of watchtower 1 and 2?
A. That would be Donna Harris.

Q. And I take it that when all the people are leaving the stadium, especially at the same time, to be above the crowd is a lot easier to see things that are going on, right?

This is a classic common sense question. If the witness does not answer it the way you and the jury expect, then Girardi gets an outrageous answer (the "O" of CROSS) and wins anyway. Because it is based on common sense, that principle usually forces the witness to answer the way you want. Watch what happens as the attorney tries to protect his witness.

MR. FOX: Speculation. Foundation.
COURT: It's asking for opinion testimony. Again, I would warn the jury that it's opinion testimony, and nobody has designated this lady as an expert on that particular area of observation or of security. But she may give you—you may give an answer if you have one.
WITNESS: Sir, I've never been in this watchtower, so I couldn't honestly tell you that. I'm not sure what you can see from there, but I would imagine that you get a bird's-eye view, yes.

Q. OK. Thank you.

It was a question that called for an obvious answer. But when defense counsel protests, the objection signals to the jury that the defense is worried about the fact that the watchtower should have been occupied.

***

Q. So this is the deployment sheet like before, and under watchtower Lot 1 and 2, who's assigned to it?
A. There's no name, sir.

Q. And watchtower 3 and 4, there's nobody there either, right?
A. Correct.

Q. And this was opening day 2011?
A. Yes, sir.

Q. And you have no clue as to why there were people in the watchtowers the two previous years that we've shown you and nothing on this opening day?

MR. FOX: Argumentative, your Honor.
COURT: Objection sustained.

Q. Do you have any opinion of why all of a sudden in this opening day, there's nobody in the watchtower to overlook Lot 2 when there were people overlooking Lot 2 the two previous years?

MR. FOX: Foundation. Argumentative.
WITNESS: Sir, I'm not sure why there were no bodies assigned to this particular location. I didn't handle the deployments themselves.

Email Regarding Security Problems

Q. Have you seen this document before?
A. The email? I'm sure I have. It's directed toward me.

Q. It is directed to you, is it not?
A. Yes, sir.

Q. And does it indicate any concerns with the ushers?
A. Yes, sir.

Q. And this is part of the Dodger record about security atmosphere, is that correct?
A. Yes, sir.

Q. And it indicates what with respect to the security?
A. It says, "Security sitting and watching while drunk fans yell at each other."

End Strong

Q1. Now did you investigate this particular accident or this assault?
A. I did not formally conduct an investigation on the assault, but I did review the business records, sir.

Q2. Did you find out that there were no Dodger people in Lot 2 when the assault occurred?
A. No. That's not what I found out, sir.

Q3. You didn't find that out?
A. No.

Q4. Who was there in Lot 2 when the assault occurred?

MR. FOX: Speculation. Foundation.
COURT: Overruled. If you know.
WITNESS: I'm not sure who was in the lot, sir.

Q5. Was there somebody there?

MR. FOX: It lacks foundation on the last answer.
COURT: The question is the knowledge of the witness. The witness may answer.
WITNESS: I'm not sure. I'm not sure who was in that lot, sir.

Q6. Wouldn't it be pretty important to you overlooking stadium operations where you had a huge, massive problem that took place in lot 2 to find out who the heck from Dodgers was there for security?

MR. FOX: Argumentative.

Q7. Wouldn't that be important?

COURT: Sustained.

Q8. Ma'am, if you have an incident like this and you're in charge of overall Dodger everything, wouldn't it be important for you to find out what the heck happened?

MR. FOX: Argumentative.
COURT: Overruled. You may answer that.
WITNESS: When I was aware of the situation, I called LAPD immediately who had taken over the incident.

Q9. Did you find out whether or not you had any security in Lot 2 when the assaults occurred?

MR. FOX: Asked and answered, your Honor.
COURT: Objection sustained.

Q10. Is it true that as you sit here right now you're going to tell this jury you have no idea if the Dodgers had security in Lot 2 when this incident happened?

MR. FOX: Asked and answered. Argumentative.
COURT: Sustained.

Q11. That's all I have, your Honor.

Although the objection is sustained on the last question, Girardi gets the intended effect from his question. The jury can decide if Hughes should have at least learned by the time of the trial what Dodgers security personnel should have been in Lot 2.

Did you also notice how persistent Girardi is? Q6 is determined to be argumentative but Q8 is not. There is very little difference between them. As a lawyer, it is sometimes hard to know why a judge rules the way he does. If you are unsure of the reasoning behind a judge's ruling, just ask. But Girardi does not want to interrupt the flow of his questions and changes the question slightly from asking about if it was important to find out who was in Lot 2 (Q6) to if it was important to find out "what the heck happened" (Q8), which is a broader question. The lesson to learn is that if you get an argumentative objection sustained, change the question slightly and you will often succeed. The second time you ask it, the judge will have more time to think about his previous ruling and appreciate the change you made, and if your second question is reasonable, you will win.

Recross

Hughes was called as an adverse witness by Girardi in his case-in-chief. That means that he could begin by cross-examining her before the Dodgers' lawyer could conduct a direct examination. After Girardi asked his last question above, the Dodgers' attorney conducted a direct examination where the witness stated that there was security in section 149 where Sanchez had been arguing with fans since the second inning. The witness further stated that there was protection for the fans in section 149. Girardi responded on recross with this common-sense question.

Q. I want you to assume that in section 149 where Sanchez was, starting in the second inning, he was throwing peanuts and food at two people wearing Giant uniforms right across the row. I want you to assume that he was obviously very intoxicated, obnoxious. I want you to assume that he was yelling massive obscenities we won't even talk about all throughout the game. I want you to assume that then in the ninth inning, they threw a Coke at Katie Gillepsie, drenching her, and then I want you to assume that then he came over to pick a fight with her boyfriend who was there. If all that happened, would you say to this jury that the security was just fine in 149?
Mr. Fox: Objection, your Honor. Incomplete and inaccurate hypothetical.
Court: Overruled.
A. I would say that if we observed it, the behavior, that it would have been stopped, sir.

Q. Well, you can't let – your whole job there was to observe, wasn't it? That was the job of the security people, to look at stuff like this, right?
A. Sir, they are tasked not only with that, medical issues, slip and falls, anything that happens on that level.

Q. Were there any slip and fall issues on 149?
A. I'm not sure, sir.

Q. The fact of the matter is if you have somebody behaving in this outrageous fashion for two hours and 30 minutes during a game, would you expect that just maybe all of these security people that were there would do something about it?
Mr. Fox: Argumentative. Incomplete hypothetical. Inaccurate hypothetical.
Court: Overruled.
A. I would expect if it was witnessed or observed by any security staff, that they would respond, sir.

Q. But they were supposed to be there to witness it, weren't they? That's what they're there for.
A. They're not there just for that, sir.

Q. Now, then, Mr. Arellano, he actually gave testimony that he was in 161. Do you know that?
A. No, I don't know that.

Q. Getting back to the fact that you had so many security people there, more than ever, I take it that the number of security people is not as important as where those security people are located, isn't that true?
A. I'm not sure what you mean.

Q. For example, let's suppose you have 200 security people, and they're all sitting in the right field bleachers and they're not anywhere else. That wouldn't be very good, would it?
A. No, it wouldn't be.

Characteristics of a Tom Girardi Cross-Examination

1. He starts and ends strong.
2. He knows that eye contact with witness is paramount. No detailed notes. Instead, he uses an outline with one word for each topic.
3. His cross is efficient and short, highlighting main points instead of diluting them.
4. He always listens to make sure the witness directly answers the question.
5. For emphasis, he will sarcastically repeat a witness's disingenuous answer as part of his next question.
6. He only asks the ultimate question after he gets three or four yeses in previous questions that set up the ultimate question. That way, when the witness denies the proposition in his last question, the jury won't believe the witness.
7. He uses memorable themes on cross to attack the witness and then reminds jurors of those themes in his closing argument. The themes tie into his bottom line message for the case that the Dodgers would not take responsibility for fan safety but instead blame others: Anyone But the McCourt Dodgers (ABMD defense).
8. He understands that he is in the persuasion business. Be likeable, prepared, and make your best argument.

5.6 AFTERMATH

The jury returned a verdict of $17,914,238 for Bryan Stow. It assigned a percentage of negligence to the following parties: 25 percent for the Dodgers, 37.5 percent for Louis Sanchez, 37.5 percent for Marvin Norwood, and 0 percent for Stow. In addition to the money awarded to Stow, the verdict had a wide-ranging impact. Girardi related that three large law firms that represent stadium owners wanted to learn from him what the stadium owners should do to prevent tragedies like the Stow case. Major League Baseball also interviewed Girardi to learn what the problems were. The results have been—among other things—that some stadiums have cut down on drinking by fans outside the stadiums before they enter, made it more difficult to sneak alcohol into games, and tightened security once fans are inside.

In a criminal proceeding, Louis Sanchez pled guilty to mayhem, and Marvin Norwood pled guilty to assault by means likely to produce great bodily injury. Sanchez and Norwood were sentenced to eight years and four years in prison, respectively. At the sentencing hearing (an excerpt can be seen on this book's website), Stow's father spoke about the pain Sanchez and Norwood had caused, and Bonnie Stow, Bryan's sister, said, "I envy those people who can forgive others who commit crimes against their loved ones. I'm not one of those people."

As Judge George Lomeli delivered the sentence, Sanchez chuckled, which drew further ire from the judge. "Rarely, do I comment, but this is the kind of case that demands it. Even now, with your smirks, you show no remorse. Not only did you blindside Mr. Stow, you continued to hit him on the head and kick him in the head. You're complete cowards."

5.7 CHAPTER CHECKLIST

Girardi's Cross-Examination Strategies

1. The trick to successful cross-examination is to be "limited and pinpoint," because as soon as you get too far afield, you let that witness argue for the other side.
2. Don't dilute your good points by conducting a three-hour cross-examination when it could be a lot shorter. Keep the jury's attention.
3. Lawyers forget that they are in the persuasion business and that the skills they use to persuade outside the courtroom should be used inside it as well.
4. "How do you get somebody to say, 'I'll marry you?' Is it with a 20-paragraph thing and then she says, 'I'll marry you,' or is it 'I love you' and she comes back and says that?"
5. Girardi does not use a bunch of notes in the courtroom that will put the jury to sleep. "The last thing you want to do is walk up there with your notes and read them. On the other hand, you don't want to forget certain issues. So I'll have a little piece of paper and I'll have ten words on it just to make sure I cover each of those ten subjects. And that's all you need and then you never read it. As you're finishing one thing, you kind of glance down and remember what the third thing is and then you talk about that. So it never looks like you're reading anything."
6. A good cross is like a boxing match: Three left jabs set up the right-hand knock-out punch. That is much better than trying to make every question a knock-out punch and being argumentative and high pitched. That will turn off the jury.
7. Resist the temptation to call the witness a liar. "Here's the thing that you gotta remember. I don't wanna call this witness an ass, a liar, a cheat, or a thief. I wanna lay it out, and I want the jury to go into the jury room and say, 'That guy was a liar.' You want them to say it, not you to say it."
8. When the witness is likeable, "you better not be laying into that guy, baby, because that jury loves him. And if you start being an asshole in front of

him, you've lost everything. In such a situation, limit yourself to your best points and be content."

9. When asking the ultimate question, set it up by getting the witness to answer yes to your preceding three or four questions. Then, when you ask the ultimate question, it won't matter that the witness denies your proposition, because his answer won't be believed.
10. Don't rely on others to help you prepare for cross-examination, "It's all you, baby."
11. When cross-examining at a deposition, do not use your knockout punch. Save it for trial. Even if the case settles, you can use the knockout punch at the settlement conference for great effect. If you use the knockout punch at the deposition, the other side will be able to fix the damage by the time of trial.
12. Start strong to get the witness defensive after a good direct examination so that the jury will see the change in confidence.
13. Don't be subtle on cross and save the points you want to make for closing. You need to be clear so the jury can follow you and because jurors do not wait until closing arguments to decide the case.
14. Use themes from your cross-examination that are the same or relate to your bottom line message for the trial. Tie everything together so it is clear to the jury exactly what you are trying to prove on cross-examination so that you can remind them in closing of the points you made on cross.
15. For expert witnesses, you have to be doubly prepared because the other side is certainly prepared for yours.

Lessons from transcripts

1. Girardi's cross-examinations are very clear and efficient. His cross of the defendant's expert took only 25 transcript pages.
2. With both witnesses, he started with very strong points he knew he would win.
3. Girardi's themes were clear. With Squires, his questions fell into three simple categories: 1) the law the Dodgers had to follow to protect their fans, 2) the expert's lack of qualifications, and 3) an expert's opinion that defies common sense.
4. If your point is important, find a way to repeat the question so that the jury will be certain not to miss it. Asking a witness how certain he is of his answer is one way to do it.
5. For an expert, attack his lack of training and publications if they are considerably worse than your expert's.
6. When the witness does not answer a question, Girardi uses a variety of tactics. One is that he sternly responds with "no" and then repeats his ques-

tion. For example, he asked the expert, "What security courses have you taken?" When the witness answered, "I actually teach a course," Girardi responded, "No. Which ones have you taken?"

7. A second technique Girardi uses when a witness does not answer a question is to follow the evasive answer with a question that begins, "Once again, sir, [repeat question]."
8. A third technique is to use a disingenuous answer as part of your next question. Here is an example. Q. Now, all this [fights in the stands] was going on under the careful watch of the security people and ushers at Dodger stadium, right? A. Well, once again, as I stated earlier, when everybody is standing up, it's a pretty tough thing to see. It was the end of the game, correct? Q. It's OK to assault people at the end of the game if you have the responsibility to keep things safe?
9. Girardi uses his boxing match analogy to set up the ultimate question (right knock-out punch) by first asking three or four questions he knows the witness will answer yes to (left jabs).
10. Tie the admissions you have obtained on cross to the points you are going to make in closing argument. In his closing, Girardi refers to the specific testimony he got from the defendant's expert witness. "Our best expert, I think, was their guy Squires. Squires said that it met protocol to assign these two people to Lot 2, but apparently you didn't actually have to have the people there [said with sarcasm]. You just had to assign them there, and then that's all you had to do, and then we've done what we should do."
11. Connect your themes on cross to your themes in closing. Here, Girardi ties the theme of Francine Hughes, who tried to deflect responsibility on cross, to his theme in closing that the Dodgers tried to blame others instead of taking responsibility for their mistake.
12. Use cross-examination to point out that the witness is unprepared. Girardi points out to the jury that witness Francine Hughes should have investigated the cause of the assault more than she did, if she truly cared about stadium security.

CHAPTER SIX

Mark Lanier Cross-Examines DePuy's Head of Clinical Research

"On cross-examination, think in terms of presentations and teaching rather than arguments and examinations."—*Mark Lanier*

In the next three chapters, we will examine in-depth three cross-examinations from a trial stemming from almost 10,000 lawsuits involving the DePuy hip implant. Billions of dollars were at stake. The witnesses had all been deposed and testified multiple times at trial. Consequently, they were well-seasoned witnesses who would not be easily intimidated. In addition, the witnesses had been prepped for their depositions and trial testimonies for hours on end by some of the best attorneys in the country.

Because the witnesses were so well prepared, the analysis that follows reveals some very creative ways to conduct cross-examinations against witnesses who will not give an inch. But before we get to the trial, let's learn more about the lead plaintiffs' attorney for these cases, Mark Lanier, who took on DePuy and its parent company Johnson & Johnson and its team of lawyers.

6.1 THE PLAINTIFF'S LAWYER, MARK LANIER

In 2018, *The National Law Journal* recognized Mark Lanier as the "Outstanding Trial Lawyer of the Year." In 2015, *National Trial Lawyers* named Mark Lanier "Trial Lawyer of the Year." In 2010, *The National Law Journal* declared Lanier as "one of the decade's most influential lawyers." After a record-setting verdict against the pharmaceutical giant Merck, *The New York Times* reported that Lanier's victory "cemented his place as one of the top civil trial lawyers in America." In 2017, he was inducted into The National Trial Lawyers' Hall of Fame. He has achieved

> **CHAPTER ROAD MAP**
>
> - Think of cross-examinations as teaching opportunities instead of arguments.
> - Use the Folder Method to organize your cross.
> - Connect your themes from your opening to the themes on your cross.

many record-setting verdicts. In 2018, Lanier won a $4.69 billion verdict for 22 women and their families who had alleged that Johnson & Johnson's baby powder contained asbestos that caused the women to develop ovarian cancer.

Lanier's journey to becoming one of the most successful plaintiff's attorneys in the country was not without its detours. He graduated from Lipscomp University with a B.A. in Biblical Languages. He wanted to become a preacher but realized that by becoming a lawyer he could pay for his love of preaching without the hassles of becoming a permanent preacher. He never had an overwhelming desire to become a lawyer and make a lot of money. Says Lanier, "The motivation in my life is teaching and preaching, and taking care of my family—and law is that third priority that funds me to do it. I just happen to be really efficient at being a lawyer in a way that my skill set . . . makes money."

6.2 LANIER'S STRATEGIES

Lanier believes the biggest mistake lawyers make on cross-examination is not putting in the time to be prepared. He adds for emphasis, "It is the most important thing." I have personally observed that when Lanier cross-examines a witness, he always can quickly find a document to rebut a witness who fails to answer one of Lanier's questions correctly.

The most unique technique that you will see Lanier use in the next three chapters is that he constantly presents interesting and understandable visual aids to the jury during cross-examination. I asked him where he came up with this idea. He explained that he teaches theology each Sunday to 700 people. So, he has spent his life trying to figure out how to "make the complicated understandable by the masses." That is how he developed his style. To get a sense of his presentation style, you can find a link to a video of his adult Sunday school class at www.winningatcross.com. Consequently, he teaches his lawyers to "think in terms of 'presentations' and 'teaching' rather than 'arguments' and 'examinations.'"

Not only does he make the complicated understandable, but he makes it memorable. Lanier told me his drawings and the demonstrative exhibits he uses on cross-examination—one of the many examples is the box of doughnuts he used in his cross of a witness we'll soon discuss in this chapter—are also an effort to bond with the jury and create a moment they will remember. Lanier relates that studies show there are three types of long-term memory. The first is procedural memory. Procedural memory is a type of unconscious long-term memory that involves those things that have become ingrained in your muscle memory. For example, you may not have ridden a bike in a long time, but you haven't forgotten how to do it. The second type is episodic memory, which involves your ability to recall past events or powerful episodes, such as your first romantic kiss.

Semantic memory is the third type of long-term memory. Semantic memory is the storage of words, facts, ideas, and other information that form our knowledge of the world. Information stored in semantic memory is the first of our long-term memories to be forgotten. As such, you will often forget the names of people or things from past episodes or procedures before you will forget the procedures or episodes themselves.

At trial, jurors use their semantic memory. Unfortunately, it is the first to fail. Instead, what if you could get them to use their episodic memory, and as a result, they would remember your points better? Ideally, you would want them to ask the witness questions and participate in court room demonstrations. But the rules do not allow for this. Lanier explains that the next best thing you can do is to tell stories and create demonstrative exhibits that engage jurors and help them become involved and approximate an episode so that they will remember your questions. There is no attorney who implements this technique better than Lanier.

Lanier's belief in these studies about memory also explains why he creates very simple drawings to make his points. I asked him why he did not use a graphic designer to create sophisticated illustrations instead of the very basic ones he uses. He explained, "When you create on the spot, it shows it is genuine and goes to authenticity. When you aren't the best at it, it shows that you're human. And although you may be able to command a courtroom, many jurors will know they are better than you at something." It is just another way he creates a bond with the jury and creates a memorable moment.

I asked Lanier how he prepared for the cross-examinations of the three witnesses analyzed in these chapters. He responded that it is the same for any witness: the Folder Method. First, he assimilates all the documents he plans to use. When you are trying to find the best documents out of the millions obtained in discovery, this takes a lot of organizational skill. "Focus and discipline is enforced by the Folder Method," Lanier says, "It means massive preparation, but it works!"

He explains how his Folder Method works. After finding the documents to "drive the points he wants to make," he creates a "road map" of the major points he wants to present in front of the jury. He then puts all the documents in folders, pre-marked so he knows where to find the relevant passages in the documents. Next, he organizes the folders to put the "best flow to things." He places the folders in Redwelds (red expandable file folders) in a Bankers Box and naturally divides them with appropriate labels. Consequently, when you watch Lanier at trial, you will see him at the podium with two to three Banker's Boxes filled with Redwelds. He swiftly finds whatever document he needs to show the jury.

For example, let's look at figure 1. There are seven areas of testimony that Lanier wanted to cover with Pam Plouhar, the head of clinical research at DePuy. This is a document that Lanier created and that was shown to the jury during cross-examination. It was displayed on an ELMO (a platform document camera). As an aside, all of Lanier's ELMO notes discussed in the following chapters were not marked as exhibits and did not go back to the jury room during deliberations.

Lanier would have had a separate Redweld for each area of testimony. For area number one, he would have labeled the Redweld "Rush to Market." Within that Redweld, he would have had individual folders with exhibits that would support

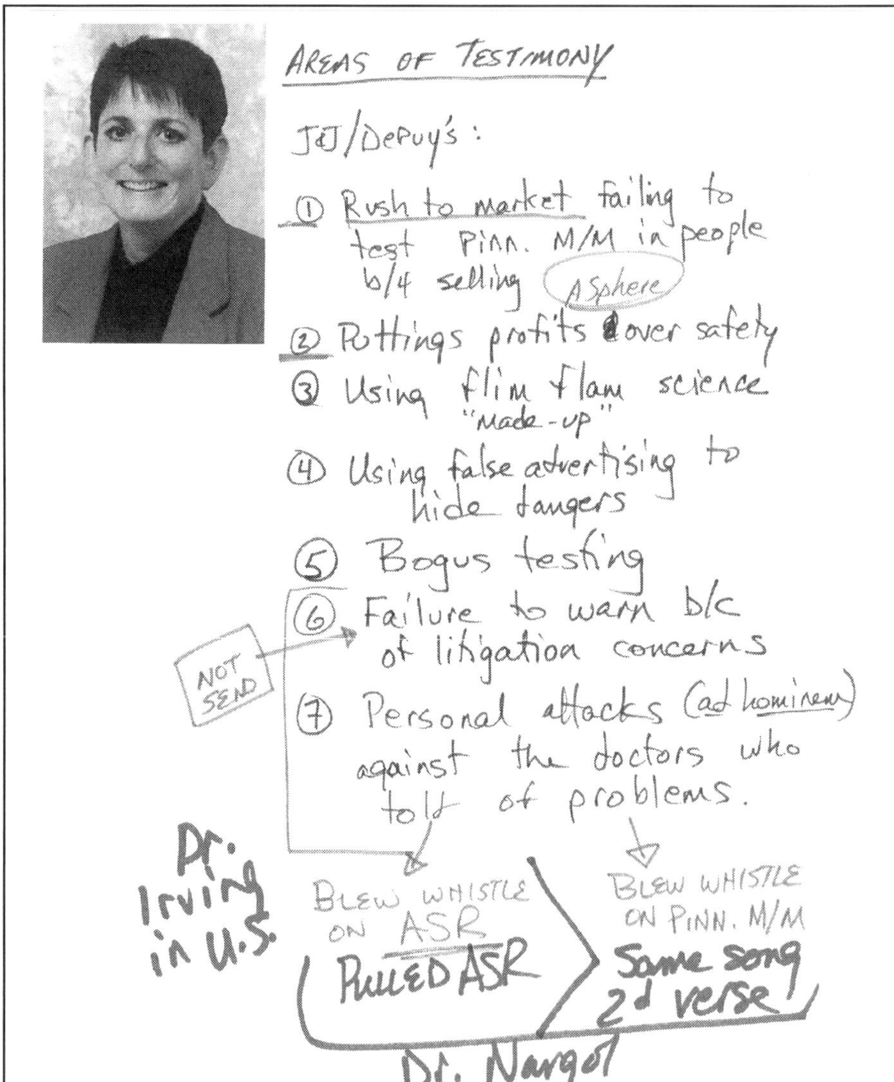

Figure 1. Seven areas of testimony Lanier wants to cover with Pam Plouhar.

his point that DePuy rushed to market its hip implant. Those folders would be labeled with the name of the document inside (i.e., Plouhar email dated _____), and he would have three copies of each exhibit (one for the witness, one for defense counsel, and one for himself).

In the Bankers Box, he also would have had a Redweld that would contain folders with documents responding to specific themes he expected the defense would assert at trial. For example, any time a witness might assert a particular defense theme, Lanier could quickly pull a folder that had documents in it that would refute that theme.

As we will see, one of the biggest challenges Lanier had for the three witnesses is that the witnesses had been deposed and testified at previous trials where Lanier had cross-examined them. I asked Lanier how he overcomes the witness who has already seen his best shots. He responded that the challenge is to "keep it fresh and launch new assaults. The solution? WORK!"

Another fascinating trait of Lanier's is that when you watch him conduct a multi-hour cross-examination, he never looks at any of his outlines. His eyes are always on the witness, or he is writing questions or making drawings on a blank sheet of paper or marking on a trial exhibit on the ELMO that is then projected on a monitor or screen in the courtroom. But appearances are actually deceiving. Lanier has a cheat sheet of his outline in one of the folders in his Redwelds. But having watched him at length in trial, I have never seen him look at it. He is that subtle. This is a much better system than that of the vast majority of attorneys who take a detailed list of questions to the podium, read them to the witness, and then check them off. This is the worst way to conduct a cross-examination, because it bores the jury, and when the jury is not paying attention, you are not accomplishing anything.

As an aside, if you watch Lanier long enough in trial, you will see that he occasionally writes something in a leather-bound journal when he is at counsel table. It is not a trial notebook, but a "running journal in life," where he writes important thoughts and to-do lists. It is a great source for creating themes for his cases and cross-examinations. It may be an odd place or time to do so, but when he thinks of an important idea for one of his trials, he immediately writes down the thought in his journal.

Finally, I asked Lanier if he treats a cross-examination differently if it is done at a deposition rather than a trial. He explained that he treats them the same, unless he thinks the case is going to trial and the witness will testify live at trial. "In that singular exception, you save your bullets for trial rather than shoot them in a deposition."

Another strategy tip to keep in mind is that if Lanier has to play a deposition at trial instead of calling the witness live, he uses three cameras at the deposition: one on the witness, one on himself, and one on the ELMO. Lanier calls this the three-camera deposition (see section 3.16). By using this technique, the jury can easily see the exhibits the witness is being shown at the deposition and can see Lanier's mannerisms as he asks his questions. What makes it even more effective is that Lanier has the deposition edited meticulously so that the video switches seamlessly from Lanier when he asks the question, to the witness when she answers the question, to the document that is being shown to the witness. It's as if the witness was actually present in the courtroom. In short, he recreates as best he can what a jury would see if the witness had testified live at trial.

Although a lot can be learned from examining the nuts and bolts of Lanier's cross-examination techniques that follow, he has many intangible skills and traits that are not readily apparent from a cold transcript. But if you look closely, you will find them. If you were a juror, they would be very obvious, since you would see him perform in person.

Lanier's most striking quality is his love of teaching. When you see him in trial, he enthusiastically presents evidence on direct examination and passionately cross-examines witnesses so that the jury stays extremely interested and understands what is happening. His presentation is sincere and easy to follow. He always uses visual aids and chooses words that are descriptive and uncomplicated, such as "That's a gimme," "flimflam science," "Put your money where your mouth is," and "hocus pocus."

He is also extremely likable and charismatic. He explains that when he was growing up, his parents were constantly moving all over the country. He learned to make new friends quickly and adapt to different cultures. In short, he learned how to fit in and be liked.

When I saw him in a recent trial, he was grilling an expert witness on cross-examination. The expert was battling back and would not give an inch. The expert sneezed; Lanier immediately interrupted his examination and said, "Bless you." I asked him how he could so quickly switch from an intense cross-examination to a kind gesture toward the witness. Lanier's answer reveals his courtroom demeanor and should be a model for others to follow:

> There is a difference between dealing with an issue and dealing with a person. If I've got an expert on the stand that I am cross-examining who I think is putting a bunch of hooey out there for the jury, well, I'm going to dissect the hooey, and I am going to try and force that witness to accept the fact that what he is saying is bogus.
>
> That doesn't change the fact that I care genuinely for each person. They've got to sneeze—well, "Bless you." It's not personal, it's business. Even if I think that they are selling their soul for money, that they are a testifying

prostitute, a jukebox you just put your money in it and they'll sing any song you want them to sing it's not going to cause me to wish them ill. I want them to be the best they can be. I want their life to be good. I hope that's part of being genuine.

The importance of this likability factor cannot be overstated. Although Lanier is involved in a very high stakes trial against multiple law firms, his courtroom demeanor sets the gold standard. He is pleasant with the judge and opposing counsel, which is something that can be very difficult to do over a long and contentious trial. When it is his turn to examine a witness, he literally jumps out of his chair to get to the podium, where he brings energy and enthusiasm that was not there before. His excitement is literally contagious, and the jury becomes captivated.

In addition, Lanier is the best prepared person in the courtroom. That means he not only knows the facts and law better than opposing counsel, but he also knows the facts and documents better than any of the witnesses. Obviously, this preparation begins before trial. Lanier obtains damaging documents through such discovery tools as interrogatories, requests for production of documents, and subpoenas. He invests in experts to help him review voluminous documents to find the key ones he can use at trial. He also gets critical information from depositions. You will see that, throughout his examinations, he forces the witness to give him the answer he wants because the witness must admit what the words on a damaging document say. A witness cannot argue with what is written in black and white.

The flow of his questions always makes sense. He transitions from one topic to another effortlessly. In fact, he shows the witness a list of topics that he wants to discuss, each framed in a persuasive way for his clients. The jury can easily follow these topics. However, when it is advantageous, he will take advantage of a witness's answer to pivot to a related topic where that answer will help. At other times, when he succeeds on a line of questions, he immediately builds on that success by quickly digging deeper into that topic to get even more damaging admissions.

The point is that Lanier stays flexible during cross-examination. He listens carefully to the witness's answer. If the witness is careless and makes an admission or creates an opening for Lanier to pursue, he jumps on it. He knows that some of the biggest points made on cross are the surprises you get by taking advantage of mistakes the witness makes in his testimony.

Finally, watching Lanier in the courtroom is like watching David take on Goliath. While both sides have a team of lawyers and assistants in the audience for help during breaks, it is an incredible feat that Lanier conducts almost the entire trial by himself, except for the presentation of some of the plaintiffs' direct examinations because some of the plaintiffs are clients of another attorney. In a six-week DePuy trial, Lanier delivered the opening and closing arguments, and conducted cross-examinations of all the witnesses including all of the expert witnesses, as well as the direct examinations of the plaintiff's expert witnesses and nearly all the other witnesses. In addition, he made all the pretrial motions to the court, as well as all the evidentiary arguments during the trial.

On the other side of the courtroom, DePuy had three lawyers at counsel table who shared responsibilities for the trial. They would often alternate which witnesses they examined, and would pass notes or whisper comments and strategies to each other. In addition, while Lanier found the exhibits himself from the folders he had at the podium, the other side constantly relied on assistants to find exhibits and display them for the jury.

Lanier does it all by himself because when you have one presenter, all the themes stay intact. "All of the focus is sharp and unidirectional," he explains. "The jury bonds more readily. It is more efficient." However, we need to stop and have a reality check. The physical and mental stamina it takes to try a six-week trial all by yourself is daunting. I asked Lanier if it were realistic to expect lawyers to duplicate his mastery in the courtroom. He responded that "everyone must play with their own skill set." But he emphasized that he has never seen anyone who cannot learn to be organized, and "that is a game changer, regardless of your skill set." That philosophy is consistent with what I believe: never underestimate your opponent, and be the best prepared attorney in the courtroom.

In the following cross-examinations, you will see many creative themes. These were not born by accident; they were carefully created and developed by Lanier. As soon as the case comes through the door, Lanier starts to think of themes for the overall trial and each cross-examination. But it does not stop there, as he continues to think about his themes for trial and cross-examination, right up until the eve of trial and the night before his cross-examinations. It is a creative process that never ends and is always being perfected.

In the opening statement of the case that follows, Lanier used Hurricane Harvey's then recent devastation of Houston, Texas, as a springboard for the analogy that the jurors were like home inspectors who would write a report on the house that Johnson & Johnson had built. He also used another theme in which he argued in opening that the plaintiffs had trusted a doctor and a product, and had gotten terrible results. He referred to these themes in his cross-examinations and created others for each cross, which will be discussed shortly in detail. Let's get some context for the cross-examinations and then learn from a master.

6.3 BACKGROUND OF THE DEPUY HIP IMPLANT LITIGATION

Over 9,000 plaintiffs filed suit against DePuy Orthopedics, Inc., and its parent company, Johnson & Johnson, regarding the alleged defective design and deceptive advertising of the Pinnacle Acetabular Cup System hip implants. The implant was used to help patients who had diseased hip joints. Patients were told that the implant would alleviate their pain and allow them to regain motion in their hips. Pursuant to the United States Judicial Panel on Multidistrict Litigation, approximately 9,000 lawsuits were consolidated in the United States District Court in the Northern District of Texas for pretrial proceedings. After consolidation, DePuy and the Plaintiffs' Executive Committee agreed to a bellwether trial process, where several trials would take place so that the parties could value the pending cases. There were four bellwether trials. The lead plaintiffs' counsel for all the trials was Mark Lanier. In the fall of 2014, the first bellwether trial took place (the Paoli trial). A single plaintiff lost to DePuy. In January to March of 2016, the Aoki trial occurred, which involved five plaintiffs. The jury returned a half-billion-dollar verdict against DePuy, and the Fifth Circuit reversed and ordered a new trial.

In the fall of 2016, Lanier represented six California plaintiffs in the Andrews bellwether trial. After that two-month trial, the jury found for each plaintiff and returned a verdict of $1.04 billion, which consisted of $28,361,648 in compensatory damages to the six plaintiffs, $4 million in compensatory damages to the spouses of four of the plaintiffs, and $1,009,000,000 in punitive damages. In the fourth bellwether trial, known as the Alicea trial, the jury awarded the five plaintiffs $247 million. (In separate litigation, Johnson & Johnson, which owns DePuy, paid a $2.5 billion settlement to 8,000 patients who claimed they were hurt by DePuy's Articular Surface Replacement (ASR) Hip Resurfacing System. The ASR system will be referenced in some of the testimony to follow.)

In short, the plaintiffs argued that DePuy negligently designed and deceptively marketed the Pinnacle system metal-on-metal hip implant ("MoM") to patients. The plaintiffs' major complaint was that the Pinnacle system was sold without testing it in humans first. DePuy argued that the FDA approved the Pinnacle system and did not require human testing before it was marketed. DePuy also argued that the plaintiffs' complaints were not due to a defective product, but rather to metal hypersensitivity or problems with the angle of the plaintiffs' hip bone that caused the implants to not work properly. In addition, doctors were aware of the risks and determined that the benefits far outweighed the risks and therefore recommended the implants to their patients.

The plaintiffs countered that DePuy paid large sums of money to very influential hip surgeons to market the hip implants and failed to heed warnings from doctors that there were dangerous complications after surgery.

The Pinnacle system was implanted in approximately 150,000 Americans, and many others in Great Britain and Australia. The system was taken off the market in 2013, but not until after DePuy had made enormous profits from what it called its "Billion Dollar Baby." DePuy said that it was taken off the market due to a decline in sales and not because of safety risks.

The plaintiffs claimed the complications for patients were disastrous. As the metal on metal system moved with each motion of the leg, metal ions were released into the blood stream with potentially toxic results for the body. In addition, around the area of the implant, irreversible damage to the muscles and bone often occurred.

In 2007, the United States government entered into a deferred prosecution agreement (DPA) with DePuy, where DePuy, without admitting wrongdoing, agreed to 18-month independent monitoring and new compliance procedures in exchange for the government's dismissal of charges that it violated the Federal Anti-Kickback statute by paying orthopedic surgeons through consulting agreements to use DePuy hip implants. DePuy also paid $84.7 million in civil fines.

Dr. Nargol, whose name is mentioned below, is a former consultant to DePuy. He warned DePuy of the problems he was seeing in patients after implanting the Pinnacle system at his hospital in England. Instead of listening to his warnings, Nargol claimed at trial that DePuy attacked him and labeled his patients' experiences as outliers. A video of an investigation done by ABC7 in Los Angeles can by found at www.winningatcross.com.

In this chapter and the next two, there are three cross-examinations from the fourth bellwether trial, the Alicea trial. As mentioned at the outset, these witnesses had testified in the previous bellwether trials and had also been deposed. Consequently, they had heard many of Lanier's questions before and had a lot of time to craft their answers. As a result, Lanier had to execute cross-examination skills at the highest level in order to succeed. To give you a visual of how these cross-examinations took place, an excerpt of the video depositions of these witnesses can be found at www.winningatcross.com.

6.4 CROSS OF DR. PAM PLOUHAR[1]

Introduce the Witness and Your Topic

Q. How long have you worked for either DePuy or Johnson & Johnson in your life?
A. I started working for DePuy in 1989, and DePuy was acquired by Johnson & Johnson in 1998.

Q. Now, you have a Ph.D. You are a woman of science, fair?
A. Yes.

Q. Your Ph.D. is in chemistry, if I recall correctly.
A. Yes. With a concentration in biochemistry.

It may seem unusual for an attorney to bolster the credentials of an opposing witness, but Lanier wants to show the jury that she is an expert so that he can later undermine DePuy's decisions by showing that DePuy should have known better, particularly the decision to market the Pinnacle hip implant before testing it on humans.

Q. *I want to talk to you, ma'am, about your role and the company's decisions and actions involving the Pinnacle metal-on-metal. OK?*
A. Yes.

Q. *If the jury's going to understand this best, I think it's important that they know that at the time we're going to be looking at—when the Pinnacle metal-on-metal was being developed and sold—for a good bit of that time you were the head of clinical testing. Is that right?*
A. Head of clinical research.

Q. *That includes testing, doesn't it?*
A. Yes.

Lanier always introduces the witness to the jury. Whether it is direct examination of a friendly witness or when he cross-examines a hostile witness as he does here, he explains to the jury why he is calling the witness. In contrast, most lawyers just start with a bunch of meaningless questions that can go on for 10 or 15 minutes. The jury hears the information and quickly loses interest because it has no idea why the witness's testimony is relevant. Once you lose a jury's attention, it is very hard to get it back.

> **Practice Tip**
>
> At the beginning of questions that ask about a complicated or new topic, use Lanier's phrase, "So the jury understands. . . ." You will immediately win friends on the jury.

Lanier Asks Witness to Explain the Pinnacle Hip Implant to the Jury

Q. *Doctor, so that we're all on the same page, because we're pretty new at this, metal-on-metal means that within the Pinnacle shell goes a metal liner, and then on the Pinnacle stem goes a metal ball, and the metal ball rubs against the metal, correct?*
A. So the stem is a femoral stem?

Q. *Yes. The stem goes into the thigh bone instead of my pinky.* **[Lanier uses his pinky to demonstrate.]**

Lanier, the master teacher, is always aware when the jury is hearing information for the first time. Plouhar is one of the early witnesses in the trial. Lanier does not make the mistake most attorneys do of assuming that since they have lived with the case for years and years, the jurors bring similar knowledge of the case to trial. You need to remember that jurors know nothing about your case.

> **Practice Tip**
>
> Lanier always has a visual aid on the ELMO projector. Often it is a trial exhibit, but other times he is writing testimony down, making a list, or creating a drawing.

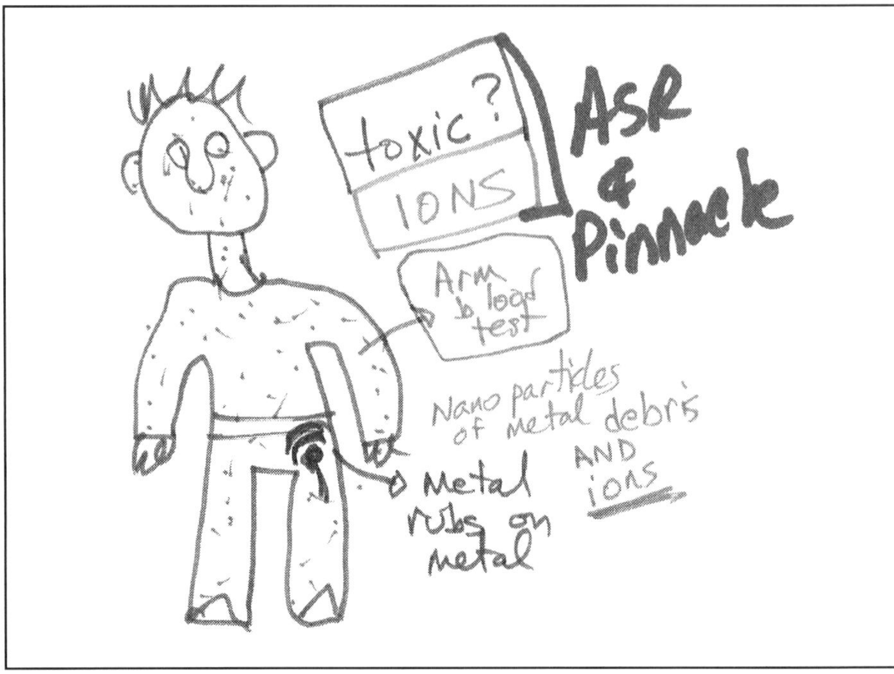

Figure 2. Drawing of human figure by Lanier.

Here, Lanier holds up the actual Pinnacle hip implant at issue in the trial and shows each part to the jury. There is no better way to explain it than with the real parts themselves.

In the following excerpt, Lanier draws the human in figure 2. Obviously he could have paid a graphic designer to create a demonstrative exhibit, but there is something very simplistic about the drawing that provides the perfect contrast to the defendant's complicated efforts to not address the problem of metal-on-metal hip implants. It makes Lanier and his clients seem relatable and his opponent seem legal and technical. It also humanizes Lanier and allows the jury to connect with him. See if you agree.

Use Drawings to Enhance Questions

Q. *You've been with me enough to know I'm not very good at drawing, right?*
A. Yes.

Q. *OK. So this is a person.* **[Lanier draws the person in figure 2]** *All right. You got it?*
A. Yes.

Q. *This person has a—a metal-on-metal Pinnacle hip implant right here.* **[Lanier draws the hip implant on left hip on figure 2.]** *He's got the ball, the stem that goes into the thigh, and it's got the liner and the cup, so that metal-on-metal rubs.* **[Lanier writes "metal rubs on metal" on figure 2.]** *Do you see it?*
A. Yes.

Q. *Metal rubs on metal. Now, you know that when it does that it puts off millions upon millions of little tiny pieces of metal, nanoparticles of metal, right?* [**As Lanier asks this question, he simultaneously fills the inside of the human in figure 2 with lots of tiny red dots to signify the nanoparticles. His use of red ink to convey danger is not lost on the jury. After making the dots, the human figure looks very ill as if he has a terrible infection.**]
A. I don't know—I don't remember the size distribution. There are—there is particle debris generated by the metal-on-metal articulation [**i.e., metal parts rub against each other**].

Q. *And the metal also produces something called—so it produces nanoparticles of metal debris and ions, metal ions that go in the body, correct?*
A. Yes.

Q. *And there are blood tests to see what your metal ion levels are, aren't there?*
A. Yes.

Q. *And the blood that shows those metal ions comes out of the arm generally for the blood test, right?* [**Lanier writes "arm blood test" and draws an arrow from the elbow on figure 2.**]
A. Yes.

Q. *So even though those metal ions are happening in the hip, they go throughout the entire body, such that you can even find them in the blood in the arm, can't you?*
A. Find them in the blood, yes, as it's drawn from the arm.

Q. *And there was serious trouble about how poisonous or toxic those ions might be, wasn't there?* [**Lanier writes "toxic ions" on figure 2.**]
A. I don't think that the—so the long-term effects of the metal ions, I think it's still being understood.

Notice how Lanier links his questions to what he draws. This not only helps the jury understand his questions, but it will also help them remember the testimony several days later. In the first bellwether trial, a defense attorney complained (and lost) to the judge that Lanier's drawing of money bags was unfair because the jury looked at it too much during testimony.

> **Practice Tip**
>
> Remember, a study has shown that three days after hearing information, people can only recall 10 percent of what was said. If the information is combined with a visual aid, retention increases to 65 percent.

Lanier then shifts from asking questions about his drawing to asking about a DePuy PowerPoint presentation that was used internally to discuss strategies.

Questions about DePuy's PowerPoint

Q. *So, for example, if we look at what the PR [public relations] man was helping coordinate on slide 15, we'll see the following: The question is asked: "Where do we take the*

Pinnacle brand?" This is after the ASR has been recalled—the ASR metal-on-metal is recalled, and so the issue is "Where do we take the Pinnacle brand?" [**The ASR was a hip implant system where the shell and liner were combined into one piece instead of two pieces as found in the Pinnacle Ultimet implant at issue in this trial. The ASR was recalled and taken off the market while the Pinnacle was still being used, but it had a similar progression of marketing promises, surgeon complaints, and failure in patients as the Pinnacle did.**] *Do you see that?*
A. Yes, it's page 15.

Q. *Now, so the jury is clear on this, the ion story is a concern because you get these metal ions that come around the body whether it's ASR or Pinnacle metal-on-metal, don't you?*
A. So the question is—is whether or not the ions are—that you have ion levels with Pinnacle as well as with ASR, yes?

Q. *Exactly. That's my point. This ion question of whether or not the ions are toxic, that is a question for both ASR and Pinnacle, because they're both putting out ions, aren't they?*
A. Yes.

Q. *And so the company is concerned that this might threaten the company's business if the patients find out about it. Right?*
A. I don't know.

Q. *Well, that's on slide 19, where they describe the situation. And they say here are the strengths, here are the weaknesses, here are the opportunities,* ***here are the threats****. So here are the threats that they were having to be confronted.* ***Do you see those threats?***
A. Yes.

Q. *"Ion story goes 'patient.'" Do you see that?*
A. I do.

Q. *I mean, this could include in a "Move to metal-on-metal: payer backlash, consumer backlash, institutional backlash." It's threats to the business, isn't it?*
A. That's what this says, yes.

As we will see throughout the cross-examinations, Lanier phrases his questions from the exact words he has in the document to force the witness to answer yes. Here, the document discussed threats, and the witness had to answer yes.

Q. *And so within the framework of this, you are seen as a* ***critical stakeholder*** [**In testimony not shown, Lanier had shown the jury a DePuy document that listed the witness as a critical stakeholder**], ***and not just a critical stakeholder, you are—let me go back to the sheet with you. You're not only a critical stakeholder, but you get media trained. Right?*** [**Lanier puts figure 3 on the ELMO and writes "media trained" below the other filters Lanier has written to indicate how the jury should view the witness's testimony.**]
A. Yes.

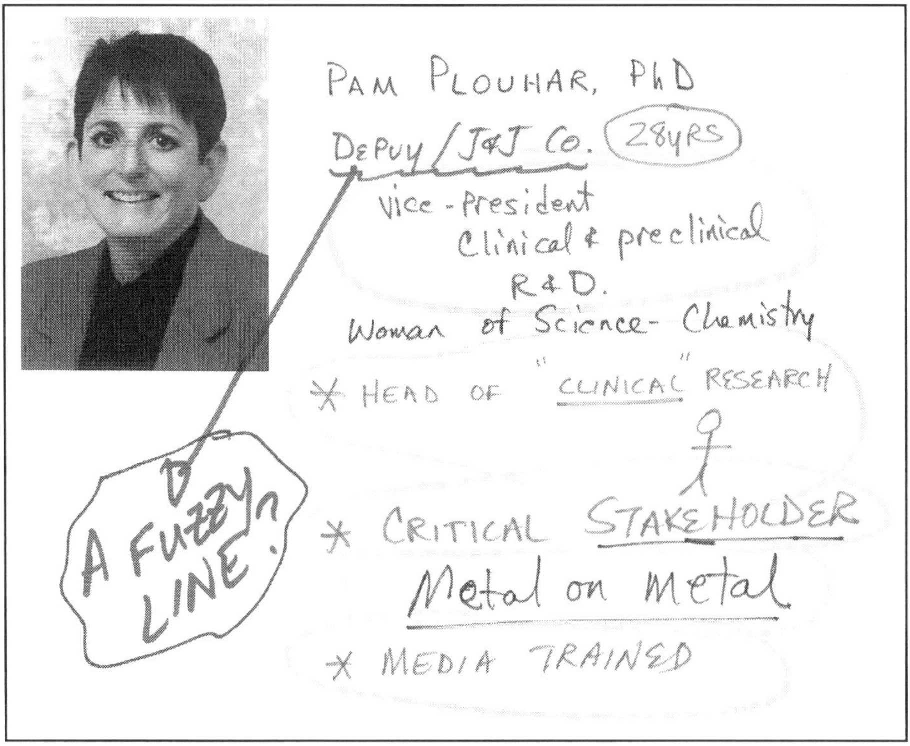

Figure 3. ELMO exhibit with details about Pam Plouhar.

Q. *In other words, the company spends, oh, tens of thousands of dollars to train you to be the front person for the company with the media, to try and keep the story OK for the Pinnacle metal-on-metal. Correct?*
A. Well, I don't—I'm not sure how accurate that portrayal is, because I don't know how much—**I had a few meetings with a media consultant** to talk about how to address media questions.

Q. *Plaintiff's Exhibit 7421 is the later unfolding of this Pinnacle response plan, and it's a P.O. for A-P-C-O or APCO. Tell the jury what P.O. stands for?*
A. P.O. stands for purchase order.

Q. *In other words, this is the way you get money for something within the company, or one of the ways, right?*
A. Yes.

Q. *And so the company is being asked to issue $100,000 charged to the communications budget. That's not science. That's marketing, isn't it?*
A. It's the communications budget.

Q. *Yeah. Not the science budget, correct?* **[Lanier repeats the question.]**
A. That's correct.

Q. *All right. So they take you, and they put aside 25,000 for website development, but 60,000 is for media training and desk-side briefings. Do you see that?*
A. I do see that, yes.

Q. *And here's the concept: "Proactively convey fact and science-based messages about joint and hip replacement to encourage balanced media coverage and help create an environment in which an accurate understanding of hip replacement can be achieved." This is to "counter or mitigate existing false perceptions about Pinnacle among general top-tier media and trade reporters." Did I read that correctly?*
A. That's what it says.

Q. *The tactics. You're here under tactics, aren't you?*
A. I am.

Q. *"Conduct media training with Pam Plouhar,* ***preparing her as lead clinical spokesperson*** *for future media engagement opportunities." So as the jury listens to you, they are listening to someone who was media trained to talk about these subjects, fair?* **[Lanier then shows the jury figure 3 again, where he has written "media trained" beneath Plouhar's picture.]**
A. About the subjects identified there, yes.

List Topics for the Jury

Lanier does something that very few—if any—attorneys do, but with his success rate, you need to do it, too. As he asks the witness about each topic, he writes them down on a sheet of paper with the witness's picture on it (see Fig. 1). At first, you might think this is too tedious and the jury would lose its attention. Here is the key: write quickly and clearly. If you cannot write quickly enough, write the list before the cross begins. But use your handwriting to keep it authentic and give your cross the feel of a spur of the moment emphasis. If your handwriting is bad, what should you do? It should be no surprise that Lanier told me that you should practice it.

The beauty of what Lanier does is that he creates an easy-to-remember list for the jury. Because it takes a little longer for him to write out the list instead of just talking about it, each point is in front of the jury both audibly and visually for a longer period of time, which makes it more memorable.

> **Practice Tip**
>
> After making your list of topics, display it to the jury as you begin each new topic, to remind them of what you have proven and what topics you are going to cover.

Have you noticed how different Lanier's strategy is from Irving Younger's advice in his ten commandments, which was discussed in chapter 2? Unlike Younger, who suggests that you should hide the ball until closing and then explain what your subtle questions on cross meant (that the jury has certainly forgotten), Lanier makes it very clear what his themes are on cross. He not only tells the witness and the jury, he writes it out for them.

As an aside, you will notice that Lanier breaks the rule of three discussed in chapter 3 by asking the witness about seven topics. He is one of the few lawyers whose preparation and captivating presentation allow him to effectively cross-examine on more than three points. His philosophy is that if you can annihilate a witness, then bring everything you have.

Q. ***My areas of testimony, so that you and the jury and the court have a clue of where I'm going, are the following:*** *I want to talk about, one, the rush to market and how your companies rushed to market in failing to test Pinnacle metal-on-metal in people before you sell it. You understand what I mean by that?* **[Lanier writes the description beside the number one in figure 1 as he asks the question.]**
A. Yes.

Q. *All right. We will talk about that first. Then we also need to talk to you about the company putting profits over safety. You understand that concept, even though I'm assuming you don't agree with me, that the company did it, right?* **[Lanier writes the description next to number two on figure 1. He will do the same for each of the following questions.]**
A. You are right.

Q. *The third thing that I want to talk to you about, the third area of testimony, is using what I call flim flamscience. That's probably not a science word, so maybe instead I should say made-up science.* **["Made-up science" is really not more of a scientific word than "flimflam science." Lanier's brilliance lies in using language and ideas that align him with the common sense that the jury brings to the case, as opposed to the overly sophisticated and complicated presentations that the defense makes.]**

Again, not anything you'd agree with me on, I'm sure, but you certainly understand what I'm at least referencing, don't you?
A. I do.

Q. *And then, four, using false advertising to hide the dangers of the product. Again, I'm sure you don't agree with me, but you understand what I'm going to be talking to you about, right?*
A. Yeah.

Q. *Five, bogus testing by the company. You understand what I'm talking about there, though I'm sure you don't agree, right?*
A. I'm not sure what is encompassed in bogus testing.

Q. *We'll get to it, and I think it will make sense to you once we're there. A failure to get out a warning letter. A failure to warn because the company wants to—is concerned of litigation. Again, I assume you don't agree with me, but you at least understand the concept I want to talk to you about, right?*
A. Yes.

Q. *And then finally are the personal attacks, or as Mr. Quattlebaum used the Latin, ad hominem, against the person, y'all's personal attacks against the doctors who were telling you about the problems. You know about the issue that I want to talk to you there on, don't you?*
A. Yes.

Q. *All right. So within these areas let's start out with the rush to market . . . .*

Use Themes from Your Opening Statement on Cross

As mentioned earlier, Lanier created his opening statement around the theme of Hurricane Harvey, which had devastated Houston just a few weeks before the trial. He told the jury that the devastation to homes made him think about the home inspectors. He asked the jurors to think of themselves as home inspectors. They would need to inspect DePuy's house. He told the jury that his job was to show them everything they needed to file a home inspection report. He would prove to them that DePuy built its house on a bad foundation, used shoddy equipment, and caused significant damage. He told the jury that the defense counsel would put fresh paint on the house to hide its problems, but if the jury gave Lanier the time, he would show them it was a poorly constructed house.

Cross-examination textbooks don't even bother to discuss using themes in opening statement or on cross the way Lanier does (as follows). That is because their authors fail to realize the importance of boiling your case down to a key message (or, as previously stated, a bottom-line message) as to why you should win in your opening and then using that theme—in this case being a home inspector—throughout trial. Not Lanier—he knows how to win.

Moreover, Lanier's theme is all the more persuasive because it empowers the jury to take action. He gets the jurors involved by inviting them to become home inspectors. He draws them into the case at the very beginning and puts them in charge. This trial is not going to be a passive experience for them. By doing this, he creates a bond with them from the outset. He will provide them with the evidence so they can fill out their report. They are going to work together to hold Johnson & Johnson accountable.

Q. *Now, here's my premise, and I want to know if you will agree with me on the premise. My premise is DePuy/Johnson & Johnson rushed Pinnacle metal-on-metal to market, never testing it in people before selling it. Agree or disagree?*
A. I disagree.

Q. *Now, you don't disagree with the whole thing, right?*
A. That's correct.

Q. *Because you do agree that DePuy/Johnson & Johnson never tested the Pinnacle metal-on-metal in people before selling it. That part you agree with, right?*
A. That's correct. Pinnacle Ultamet or Pinnacle metal-on-metal was not tested in people before it was sold, that—that product.

Q. *The only—right. The only thing you disagree with is whether or not it was rushed to market, correct?*
A. Yes.

Q. *Now, you were not here for the opening statements, obviously. Did you at least get a chance to hear them or read them?*
A. I did not read them, nor did I listen to the opening arguments.

Q. *The illustration I used for the jury in opening was this idea if you were a housing inspector, you need to not just go into the house and see fresh paint and nice furniture, because what you see on the surface is not always what's really there. You're familiar with that concept, aren't you?*
A. Yes.

Q. *Things are not always as they seem on first appearance. You can spiffy it up and make it look pretty good until someone gets a little closer for the examination. Do you follow me?*
A. Yes.

Q. *In this trial the jury gets to look under the rug. The jury gets to look behind the sofa. Heavens, the jury gets to know whether or not the walls were built with the 2-by-6 specified [indicating] or whether the builder used a 2-by-4 instead, figuring nobody would see it.* **[Lanier indicates this on a slide he used in opening statement.]** *The jury gets to see all of that in the trial, you understand?*
A.Yes.

Q. *And I say that because you know, don't you, that this rush to market is a big issue with me? From our past you know that I am very concerned about the rush to market, right?*
A. Yes.

Q. *Mr. Quattlebaum in his opening used a—an interesting exhibit. It was slide number 16. I'm putting it up for you to see. Do you see that?*
A. I see it, yes.

This technique is as brilliant as it is bold. Imagine what must be going through the witness's and defense counsel's minds. Lanier is going to take a slide that the opposing attorney relied on in his opening statement to undercut the witness's testimony. Both the witness and the attorney are frantically trying to figure out where Lanier is headed. Consequently, Lanier now has this very well-prepared witness off-guard and exploring areas that could not possibly have been foreseen in witness preparation.

Is Lanier really going to get the witness to admit that her attorney was wrong in what he argued to the jury in his opening statement? Let's see.

Q. ***We—we've got teachers, we've got an architect, we've got lots of different folks with a lot of different education, parents, moms on the jury. You follow me?***
A. Yes.

Great lawyers like Lanier remember their jurors' occupations from information provided during jury selection so they can connect to them and tailor their evidence to them.

Q. *They know what an optical illusion is. You do too, don't you?* **[Lanier is aligning himself with the jury against the witness.]**
A. In general, yes.

Q. Well, here. **[Lanier was going to create the drawing anyway. But when the witness hesitates by saying "in general," Lanier pounces on it and says, in essence, "If you're not sure, let me draw an example for you." Once again, he makes the witness look evasive.]** *I can take a blank sheet of paper and I can take a ruler. And I can with this ruler draw a line that's one inch. And I can draw another line that's one inch. Those lines are the same size, right?*
A. Yes.

Q. But if I take this line and I do an arrow like that [indicating], and I take the second line and I do an arrow like that, to the eye it looks like that second line is longer than the first one, doesn't it? Do you see what—oops. I'm sorry. Do you see what I'm talking about?
A. I understand, yes.

Practice Tip

You need the right tools to employ Lanier's techniques:

1. Lots of blank cardstock sheets (so ink doesn't bleed) with the witness's photo in upper left-hand corner.
2. Pens, highlighters, and markers with different colors.(Lanier prefers Paper Mate markers.)
3. Wireless microphone or other setup so the jury can hear you when you write on paper and are away from podium microphone.
4. It never hurts to have a ruler. You never know if you might need it.

Not many attorneys bring a ruler to a courtroom. Lanier is setting the groundwork for an important point he is about to make. He demonstrates how easy it is to create an illusion by using what we have all seen since grade school. It is called the Müller-Lyer illusion, where two lines of equal length do not appear to be the same length when one line has arrow heads on each end (appears shorter) and the other line has arrow tails on each end (appears longer).

Q. That's an optical illusion, also known as visual hocus pocus, right?
A. I don't know about that.

Q. That may just be a Lubbock term. Have you ever been to Lubbock, Texas? **[Lanier uses this opportunity to remind the North Texas jury that he is from a relatively small Texas town known for its salt of the earth people and that the witness is not. Also, visual hocus pocus sounds more sinister than optical illusion. David is taunting Goliath.]**
A. I don't believe I have.

Q. OK. You've got a lifetime of experience in front of you. The optical illusion, the visual hocus pocus, is what Mr. Quattlebaum and your team did in his opening here, isn't it? He tries to—
A. I don't know what you're referring to.

Q. He tries to make this look like it was a long time and not a rush to market. So he paints the Pinnacle and Ultamet development as if it lasted from 1994 until 2001. Do you see that? **[Lanier shows the witness a printed PowerPoint slide on the ELMO that was used by defense counsel in opening statement.]**
A. I do.

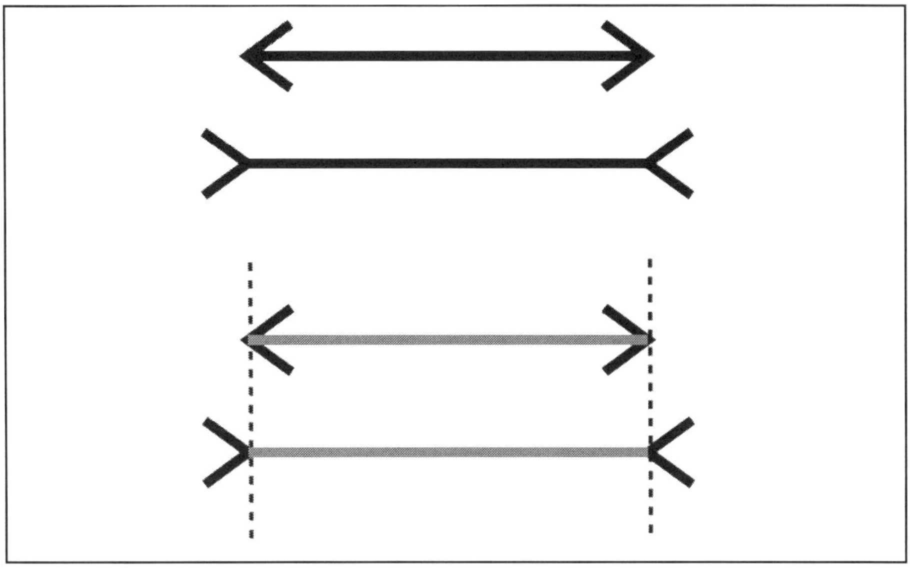

Figure 4. Müller-Lyer illusion.

Q. *And not only does he do that, but y'all have got 1998 in there three times to make it look even longer. Do you see that? 1994 is one inch, 1995 is one inch, 1996 is one inch, 1997 is one inch, 1998 is one inch, plus another inch, plus another inch. This is 1998.* **[Lanier puts a ruler on top of the printed slide to measure.]** *That's visual hocus pocus, isn't it? Makes it look long, but that's an optical illusion, right?*
A. The line defines it as seven years. **[The witness does not answer the question but instead responds that the timeline defines seven years. Lanier will follow this evasive answer by highlighting the point he wants to make.]**

Q. *Sure. That wasn't my question, ma'am. Visual hocus pocus. You've got an optical illusion built into the chart when he's trying to explain to the jury what this case is all about, already sowing these seeds. Do you see that?*
A. I see that there is two—two segments that are 1998.

Q. *And then there's this—no, three actually. See this segment here, that's 1998, too. In other words—*
A. OK. It's just not labeled as 1998.

Q. ***Right. They didn't even label it there,*** *but it is. Look at this, 1998, that whole block is 1998. You see?*
A. Yes.

When the witness tries to help her company and attorney by saying there are only two segments, not three for 1998, Lanier highlights the fact that that is even further evidence of visual hocus

Practice Tip

Not only should you use your opening statement theme on cross, but be sure to also use your opponent's exaggerations and misstatements from his opening statement against his witness.

pocus because it's not labeled. This point is made even stronger by Lanier's earlier drawing of the two lines.

Q. *And this is just—With due respect to Mr. Quattlebaum and your team, this is just false. It's untrue, isn't it?*
A. So I—I disagree. I think that the development actually did take place over seven years.

Use Demonstrative Exhibits to Make Your Point

The plaintiffs claimed that the metal hip implants they received had a different hardness, coating, and grain size than the ones Johnson & Johnson had tested in its lab. Lanier wanted to use a demonstrative exhibit to show the jury that the witness, who was the head of testing, should have tested the different hip implants before marketing them to the plaintiffs. He also wanted to create an episode that the jury would remember when other witnesses were examined.

Q. *Can we agree one of the most fundamental rules of doing a study—like we can call it I think rule 1. If you're going to study a product, you need to use the product. Right?*
A. Yes. . . .

Q. *Do you eat doughnuts?*
A. Occasionally.

Q. *This is like my downfall. OK? Have you ever eaten a Dunkin' Donut?*
A. Yes, I have. . . .

Q. *You've got a box of Dunkin' Donuts, OK? That's free. Those are yours. All right. Now, ma'am, I want to do a test, and I want to test whether or not Shipley's Do-Nuts are better than Dunkin' Donuts. OK? Are you with me?*
A. Yes. . . .

Imagine the dramatic effect of a box of Dunkin' Donuts on the witness stand and a box of Shipley Do-Nuts at the podium where Lanier stands. This demonstration is also a wonderful example of making things simple for a jury.

Q. *So here's my test. I believe, Mark Lanier—I'm going on record right now. I believe that in a taste test that Shipley's . . . tastes better than Dunkin' Donuts. . . . That's what I want to test. OK? Now, y'all don't have Shipley's up there in Indiana, do you?*
A. No. **[By choosing Shipley Do-Nuts, Lanier not only chooses a great product, but one that is only available in Texas and the deep South. Consequently, it provides an opportunity for him to remind the Texas jury that the witness is from out of state and represents a large national company that may not have the same values as the local people on the Texas jury.]**

Q. *It's one reason Texas is a more populated state than Indiana. I've got some Shipley's Do-Nuts, and I want you to taste them to see whether or not they taste better than Dunkin' Donuts. OK? Are you with me? Are you following me?*
A. Yes.

Q. *Go ahead and taste and see if they're better.*
A. I don't have any Shipley's Do-Nuts.

Q. *You don't have any Shipley's Do-Nuts. Well, just eat one of the Dunkin' Donuts and tell me if Shipley's is better. You can't do that, can you?*
A. No.

Q. *It's impossible. And I can't make you eat a doughnut anyway. That's not fair to you. But my point isn't eating the doughnuts. My point is if you don't have a Shipley's Do-Nut so that you can taste it, there's no way you're going to be able to answer that question, can you?*
A. That's correct.

Q. *You can eat as many Dunkin' Donuts as you want, but if you can't eat a Shipley's Do-Nut, you're not really testing the Shipley's Do-Nut. You've got to have the product, right?*
A. Yes.

Q. *Now, here's the reason I go to such a length to talk about this. Your company was never testing the right product. It was never testing the product that was put in these plaintiffs. Did you know that?*
A. I don't know what you're talking about.

Q. *I'm talking about the fact that y'all had the wrong donuts. You're testing the—you're eating Dunkin's when you're supposed to be eating Shipley's. Y'all didn't use the right product. Did you know that?*
A. I'm still not sure what you're referring to. . . .

Q. *The doughnuts, or the pieces that you tested in the lab to get this cleared are a different kind of doughnut than what you were putting in the people. Y'all didn't use the right—y'all changed it up, didn't you?*
A. I don't know what you're talking about. I don't know.

Q. *Well, OK. I'm not a great baker, but I actually do bake. The ingredients that Shipley's says is on their doughnuts: flour, shortening, two other kinds of flour, sugar, eggs, milk, and salt. Do you see that?*
A. Yes.

Q. *I would venture to say that some kind of flour, some type of oil, still flour, sugar, eggs, milk, and salt are also in a Dunkin' doughnut. That's pretty fair, isn't it?*
A. Yes.

Q. *But they taste very different, because they may be in different proportions, right?*
A. Yes.

Q. *So here's the predicament we're in. If the lab tests have one kind of implant but in the plaintiffs we have—the plaintiffs have a second kind of implant, your testing is bogus. I mean, it's just wrong, isn't it?*
A. If that is true, but I'm not sure that it's true.

Q. OK. That's fair. We'll look at that together. But if true, testing is wrong. Because rule number 1, whether it's doughnuts or hip implants, is if you're going to study a product, you've got to use the product, don't you?
A. Yes.

While the witness never admitted that Johnson & Johnson had not done the correct tests because she did not have personal knowledge of the tests, Lanier had made an important point with the witness through the analogy and could use it with other witnesses who would testify later who had more knowledge. The doughnut comparison created an episode for the jury that would be easy to remember throughout the trial. Whenever a witness would give complicated answers about the tests that Johnson & Johnson conducted, Lanier would use the doughnut analogy to prove his point.

Break Up Topics

Q. Well, I've talked to you about the rush to market, failing to test the Pinnacle metal-on-metal in people before selling it, thereby putting profits over safety . . . . Now I want to talk to you about a brand-new subject, our ***after-lunch subject****: using made-up science. Now, this is under your watch, isn't it?*
A. I'm not sure what you're referring to, though I'm sure we'll get to it.

Q. Well, let's start out with a couple of things. And this is "film flam." [It] sounds like a bad phrase. There's got to be a better—illegitimate, illegitimate science, is there such a thing? You know what I mean if I say, "illegitimate science"?
A. I think we'll talk about it, right?

Q. Yes, ma'am.

Lanier knows the importance of summarizing important testimony and highlighting upcoming topics. Applying the principles of primacy and recency, that is, that people remember better what they hear first and last, Lanier uses the moments after a break and just before one to discuss important facts with a witness. Here, Lanier has just finished up a major topic, and begins this new one shortly after the lunch break and immediately launches into it.

> **Practice Tip**
> Divide your topics around the major breaks in the day.

Space does not permit an analysis of Lanier's entire cross. Let's fast-forward to his recross.

Recross Examination

After defense counsel conducted her direct examination, Lanier began his recross. If my terminology is somewhat confusing, here is a brief explanation.

Plouhar was called as an adverse witness by Lanier in his case-in-chief. Generally, when you are examining a witness in your case-in-chief, you are putting on neutral or friendly witnesses, and your examination is called direct examination. After you conduct your direct, opposing counsel conducts a cross-examination, and then you finish with redirect examination to address issues raised on cross and clear up any confusion.

But when you call an adverse witness, that is a witness who is aligned with the other side, your direct examination becomes a cross-examination. After that, opposing counsel can conduct a direct examination (since the witness is aligned with him), and then many courts will allow a recross such as the one that follows.

As he did at the beginning of his cross, he lists his topics for recross and tells the jury what he is going to prove (see Fig. 5). Let's look at another analogy Lanier uses to help the jury remember his points.

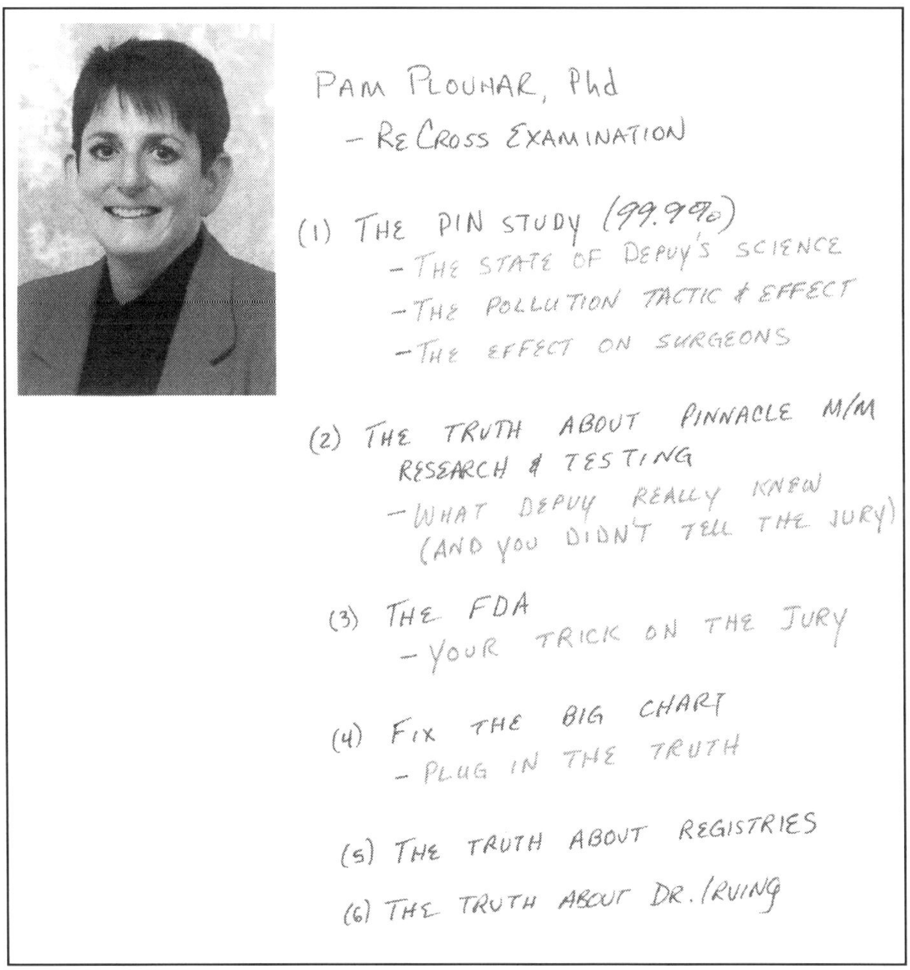

Figure 5. ELMO exhibit with list of topics that Lanier has for recross.

By way of background, the witness explained on direct that the mistake DePuy made by stating that its hip implants were 99.9 percent effective five years after surgery did not matter, because there was no proof that doctors relied on that specific information when deciding whether to recommend it to a patient. In fact, one study showed that the survivorship rate was only 15 percent after five years, which is a huge failure rate. Lanier uses the analogy of tainted milk to show how DePuy was trying to let its incorrect information seep into the marketplace.

Use Analogies to Argue Your Case

Q. *Now, you also said yesterday there's no evidence of reliance by Dr. Terhaar* [**a surgeon who put a Pinnacle hip implant in one of the plaintiffs**], *etc., relying on the PIN study* [**that incorrectly claimed a 99.9 percent survivorship after five years**] *and all the rest of this stuff. But, ma'am, this tactic is a little like putting ink in the milk. You've got a glass of milk. You've got an eyedropper of ink. You put a little ink in that milk—you tracking with me?* [**Lanier draws figure 6.**]
A. Yes.

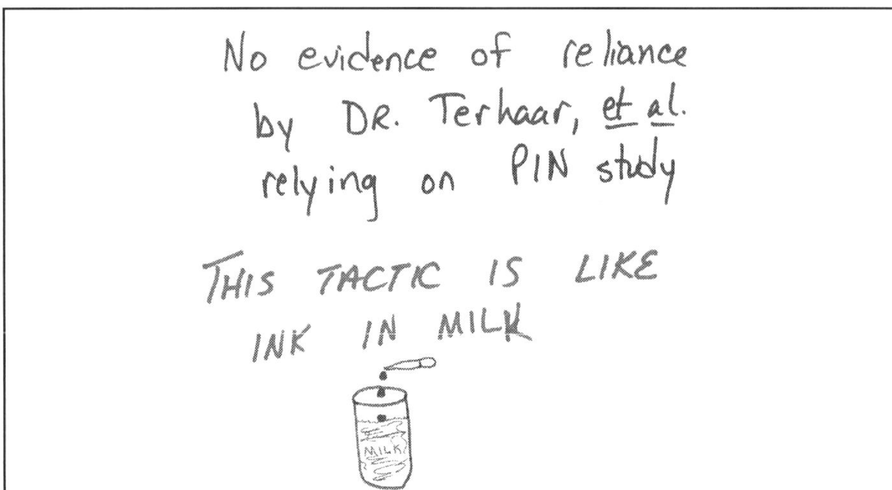

Figure 6. Lanier's drawing of ink being dropped into a glass of milk.

Q. *Now, the ink may have just hit some of the milk there at the top, but it disburses throughout the milk and makes it cloudy, because it has an effect on the rest of it, doesn't it?*
A. The milk, yes.

Q. *Yeah. You're not going to drink that milk, are you, unless you're mighty thirsty?*
A. I was going to say it depends on how thirsty I am.

Q. *I know. I know. I saw your chemistry mind working on that one. Unless you're mighty thirsty and you've got no other choice, you're not drinking that milk, are you? See,*

what y'all did is you took the 99.9 percent, and you put it in all the journals. You gave it to the FDA. You kept the falsehoods in it all the way around. You had all the doctors talking about it. You didn't just give it to the FDA back then, in 2009, you gave it to 'em again, didn't you?
A. I think I'll have to—refresh my memory.

Q. *Remember when they were thinking of taking metal-on-metal off the market in 2012? Y'all made a presentation to 'em, and in that presentation you used the 99.9 percent again?*
A. I think it was referenced in that presentation.

Q. *Yeah.*
A. But I think that presentation was mostly based on the national joint registries.

Q. *In other words, "yes, Mark, we used it, but we used a bunch of other stuff, too. Right?"*
A. Yes.

Lanier shows some exasperation at the end of this excerpt that probably mirrored the jurors'. While jurors are listening to the facts, their primary activity is deciding who they like, the attorney asking the questions or the witness.

> **Practice Tip**
>
> Whenever the witness does not answer a simple question, the lawyer wins because it shows the witness is afraid of the simple answer.

Lanier Continues to Connect His Opening Statement to Cross

Q. *Now, you were asked this question by Ms. Renfroe: Why didn't DePuy study Pinnacle metal-on-metal in people before selling it? Do you remember that?*
A. Yes.

Q. *And the jury knows that I'd written that on a tablet in opening, challenging Mr. Quattlebaum to answer it.*

MR. LANIER: There we go. Thank you. [**An assistant gets the tablet from opening statement.**]

Q. *Challenging Mr. Quattlebaum to answer it: Why didn't you test the Pinnacle metal-on-metal in people before selling it? You cannot see the tablet, but it's the same thing I've written on the ELMO, so that you've got it. OK?*
A. Yes.

In Lanier's opening, he ended on a very strong point by writing three questions on an easel in front of the jury. He told the jury that defense counsel should answer these simple questions in his opening, and to be completely fair, Lanier was going to give defense counsel five minutes of his time so that defense counsel could not complain that he would be short on time if he answered them. The three questions were: 1) Why didn't DePuy test its product on people before selling it? 2) Why did it compromise on the hardness and coating of parts? and 3) Why won't you bring company executives to testify live?

It was a powerful moment in the opening statement. The questions pinpointed where Lanier felt the defense was weakest. Defense counsel did not answer the questions in his opening but told the jury the questions would be answered during the trial. After delivering his aggressive opening statement, Lanier never let up, and he would later follow up on the unanswered questions during his cross.

Q. *Now, if I understand your answer, the first thing you said was, well, we tested a different product. We tested the Ultima instead. Is that right?* [**The Ultima was another DePuy metal-on-metal hip implant that was marketed just before Pinnacle. Pinnacle was based on the Ultima.**]
A. Yes.

Q. *We know not only that metal-on-metal products differ, but rule one, as we discussed yesterday, is you got to test the right product. Right?*
A. Yes.

Q. *You can't confirm for me Shipley's is a better doughnut unless you taste a Shipley's Donut, right?*
A. Yes.

Q. *OK. So the fact that you tested a different product is absolutely useless in telling us whether or not the Pinnacle metal-on-metal is going to work, isn't it?*
A. Well, FDA accepted it as a comparable articulation.[**There was a loophole at the FDA where companies could get medical devices approved without testing in humans if it was substantially equivalent to another product that had been approved.**]

Q. *Wasn't my question. Please answer my question.*
A. We didn't test the Pinnacle metal-on-metal articulation.

Q. *No. And the tests that you did do on the Ultima was a short-term test. It wasn't a five-year test, was it?*
A. No. It typically would have been two years.

Q. *And you didn't even have all two years done by the time—and analyzed by the time you started getting your metal-on-metal cleared by the FDA, did you?*
A. I don't recall the exact timing, but I don't believe that they had follow-up on all of the patients that were enrolled in that study, at two years.

* * *

Below, Lanier continues with the doughnut analogy. We pick things up with Lanier attacking the witness's direct testimony where she discussed the testing that was done. Another issue (discussed next) is that DePuy was changing vendors every couple of years for the manufacture of its hip implants. The specifications varied through the years for the hardness, coating, and dimensions among others.

Q. *Well, ma'am, even aside from that, because this is a 2006 study we know for a fact if the metal hardness* **[on DePuy hip implants]** *changed dramatically again in 2006 to '7, then all of the Pinnacle metals that are being compared there that you're using in all of these numbers as you chart them across, these are Dunkin' Donuts numbers, not Shipley's, right? These are all Dunkin' Donuts numbers, aren't they?*
A. I think we talked—I think we talked about this this morning, and I told you that all of the patients were enrolled in the study by the end of the 2006.

Q. *Exactly. I mean, you're not—you're not even comparing the same shell, the same ball, the liner, the hardness. You've got a totally different product that y'all are trying to tell this jury they should look at the results on.*
A. And I don't know that for a fact.

Q. *OK.* ***If it turns out that the documents are truthful and accurate and that that is the fact, then the jury ought to disregard all of your numbers up here, shouldn't they?***
MS. RENFROE: Objection, Your Honor, argumentative, assumes facts that are not established, not in evidence.
COURT: Overruled.
WITNESS: I don't know. **I think you'll have to talk to Leanne about that.**

This is a devastating tactic to use with a witness. If you cross a witness early in the case and she argues that data is wrong or that a document does not purport to be what you tell the jury it is, ask the witness to agree that, if it is proven that the document is true, then her testimony must necessarily be incorrect.

> **Practice Tip**
>
> When the witness tries to pass the buck by answering that you need to ask another witness the question, force the witness to at least admit what the document says.

Write an Important Question and the Answer for the Jury to See

Q. *But I'm just talking about you because of these numbers. If the evidence shows that a significantly softer metal was used in these patients than the ones that were used in all of your little tests that y'all did, if it is true, then the jury needs to know that this is apples-to-oranges, or Shipley's to Dunkin'. I mean this is different, right?*
A. And, again, all I can say at this point in time, because I don't have—I don't know, is that I can tell you when all of the patients were enrolled in the studies and enrollment was completed in October/November of 2006.

Q. *All right. But maybe I'm not asking it clear. I'll write it down and see if that helps you follow it.* **[Lanier writes the question on a blank sheet of paper in large words for the jury to see on the ELMO. (See figure 7)]** *Here's the question: If the liners in the study, liners and balls in the study are significantly different then the results do not necessarily apply. Fair?*
A. So I do not know if the liners or Balls—and balls are significantly different.

Lanier often does this with a witness. It intimidates a witness to see her own words blown-up on a projection screen. By writing the question and answer down (see figure 7), Lanier accomplishes several goals. First, he highlights the witness's answer by taking the time to write out the question and answer. This ensures that the particular question and answer remain before the jury for a long time and is easier to remember. He essentially creates a slow-motion highlight of the testimony.

Second, he intimidates the witness by giving permanence to the answer by writing it down. Third, he provides an easy reference to this question-and-answer exchange that he can refer the witness to later in the testimony and show the answer when cross-examining other witnesses about the accuracy of the answer or to get an agreement with it.

Q. *Right.*
A. And I don't know how it would affect, so I don't know that I can answer this. The results may or may not apply. I don't know.

Q. *So I put maybe? That's the—***[Lanier writes the word "maybe" in quotes in a different color ink below the statement he has written.]**
A. I would say I—**the best I can say is I don't know**. But all I can tell you is that all of the devices were implanted in the subjects by the end of 2006.

Q. *So if those devices are different than the devices the plaintiffs have, you think that's OK to test the wrong device and say that the plaintiffs should have a good result?*
A. I don't know that the devices are different than what the plaintiffs received. **[Lanier writes "I don't know" beside the word "maybe." This accomplishes two things. It shows the jury that Lanier is fair in making his notations and shows that the witness is struggling to try and put an answer together.]**

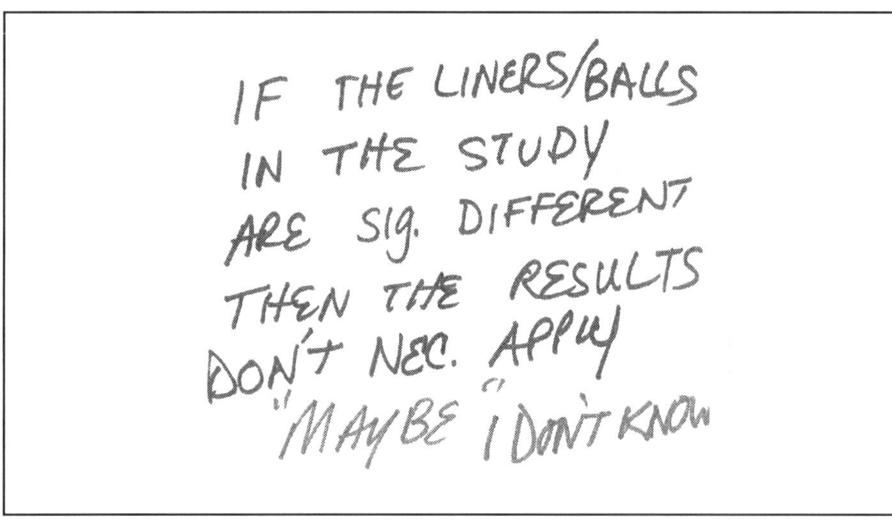

Figure 7. ELMO exhibit by Lanier to highlight the witness's answer for the jury.

Listen for Too Many Objections

If you get too many objections to a well-crafted line of questions, it means that you are striking gold and that opposing counsel fears the witness's answers. It is important to always be aware of what is happening in the courtroom.

Q. Ma'am, let me show you some documents that are so fundamental on this issue. I'd like to show you—

MR. LANIER: Your Honor, I would offer into evidence Plaintiff's 7430. Does it help you if I give you a copy again?
(Pause.)
MS. RENFROE: Your Honor, I apologize for the delay. My objection is 401 and 403, also no showing of any foundation or personal knowledge by this witness as to this document or subject matter.
COURT: Overruled.

Q. Ma'am, this is a sample document from your company with people who actually run tests for a living in the lab—do lab tests as well. You know these fellows. You know Andrew Goldsmith, don't you?
A. I don't know Andrew Goldsmith.

Q. Do you know Jim Lancaster?
A. I do know Jim Lancaster, and I know Graham Isaac.

Q. All right. So you know two of the three involved in this. "We need to be testing components that represent the final design." **[Lanier reads from the sample document.]** *Do you agree or disagree you ought to be testing the product, the actual product?*

MS. RENFROE: Calls for speculation, Your Honor, in view of the lack of any showing of any connection between this witness, this document, and this subject matter.
COURT: Overruled.

Q. Ma'am, that's a gimme. That's rule 1.

MS. RENFROE: Same objections.
COURT: Overruled.
WITNESS: Yes, they should be testing components which represent the final design.

After the vociferous objections of the defense counsel, Lanier doesn't even let the witness answer but responds to the long objection by saying, "that's a gimme." And amazingly, he gets another objection. The opposing lawyer, in an effort to protect the witness and the record, doth protest too much. In addition, by saying, "that's a gimme," he aligns himself with the jurors who want witnesses to answer the simple questions that are asked. He wins by using a simple down-home phrase in a question that is met by objections and a complicated answer.

MR. LANIER: Your Honor, we move into evidence Plaintiff's Exhibit 7427.

Q. It's just another example from the files, trying to make sure everybody is on the same page. "Contrary to Jim's thoughts, I believe it is imperative that the components for this

test must reflect our production items." **[Lanier is reading from the Depuy document here.]** *If you're going to claim that the test results are valid, they have to test the right product. True?*
A. Yes.

Q. *It goes back to where I started this with you. You cannot tell me if the Shipley's doughnuts taste better unless you taste one. Right?*
A. Yes.

Q. *You can eat all the Dunkin' doughnuts you want, you could eat five dozen, but you can't tell me if Shipley's is better if you never eat the Shipley's, right?*
A. That's correct.

When the witness stated earlier that she does not know if the results of the study of a different product should apply to the Pinnacle hip replacement, Lanier shows her a DePuy document that states that the tests should be conducted on the actual product being marketed. Lanier hammers the point home again by using the doughnut analogy.

DePuy's problem is that it had never done any tests in humans before selling the Pinnacle implant and only had data from patients after it had put the implants in them. Lanier highlights this problem.

Lanier Draws a Building to Illustrate an Analogy

Let's look at one more analogy that Lanier uses, which is that of a building. Lanier builds momentum as he approaches a break in the day, and starts off quickly after a previous break to make his points memorable and keep the jury interested. Here, he begins his question right after an afternoon break.

Q. *And I went to page 7 of it—I mean, ma'am, y'all are putting up statistics for how the Pinnacle metal-on-metal is doing after four weeks and after three months. Right?*
A. Yes. That's what this is.

Q. *You understand, y'all have promised these people that these hips are supposed to last like 20, 30 years.*
A. This was the progress report with the data we had on file.

Q. *Wasn't my question, ma'am. These hips were supposed to last 20 or 30 years. That's why they're putting 'em in. I mean, the metal-on-poly works for a good 20 without any trouble.*
A. These are short-term results. **[The witness does not answer the question as to what the patients were promised, but Lanier decides to pounce on the witness's choice of words, "short-term."]**

Q. *Not—not short term. These are like real short-term. I mean, these—these—these results are irrelevant, aren't they?*

MS. RENFROE: Argumentative, Your Honor. [**The constant argumentative objections are surely viewed by the jury as trying to prevent damaging answers.**]
COURT: Overruled.

Q. *These results are irrelevant, aren't they?*

MS. RENFROE: Argumentative.
COURT: Overruled.

Q. *These are irrelevant, ma'am? Ma'am, answer please.*
A. In terms of long-term results, they are not relevant. They are only short-term results. [**Lanier wins.**]

Q. *OK. Thank you. And then—the ones that have medium term, or actually still short. But the five- and eight-year studies on there, those came from the Engh* [**the author of the studies**] *studies, the doctors, right?*
A. Some of them, yes.

Q. *Yeah. And—and the reason is—I mean, this is the drawing I was doing over there while you were doing the direct testimony.* [**See figure 8.**] *Have you ever heard about the fellow who falls off the—the—the top of the building, and as he's falling down to the ground, he yells out as he passes the twentieth floor, "so far so good"? That—that—that doesn't matter. I mean, you're talking about what happened after—after four weeks. It takes a long time for this reaction in the body to the metal debris to—to happen, doesn't it?*
A. It does take time, yes.

Q. *OK. I mean, you can't have the fellow falling off the building yelling "so far so good" in the middle of the fall. You've got to wait and see how he's doing once he hits the bottom. Fair?*
A. I don't know if it's a good analogy, but I guess so. [**The witness doesn't like the analogy or the drawing. But watch what Lanier does with her answer. Do you think Lanier is going to give in?**]

Q. *It's a pretty good one though, isn't it? I mean, realistically that's—that's the issue. When you test you need to test for a good length of time, and you need to test with enough people to get the results. Those are fundamentals of science, aren't they?*
A. Typically, yes.

Q. *Yeah. Typically. It's called duration and power. "Duration" means you have to test long enough. And "power" means you have to have enough people in the test to get some results. Right?*
A. Yes.

When the witness questions the building analogy and then defends what DePuy did and quarrels with Lanier about his use of the phrase "fundamentals of science" by suggesting that that is what is typically done, Lanier fires back with the scientific terms of duration and power to force the witness to admit how a proper study should be conducted. The lesson here is to be colloquial when you need to be but be prepared to use scientific terms when necessary. It is a great one-two punch.

> **Practice Tip**
>
> It is impossible to get a jury to remember one point you made with a witness at one moment out of an eight-week trial. But if you have a memorable analogy and a picture to go with it, you will succeed every time.

Lanier also shows the witness and the jury that he knows the meaning of the phrase *duration and power*, which is used to determine if a study is reliable. Lanier is not intimidated by the witness with a PhD in chemistry who he is cross-examining but, instead, shows her that the science backs up his questions.

6.5 THE POWER OF LANIER'S VISUAL AIDS

At the beginning of the chapter, we learned that in 2018, Lanier won a $4.69 billion dollar verdict for 22 women and their families who claimed that Johnson & Johnson's baby powder contained asbestos, which caused the women to develop ovarian cancer. Figure 8 is a drawing that Lanier used in that trial also.

Let's examine a video clip where Lanier recreates a cross-examination of Johnson & Johnson's expert and uses the drawing of the man falling off

Figure 8. ELMO exhibit with drawing of a building by Lanier to help the jury remember his points.

the building. You can find the video at www.winningatcross.com. It is called "Crossing J&J Powder Expert." The expert had relied on four studies to explain to the jury that the baby powder did not cause ovarian cancer. The studies showed that seven to nine years after exposure, people who had used the baby powder did not develop any cancer.

The challenge for Lanier was to undercut that powerful testimony in a memorable way. What is remarkable is how easily Lanier explains complicated ideas so simply. In the second drawing on the video clip, Lanier diagrams the definition of "latency" perfectly. His simple drawing helps you understand the word and remember it.

He then draws the same building (Fig. 8) that he used with Dr. Plouhar to make his point with J&J's expert witness. Long after he has drawn the building, the jurors are certain to remember the image and the point he makes.

In the video, pay attention to the pace of Lanier's questions and his drawing. He is not rushed nor is he afraid that he has to pause during his questioning while he completes a diagram or drawing. Lanier could have easily prepared these visual aids prior to the cross-examination, but by drawing them in front of the jury, he creates anticipation and engages the jury. For example, in the last drawing, the jury becomes curious about what the finished building will look like, what the person falling off of it will look like, and most importantly, what is the point of the drawing. When Lanier delivers the punch line, his point is much more memorable than if he had asked all his questions without the use of visual aids.

Before we move on to another witness, let's review the effectiveness of Lanier's visual aids on Dr. Plouhar's cross-examination. There is simply not enough space in this book to show you how often Lanier writes on a blank sheet of paper. We have seen only eight examples out of the dozens and dozens of separate documents he created for this witness. As mentioned earlier, when he wasn't writing, he was showing the witness a trial exhibit and highlighting the passage he was reading from.

The sample illustrations used in this section give you a very good idea of the different types of documents Lanier created. Figure 3 presents a summary of the witness's background to show her expertise and heavy involvement with the product, and that she was media trained to discuss the problems with the Pinnacle system. Figures 1 and 5 list the arguments he would make on his initial cross and recross. Notice that I did not state "topics." Lanier writes down for the witness and the jury the contentions he will prove.

The handwritten lists that he writes in real time while the witness is on the stand give the jurors the sense that his cross-examinations are going to be down-to-earth, direct, and simple, even though the topic of the cross would be overly complicated in the hands of most attorneys. In addition, Lanier also creates anticipation with each item he writes. That anticipation—what is he going to write or draw next?—engages the jurors. It is another way to create a bond with them.

Figures 2 and 8 are illustrations of a man with toxic ions in his body and a man falling off of a building, respectively. The images are memorable, and they make the problem with studies of short duration and the way that toxic ions spread through the bloodstream easy for jurors to understand. Finally, figure 7 reveals the powerful effect of writing down a simple question for the witness and then writing down a response that does not answer it.

6.6 CHAPTER CHECKLIST

Lanier's Tips and Strategies

1. The biggest mistake lawyers make is not putting in the time to be prepared. "It is *the* most important thing."
2. Use the Folder Method to organize your cross. Find the important documents and create a road map of the major points you want to make. Put three copies of each document in an individual folder with a label on it, and then put all the folders related to one topic in a Redweld with a label on it. Then put the Redwelds in Bankers Boxes according to a logical organization.
3. Unlike the advice in Irving Younger's ten commandments, where he suggests that you should hide the ball until closing and then explain what your subtle questions on cross meant (that the jury has certainly forgot), Lanier makes it very clear what his themes are on cross. He not only tells the witness and the jury, he writes it out for them. He is very direct.
4. Lanier always has something displayed for the jury, whether it is a sheet of paper with a list of the topics he is covering with the witness, a trial exhibit, a drawing he is creating, or his writing of the answer to an important question he has just asked.
5. You need the right tools to employ Lanier's techniques: lots of blank sheets with the witness's photo in upper left-hand corner; pens, highlighters, and markers with different colors; and wireless microphone or other audio setup so the jury can hear you when you are away from podium microphone.
6. At the outset, tell the jury why you are putting a particular witness on the stand. It provides essential context so jurors can understand why you are asking your questions.
7. Try to create an episodic memory for the jury by using creative, demonstrative exhibits, such as the box of Shipley's Do-Nuts Lanier used.

8. Bond with the jury by creating simple drawings instead of employing an expensive graphic designer.
9. Make constant eye contact with the witness.
10. Keep a journal at the counsel table to jot down ideas in the heat of the moment that might help you later in the trial.
11. If you must play a deposition at trial because a witness is unavailable, use the "three-camera deposition" explained earlier. You want to create a realistic and interesting presentation for the jury. Meticulous editing is the key.
12. Lanier conducts the entire trial himself in order to provide coherent themes and bond with the jury.

Cross of Plouhar

1. Lanier writes key bio facts on a blank sheet of paper that has the witness's photo in left-hand corner and name at top. Lanier refers to this document throughout the examination to remind jury of the witness's qualifications—or lack thereof—and bias. For example, he emphasizes that she was "media trained."
2. Lanier phrases his question from the exact words he has in the document to force the witness to answer yes. For example, he asks, "You were a critical stakeholder?" when the document says so.
3. At the beginning of some of the questions that ask about a new or complicated topic, Lanier uses the phrase, "So the jury understands . . . ." This helps create a bond with the jury.
4. Use your theme from opening statement in your cross. Lanier tells the witness that he told jurors in his opening statement that one of his themes was that they were home inspectors who needed to decide if DePuy's house was up to code. Then he asks the witness questions based on that theme.
5. Furthermore, he uses exaggerations and misstatements from his opponent's opening statement against his opponent's witnesses during his cross.
6. Divide your topics around major breaks in the day. Applying the principles of primacy and recency—that is, that people remember better what they hear first and last—Lanier uses the moments just before and after a break to discuss important facts with a witness.
7. Listen carefully to questions on direct. You may find that the witness answers her lawyer's question slightly less favorably than the lawyer might expect because the witness wants to make sure she's telling the truth. Such an imprecise answer may give you an opening on recross.
8. Whenever the witness does not answer a simple question, the lawyer wins because it shows the witness is afraid of a simple answer.
9. Use analogies to make your points more memorable. Lanier complains that DePuy uses studies on a different implant product to claim that its Pinnacle

system is safe. Lanier says that is like eating Dunkin' Doughnuts and saying they are better than Shipley's Do-Nuts without ever trying Shipley's Do-Nuts. He also uses a drawing of a man falling off a building who exclaims, "So far, so good!" as he passes the tenth floor on his way down. Lanier points out that DePuy does the same thing when it claims its very short studies are trustworthy for long-term results.

10. If you call a witness early in the case and she argues that data is wrong or that a document does not purport to be what you tell the jury it is, ask the witness to agree that, if it is proven that the document is true, then her testimony must necessarily be wrong.
11. When a witness passes the buck by not answering the question and tells you that you need to ask another witness that question, force the witness to at least admit what the document says.
12. Write important questions down on a blank sheet of paper for the jury to see. Remember to write large words so it is easy to see on the ELMO projector.
13. If opposing counsel starts objecting a lot, you know that you are striking gold. Opposing counsel's fear is confirmation that your questions are good.
14. It is very difficult to get a jury to remember the point you made with a witness at one moment out of an eight-week trial. But if you have a memorable analogy *and* a picture to go with it, you will succeed every time.
15. Lanier uses simple drawings of a man filled with dots to represent toxic ions that have been released from the rubbing of the metal parts of a hip implant and a stick figure of a man falling off a building to represent studies that were cut short. Simplify, simplify, simplify.

CHAPTER SEVEN

Mark Lanier Cross-Examines the President of DePuy

"Let's see if this document bears out your view of it or mine."
—*Mark Lanier*

Andrew Ekdahl, who was president of DePuy during the relevant time of this litigation, is the second witness whose testimony we will study from the DePuy hip implant trials. This witness presented many different challenges for Lanier than the ones we saw in the previous chapter. Ekdahl was obviously ranked higher in the company than Plouhar, which made the stakes very high. He also resisted answering Lanier's questions in a different manner than Plouhar. As a result, you will learn from the different techniques that Lanier used with Ekdahl. You will also see the different demonstrative exhibits that Lanier used, which highlight Lanier's versatility and effectiveness.

7.1 CROSS OF ANDREW EKDAHL

Andrew Ekdahl appeared at the trial via satellite. After he was sworn in and stated his name and where he worked, Lanier began his cross as follows:

Lanier Announces His Theme for Cross

Q. ***I want to get right into things with you,*** *and we will explore a little bit more about your qualifications as we go along, but let's start out with a general premise. And* ***this is my theme for my cross-examination*** *of you—and so the jury is clear, you are what we call an adverse witness. You work for the other side, don't you?*
A. Yes.

Q. *We served you with a subpoena to force your testimony today?*
A. I believe you served my attorneys with a subpoena.

> **CHAPTER ROAD MAP**
>
> - Draw pictures of your themes to give them more impact.
> - Learn several phrases you can use when a witness does not answer a simple question.
> - Learn how to make the complicated simple.

Q. They accepted it on your behalf, but it was a subpoena; — you are here under a court order to testify, aren't you?
A. Yes.

Lanier makes it very clear to the jury that Ekdahl is not a neutral witness. Ekdahl's motives are not aligned with Lanier's. Use this technique at your next trial. Imagine how happy the jury was to hear Lanier's words, "I want to get right into things with you," rather than the lengthy preambles that they hear from most other lawyers.

Q. All right. Here's my theme for you, sir: ***I want the jury to hear from you how marketing and sales ran the company during the relevant time periods, not science.*** *You understand what I mean when I say that?*
A. I disagree with it, but, OK.

As briefly discussed in chapter 3, Lanier does not make such subtle points on cross-examination with the hope that he can argue them more strongly in closing—as Irving Younger suggests you should do in his ten commandments. Instead, Lanier does just the opposite, and with great effect. He boldly tells the jury—as he did earlier when questioning Plouhar and as we will see him do later with Dr. Schmalzried—what his theme is for the cross.

Why will Lanier win this cross? You should know the answer to this question by now. But if not, here's the answer: He has chosen topics that he can win on because the documents (e.g., trial exhibits, such as prior statements by the witness) and common-sense reasoning will back him up. Cross-examination is really that simple. But Lanier executes these strategies very effectively.

In your next cross—whether it is in deposition or at trial—start it just the way Lanier did: "I want the jury to hear from you. . . ."

Q. I know you disagree with it, but you at least understand what I mean, right?
A. Believe so.

Q. All right. ***So let's put it to the test.*** *. . . Have you ever heard the expression* ***"Put your money where your mouth is"?***

Lanier links this line of questioning about budgets, a topic that tends to be rather dry, to a famous everyday saying, so that the jury can understand his theme and remember it during deliberations. The phrase also aligns him with the jury. That is, Lanier is going to ask common-sense questions, the jury is going to apply its common-sense reasoning, and the witness will need to answer using common sense or suffer the consequences.

A. Yes.

Q. *And the reason I say that is, if we wanted to look at the budget—and I've got a copy of it if we need to mark it as an exhibit, but I don't think we'll need to.* [**Lanier intimidates the witness by letting the witness know that if he denies the obvious or does not remember something Lanier thinks he should, the witness will suffer the jury's wrath for making Lanier go through the time-consuming details of the budget. But Lanier is always ready with a document if the witness denies an important point.**] *If you look at the budget for the companies, the truth of the matter is more money was spent on sales and marketing than was spent on R&D* [**research and development**].

A. On the combination of sales and marketing?

Q. *Yeah. In other words, y'all were spending more on a combination of sales and marketing than you were on a combination of R&D, research and development, the science. True?*

A. Yes. That's correct.

Lanier brilliantly makes a subtle adjustment. The witness tries to make it sound as though it should be no surprise that the *combination* of two items, sales and marketing, should be bigger than one item, R&D. But Lanier rephrases his question to put them on equal footing by referring to R&D as the combination of research and development. Lanier is flexible here as he thoughtfully listens to each answer. He then moves on to his next point.

In figure 1, as Ekdahl answers "yes" to that last question, Lanier draws a seesaw, with money bags tipping the seesaw to the sales side. Drawing pictures accomplishes several goals. First, it makes the information more interesting and entertaining for the jury. It is no easy task to keep a captive audience engaged for eight hours a day. Second, it makes the testimony more memorable. There is enormous research that proves that we will retain more information if we both see and hear it as opposed to just hear it.

By the end of Lanier's cross, he will have drawn eight pictures on one page that prove his case. In a long trial, he wants to make sure the points he makes with the key witness are remembered during deliberations.

> **Practice Tip**
>
> Use visual aids on cross to aid jurors' recall. Tests have shown that when people were shown 2,500 photographs for 10 seconds each, they could recall them with 90 percent accuracy several days later. A year later, the accuracy rate was 63 percent.

Q. *So we can talk about it in terms of money, but* ***we can also talk about it in terms of the workforce****, because the truth of the matter is if we look at the workforce of the company, more employees worked for sales and marketing than worked in R&D. Correct?*

A. Off the top of my head that's **probably correct**.

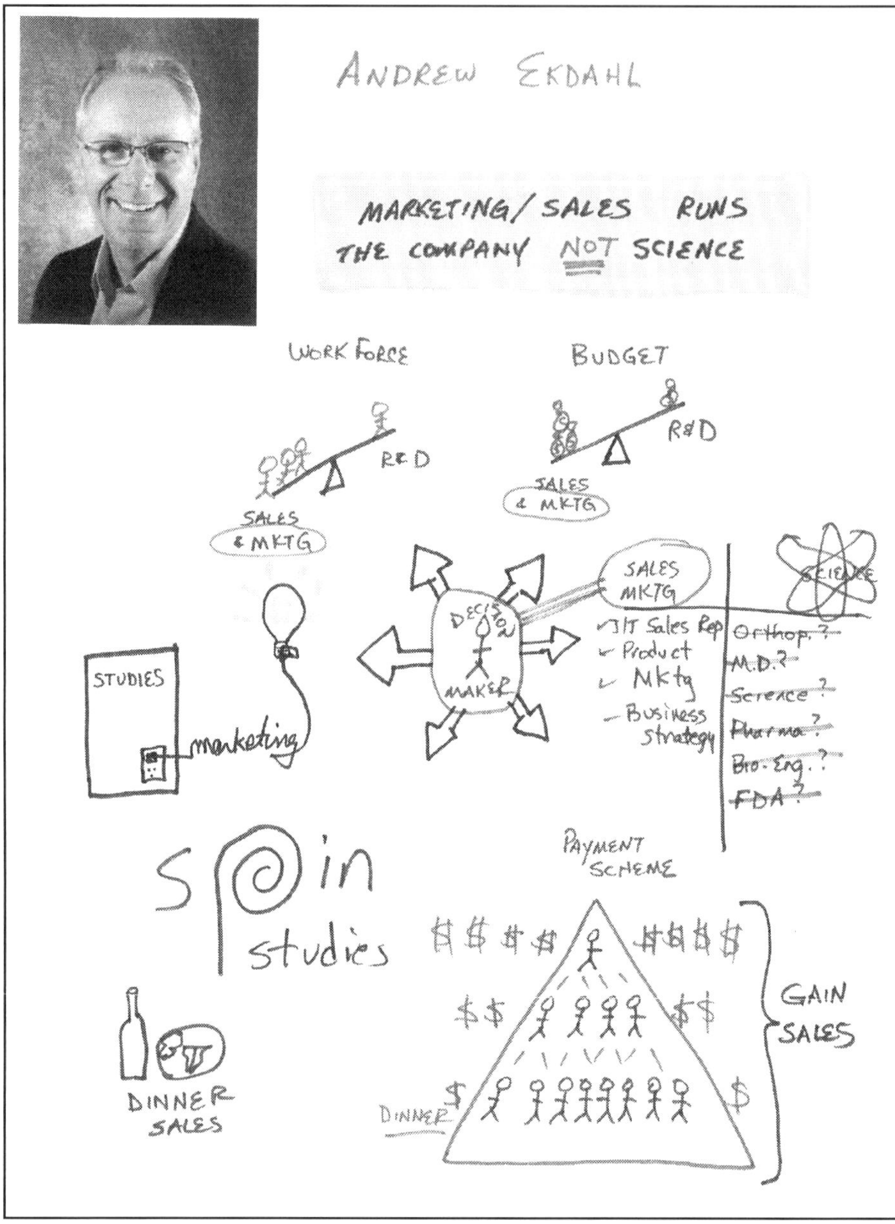

Figure 1. Handwritten trial notes made by Mark Lanier.

Q. Well, and you don't have to do it off the top of your head. I've asked you this question before, and you've already testified to this effect, haven't you?
A. Yes.

Here, Lanier has the line and page number ready if the witness says anything that is less than absolute. On figure 1, Lanier draws another seesaw that tips to the side of sales under the heading "work force." Lanier transitions to his third point.

Ekdahl's Background Is in Sales and Marketing, Not Science

Q. All right. So we can look at it in terms of the budget, and we can look at it in terms of the workforce, but we can spread out from there and also ***consider the decision-makers****, the person who's making decisions for the company. And, in fact, for a good bit of time that was you, wasn't it?*
A. I was **among** the decision-makers for the company, yes.

Q. Well, you ***were*** *the — **the president** of the company, weren't you?*
A. Yes.

When the witness tries to qualify his answer by minimizing his role, Lanier points out that the witness was the head decision-maker. As Lanier goes through the next series of questions about Ekdahl's roles at the company, he makes a list of them in a column on the right side of figure 1 under the heading "sales." He also draws pictures to accompany his cross. By doing so, Lanier gives the jury a visual aid to associate with each of his main points and topics. This will help the jurors remember his points better. Also, having the pictures all on one sheet helps to keep the picture that is associated with his theme in front of the jury for a longer period of time.

Although the images might look small, Lanier has the ELMO zoomed in as he is drawing them. For example, when he is drawing the science symbol and making the list below it, the jury can easily see the text because the ELMO is zoomed in. Then, when he goes to another picture on the document, he zooms out, so the jury can see all the pictures and put them in context.

Q. Sir, you started out as a sales representative for Johnson & Johnson, didn't you?
A. Johnson & Johnson Medical Products in Canada, yes.

Q. A Johnson & Johnson named company in Canada, right?
A. Part of the Johnson & Johnson family of companies, yes.

Q. You were one of the sales reps that went to the doctors and sold to the doctors, weren't you?
A. Correct.

Q. And then you moved over to DePuy, and you became the product director within DePuy. And this would have been around 1999. You were the product director for hips, weren't you?
A. Yes.

Q. Then you became the group product director for hips, didn't you?
A. Yes.

Q. Then you became the director of marketing, didn't you?
A. I did, yes.

Q. Then you became the vice president for marketing, didn't you?
A. Yes.

Q. Then you became a vice president for business strategy. And you were over business strategy, weren't you?
A. Yes.

Q. Then you became the franchise vice president, still involved in hips, right?
A. That's correct.

Q. Then you became president of the company, served in that role from 2011 to 2013, correct?
A. Yes.

Q. So you as the decision-maker, or one of the decision-makers, let's try and look at who you are, comparing you to the issue of are you sales and marketing or are you a science guy. Which are you? You got me. You following me?
A. Yes.

Practice Tip

When a witness lacks expertise or has failed to do something, ask questions that get "no" answers so the jury repeatedly hears what the witness did not do or doesn't know but should.

Lanier then fills out the second column under the science icon. He does something that most lawyers forget to do, but should not. He gets the witness to answer a series of questions with "no" or in the negative. Keep track of how many times the witness says "no" or its equivalent.

Q. All right. So if we want to look and see which is you as the decision-maker, are you or have you ever been an orthopedic doctor, an orthopedic surgeon?
A. No.

Q. In fact, I don't think the company even had an orthopedic surgeon that worked there during the relevant time, did they?
A. I'm not sure what the relevant time is.

Q. Well, let's go 1998 to 2013.
A. Don't know the answer.

Q. Hmmm. How about while you were president of the company, did you have an orthopedic surgeon working for the company then?
A. I'd have to go—honestly, I'd have to go back and look. Don't recall.

Q. You're not a medical doctor, are you?
A. No, sir.

Q. You as the president, the decision-maker, you don't even have a science degree. You don't have a science background, do you?
A. No, sir.

Q. You don't have a pharmaceutical background, do you?
A. No, sir.

Q. You're not a bioengineer, like Dr. Bernstein, are you?
A. No.

Q. You're not someone from the FDA. You don't have FDA credentials you bring to the job, do you?
A. No, sir.

Q. If we look at your background for being the decision-maker as the president, you really do have a background as a Johnson & Johnson company sales rep. True?
A. True.

Q. You have a background as—well, all these things we went through. As the product director, you have a background in marketing. You have a background in business strategy. These are the types of jobs that you've held in the past which propelled you to be the president, right?
A. They're my past experiences, that's correct.

Q. So if we look at you as the decision-maker, again, we've got sales and marketing, not science. True? **[Lanier draws lines that connect the decision-maker drawing to the sales and marketing column in figure 1 to illustrate Ekdahl's sales experience and lack of science experience.]**
A. As—as being someone **who's among the decision-makers**, correct.

What do you think Lanier is going to do when the witness minimizes his role. Of course, you know the answer, but I thought I would give you an easy test question. Lanier is going to hammer him with the truth.

Q. Well, as ***being at the top****. You were the* ***president*** *of DePuy, weren't you?*
A. Yes.

Q. OK. Now, so now we've got—we've got a question on whether marketing/sales runs the company instead of science. We've looked at the budget. We've looked at the workforce. We've looked, at least, at you as the decision-maker.

As Lanier asks this question, he points to the different pictures he has drawn in figure 1 referenced in his list in the question above.

> **Practice Tip**
> Summarize the points you have made when you transition to a new topic.

Lanier Maintains Marketing Influenced How DePuy Conducted Studies

Q. Now I want to go to another area. I want to talk about the studies that were done. The company has conducted studies, right?
A. Correct.

As Lanier talks about the studies, he draws an electrical socket (fig. 1) to show that marketing was plugged into the studies. Lanier then proceeds to go through a series of confidential studies that DePuy conducted to support his argument that marketing needs influenced DePuy's studies.

***

Q. ***Let's see if this document bears out your view of it or mine***.

This question should be one you keep in your arsenal. It is a perfect response to a witness who disagrees with your inferences. Lanier then will back up his assertion with the document.

Next is an instance where the witness argues with Lanier. Watch how Lanier does not cede any ground and further makes the witness pay for not answering a simple question.

Q. *Of course, sir. [The scientific studies are] what your salesmen want [in order to] sell the product. I'm not fussing that. That's my point.*
A. **I would frame it differently** than "our salespeople want." I'm saying it is what surgeons like to see before they're going to prescribe the device.

Q. *Well, we're going to look at* ***your art of framing***. *I've got some of your emails where you talk about how to spin things so that they sound better. We'll look at your spin in a little bit, but right now just focus on my question. My questions are very clear. Here's another study . . . .*

> **Practice Tip**
>
> One technique to control a witness who does not answer your question is to declare, "My question is very clear," and ask your question again.

In your next deposition or trial, listen for words a witness uses to couch his answer and then use them in your next question. In the testimony you just read, Lanier adapts the answer, "frame it differently" into part of his question that explores the witness's "art of framing."

Lanier Argues That DePuy Spun the Results of the Studies

Q. *And Paul Berman emails and says, "Team, we need to get our heads together on this one [a study] . . . we'll need to provide spin for the sales force." Do you see that?*
A. I see where Paul has written that, yes.

Q. *"The abstract does not paint a great picture around Pinnacle deflection . . ." That means how it causes the product to bend or deflect, right?*
A. You mean the Pinnacle shell to deflect?

Q. *Uh-huh.*
A. Yes.

Q. *OK. And you took it, you not only read it, you had your assistant print it out for you, didn't you?*
A. Looks that way, yes.

Q. And so as y'all would spin studies for the sales force, you took an active role, and we'll see it in more detail, in excruciating detail later with the way you personally spun the 99.9 percent study. Remember that?
A. Do I remember the study?

Q. Yes. And do you remember your role in spinning it?
A. No.

Q. All right. Well, we'll get into that in a little bit. . . .

As Lanier talks about spinning the studies, he makes another illustration on figure 1 to indicate "spin studies." Notice how creatively Lanier writes the "p" of spin. That is a perfect example of creating an image for jurors to associate with a word. The playful drawing also taunts Goliath. Lanier is using the drawing to make fun of the so-called studies. It also reminds one of a hypnotic spiral that would captivate you no matter how hard you tried to resist, which was the intent of DePuy's studies. In short, with just one picture, Lanier has conveyed many meanings that the jury will not forget.

Now, let's fast-forward to a later moment in this two-day long cross-examination. In this section, Lanier wants to show the jury a timeline to indicate that DePuy knew that metal-on-metal hip implants could cause toxic ions to enter the bloodstream long before it stopped marketing the product. See if you can find out another skill Lanier uses before it is revealed after this section.

The context for this section is that the End Game memo was written by Graham Isaac, a leading global authority on medical devices who worked at DePuy. He wrote this memo in 1995, years before DePuy put the Pinnacle Ultimet on the market. He concludes that metal-on-metal hip implants are far from satisfactory and that polyethylene combined with metal has been doing really well. The problem for DePuy was that other companies made the polyethylene combinations, and DePuy was trying to find a way to capture a share of the market with a metal-on-metal hip implant that its own engineer concluded was far from satisfactory.

Q. You understand all these plaintiffs have metal-on-metal in their hip. Or had it. Had to take it out. You understand that?
A. I do.

Q. You understand it was a metal-on-metal project that needed the question answered about the long-term effects [of metal-on-metal implants] because toxic debris would be generated that required a clinical trial that your company didn't do. We're talking metal-on-metal here. You understand that?
A. I do, yes.

Q. Your company was looking at a lot of different things. We know that because of the End Game memo by Graham Isaac; it's Plaintiff's Exhibit Number 1. Also 1995. We're still

in that year. And he's looking at the alternatives. He's looking at ceramic-on-ceramic [hip implants], and he's looking at metal-on-metal [hip implants]. Correct?
A. That's correct.

Q. *And when you look at what he says about metal-on-metal, he says in the past it hasn't done very well. "It is clear from literature survivorship of cobalt-chrome metal-on-metal in the past has been far from satisfactory." He's got the McKee-Farrar [the original metal-on-metal hip implant study from the 1960s], showing [the hip implant] survives 27.5 percent of the time at 20 years. Stanmore [showing the hip implant] survives 53 percent of the time at 11 years. That's poor survivorship. Do you see that?*
A. I see where he's written that, yes.

***

Q. *So in 1995, we also know that according to the company [DePuy] the only combination—because y'all were looking at different types—the only combination likely to give rise to toxic levels in the body is metal-on-metal. Right?*
A. That's where it's been written, yes. Graham has written that.

The new skill we learned is that Lanier always labels his most important exhibit as number one. This multi-week trial had thousands of exhibits. What is the first exhibit the jurors are likely to look at during deliberations? The first one. In this case, it's the End Game memo that proves DePuy knew of the problems with metal-on-metal hip implants long before it manufactured the Pinnacle system that was put in the plaintiffs over ten years later.

Use of Documents to Support Claim that DePuy Knew of Toxicity

In this next section, we will see how Lanier wins battles with witnesses because he has documents to back up the exact words he uses in his questions. I have highlighted in bold the exact phrases in his questions that are supported by the documents.

Q. *Well, we at least know the company is still aware [in 2007] because the company is in a panic about this issue over ions and toxicity. It's a* ***threat to the company****, isn't it?*
A. **I don't think it's a threat to the company.**

Q. *Well, that's what we got from Plaintiff's Exhibit 444, where the company calls it a threat.*

Q. *Here's the Worldwide Hip Business Team meeting. Right?*
A. Yes.

Q. *And that is the hip business team, worldwide. Do you see it?*
A. I do.

Q. *If you'll go to slide number 3. And it's a weak copy. I'm going to have to blow it up. But you'll see up at the top DePuy/Johnson & Johnson. Do you see that?*
A. I see that, yes.

Q. *And I say it was a threat and you said, no, it wasn't a threat.* [**Lanier knows he is about to win because the document supports him, but Lanier reminds the jury that the witness has denied his proposition.**] *I'll represent this is July 2007. Look at the threats. Do you see them?*
A. Yes.

Q. *The very first one: Metal-on-metal backlash. That's the bold first threat you've got. Do you see that?*
A. I see that, yes.

Q. ***So it was a threat. It was viewed as the number one threat to your company**, in what you listed anyway, wasn't it?*
A. I don't know whether it's the number one threat or if this is a ranking—I don't know how they got to this order. I wasn't at the meeting.

Q. *It's at least listed first in bold print. I mean, you've got more details later on. You can see metal ions also listed under the threat. You see that? Metal ions?*
A. I see that, yes.

Q. *So, July of 2007, right after Mr. Barzel's implant* [**one of the plaintiffs**], *the company is still seeing these ions as a threat to the business, isn't it?*
A. I see where someone has put that in a slide, yes. [**Lanier is going to pounce on this minimalization**.]

Q. *Not just* **someone**. [**said with emphasis**] *This is a major presentation. This isn't some, oh, gee, Lanier found in the midst of our millions of documents some weird document that somebody wished they hadn't written. This is—this is a presentation that's going down. This is a major business presentation, isn't it?*

Lanier directly takes on the suggestion in Ekdahl's answer that he is cherry-picking helpful information from documents. In response, Lanier uses everyday language to explain where he got the words. If Lanier is proven right by the document, he wins. If not, the witness wins. What do you think will happen?

A. I wouldn't—I wouldn't know if I would characterize it as a major business presentation. This is a group of people that got together and talked about the hip business worldwide using a standard analytical tool of the strengths, weaknesses, opportunities and threats, and they have got lists—long lists of them.

Q. *This is the Worldwide Hip Business Team meeting where y'all all convened from around the world in Chicago. And it's a multipage slide presentation where y'all not only analyzed your company, but you looked at your opponents and what their strengths and weaknesses and the threats from them. Remember?*
A. Yes.

Q. *Because this is a time where even though the company is still concerned about ions and toxicity, even though the company has answered a bunch of questions out of England where the metal ions caused these problems, in spite of that, the company just gets* ***deeper and deeper*** *into metal-on-metal, doesn't it?* **[Lanier has basically summarized his case theory and then uses the precise words from a document he will show the jury if the witness doesn't answer "yes."]**

A. I don't know what deeper and deeper means in your mind.

Q. *I'll use your mind, your company's mind.* **[Lanier never lets the witness gain control. He listens for responses that don't answer the question and uses the words in the witness's answer to create his next question. When the witness states that he doesn't know what "deeper and deeper" means in Lanier's mind, Lanier turns that answer against the witness.]**

A. I don't know what that means.

Q. *Getting deeper and deeper into metal-on-metal. Hey, that's a risky move, that's high risk, isn't it? Right?*

A. I don't think so. No.

Q. *Well, look on slide number 6, what's around the corner. "We are getting deeper into metal-on-metal high risk if any complications are shown." Do you see that?*

A. Yeah. I see where someone has written that. **[Again, Lanier won't let the witness deflect the importance of the PowerPoint presentation.]**

Q. *Where it was presented to the* ***entire Worldwide Hip Business Team****. Do you see that?*

A. I see that.

Q. *I mean, y'all were* ***scared most*** *about metal ions. This was scary to y'all. Right?*

A. No.

> **Practice Tip**
>
> If the witness gives an outrageous answer, repeat it. For example, Lanier repeats the denial "no" for emphasis.

Q. *Did you say no? Look at the next slide, slide 7: What scares us most in the year ahead. Metal ion backlash. Scared metal ion backlash. Right?*

A. I see where someone has written that. **[What do you think Lanier will do next?]**

Q. *No, not where* ***someone*** *has written that. Sir, these slides undergo editing. Y'all will email these slides around before the presentations to say anybody got any comments? Does this seem right? Won't you agree?*

A. I wasn't part of it. I don't know. I don't know how they got to this document.

Q. ***So in 2007 you weren't a part of any of this.*** **[On recross, Lanier will find documents to prove that the witness was involved.]** ***What were you doing in 2007? What was your job?***

A. I can't recall what my job was in 2007. **[Lanier is a master of facts and knows precisely what the witness's job duties were better than the witness remembers.]**

Q. *You can't recall? You were the vice president for marketing in 2007 for hips, about to move into business strategy as the vice president. Remember?*
A. Yeah. I don't remember what time of year I moved from one job to another.

Using Logical Reasoning to Prove Your Point

Later in the cross, Lanier undercuts Ekdahl's assertion that he had nothing to do with the PowerPoint presentation and the inference that he wasn't even aware of it. But for now, let's look at this next section. Lanier does not have documents to prove his point, but he has the power of logical reasoning on his side. He will prove to the jury that the witness has made an apparently outrageous statement, specifically that he was unaware of what happened in Chicago. This technique is the "O" of CROSS.

Q. *So you want us to believe that the vice president for marketing doesn't know what scared the company the most in marketing, didn't know—*
A. I'm saying.

Q. *—the risks, that y'all were getting deeper into metal-on-metal—*
A. I'm sorry—

Q. *—and didn't know the threats.*
A. I'm saying I don't believe I was at this meeting, I don't know how the information was gathered, and I don't know how it was discussed.

Most attorneys would stop here. But if you have logical reasoning on your side, it does not matter how the witness answers your question. The trick is to present your question in a clear manner so the jury can decide who to believe.

Q. *But are—regardless of whether you were at the meeting, are we to believe you were so out of step that the vice president of marketing did not know these things, the major threat, what you were scared most of, the high-risk move that y'all were making, and somehow you, not knowing that, got promoted to vice president of business strategy that year?*

It does not matter what the witness answers. If you the reader—and more importantly the jury—believe the propositions in Lanier's question, then any attempt by the witness to deny it will not make sense, and the cross-examiner will have won the battle.

A. No, I'm saying, Mr. Lanier, I don't know how this document was created, the form in which they did it, how they did it, or how it was debated. So it's very difficult to comment on it the way you're asking me to comment on it.

Q. *Well, but I'm not even asking — OK. 2008. As we roll forward, in 2008, with all of this going on along comes Hazel Miura [a plaintiff], and she gets her implant in 2008. May of 2008. I think it was May the 2nd. May 2nd of 2008. With all of this going on in y'all's*

mind, y'all are still out there hyping these **[implants]** *to the doctors, aren't you?*
A. Is metal-on-metal available for doctors to prescribe? Yes.

Q. No. That wasn't my question.

MR. LANIER: Objection, nonresponsive.
COURT: Sustained.
MR. LANIER: Ask the witness to be instructed to answer the question.
COURT: Please answer the question, sir.
WITNESS: Repeat it, please.

Q. Yeah. Y'all were still out there hyping this to the doctors, weren't you? You were giving the sales force the sales pitches to use, right?
A. Yes.

This is a damaging admission, and all the more so because of the way in which Lanier has contrasted DePuy's fears at the worldwide meeting in Chicago with how DePuy was at the same time hyping metal-on-metal implants to doctors, one of whom put the Pinnacle system into one of the plaintiffs.

Research a Witness's Answers During a Break

Lanier then moves on to another subject, but observe what happens after a scheduled break. While most attorneys would not have Lanier's team of lawyers and paralegals to find documents so quickly during a break, nonetheless, always check what a witness says in a deposition or at trial. Many times you can find a mistake—even without Lanier's resources—and bring it to the witness's attention while the witness is still testifying. Such a moment can be very powerful.

Q. All right. Mr. Ekdahl, we're going to perhaps be back to where we were in the morning, but before I totally leave this timeline, this break afforded us a moment of time to check something. OK? I kept asking you questions about Plaintiff's Exhibit 444, and I was suggesting surely you at least knew what was going on at the Worldwide Hip Business Team meeting, because—you remember me pointing that out?
A. Yes.

Q. You remember I was showing you these major threats and what scared y'all the most and what's around the corner and getting deeper into metal-on-metal and the high risk of that move, and you were saying, well, that's what one person wrote or I see that's written in this document and just left it there as if this is maybe some renegade document. Do you remember your comments?
A. I don't remember them exactly, but OK. **[Lanier gets witness to agree to Lanier's summary of trial testimony earlier in the day.]**

Q. This was the Worldwide Hip Business Team in Chicago. 2007, WWHBT. The July agenda. You got it sent to you, didn't you?
A. Yes.

Q. *Not only did you get the Agenda sent to you, but you went to the meeting. At least you had a hotel room at the Westin from July 30 to August 2. That's on page 5. Do you see that?*
A. I see that.

Q. *Not only did you have a hotel room, not only did you get the agenda that you say you knew nothing about, but on July 30, it was requested that you attend. On July 31, it was requested that you attend. . . .Do you see that, sir?*
A. I do.

Q. *So your attendance was requested. And lest you wonder if you actually showed up to your hotel room and attended, y'all listed the people that did not attend. And you're not on there, are you?*
A. I'm not.

Q. *And lest there be any other doubt about this, you not only were sent the agenda, had a hotel room, were a requested attendee who seems to have appeared, but you were presenting a bunch of this stuff, weren't you? Look on page 2. You are a presenter for the ASR platform next steps review...Do you see that?*
A. I see that.

Q. *And the next morning when everybody gets together on July 31, the first time that's done at 8:30—8:00 to 8:30 in the morning is for reviewing the agenda and making adjustments and the year-to-date business round table. And do you know who owned that project? You did.*
A. OK.

Q. *This isn't just, gee, somebody put together a PowerPoint that may have said something but you have no knowledge of it. That's not honest testimony to the jury. Now, maybe you had forgotten. But you knew this stuff. You were there. You oversaw the agenda. Correct?*
A. Yes.

Q. *So we can take back all of those comments you made about, well, one person said that in a PowerPoint, I didn't know, I didn't know, I didn't know, I didn't know. You knew these very things about getting deeper into metal-on-metal, it being a high risk, it was a threat to your business, and y'all were scared of metal backlash. You knew those things, didn't you?* **[Lanier does not expect Ekdahl to answer yes. He is merely arguing his case to the jury and showing how outrageous the witness's answer will be when he again denies it. Remember, one of the greatest myths of cross-examination is that you can get the witness to confess. All you need to do is what Lanier does: show the jury that the answer is outrageous.]**
A. Well, again, like I said, I don't recall this PowerPoint. I can't—Was I in the room? Yes, let's say I was in the room. I don't know who generated it, how it was generated, and if it was generated just for a discussion and a dialogue. So it's very difficult for me to answer that.

Lanier has won the battle. Let's skip ahead to another part of Lanier's cross-examination.

Bless You

Q. OK So we've got a Pinnacle metal liner, and we've got a Pinnacle shell. And those are different parts, aren't they?
A. Correct.

Q. And you can have the Pinnacle shell but use it with either a metal liner or you could use it with a poly liner, couldn't you?
A. That's correct.
(Someone sneezes.)
MR. LANIER: Bless you.

What I am about to say may seem odd at first, but hear me out. There are two words that Lanier utters that may be the most important part of the entire cross-examination. The words are "bless you." Many attorneys get too antagonistic during cross-examination. One of the many problems with such an approach is that when you let your emotions get the best of you, you cannot think clearly. Remember, billions of dollars are at stake because the outcome of this bellwether trial and the other ones will affect the settlement value of all the other pending lawsuits. It is easy to be kind and say "bless you" when you are at work or out with friends, but in a courtroom with extremely high stakes, it is a different matter.

Another problem with being too emotional and argumentative is that the jury sees you as biased and no longer the truth teller in the courtroom. Lanier is always professional and very aware of his surroundings. He does not let emotions get in the way of forming his next question.

> **Practice Tip**
>
> Don't get angry on cross. Instead, be firm with the witness and give the jury the documents and answers from the witness you need to win. Jurors trust the lawyer who is knowledgeable, fair and likable, instead of one who is biased and angry.

Lanier Admits Mistake

Lanier questions Ekdahl about his efforts to change a press release about the hip implant so that it is more favorable after it had already been approved for release by the legal team at Depuy. Ekdahl claims he was wondering whether a change could be made, and Lanier argues that Ekdahl was really directing that the change be made.

Q. This [email] is not you asking whether it can be done. You've already made your edits, and before they make the change, the powers that be are saying can you confirm we can do what Andrew [Ekdahl] told us to do.
Mr. Quattlebaum: Objection, Your Honor.

Q. Do you see that?

MR. QUATTLEBAUM: Misstates the document.
COURT: Overruled.

WITNESS: I got to be honest. I read it much differently than you do. I look at the note from Jessica, "I realize the hip launch release has already been routed and approved, but Andrew Ekdahl is wondering—seems to me to be a question—if we can make three edits on the second page. Can you please review the attached and let me know what you think?" I think she's very openly asking for additional guidance based on an inquiry of mine. And then she goes on in another email—for an inquiry.

Q. Well—
A. OK. So I—

Q. All right.
A. —I'm sorry. To me, it seems like very reasonable dialogue between colleagues.

Q. Well, it radically—regardless, I'll leave aside— I'll give you the best deference in the world to that, and you were "wondering."

Although it rarely happens to Lanier, this exchange was an instance where Ekdahl had a more reasonable interpretation of a document than Lanier. This was a very heated exchange between Lanier and the witness. But not so heated that Lanier stopped listening or tried to prove his point at all cost. Lanier is always listening to the answers and staying flexible.

We can learn from Lanier that the goal is to keep the jurors' trust and prove your case. By giving the witness the benefit of the doubt, Lanier maintains his credibility and simply moves onto another topic where he is certain he can win.

On the flip side, opposing counsel asserted the argumentative objection 17 times in one day and was overruled each time. There is no excuse for such a failure rate. Jurors hate objections. They make the testimony last longer, and they interrupt the witness's answers. Most important, jurors believe that lawyers object to hide the truth from being heard. You don't want to be perceived that way by the jurors even if you are making legitimate objections. Often it is better to not object even if you have reasons to do so for the reasons I just stated. Choose your objections wisely.

While some of the argumentative objections were made in conjunction with other substantive objections to preserve issues for appeal or win the evidentiary point at trial, the fact is that the jury heard opposing counsel protest that Lanier was being unfair to the witness 17 times, and the judge disagreed every time. That means that the judge affirmed that Lanier was not being argumentative every time that defense counsel objected to his being so. Anyone would love to conduct a cross and have the judge give you 17 additional victories.

Before and After Breaks

During cross-examination, Lanier will periodically look at the clock in the courtroom. He does this because he wants to make sure he ends on a strong point before an important break in the proceedings, such as lunch or the end of the day or the end of the week. Just as basketball teams are taught to finish quarters strong, Lanier wants to make points that will be remembered.

There are several things to learn from Lanier in this next segment that concluded the first day of Ekdahl's cross-examination. His theme for this part of the cross-examination was that Johnson & Johnson was intertwined with DePuy. Lanier wanted to hold Johnson & Johnson liable for the punitive damages for DePuy's actions. Johnson & Johnson contended that it was not liable because DePuy was a separate entity.

As the end of the day approaches, Lanier looks at the clock in the courtroom and makes sure he concludes with his strongest points.

Q. By the same token, Johnson & Johnson is who made it mandatory that y'all put their logo on your products, didn't they?
A. I don't know that.

Q. At least you would agree that it was mandatory to put the logo on the product, right?

MR. LANIER: OK. Your Honor, move into evidence Plaintiff's Exhibit 7199.
MR. QUATTLEBAUM: 401, 403, and foundation, your Honor.
COURT: Overruled. Plaintiff's 7199 is admitted into evidence.

Q. Sir, I just asked you: "Q. At least you would agree that it's mandatory to put the logo on the product." [**Lanier reads from the real-time trial transcript that is fed to his computer in order to emphasize Ekdahl's claim that he does not know the policy regarding logos.**] *You said, "I don't know that." Correct?*
A. Correct.

Q. But here we look at the Pinnacle acetabular cup system creative brief in February of '06. It's got mandatory executional guidelines. "All advertising and promotions must feature the DePuy log with, quote, a Johnson & Johnson company." Do you see that?
A. **I'm trying to catch up.**

Q. Page 17.
A. OK.

Lanier never fumbles with a document. He anticipates that the witness may not remember or will not know an answer, and Lanier has the document and page number ready to show the witness and jury.

Unlike most attorneys, Lanier does not make the mistake of just talking about what is in a document. He uses a highlighter to mark each word as he reads it from the document. He often will then circle important words with a felt tip pen to highlight them even further.

Q. *That's what it says. It was required to use the Johnson & Johnson company on the logo. That was mandatory, wasn't it?*
A. That's what it says.

Q. ***You said I didn't know that.*** *Look at the approval down here. You're on it. You had to approve that, didn't you?*
A. I see that, yes.

Q. ***So it's not fair for you to say I didn't know that. You did know that, didn't you?***
A. I did not know that to be candid. As I've said, I didn't know that.

Not only has Lanier shown that it was mandatory, but that Ekdahl had to approve it. He then highlights for the jury that Ekdahl had previously stated that he had no knowledge of this.

Q. *If we go and look at the funding, for example, that huge Coach K* [**the well-known Duke University basketball coach, who had a DePuy hip implant and then was featured in DePuy advertisements**] *campaign that y'all did, most of the funding was Johnson & Johnson, wasn't it?*
A. Don't know.

MR. LANIER: Move into evidence Plaintiff's 16, your Honor.
MR. QUATTLEBAUM: 401, 403, foundation, and postdates some of the implant dates in this case, your Honor.
COURT: Understand that. Overruled. Plaintiff's 16 is admitted into evidence.

Q. *June 2, 2008, DePuy advertising campaign during the Olympics. This is for the DePuy advertising campaign. You see that? Bottom of the first page?*
A. I see that.

Q. *If you look under the second page under the financials about this funding "We received tremendous support from Johnson & Johnson Corporate in creating the campaign and Sheri in the surgical care [section] to support* ***80 percent of the funding.****" Do you see that?*
A. I see that.

Q. *Y'all got support from the "best consumer marketing and advertising experts in Johnson & Johnson, and it will be an exciting campaign." Do you see that?*
A. I see that.

Q. *"That this campaign was a great opportunity to harness the power and scale of national registry and using Coach K as a persuasive spokesperson because J&J is a major*

sponsor of the Olympics and is going to spend over 40 million bucks during that two-week time." Do you see that?
A. I see that.

MR. LANIER: Your Honor, a good stopping point.
COURT: OK. Ladies and gentlemen, be back at 9:00 o'clock in the morning.

Lanier ends with one of his best points. After Ekdahl states that he doesn't know if Johnson & Johnson provided most of the funding for one of DePuy's largest advertising campaigns for hip replacements, he proves it through a document whose force is all the stronger because of the witness's denial.

When Lanier continues with his cross the next morning, he reminds the witness—but he really intends to remind the jury—what the topic was from yesterday, and then he transitions to his next point.

Q. *Well, let's pick up where we left off before the break last night. And what I was doing was walking through a section with you where we were looking at the different roles of Johnson & Johnson versus the roles of DePuy and how the two intermingled. Do you remember that?*
A. I remember we were talking about this, yes. . . .

Q. *We had Johnson & Johnson funding the Coach K material before. That included the Olympic funding that we were specifically looking at. Do you recall that?*
A. I recall you read from an email, yes.

***

Q. *[Another] area that I wanted to talk to you about in this relationship was the fact that one of the problems DePuy had is some of their advertisements and commercials were deemed to be may be improper, and when that happened it was Johnson & Johnson who jumped into the picture to try to save the reputation for this direct advertising. Do you recall that, sir?*
A. No, sir.

Lanier then showed the witness several letters written on Johnson & Johnson letterhead by an attorney to all the major networks stating how DePuy's ads for hip implants met regulatory guidelines.

What to Do When Witness Tries to Take Control by Asking a Question

Attorneys will often get thrown when a witness asks them a question. It may be in the form of "May I explain?" or another such phrase that the witness is using as an attempt to take control of the examination. Your job is to maintain control but also appear fair to the witness in front of the jury. Here is an exchange where Lanier does both. In this example, Lanier questions Ekdahl about an email from DePuy's head of marketing.

Q. Here's the aSphere head's positioning statement. "DePuy Orthopaedics is currently the number one hip market share company in the U.S. ***A key driver of the U.S. hip growth has been a clear dominance of metal-on-metal."*** *Do you see that?*
A. I see that.

Q. So that we understand this, y'all have become the number one hip company in the U.S. by market share and a key reason why was your ***dominance in metal-on-metal****. Y'all were the 800-pound gorilla, weren't you?*

Lanier uses another colloquial phrase to create an image for the jury to remember. The "800-pound gorilla" is a phrase that has a long history in the English language of referring to an organization or person that is so powerful that it can do whatever it wants. There is also a joke associated with the phrase that some of the jurors may have known: Where does an 800-pound gorilla sit in a room? Answer: Anywhere it wants.

MR. QUATTLEBAUM: Object to argumentative, your Honor.
COURT: Overruled.

WITNESS: A key reason we're the number one hip company is because of the **quality of our products.**

Q. Where did it say that?

Imagine the scene in the courtroom. Lanier has the email enlarged on the ELMO. He has just highlighted the exact words from the email as he read them to the witness. Then, the witness, instead of answering the simple question, responds that the key reason was the quality of the products. Lanier then points to the words in the email and asks incredulously, "Where did it say that?" The witness's answer appears biased for DePuy. Then, the witness digs himself a deeper hole.

A. I'm telling you that's why we're the number one. He says this is a key driver. It's not all of them. It's a key driver.

MR. LANIER: Objection, nonresponsive.
COURT: Sustained.
MR. LANIER: Ask the witness to be instructed to answer the question.
COURT: Please answer the question that was asked.
WITNESS: **All right. Let's reread the question**.

Most lawyers would reread the question from the real-time trial transcript. But not Lanier. Why? Because Lanier is not going to lose control just because the witness tries to tell Lanier what to do. Lanier ignores the request and firmly states that he will re-ask it. Watch what happens next.

MR. LANIER: I'll re-ask it, sir. This does—this says very simply—
MR. QUATTLEBAUM: Excuse me, your Honor. I would ask that Mr. Ekdahl—his request be honored which is to reread the question that was asked.

Without looking ahead, what do you think the court will say? Given defense counsel's lack of success for all of the argumentative objections during this cross, you should know the answer. But the court supplies the legal rationale as well.

COURT: You can cross the way you want—I mean direct the way you want to, but I'm not going to make him do that. No. You don't have to ask him—
MR. LANIER: Thank you.

By Mr. Lanier:

Q. ***Sir, I think I'm going to hit it pretty much word for word anyway****. It says, "A key driver of DePuy's U.S. hip growth has been a clear dominance of the metal-on-metal bearing segment." Y'all were the number one hip company, and the key driver behind it was the fact that y'all were dominating the marketplace on metal-on-metal. That was where you were the 800-pound gorilla, true?*
A. It says here, we—it was a key driver of our growth, yes.

Q. *OK.* ***I'm not fussing****.* **[Again, Lanier uses informal language in his questions to align him with the sensibilities of the jury against the giant corporation.]** *I'm just living by the words of the document. OK?*

Lanier maintains control but signals to the jury that he is going to re-ask it "pretty much word for word anyway" so that jurors don't begin to have sympathy for a witness who asks for a question to be reread.

End on a Strong Point

Q. *I want to end with one more thing, and this is kind of an issue of how well you remember things and how well you've testified. OK?*
A. OK.

Q. *You remember the PowerPoint presentation of Dr. Schmalzried that had offensive slides in it and offensive language in it with all of the double entendres and the rest. Remember that?*
A. I do, yes.

Q. *And I asked you about it in terms of maybe even just saying, man, we shouldn't have sponsored that, I'm sorry about it. And your reply was you know nothing about it at all. Remember that?*
A. I don't remember exactly what I replied.

Q. *Well, I've got the testimony here. We can go through it. I think your comment on page 61 of volume 8 was: "I've never seen anybody give this presentation." Do you remember that, sir?*
A. I remember that, yes.

Here is the context for this excerpt. Dr. Schmalzried used a PowerPoint "Big Balls and Thin Liners" to promote metal-on-metal hip implants. There were inappropriate slides in it. For example, one had a picture of an obese woman's rear end with a thong and a thin woman wearing a thong with the caption, "Which is better?" Other slides had phrases that had a double entendre with sexual undertones (see testimony to come). The point is, it is not a PowerPoint that would be easy to forget seeing. The previous day, Ekdahl testified that he had never seen it. Lanier zeros in on this statement.

Q. *I mean, I said: You are claiming that all you are paying [Dr. Schmalzried] for is education. You said, look, he made some offensive statements in a presentation, I don't believe we paid for this presentation. That was also added to your testimony yesterday. Remember that?*
A. Yes.

Q. *Just so the jury gets a feel for how selective maybe you remember some things, let's go ahead and be up front about it now. You were there when he gave the presentation, weren't you?*
A. No, I don't believe I was.

Q. *Well, you were at least at the conference where he gave the presentation, weren't you?*
A. I don't know. I don't know where he gave it.

Q. *Sir, if you look at Plaintiff's Exhibit 7467, page 3, Eighth Annual Current Concepts in Joint Replacement, spring 2007, Las Vegas, Nevada, May 20 through 23, 2007. Do you see that?*
A. OK. I see that.

Q. *And this is a—this is a massive program with a large faculty, including on the faculty Dr. Schmalzried. Do you see that?*
A. OK. I see that.

Q. *And if you'll look in the midst of all of the presentations that were going down here, you've got the sessions that start on Monday, and they work through. And most of them—I mean, they all look pretty normal and legit to me, until we get to the one on page 9 of the exhibit, session 23: "Big Balls and Thin Liners: A Triumph of Hope Over Reason." Schmalzried [presenting]. Do you see that?*
A. OK.

MR. LANIER: If we go, Juan, please, to the computer.

Q. *That is the presentation that we've got, the offensive one. Right? Exhibit 69?*
A. Yes.

Q. *And then if you turn the next page to the Excel spreadsheet, where it's got the reservations arriving and staying for the entire trip, it's got you, Andrew Ekdahl, as one of the attendees. Do you see that, sir?*
A. I do.

Q. *So you were actually at the seminar where the slide presentation was being made, where it was claimed in the slide presentation that it had been supported and funded by DePuy, and you weren't the only one. There were 30 people from DePuy who were there. Berman to Zellner* [**the beginning and ending names on the spreadsheet**]. *Do you see that?*
A. I see that.

Q. *And you expect us to believe that with 30 people there a presentation like that could be made where at the end of the presentation it says it's supported by DePuy, and not one person out of the entire 30 that were there saw that presentation, pulled Schmalzried aside or said anything at all to him in regards to this?*
A. Well, I guess I don't know—first of all, I don't recall seeing it. That's what I—that's what I testified to. And I don't recall seeing it. And I also don't know if this is the **exact presentation** he gave. Well, we don't, right? I mean, I don't know if it's the exact one he gave.

The witness ends his testimony by minimizing what he knows by suggesting that Schmalzried might not have given this "exact" presentation. Schmalzried will testify later in the trial that he gave this exact PowerPoint presentation.

Recross

As soon as opposing counsel finishes, Lanier quickly gets out of his chair and rushes to the podium. His eagerness shows confidence and an appreciation for the jury's time.

Q. *Mr. Ekdahl, I've got a lot to cover with you. You covered a lot of material and a lot of new stuff with Mr. Quattlebaum, so we've got a lot of work to do. I'll try and move as quickly as we can, but we must cover these things. OK?*
A. OK.

Lanier is planting the seed in the jurors' minds that if he cannot get to all of the topics because of a delay, it will be the witness's fault, not Lanier's. He also signals to the jury that he has an answer for every major point that was brought out on direct.

Q. *And what I'd like to do is I really want to focus you in now on the truth. You understand that's what we're here about, right?*
A. Yes.

Q. *We're — we're not interested in cherry-picking* [**Lanier uses a colloquial phrase.**] *a sentence here or a sentence there. We're not interested in the spinning of something, or word games. We simply want to talk about the whole truth. That's a fair thing to ask, right?*
A. Sure.

Q. *And I used an analogy with the jury when we started this trial about inspecting a house and talked about how important it is to look under the rug, see if anything had*

been swept under the rug, to look behind the sofa, to check for termite damage, you know, all of those types of things. I'd like to do that with you, OK? Figuratively speaking. OK?
A. OK.

This is a perfect example of why you should spend time on your opening statement to develop a powerful theme. It ties your whole case together. As he did with Plouhar, Lanier reminds the jury of his opening statement during cross.

Q. So let's use—here's the way we're going to do this. ***We're going to start with where you ended, because it's freshest in our minds.*** *And then we're going to move forward through the things you did yesterday and the things you've done today up to this point and try to cobble them together in an order that makes sense. OK?*
A. OK.

Lanier shows the importance of being flexible in recross. Most attorneys are stuck with an outline from which they never budge. Why not start with the last topic opposing counsel discussed? Once you prove that argument wrong, then everything else will be easy. But you have to be flexible, because obviously you won't know what that topic will be until opposing counsel finishes. It might even be a topic you have not anticipated. If it is, then pull your impeaching documents together and attack it.

> **Practice Tip**
>
> If opposing counsel ends direct on a strong point, don't show weakness by not confronting it immediately. If you do, the strong point opposing counsel has made will linger longer than it should.

Q. We're going to begin with the truth on why the company stopped selling the Pinnacle metal liner. OK? Are you tracking with me?
A. OK.

Q. We've got your letter. We've heard your testimony. But I'd like to put it under the microscope for a moment. The truth of the matter is the FDA put the brakes on metal-on-metal absent more testing, human testing, PMA **[premarket approval]** *testing. True?*
A. Yes. The FDA wanted—I—I believe what the FDA was asking for were PMAs on metal-on-metal.

Q. Yes. In other words, testing in people. Right?
A. They were asking for PMAs.

The witness again tries to spin what the FDA said and minimize the damage of Lanier's question.

Q. Which means testing in people, as we've already heard from the head of clinical research at the time for DePuy, Dr. Pam Plouhar. That's what it means, simple truth, right?
A. Yes. The simple truth is the FDA was **asking** for PMAs.

Q. ***Not asking. Mandating.*** *There's a difference between the two.*
A. Mandated.

Doesn't this exchange confirm Lanier's point at the beginning of his recross? He told the jury he was asking for the simple truth, and it took several questions for the witness to admit that the FDA prohibited DePuy from continuing to sell metal-on-metal hip implants without human testing.

7.2 USING THE "SIMPLE TRUTH" IN A QUESTION

Now that we have seen Lanier use the phrase "the simple truth" in the last example, let's see him explain this further in a video clip which can be found at www.winningatcross.com under the heading "The Simple Truth." In the video, much like the last example, Lanier contrasts his basic question that asks for the simple truth with a long-winded answer that does not answer the question.

Notice how Lanier gives another tip to use if the witness does not answer a simple question with a simple answer but instead gives an unnecessarily complicated answer. He explains that you can ask the witness if he understands what a true false question is, like the ones that were given in school. Of course, everyone on the jury remembers those tests, including the fact that there were only two possible answers to such a question and that there was never a third option that allowed for an explanation. By asking the witness if he remembers those tests from school, it provides another way to highlight to the jury that the witness is avoiding an answer that hurts him by giving an irrelevant long one instead.

Not only is using "the simple truth" a great phrase to use in your questions, but it can also be an entire theme for your cross-examination. For example, you could begin your cross by telling the witness that you now wanted to talk to him about the simple truth, in contrast to what he just told the jury on direct. Then, you could pepper your questions with the phrase "the simple truth" to remind the jurors of your theme throughout the cross-examination.

7.3 CHAPTER CHECKLIST

Since some of the skills Lanier executed on Plouhar were also used on Ekdahl, only the different ones will be summarized below.

1. Lanier begins by drawing clear battle lines: "I want the jury to hear from you how marketing and sales ran the company, not science."

2. When a witness denies a proposition, Lanier proclaims, "Let's put it to the test."
3. Lanier is always ready with a document to make a point, whether the witness denies an obvious or subtle fact.
4. Lanier draws eight pictures on one page that illustrate each proposition he wants to prove on cross.
5. When a witness lacks expertise or has failed to do something, ask questions that get "no" answers so the jury repeatedly hears what the witness did not do or doesn't know but should.
6. When the witness minimizes his responsibility, such as when he says he was "among the decision-makers," Lanier fires back, you were "at the top. You were the president of DePuy."
7. Summarize the points you have made when you transition to a new topic.
8. When a witness denies an inference you are making from a document, respond by saying, "Let's see if this document bears out your view of it or mine."
9. One technique to control a witness who does not answer your question is to declare, "My question is very clear," and then ask your question again.
10. Out of the thousands of exhibits, label your most important document number one so jurors will look at it first during deliberations.
11. If the witness gives an outrageous answer, repeat it. For example, Lanier repeats the damaging denial "no" for emphasis.
12. Use logical reasoning to get an outrageous answer. It does not matter what the witness answers. If the jury believes the propositions in Lanier's question, then any attempt by the witness to deny it will not have the ring of truth and the cross-examiner will have won the battle.
13. Research a witness's answers during a break so you can confront the witness with the truth.
14. Don't get angry on cross. Instead, be firm with the witness, and get the answers from the witness you need to win. Jurors trust the lawyer who is knowledgeable, fair, and likable, instead of one who is biased and angry.
15. Maintain your credibility with the jury and freely admit any mistakes you make.
16. When showing the witness a document, Lanier reads the relevant passage as he highlights it and then circles the important words in the highlighted passage.
17. At the start of each day, summarize for the jury the topics you covered the previous day with the witness.
18. When a witness denies his previous testimony, Lanier does not pause in his presentation while he searches for the previous day's testimony. He has it ready and quickly confronts the witness with it.

19. Conclude your cross with your strongest point.
20. Use "the simple truth" as a theme for your cross and also as part of your questions. For example, "Ms. Witness, the simple truth is. . . ." When the witness does not give a direct answer but instead a long irrelevant explanation, the fact that you have used the phrase "the simple truth" in your question highlights for the jury the non-responsive answer.

CHAPTER EIGHT

Mark Lanier Cross-Examines Dr. Thomas Schmalzried

"Here is my theme for you. I find you to be a man of many hats."—*Mark Lanier*

This is the third and final witness we will examine from the DePuy hip implant trial. Dr. Thomas Schmalzried is a well-known orthopedic surgeon. During the trial, Lanier asserted that Schmalzried was an opinion leader in the medical community in regards to DePuy's Pinnacle hip implants and that he helped sell and market them. He was also on the design team for DePuy's Pinnacle and ASR hip implants, but his exact role wasn't clear, as we will soon see Lanier explore. Schmalzried had also been deposed and had been a witness in previous bellweather trials, so he had been battle-tested in the courtroom.

> **CHAPTER ROAD MAP**
>
> - Think creatively how to use demonstrative exhibits to prove your point.
> - Learn how to display and highlight documents to cross-examine a witness.
> - Write down a list of a witness's admissions underneath your theme's heading for the jury to see.

Lanier is aware that in a long trial, you can never afford to lose the jury's attention. Consequently, you cannot use the same demonstrative exhibits for each witness. Instead, Lanier wants a jury to be looking forward to what he is going to do differently with each witness. To give you a sample of his creativity, this book examines three of the witnesses from the trial. For this witness, Lanier does not disappoint. Right off the bat, Lanier used a different tactic than he used for the previous witnesses, which made the cross-examination entertaining and memorable.

8.1 CROSS-EXAMINATION OF DR. THOMAS SCHMALZRIED

Lanier Introduces Theme That Witness Had Many Roles

Q. Dr. Schmalzried, here is my theme for you, if you will. I find you to be a man of many hats. Would you agree with that? **[Lanier expects the witness to be caught off guard. He is taunting Goliath.]**

A. I—I'm not sure what you mean, sir. **[The witness is already on the defensive. He has been through this dance with Lanier before, but he senses something different is about to happen.]**

Q. *Well, what I mean is when it comes to—when it comes to Johnson & Johnson/DePuy you wore many different hats. You wore the hat of—let's see, you wore the hat of a salesman. You wore the hat of a marketer. You wore the hat of a doctor. True?*

As he asks each question, Lanier puts on one of three different navy baseball hats, each with one of the words of his theme—"doctor," "salesman," or "marketer"—embroidered on the cap's front in white letters. If you were in the courtroom and were on Johnson & Johnson's side, you could not help but smile at Lanier's creativity. But if you were on the jury, you would see an attorney making very direct points with images that would be impossible to forget.

A. No, I—I disagree with that, sir.

Q. *Well, you and I have been through this before, and I think you would tell me and you would tell the jury you were a doctor. No more. No less. You do not like my insinuation that you wore the hat of a salesman, correct?*

A. I'm a surgeon. A physician, a surgeon, sir. **[The witness gets testy and does not like being referred to as a mere doctor.]**

Q. *OK. I'm not going to fuss that you have a doctor's hat and you wore that. I'm not going to fuss that. You did wear a doctor's hat. But beyond just a doctor's hat, sir, you also wore the hat of a salesman, didn't you?*

A. I—I don't believe that's correct. I think that mischaracterizes my career.

Q. *All right. That's where we're going to start. We're going to start out with, did you wear the hat of a Salesman?*

As mentioned in previous chapters, Lanier does not follow the bad advice given in Younger's "Ten Commandments of Cross-Examination." He does not hide the ball from the witness or the jury. Instead, he begins with a full-frontal attack.

Imagine how much confidence you must have to put baseball caps on your head in front of the jury. Doing so is a gamble: if Lanier can prove his points, the jury will remember his success for the remainder of the trial, and it will influence how the jury assesses the other DePuy witnesses. But if Lanier fails to prove his points, it will be impossible for him to recover his lost credibility.

Why is Lanier so confident? As we learned earlier, you have the power to choose your topics for cross-examination. Lanier knows that he will have emails, videos, and other documents to prove each one of his themes.

Also, notice how Lanier's theme of Schmalzried as a man who wears many hats fits with his opening statement's bottom line message that the plaintiffs had trusted both a product and a doctor—and in the end, got terrible results. Lanier will emphasize that Schmalzried, as a doctor, took on other surprising roles, all of which ultimately undermined his trustworthiness.

Schmalzried's Role as Salesman

Q. *And what I'd like to do is just walk through some basics of this.* [**"Basics" is an everyday word that simplifies the issue for the jury, not because the jury is dumb, but because jurors want lawyers to get to the point so that they can decide the case.**] *So basic number one, you would agree with me that you were paid a percentage of the sales of the product, weren't you?*
A. I earned a royalty on some DePuy products.

Q. *Well, you can say, "earned a royalty," but that makes it sound like you were an inventor. We're going to get into exactly whether or not you were an inventor later, but you're not on a patent for the products, are you?*
A. Depends on—on what products you're talking about, sir.

Q. *I'm talking about the products that earned you $30 million in this litigation. How many of those had you—how many of those products were you on the patent for?*

MR. QUATTLEBAUM: Objection, Your Honor. Misstates the evidence.
COURT: Overruled.
WITNESS: So I know I'm on a Summit stem patent.

Q. *OK. That's one out of many products where you were getting a cut, right?*
A. Well, there were intellectual property contributions to every product in the royalty.

MR. LANIER: Objection, nonresponsive. [**Lanier keenly listens to the answer and knows that the witness does not answer the question of whether he is getting a cut, but instead tries to argue he had made intellectual property contributions for every product he received a royalty on.**]
COURT: Sustained.
MR. LANIER: Ask that the witness be instructed to answer the question.
COURT: Just answer the question you're asked, sir.

Q. *Can you answer the question?*
A. I apologize. Can you please repeat the question?

Q. *Yeah. The Summit stem is just one of many products that you were paid a royalty or a cut on, correct?*
A. It's one of several products that I received a royalty on.

Q. *Yeah. You received I think somewhere in the ballpark of $30 million or more, haven't you?*
A. I think $30 million is—in that ballpark, yes, sir.

Q. Yeah. And so—and so the jury understands though, what you would get paid is a percentage of sales, whether you were on the patent or not, correct?
A. No. You don't have to be on the patent to be paid a royalty.

MR. LANIER: Objection, nonresponsive.
COURT: Sustained. **Just answer the question, sir.**
WITNESS: I'm sorry. Repeat the question, please.

Q. Yeah. You were paid a percentage of the sales whether you were on the patent or not, true?
A. Yes.

Q. OK. And so every quarter or so you would get a payment in the mail. A check. Right?
A. No, sir.

Q. Well, maybe not every quarter, but pretty frequently you would, wouldn't you?
A. The misstatement was it was a direct deposit. [**The witness quibbles with Lanier and loses credibility for not answering a simple question**.]

Q. Oh, it wasn't a check; it was a direct deposit. All right. So every quarter you would get a direct deposit of a check.

Lanier executes two skills in this passage that you should incorporate into every cross. First, as with the other witnesses, he makes a list of the points he wants the witness to admit to on a sheet of paper that is displayed for the jury during cross. See figure 1.

Second, Lanier listens very carefully to the witness's answers. Every time the witness fails to answer a question and instead qualifies his answers or argues with Lanier, Lanier decides whether to repeat his question again, rephrase it, or object that the answer is non-responsive.

Q. Here's an example, sir. This is a copy of a check that was provided to us by—actually, I thought by your office, but it may have been through DePuy, but I think this was from your office. [**Lanier puts the check on the ELMO so the jury can see it.**] *It's a payment by DePuy Orthopaedics, by Johnson & Johnson Services, I think, as the paying agent, made out to you. And this happens to be for $326,000 this quarter. Is that right?*
A. That's the amount on the check, sir.

Lanier then proceeds to question the witness and display for the jury several checks to show that Schmalzried received similar checks each quarter.

Q. And the reason you got paid a percentage of the sales is, in essence, because of your other work on the product beyond simply being a contributor of ideas to its development. Fair?
A. No, sir. Not fair at all.

Once again, Lanier gets to the heart of the matter with the question above. The witness then complains that Lanier is not being fair. Let's watch what happens

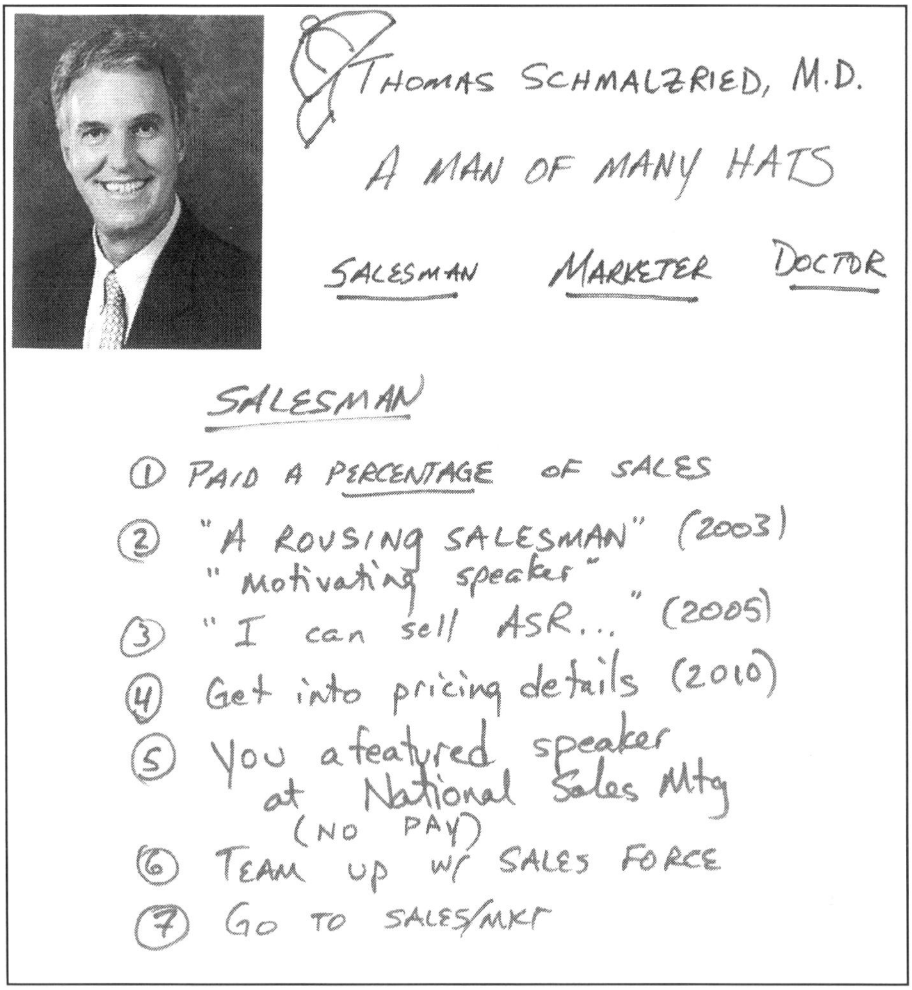

Figure 1. ELMO exhibit with major points Lanier wants to address during cross.

next. Remember, Lanier has already taught the jury to expect that he will have documents to prove his points in black and white.

Lanier Contends DePuy Viewed the Witness as a "Rousing Salesman"

Q. *Well, let's look at your work as a salesman beyond the percentage. Would you agree with me that the company saw you as a* ***rousing salesman*** *in 2003?* [**Lanier uses the exact words that are on the document he is about to show the jury.**]

A. I don't know about that.

MR. LANIER: Well, your Honor, we move into evidence Plaintiff's Exhibit 7281.

MR. QUATTLEBAUM: Your Honor, 401, 403, foundation, and hearsay.

COURT: Overrule your objection. Plaintiff's 7281 is admitted into evidence.

Q. All right, sir. So here's what we've got, an email about—within the company, DePuy Australia to DePuy Great Britain, July 4, 2003. Over there I guess they work on July 4; it's not as big a holiday for the British as it is for us. You see that?
A. Yes, sir.

Q. All right. Now, this is an email where they're talking about someone to present on ASR **[a DePuy hip implant that was similar to the Pinnacle that was recalled.]** *That was the other metal-on-metal [**hip implant**] product of DePuy, correct?*
A. Yes, sir.

Q. It says, "I would suggest Andrew Cobb as someone who would present well on the surgical technique and sell the implant (unless you specifically want Roger to be the surgeon). If you need a more ***rousing salesman*** *and motivating speaker, I would suggest—"*

MR. QUATTLEBAUM: Objection, your Honor. Mr. Lanier misread the document. It did not say "and."
MR. LANIER: I'll re-read that, judge.
COURT: OK.
MR. LANIER: **I want to get it just right.**
COURT: All right. Sustain your objection.

Q. "If you need a more rousing salesman motivating speaker I would suggest Tom Schmalzried."

> **Practice Tip**
>
> Whenever Lanier reads a document that is displayed on the ELMO, he either highlights or underlines the passage he reads so the jury can follow along easily. Most attorneys make the mistake of just reading the document or pointing to a paragraph with their finger.

It makes no sense that plaintiff's counsel would object that Lanier misread the document because he left out the word "and." All defense counsel did was give Lanier a chance to highlight the words "rousing salesman" again for the jury. Just because you can make an objection does not mean it is wise to do so.

Q. You weren't being suggested for your surgical technique or your product know-how, you were being suggested by the company as a "more rousing salesman motivating speaker." ***Do you see that?*** **[This is a common refrain Lanier uses in his cross-examinations. There is only one truthful answer the witness can give, "Yes, I see what is written." The refrain emphasizes to the jury the point that is proven by the document.]**
A. Yes, sir.

Q. And yet you say you didn't wear the salesman hat. **[Lanier puts on the salesman cap again and takes it off.]**
A. No, sir. I'm not a salesman.

Lanier knows Schmalzried won't admit he is a salesman, but he puts on the cap again to highlight that Schmalzried's answer is the opposite of what is shown in black and white in the email.

***

Lanier Argues That the Witness Told DePuy He Could Be a Salesman

Q. *Do you recall telling the company you could be a salesman [in 2005]?* **[Lanier can ask this question with confidence because he will soon show the jury proof through an email. It makes no sense for the witness to deny Lanier's question.]**
A. No, I don't recall telling them that I can be a salesman.
MR. LANIER: Your Honor, we move into evidence Plaintiff's Exhibit 164.

***

Q. *So the [DePuy] marketing man is emailing you about Birmingham hip ad [a competitor]. . . . So there's an ad for this Birmingham hip resurfacing device, and you replied to the head of marketing. Look at what you said. You said, "Interesting—DePuy should be ready with European ASR data." ASR, again, another metal-on-metal hip, right?*
A. Yes, sir.

Q. *"We need to be ready—" now, "we" is—you've now put yourself in camp with DePuy and the marketers, right?*
A. I—working with DePuy, that's correct.

Q. *Of course, if doctors use the Birmingham hip instead of a DePuy product,* ***you don't get a cut, do you?***
A. I—**I don't have any relationship** to the BHR.

Q. *In other words,* ***true, you don't get a cut*** *if they use the—the Birmingham hip, right?* **[If a witness is evasive, Lanier will sometimes repeat the question as a statement that begins with the answer that the witness should have given, as he does here. By saying, "In other words, true," Lanier highlights how simple the answer should have been."]**
A. I don't earn a royalty on the Birmingham hip.

Q. *And a royalty or a cut that you would have earned on a DePuy hip isn't going to happen because they're using the competitive device, right?*
A. I only receive a royalty on the DePuy product.

Q. *So you said, "****We*** *need to be ready with ASR and XL—in the short term—****I can sell*** *XL versus resurfacing in the U.S." Did I read that right?*
A. Yes, sir. That's what it says. **[The witness tries to distance himself from the damaging email. Lanier, who always listens carefully, hears the discrepancy and attacks with his next question and highlights the phrase again on the ELMO.]**

Q. *No. That's what* ***you*** *said. Those are* ***your*** *words.*
A. Yes, sir. Yes, sir.

Q. *You're—you're putting on the salesman hat, you're saying I can sell the DePuy product over the Birmingham product if you get me the data, I can make that sale in the U.S., don't you?*
A. I'm using marketing vernacular when I'm talking to the marketing team.

Q. *Well, actually, sales and marketing we found out are different departments within the company. We'll go to the marketing hat in a little bit. My point is you're saying I can sell it. You're putting on that hat yourself, aren't you?*
A. No, sir, I'm not. **[Even after being shown the email, the witness denies he had a role as a salesman. This is music to Lanier's ears. He can now go through the email again for the jury.]**

Q. *Does it say, "I can sell—"*
A. Yes, sir, it does.

Q. *"—XL—"*
A. Yes, sir, it does.

Q. *Did you say, "I can sell" it?*
A. I wrote this.

Q. *So is that a yes answer? Yes, you said I can sell it?*
A. I'm using marketing vernacular to the marketing team.

Q. *Yeah. Because they won't understand normal English, is that what we're to understand?* **[Who appears more credible in front of the jury? Lanier and his plain English or a witness who qualifies the most simple answers? When the witness implies that Lanier has misinterpreted the email because the witness was using "marketing vernacular," Lanier uses plain English in the next few questions to highlight that his interpretation of the email is correct and not the witness's.]** *I mean, you—you could have said—you could have said a lot of different things. You could have said, "You can sell ASR" or "XL," but you didn't, did you?*
A. No, sir.

Q. *You could have said, "You can look at papers to do it." The point is, sir, you saw yourself wearing the salesman hat. You were going to go out and sell the product to the U.S. market, weren't you?*
A. No, sir. That mischaracterizes my role. **[This statement is a lot more outrageous after Lanier has impeached him with the above emails.]**

***

Did you notice how Lanier summarizes the witness's testimony on cross. Not many lawyers do this, and Lanier does it really well. After he makes each point on the documents he shows the witness, he writes down the admissions on a sheet of paper with the witness's name and photograph (see Fig. 1).

Also, by making a list, the jury can clearly see the points—in this case seven—that Lanier proves to establish that Schmalzried is also a salesman.

Instructing Sales Teams Versus Educating Them

In the next excerpt, Lanier questions the witness about a PowerPoint presentation called "The Second Billion" that the witness presented to DePuy's sales force.

> **Practice Tip**
>
> Ask only leading questions to force a witness to give specific answers that you want the jury to hear. However, an exception to this rule is when it doesn't matter what the answer is, because you already have proof of that answer (such as a written document). In that case, a non-leading question is acceptable.

Q. *And then you start giving them instructions on how to be a good salesperson. You're giving the sales team sales instructions, aren't you?*
A. I think I'm educating them.

Lanier knows the witness is never going to admit that he is a salesman based on his testimony in previous trials. Also, we know that a witness is not ever going to confess to making a significant mistake. This was discussed in chapter 2 as the greatest myth of cross-examination. Instead, Lanier reminds the jury of his theme and counts his victories each time the witness makes an outrageous statement (the "O" of the CROSS acronym discussed in chapter 2). Here, the witness states that he is not instructing the sales team but merely educating them. Lanier fires back with a great response.

Q. *Yeah. You're educating them on how to sell. Slide number 6. You say "Sell smart." "Know the competition." "Sell the system." "SWAT." Do you want to tell the jury what "SWAT" stands for?* **[This is not a leading question and it gives control of the examination over to the witness. But Lanier does not care what the witness says, because the definition of SWAT is written on the next slide.]**
A. Sell what's available today.

Q. *Sell you can't really read it there* **[on the PowerPoint slide.]** *Sell what's available today. That's what you're teaching them. You're giving them—*
A. Yes yes, sir.

Q. *— you're giving them sales techniques, aren't you?*
A. Yes, sir.

Lanier has now gotten the witness to admit that he was giving them "sales techniques," whereas just a bit earlier the witness would only admit to educating the sales force. Why does Lanier succeed? He uses the witness's own PowerPoint presentation to prove his point. You must have either the documents to prove your points or the power of common sense on your side in order to win. These are the keys to success. A little later in the cross, Lanier plays a video of DePuy's National Sales Meeting in New Orleans.

(Video playing.)

(Dr. Schmalzried): Thank you, Paul. Thank you very much. "Good afternoon, DePuy. Let's talk about the second billion . . . I'm finally going to get to play with Coach K. Welcome to the A team." . . . .

(Video playing.)

(Dr. Schmalzried): "Your billion-dollar baby, Pinnacle with high-performance bearings. You are the market leader. Congratulations. Give yourself a hand. I thank you. It has been not only fun but tremendously gratifying to be a member of this team."

MR. LANIER: Stop.

(Video stopped.)

[The entire video can be seen at www.winningatcross.com.]

Q. You still want to say you didn't call yourself part of the sales team?
A. I'm part of the DePuy team. I'm—I'm not a salesman.

Q. You just said, "Welcome to the A team," and then after a couple of other sentences on your next slide, you said, "It's been personal—" you thanked them. You said, "It's been personally gratifying to be a part of this team."
A. Yes, sir. I—I was definitely on the DePuy team. I'm not a salesman.

Q. All right.
A. I'm a surgeon.

Is one of Lanier's tried-and-true techniques now seeming like second nature to you? He challenges the witness with a proposition he knows the witness is going to deny. He then proves his point through documents. He asks the question again, knowing that he will get a denial, and then shows the witness the documents again, albeit in a quicker manner. By doing this, Lanier gets to show the documents twice to the jury.

***

Q. By the way, I'm going to put down here "Team up with sales force." **[Lanier writes on figure 1.]** *Even though you claim you were just on the DePuy team, not the sales team, you certainly are saying it's been gratifying to be part of the team to the sales force, weren't you?*
A. It was gratifying to be part of the DePuy team.

Lanier is referring to figure 1, where he lists the witness's admissions. He wants to be seen as fair by the jury. Even though he has proven a lot more, Lanier knows the witness cannot quarrel with what he's written on line 6: "Team up with sales force."

Dr. Schmalzried's Role as a Marketer

Q. *All right. So, now, within this framework, sir, we started this out with my suggestion to you that you wore different hats, you wore the hat of salesman, you wore the hat of marketer, and you wore the hat of doctor. Remember?*
A. I do.

Q. *All right.*
A. I remember.

Q. *So now we're going to look at you as marketer. And we'll set the salesman hat aside, pull out the marketing hat. Will you just agree with me that you wore this hat a whole bunch and it will save us some time?* **[Lanier shows the marketing baseball cap to the jury.]**
A. No, sir. That—that mischaracterizes my role.

I bet you can predict what Lanier does based on what we learned from his examination on the salesman topic. Lanier has several documents to prove his point, and the documents will have the witness's own words or those of DePuy to prove his points. Lanier knows he is going to win because he has the documents to prove it. It is that simple. The more the witness denies that he is a marketer in spite of the documents that will show otherwise just makes the cross-examination all the more devastating. Lanier begins to create figure 2, which lists the facts that support his contention that Schmalzried is a marketer.

***

Q. *Here's one of the consulting reviews that you sent the company way back in 1999. Do you see this?*
A. Yes, sir.

Q. *It was your quarterly report where you told the company a summary of your services. Do you see that?*
A. Yes, sir.

***

Q. *This is third quarter of 1999. It's your quarterly report. You want to tell the jury why you had to do a quarterly report like this?*
A. At that time I was under a consulting agreement with DePuy.

***

Q. ***Then you've got the market trends.*** *Do you see that?* ***A whole section on it.***
A. The agreement that this was produced under —

MR. LANIER: Objection, nonresponsive.
WITNESS: —Outlines the quarter's reports—
COURT: Sustained. Sustained. **Answer the question, sir.**

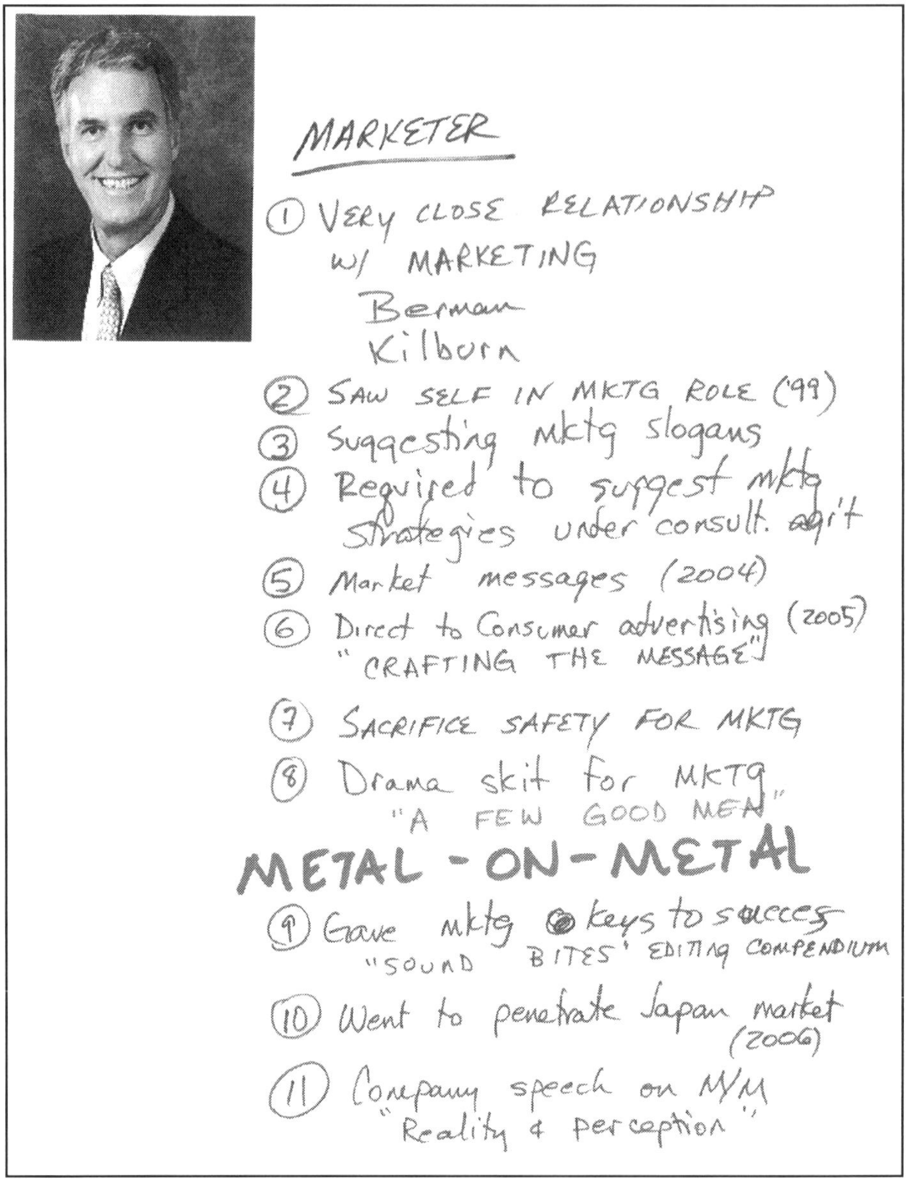

Figure 2. ELMO exhibit with facts that support Lanier's contention that Schmalzried is a marketer.

Notice how Lanier cuts the witness off as soon as he realizes the witness is not answering the question. The judge's frustration with the witness's answers only highlights the fact that the witness is losing credibility with the jury. When the witness does not answer the question after the judge's ruling, Lanier piggybacks on the judge's admonition by repeating the judge's instruction. Now it's two on one: the judge and Lanier against the witness who won't answer the question.

Q. *Answer the question. I just said do you see where you've got a whole section on market trends?*
A. Yes, sir.

Q. *And down at the end you say, "DePuy needs to develop and incorporate a marketing strategy for the whole product line: The War on Dislocation!" You're suggesting marketing strategies for them, aren't you?*
A. **Yes, sir. As was required under the consulting agreement.**

Q. *We'll—we'll get into that. So you saw yourself in the marketing role, and you are suggesting marketing slogans.* ***And now you're telling us that you were required to be a marketer under the agreement.***
A. No, sir. That's not what I said at all.

Like most witnesses, this one is minimizing the bad acts of which he's been accused. In the previous answer, he says that the reason he provided marketing strategies is not because he was a marketer, but only because it was required by the agreement. Really? Lanier dissects this spin.

Unlike most lawyers, Lanier has one advantage here: he is able to pay for a real-time transcript of the court proceedings. Watch what he does when he goes to his laptop at the counsel table and reads the transcript of what the witness just said.

> **Practice Tip**
>
> The key to becoming a great cross-examiner is to listen, listen, and listen.

Q. *All right. Let's get it exactly the way you said it, sir. What you just said is—I said "You're suggesting marketing strategies for them, aren't you"? Do you see where I'm reading?*
A. Yes, sir.

Q. *Let me see if I can—and your answer was, "As was required under the consulting agreement." Do you see that?*
A. I do.

Q. *So you're saying under the consulting agreement it was required for you to suggest marketing strategies?*
A. The consulting agreement had headers for the different categories in the quarterly report, and those definitions in that agreement were economic, environment, and marketing trends. And I was following the outline of that agreement.

Without looking ahead, what do you think Lanier is going to do with this non-responsive answer? This is a bit of a trick question. As we have seen, Lanier usually objects that the answer is non-responsive. Here, he does something different, which is just as effective.

Q. *Is that a yes or a no? I'm trying to figure out, are you backing away from what you swore under oath here when [I asked] "You're suggesting marketing strategies for them, aren't you?" and instead of simply answering yes, you added "As was required under*

the consulting agreement." So if you're telling the truth there, you were required to suggest marketing strategies under the consulting agreement, fair?
A. Yes. It was one of the duties of the consulting agreement.

Lanier wins. The witness loses. Lanier has proven that the witness wore a marketing hat. We are going to fast-forward a little bit to when the court returns from a recess. Watch how Lanier begins by summarizing what happened before the break and then highlights the next topic for the jury. As mentioned in the other crosses, always take advantage of a break to summarize for the jury what happened before it.

Schmalzried Injects Himself into a Marketing Campaign

Q. But would you also agree that you weren't simply talking to the sales force about how a surgeon sees things, you weren't just talking to the marketing about how a surgeon sees things, heavens, you were getting involved or injecting yourself into direct-to-consumer advertising and messaging, weren't you?
A. I believe I had **discussions** about direct-to-consumer advertising.

*Q. Well, but I wasn't just saying did you have discussions. What I was saying is, you were **injecting yourself**, you were saying, to use your team analogy, **"Put me in, coach, I can play."*** **[Lanier borrows a colloquial saying from the witness and uses it against him to create an image for the jury.]**

The battle line has been drawn. Lanier is careful with the words he uses. In this case, the words are "injecting yourself." The witness, like most witnesses, minimized his role and says that he only had discussions. Why does Lanier use the words "injecting yourself?" Although those exact words are not in the email that follows, Lanier knows he can prove his contention from a fair reading of the email.

Practice Tip

Even if the document does not have the exact words you use in your question to prove your claim, you will win if a fair inference from the words in the document supports your contention.

On the flip side, even if the witness had admitted that he had injected himself into advertising, Lanier would have still shown the following documents to the jury to emphasize his point. But since the witness does not admit the obvious, the cross-examination is all the more devastating when Lanier proves his claim.

*Q. Look at Exhibit 162. This is an email that you sent to the head of marketing, Randy Kilburn, concerning direct-to-consumer marketing. . . **Do you see that?***
A. I do.

***

Q. So you said, "We both have been busy with other things—so ***where do we stand*** *with the direct-to-consumer campaign?" Now, let's pause for a moment and look at the pronoun you use. "Where do we stand," who's the "we"?*
A. Well, Randy Kilburn and myself, I guess, because that's who the email is to.

Q. So the "we" is—"Where do we stand with the direct-to-consumer," it's—it's the head of—it's the marketing guy, he's the one with the umbrella pumping up and down in the Taking Share of Business [video], right?
A. Yes, sir. That's Randy Kilburn.

Q. Uh-huh. "Where do we stand," him and you?
A. Yes, sir.

Q. That's—that's marketing. "Where do we stand with the direct-to-consumer campaign? ***I remain very interested in crafting this message.*** *" Do you see that?*
A. Yes, sir.

Q. You were injecting yourself in the direct-to-consumer marketing campaign, weren't you?
A. No. I think that mischaracterizes the events.

Q. You want to know where we stand on it because you remain interested in ***crafting the message****, right?* ***That's what it says?***
A. Yes, sir. Yes, sir, that's what it says.

Q. We can put that in quotation marks, "Crafting the message." **[Lanier puts this phrase in quotation marks on figure 2, which he shows to the jury on the ELMO.]**

As you have seen, when Lanier shows a document to the witness, he first reads and highlights what is on the document and then often asks, "Do you see that?" or "That's what it says?" That way, he gets the jury to read along as he speaks and highlights the words on the document. Then, he asks the witness the perfect question about the document: "Do you see that?" The only possible answer is "yes." He doesn't make the mistake of asking if the witness is telling the truth now in court or when he spoke the words that appear in the document, because that would give the witness the chance to offer a self-serving explanation.

In short, the witness cannot deny what is written. Lanier leaves it to the jury to decide if Lanier has made his point or not through the document. Since Lanier takes the wording for his questions from the document or the obviously clear inference, Lanier always wins and the witness always loses. You can do the same by following this principle.

Schmalzried Acts in Drama Skits for the Marketing Department

Q. If we go back to looking at you as a marketer, sir, we're still looking at the marketing hat though, all right? Are you with me?
A. Yes, sir.

Q. *Are you with me? We've also got you—I mean, you're doing drama skits for the company's marketing department. Is that right?*
A. Are you asking me if I did a drama skit?

Q. *Yeah.*
A. Is that the question?

Q. *Yes, sir.*
A. I did—I did a drama skit with the marketing department.

Q. *I think it was A Few Good Men, the Jack Nicholson movie, "You can't handle the truth." Remember?*
A. I do.

Q. *And you played one of the lawyers in that marketing skit, didn't you?*
A. I think.

Q. *And, again, that's not something we typically think of our doctors as doing. You understand that that's not what typically we see with doctors?*
A. Doctors do all kinds of things.

Well, of course, doctors do all kinds of things outside of work in their free time, but that is not Lanier's point and the jurors know it. Every time the witness waffles and does not answer a question directly, Lanier seizes on it and makes his point even stronger as evidenced by what happens next.

Q. *But I think that for most people that it's not envisioned that the doctor is back working with the marketing department of a company where the doctor gets a cut of everything that's sold within a group of products and the doctor's helping them market it by doing dramatic skits. Is that typical—is that—are you saying that's the way most doctors practice medicine?*
A. That's—we're not even talking about the practice of medicine.

Q. *No. We're not, are we? We're talking about marketing, right?*
A. If I recall correctly, that skit was an internal event for the DePuy Corporation. I wasn't talking to surgeons. I wasn't—I wasn't marketing. **[Again, the witness tries to minimize what he has done. Watch how Lanier incorporates the witness's answer into his next question.]**

Q. *Yeah. That—that—trust me. I put it down here as a marketing thing you were doing because that's what you were doing. You were dealing with the marketing people—Polly Cary, Randy Kilburn, Andrew Ekdahl, Paul Berman. These are the people you were dealing with, right?*
A. I was certainly working with the marketing team, yes, sir.

***

As Lanier winds up his cross-examination, he hammers home his theme. I am not going to remind you of it since it will be obvious from his questions. In this series of questions, Lanier shows the witness DePuy documents that state the contributions the witness made to DePuy's marketing of metal-on-metal hip implants.

Q. *So here were the key elements of your contribution to Ultamet, supposedly what justified paying you quite a lot of money. Right?*
A. Yeah. I—I earned royalties, yes, sir.

Q. *Well, this is the question of how did you earn them, though. Did you earn them by uniquely contributing ideas, or did you earn them through all of these papers you wrote, the sales meetings you attended, the marketing efforts? This is — which hat were you wearing when you earned them? Do you follow?*
A. Yes.

***

Q. *Look at the next contribution. You were a "strong advocate of large head metal-on-metal for increased stability and lower wear." So you got paid for being a "strong advocate," do you see that?*

MR. QUATTLEBAUM: Objection, your Honor, to the characterization of the question. It doesn't—it doesn't say he got paid for that.
COURT: Rephrase your question.

Q. *Well, sir, this is all under the category of whether or not there's evidence of an appropriate consultant contribution to the design project, and here are the key elements of your contribution. Do you see that?*
A. Yes, sir.

***

Q. *Now, by the way, I questioned earlier whether or not Mr. Quattlebaum had been fair in his representation to the jury [in opening statement] that you were* **not** *an advocate for metal-on-metal.* ***You were a strong advocate*** *for large head metal-on-metal, if we're to believe [your contribution], right?*
A. I—that's correct.

Lanier pays close attention to opposing counsel's opening statement. He uses any misstatements or exaggerations made by the lawyer to question witnesses. By getting the witness to admit he was a strong advocate for metal on metal, he not only proves one of the themes on his cross but he undermines opposing counsel's credibility by highlighting the inconsistency in the opening statement.

Q. *Well, the truth of the matter is what you really did is work hard on convincing the world to use metal-on-metal, or at least the U.S., and you worked hard on sales and marketing, didn't you?*

MR. QUATTLEBAUM: Object to argumentative, your Honor.
WITNESS: I think that mischaracterizes—

COURT: Overruled. [**Opposing counsel fails almost every time that he asserts the argumentative objection.**]
WITNESS:—my activities.

Q. If you'll look at Plaintiff's Exhibit 3863 . . . . "Dr. Schmalzried also led the U.S. resurgence of metal-on-metal bearings [**detailed in metal bearings below**] *as a better option for large diameters, like resurfacing." That's what they credited you with, isn't it?*
A. I am credited with that.

Q. Yeah. You led the resurgence, and you did that through your assisting in sales and marketing and training doctors on how to do it and all of that and, you know, getting them to use the product, et cetera. Right?
A. No. That mischaracterizes my activities. [**Whether the witness was prepped to use this word ("mischaracterizes") or he came up with it on his own, he has used it six times in the excerpts shown in this chapter. The word is formal, and its repetition in multiple answers gives the sense that the witness is being evasive.**]

Q. Because that's the way they listed you on page 71 of this same exhibit. "Dr. Schmalzried regularly assists in the preparation of DePuy education and marketing materials where" your product knowledge, creativity and your style are invaluable. You're a favorite of the DePuy sales force, and excerpts from your presentations are commonly utilized to support the products in local markets. You've been a featured speaker at the last two DePuy domestic national sales meetings and at several DePuy international sales meetings. You're recognized as one of the best communicators in the industry. You frequently lecture at these national and international meetings and symposia. Do you see that?
A. Yes, sir.

Q. That's what you were being paid for. That's your unique contribution. These other guys ***don't hold a candle to you*** *in that regard, do they?* [**Lanier uses another informal, well-known saying to create a memorable image for the jury.**]
MR. QUATTLEBAUM: Object to the argumentative, Your Honor.
COURT: Overruled.
WITNESS: I wouldn't say that.

Q. I mean, DePuy didn't have Andy Engh, nice guy, but they didn't have him addressing the national sales conference and international sales conference over and over, or at least he wouldn't do it. Right? [**Dr. Engh is a highly respected orthopedic surgeon. Lanier suggests by his question that DePuy considered Schmalzried a better salesman than Engh.**]

MR. QUATTLEBAUM: Object to the argumentative.
COURT: Sustained.

Q. They didn't have him do it, to your knowledge, fair?
A. I—I don't know.

Here, opposing counsel gets a very rare win on his objection. What does Lanier do? He crafts a question that asks the witness to answer the question based on his personal knowledge.

Next, Lanier transitions to one of his last main points. Ironically, Lanier uses a word from his own question, "fair," to tie in the next series of questions about fairness. Use this trick next time in your cross. For example, you could use any word that helps with your theme. Instead of "fair," you could have asked a question about whether or not something was "true," and when the witness denies it, you could say in your next question, "I want to ask you some other questions about whether you were being truthful."

End Strong

Lanier knows the importance of ending his cross and the day on a strong point. He gets both opportunities with this witness. In the last four minutes of his cross at the end of the day, he challenges the witness on two points: Should the hip implants have been tested in humans before their sale, and does the witness consider his PowerPoint slides that contrast overweight women wearing thongs with thin women to be inappropriate?

Q. *Sir, if you're going to put a product in people that has not been tested in people, if you're going to sell something that's dangerous without testing it in people to see its risks level, you need to at least warn people it's not been tested so they can decide, hey, I'm willing to take the risks, or, no, thank you, I'll go with something that's already been checked out a little more thoroughly.* **[first time Lanier asks this question]**

MR. QUATTLEBAUM: Objection to compound, 401, 403, calls for a legal conclusion.
COURT: Overruled.
WITNESS: There are a whole lot of parts in there. Would you like to break it down a little bit for me?

Q. *If I can do it in four minutes. Let's try. Let's break it down this way: If you're selling a dangerous product that hasn't been tested in people, you ought to warn the people of that. Fair?* **[second time Lanier asks this question]**

MR. QUATTLEBAUM: Same objections, if that's acceptable to the court to say it that way.
COURT: Yes, sir. It's acceptable to say it that way. Overruled.

Lanier has written the proposition in red letters on a blank sheet of paper and displays it on the ELMO (Fig. 3). He forces the witness to answer a simple question. It does not matter what he answers, as long as the jury knows what the correct answer should be. Lanier knows that anyone would want a company to answer "yes" to that question. Watch what happens next.

Q. *Fair?*
A. No. I—I don't—I think that is not—that doesn't represent what happens. But you put the—the dangerous product, assuming that, yes, you know, it's known to be, as you define dangerous . . .

Figure 3. ELMO exhibit used to end cross-examination strongly.

Q. *OK. I'm removing this from the Pinnacle metal-on-metal in just a moment. We'll zoom in on that. I'm just asking you, period. I mean, surely, if you're selling a dangerous product that hasn't been tested in people you ought to warn folks of it before they buy it and put it in, shouldn't you?* [**third time Lanier asks this question**]

MR. QUATTLEBAUM: Same objections, your Honor.
COURT: Overruled.
WITNESS: So the way that you've set this up proposes that the danger is known. And I'm not agreeing that's the case.

Q. *OK. If that's your concern, I'll fix it.* [**Lanier listens, is flexible, and is fair.**] *If you're selling a possibly dangerous product that hasn't been tested, this might be dangerous to you, we don't know. Are you following me so far?*
A. Yes, sir.

Q. *If you're selling a possibly dangerous product that hasn't been tested in people, you still ought to warn folks of that, shouldn't you?* **[fourth time Lanier asks this question]**

MR. QUATTLEBAUM: 401, 403, lack of foundation, and calls for a legal conclusion.
COURT: Overruled.

Lanier uses green ink to write the word "possibly" on figure 3. Lanier is not worried. Wouldn't jurors believe that a company should still conduct tests even if the product is "possibly" dangerous?

WITNESS: —I think that every prosthetic joint is possibly dangerous.

MR. LANIER: Objection, nonresponsive.
COURT: Overruled.

Q. *I'm not asking about other joints that have been tested that may or may not be dangerous and what the tests have shown and all the rest. I'm talking about if you've got a possibly dangerous product that has not been tested in people, surely before you sell that to people you would want to warn them? Am I not—you're saying, no, don't warn them, just sell it to them. Which—what's your position—warn or not warn — Dr. Schmalzried?* **[fifth time Lanier asks this question]**

Lanier then writes in blue ink: "T.S. [Thomas Schmalzried]: WARN or NOT." He wants the jury to see and hear the answer, he wants to intimidate the witness by asking him and showing him the question with his name by the answer, and he wants to use the exhibit (figure 3) to show to other witnesses and to remind the jury in closing argument.

MR. QUATTLEBAUM: 401, 403, argumentative, compound, and calls for a legal conclusion.
COURT: Overruled.

WITNESS: I counsel all my patients on the potential risks of the surgery that they're having, irrespective of the device.

Q. *Is that a yes or no? Warn or not? If you're selling a possibly dangerous product—*
A. I —

Q. *— that hasn't been tested in people, should you warn people of that?* **[sixth time Lanier asks this question]**

MR. QUATTLEBAUM: Same objections, Your Honor.
COURT: Overruled.

WITNESS: I warn people categorically whether the product has been tested in people or not.

Q. *Is that a yes answer, you should warn? Should you tell people—* **[seventh time Lanier asks this question]**
A. I do.

Q. *Should you tell people this is not yet—this may be dangerous, this has not yet been tested in people? Should you tell that to people?* **[eighth time Lanier asks this question]**
A. That's the part where—where we diverge.

Q. *I'm not—I'm not —*
A. I tell—I tell—I'm not finished. I tell everyone of the risks of surgery, regardless of the degree of clinical testing or not.

Q. *But that's not my question, sir. My question is if you're selling a possibly dangerous product that hasn't been tested, do you warn folks of the fact it hasn't been tested? Do you?* **[ninth time Lanier asks this question]**
A. I—I—I don't—I do not warn people that it hasn't been tested, preclinical—preclinical testing. I have not done that.

Q. *Wow. OK.*

When Lanier gets the witness's answer after having asked the same question nine times, he draws a box around the word "NOT" on figure 3. Lanier wins the battle because he has the power of logical reasoning on his side. He knows that the witness cannot say a company should test a possibly dangerous product before selling it because he was part of DePuy's efforts not to do that. By writing out the question, showing it to the jury, and highlighting the witness's disingenuous answer, he creates a very memorable moment in the trial.

Also, each of the eight times that the witness does not answer the simple question, the jury votes in their mind whether the question is fair or the multiple refusals to answer is fair. Also, the jury cannot help but decide who is more likeable, the attorney or the witness.

The last point Lanier discusses is one of the witness's PowerPoint presentations. (It was mentioned in the cross-examination of Ekdahl in chapter 7.) Dr. Schmalzried used the PowerPoint "Big Balls and Thin Liners" to promote metal-on-metal hip implants. There were inappropriate slides in it. For example, one had a picture of an obese woman's rear end with a thong and a thin woman wearing a thong with the caption, "Which is better?" Other slides had phrases that had a double entendre with sexual connotations. The PowerPoint fit into Lanier's theme that Schmalzried wore hats other than just being a doctor.

Q. *Last thing I want to talk to you about is the PowerPoint that the jury has seen that you gave in Current Concepts entitled "Big Balls and Thin Liners." Do you remember that PowerPoint, sir?*
A. I do.

Q. *It was an offensive PowerPoint, agreed?*
A. Not to the audience that I presented it to. **[An incredible answer that states that the PowerPoint was appropriate for doctors and other professionals.]**

Q. *Well, sir, I put it on the screen. That's body shaming. You don't think that's offensive?*
A. I apologize for this slide. It was not intended for this audience.

Q. *It's not appropriate for any audience, is it?*
A. It was appropriate to the audience that I presented it to, in my opinion. [**The witness doubles down on his previous incredible answer.**]

Q. *Whew. And you gave it not just once. You gave it multiple times, didn't you?*
A. Maybe twice. I—I don't know the number. . . .

Q. *But now looking back, surely you'll agree, "It's not the position. It's not the material. The critical issue is the size of the butt?" You can't justify that to any audience—*
A. I'll stand by my presentation, sir.

Q. *What does the "size of the butt" have to do with anything scientific here in your presentation, aside from getting a laugh, at this lady's expense? You put this PowerPoint together, didn't you?*
A. Yes, sir. . . .
LANIER: I'll pass the witness, your Honor.

8.2 SUMMARY OF MARK LANIER'S CROSS-EXAMINATION STYLE

Now that we have studied three cross-examinations by Lanier, let's recap the techniques he has used. He begins the cross-examination by boldly telling and writing on a sheet of paper on the ELMO what he wants to prove on cross. For example, one of the themes for Ekdahl's cross-examination is that "Marketing/sales runs the company not science." For the cross-examination of Schmalzried, Lanier uses three baseball caps to show the jury that Schmalzried was a doctor, marketer, and salesman. The themes are based on the documents he has that can prove his point. It is that simple.

During cross-examination, Lanier always accompanies his questions with a visual aid such as a trial exhibit, a drawing he has created, or a list he has made. Let's examine each visual aid separately to make sure you understand them so that you can duplicate them in your next deposition or trial. When Lanier shows the witness a trial exhibit, for example, the consulting agreement to prove that Schmalzried was involved in marketing, he reads from the document and simultaneously highlights the relevant passage that he is reading. He then goes back over the document and circles the key words from the passage with a felt-tip pen. That way, the jury gets to see and hear the damaging words on the document twice. To make his points and to satisfy the requirement that a question is asked, Lanier will intersperse his reading/highlighting/circling of words with the question, "Do you see that?" The witness is forced to say "yes."

When Lanier draws his simple drawings such as a human with the red dots inside of him to signify the toxic nanoparticles, the jury cannot help but empathize with Lanier's less than professional drawing skills. The jurors, trying to be impartial, fight back smiles when Lanier begins to draw a simple picture to battle a witness who is giving disingenuous and complicated answers. More important, the drawings are so simple and straightforward that they mirror the direct questions Lanier asks the witness. Consequently, there is a rhythm that Lanier creates: direct question with a simple drawing, which results in either an admission or an evasive answer. It is a winning formula every time.

The third category of visual aids that Lanier uses is that of his writing: either a list of points that he is going to prove or the written form of the very question he is asking orally. The list provides a road map for the jury so that it knows where Lanier is headed. Lanier then will refer to the list after each point has been proven so the jury can see what he has accomplished and what is left to do.

Perhaps the most dramatic moments of Lanier's cross-examinations come when he writes out the major questions in very large letters on a sheet on the ELMO and waits to fill in the answer given by the witness. This happened multiple times with all the witnesses, but the most recent example is when Lanier asked Schmalzried if he agreed that "If you're selling a possibly dangerous product that hasn't been tested in people, you ought to warn folks of that." He then wrote, "WARN or NOT," and waited for Schmalzried's answer. Lanier got the benefit of asking the question nine times while the written question was displayed for the jury. The witness dodged or evaded eight times before finally saying that he would not warn.

Why is it so effective to write out these questions in large letters? Because Lanier knows that there is only one common-sense answer to each of them. He chooses the wordings of these questions very carefully. Consequently, as soon as he finishes asking the question and writing it, the jury immediately uses their common sense to answer the question the only way that common sense dictates. When the witness answers differently or takes a long time to answer the question, the jury discredits the answer and ultimately the witness.

Lanier's technique here also involves the creation of an episodic memory for the jury, the importance of which Lanier mentioned at the beginning of chapter 6. An episodic memory is one that people remember the most, like a first romantic kiss. Lanier approximates an episodic memory by getting the jury to participate in the question that is being asked. When the question is displayed on the ELMO, the jury gets to read the question and silently determine whether the witness dodges it or answers it head-on. The jurors becomes very active decision-makers in whether the witness is evasive or not.

In addition, when a witness does not answer a question, Lanier sometimes repeats it, but usually he objects that the answer is non-responsive and gets the judge to instruct the witness to answer the question, or he just repeats the question after the judge grants his objection. Either method is effective.

As you have seen, Lanier is a master of the documents and can quickly find an impeaching document to prove his point. He is very well prepared and extremely organized.

Finally, there is Lanier's presence. Courtroom observers, including myself, coalesce around a few adjectives to describe him. The first is likability. It is the most important quality you can bring to the courtroom. Jurors like and appreciate him because he is always attentive to their needs. He empowers them in his opening statement to help make a difference for his clients. His cross-examinations are direct, creative, and supplemented with a variety of visual aids, and his tone is firm but not argumentative. The transcripts do not have the ability to fully convey Lanier's demeanor, but if they could, you would see that Lanier's tone of voice is respectful, even in the most heated moments of a long cross-examination in a long trial. He does not lose his patience.

Lanier is also enthusiastic. He brings a love and passion for what his case is all about to his cross-examinations that creates positive energy in the courtroom. As soon as the other lawyer finishes, Lanier cannot wait to get out of his chair, dash to the podium, and get started. As mentioned earlier, his very first question gets right to the point. He is also an enthusiastic listener. If the witness makes a good point, Lanier will admit it and adjust his next question to fit that answer. Likewise, if the witness evades the question, Lanier listens carefully, seizes on the non-answer, and zeroes in to make sure the witness answers the question by repeating it. On a scale of one to 10, while most lawyers have an energy level of four and an interesting factor of three, Lanier has an energy level of eight (because 10 would be too much) and an interesting factor of 10.

On a higher level, Lanier's artistry works this way: when you see someone who deeply believes in what they are doing and performs their craft well (in this case, cross-examination), you cannot help but become very curious and interested in what they are doing. You are going to pay attention. And once you pay attention, Lanier has an opportunity to persuade you, and with his accomplished skills, it becomes "game over" for the other side.

8.3 CHAPTER CHECKLIST

Cross of Dr. Schmalzried

Since some of the skills Lanier executed on Schmalzried were the same as those analyzed in the previous chapters, only the different ones will be summarized.

1. Lanier accuses the doctor of wearing many different hats, and with each question he asks, Lanier puts on one of three different navy baseball hats, each of which has the words "doctor," "salesman," or "marketer" written on them, to match his corresponding theme and question.

2. When a witness doesn't answer a question, Lanier objects, "non-responsive," and asks the court to instruct the witness to answer the question.
3. Whenever Lanier reads a document that is displayed on the ELMO, he either highlights or underlines the passage he reads so the jury can follow along easily. Most attorneys make the mistake of just reading the document or pointing to a paragraph with their finger.
4. After Lanier highlights and marks the exhibit, he asks the witness, "Do you see that?" There is only one truthful answer. If the witness says anything different than "yes," you have shown his evasiveness and can ask the court to instruct the witness to answer a simple question.
5. Ask only leading questions to force a witness to give specific answers that you want the jury to hear. However, an exception to this rule is when it doesn't matter what the answer is, because you already have proof of that answer (such as a written document). In that case, a non-leading question is acceptable.
6. The key to being a great cross-examiner is to listen, listen, and listen.

PART III

Famous Trials

Part III analyzes the deciding cross-examination from the Proposition 8 trial where the plaintiffs challenged California's Proposition 8, which banned gay marriages. The trial was so important that it became a Broadway play performed as a stage reading. In addition, the entire trial transcripts were read by Hollywood actors and broadcast on YouTube.

Part III also examines videos of cross-examinations from the O.J. Simpson and George Zimmerman trials. Those trials were selected because of the compelling facts that caused the nation to follow them intensely. In addition, the trials were broadcast on television, so you can view videos of the cross-examinations on the book's website.

Once you see the successful application of cross-examination techniques and memorable mistakes that were made in these trials, you are likely to never forget them, given the high stakes involved. The judge has instructed that the jury be brought into the courtroom and the bailiff announces, "All rise for the jury." Let's watch the action unfold.

CHAPTER NINE

The Proposition 8 Trial

"Let me jump right to the bottom line, OK, sir?"—*David Boies*

The first trial that we are going to examine is *Perry v. Schwarzenegger*, more commonly known as the Proposition 8 Trial. Not only was the trial fascinating, but it featured David Boies as one of the principle lawyers for the plaintiffs. His outstanding skills merit close examination. Boies has been selected as one of the 100 Most Influential People in the World by *Time* magazine (2010) and has been named Global International Litigator of the Year by *Who's Who Legal* an unprecedented seven times.

He has been involved in many famous cases, including the one we are going to examine here. Boies gained widespread notoriety for his cross-examination in a deposition of Bill Gates when he represented the Department of Justice in its antitrust lawsuit against Microsoft in the late 1990s. He became a household name when he represented Al Gore before the United States Supreme Court in *Bush v. Gore*, which decided the recount question of Florida's votes in the 2000 presidential election. In a 5–4 decision, the Court essentially allowed Florida's previous certification of Bush as the winner of its electoral votes to stand.

Ironically, his co-counsel for the case below was Ted Olson, who represented Bush in that decision. Olson is a former United States Solicitor General who has argued over 50 cases before the Supreme Court.

David Boies has spoken publicly many times about his struggles with dyslexia, including how he did not learn to read until he was in the third grade. Significantly, it does not affect his writing, and he has an incredible memory and his arguments are extremely well organized.

CHAPTER ROAD MAP

- Analyze Boies's techniques for cross-examining an expert witness.
- Learn how to cross-examine to support your case.
- Discover how to handle a witness who quibbles with your question.

In *Redeeming the Dream: The Case for Marriage Equality* (2014: Viking Press, New York), his co-counsel on the case, Ted Olson, says that Boies's most notable cross-examination skills are patience and focus: "He can't be brushed aside or worn down by an evasive witness. He will calmly persevere, certain of what he is going for, and he will remember exactly, literally verbatim, what a witness said in answer to a prior question an hour before, several hours earlier, or even the previous day." Olson further states that Boies "has an avuncular style—gracious, polite, respectful—but intense and relentless nevertheless."

9.1 SUMMARY OF *PERRY V. SCHWARZENEGGER*

The bench trial of *Perry v. Schwarzenegger* started on January 11, 2010, and contains several excellent cross-examinations, one of which will be examined in-depth shortly. The trial was so momentous that it became a Broadway play performed as a stage reading. It was directed by Rob Reiner and had an all-star cast, including George Clooney, Brad Pitt, Martin Sheen, and Jamie Lee Curtis. (You can view it at www.winningatcross.com.)

It all started in May 2008, when a lawsuit known as *In re Marriage Cases* reached the California Supreme Court, and the court held that California's statutes limiting marriage to a man and a woman violated California's Constitution. But later that year, California voters—by only four percentage points—passed Proposition 8, an amendment to California's Constitution that stated that a marriage could only be between a man and a woman.

As a result, the lawsuit *Perry v. Schwarzenegger* was filed. It was brought by the American Foundation for Equal Rights (AFER) on behalf of two couples, Kristen Perry and Sandra Steir, and Paul Katami and Jeffrey Zarillo, who had been denied marriage licenses based on their sexual orientation.

On August 8, 2010, Judge Vaughn Walker ruled in favor of the plaintiffs. He found that Proposition 8 was unconstitutional under the 14th Amendment to the U.S. Constitution. The defendant appealed, and the Ninth Circuit stayed Judge Walker's ruling until it could reach a decision. The Ninth Circuit eventually upheld Judge Walker's ruling but issued a stay until arguments were heard by the U.S. Supreme Court.

On June 26, 2013, the United States Supreme Court issued a 5–4 decision that essentially preserved Judge Walker's decision that Proposition 8 was unconstitutional and that gays and lesbians had the right to get married in California. On June 26, 2015, the U.S. Supreme Court decided *Obergefell v. Hodges* and legalized same-sex marriages throughout the United States.

As mentioned above, Boies and Olson represented the plaintiffs. Charles Cooper was the lead lawyer for the defendant. His client was ProtectMarriage.

com, the official proponent of Proposition 8 and the coalition behind the 2008 "Yes on 8" campaign in California. ProtectMarriage.com intervened because California's attorney general at the time, Jerry Brown, and California's governor, Arnold Schwarzenegger, did not want to defend the lawsuit because they felt Proposition 8 was unconstitutional. Among many other accomplishments, Cooper was an Assistant Attorney General in the Department of Justice in the Reagan Administration and was listed by the *National Law Journal* as one of the top 10 civil litigators in Washington, D.C. He has argued before the Supreme Court several times and was a clerk to Justice William Rehnquist.

The litigation skills of both sides were at a very high level. But at this trial, Boies and Olson were better than their highly skilled opponent, Charles Cooper.

9.2 SUMMARY OF OPENING STATEMENTS

To better understand the following cross-examination, we need to briefly look at the opening statements and the main issues in the case as told to the judge by each side. Ted Olson began by stating his bottom line message: "This case is about marriage and equality." He then explained that "the Supreme Court of the United States has repeatedly described the right to marriage as one of the most vital personal rights essential to the orderly pursuit of happiness, a basic civil right, a component of the constitutional rights to liberty, privacy, association, an intimate choice, an expression of emotional support and public commitment, the exercise of spiritual unity, and the fulfillment of one's self."

As you will remember from chapter 1, it is important to capture the jury's or judge's attention immediately with what I call a "lightning bolt." Here, Olson cites the highest court in the country as his lightning bolt to support his bottom line message.

He further argued that "the plaintiffs are two loving couples, American citizens entitled to equality and due process under our constitution. They are in deeply committed, intimate, and long-standing relationships." He pointed out that Proposition 8 violated the plaintiffs' rights under the due process clause of the 14th Amendment. He further explained that Proposition 8 was born out of prejudice, it stigmatized same-sex couples, and procreation is not a main reason for marriage.

Charles Cooper argued for the defense that "[o]n November 4, 2008, 14 million Californians went to the polls to cast their ballots on an issue of overriding social and cultural importance: Whether the institution of marriage should be redefined to include couples of the same sex. . . ." Proposition 8 was needed to restore the traditional definition of marriage that was taken away by the California Supreme Court's ruling that same-sex marriages were legal. In short, he reasoned that a court should not impose its will against the wishes of its citizens on such a fundamental right. He said that heterosexual procreation was a main reason for marriage and that Proposition 8 did not create hatred or animosity toward gays and lesbians. Furthermore, the consequences of same-sex marriages on society and children are unclear and the voters should be allowed to decide this important issue.

9.3 SUMMARY OF DIRECT EXAMINATION OF BLANKENHORN (PART I)

David Blankenhorn was *the* key expert witness for the defense in the area of marriage, fatherhood, and family structure. Before we look at Boies effective cross-examination, it is necessary to see what defense attorney Charles Cooper elicited from Blankenhorn on direct. First, Cooper laid the foundation for Blankenhorn's ability to give an expert opinion in the three areas just mentioned. As you read the summary, think of ways you would cross-examine Blankenhorn. Then, we will look at how Boies tackles what appears to be an invulnerable witness.

Cooper established that Blankenhorn graduated from Harvard University in 1977 *magna cum laude* with a B.A. in social studies. He then obtained a master's degree in history from University of Warwick in Coventry, England.

After serving as a community organizer for several years in poor communities in the United States, he started the Institute for American Values in 1987. The organization commissions research and issues a "Report to the Nation" that focuses on fatherhood, marriage, family structure, and the well-being of children.

It also produces a periodic report, "Why Marriage Matters: Conclusions from the Social Sciences." That report is a consensus of 15 scholars from different political spectrums on the subject of marriage.

Blankenhorn is personally involved in the research and publications of his organization. He has also authored two books. His first one, *Fatherless America*, was widely reviewed. That book was a study of the consequences of having 35 percent of U.S. children living apart from their fathers. For that book, Blankenhorn interviewed fathers in six cities and surveyed scholarship on the role of fathers. The book was favorably reviewed in every major newspaper, including the *New York Times*.

His other book is *The Future of Marriage*. It looks at trends in marriages and how the institution can be improved. For this book, he held a literature review and conducted a series of consultations with an interdisciplinary group of scholars. Although it was not as widely reviewed as his first book, it led to him being asked to speak around the country. Dale Carpenter, an internationally known law professor at the University of Minnesota who is a proponent of gay marriage, said that the book was "probably the best single book yet written opposing gay marriage. Blankenhorn is a serious scholar and thinker."

In addition to authoring books, Blankenhorn has also co-edited several books, including: *The Black Fathers in Contemporary American Society; The Book of Marriage; Promises to Keep*; and *Rebuilding the Nest*. The books he has written and edited have been peer-reviewed and cited over 50 times in academic journals. His writings have also been cited in five judicial opinions.

Finally, Blankenhorn has been a member of several commissions, including the Commission on America's Urban Families, which was appointed by President George Bush in 1992 to examine the state of America's urban families. He was also asked by Vice President Gore to work with him on a program called Family Reunion. He has also provided testimony three times on same-sex marriages and fatherhood before legislatures.

After asking the witness about his expertise, Cooper asked the court to recognize him as an expert in the area of marriage, fatherhood, and family structure. The court asked Boies if he wanted to ask the witness questions (voir dire) to challenge his expertise, and Boies said, "yes."

One of the most important keys to successful cross-examination is to listen and pay close attention to what is being said. While Blankenhorn's credentials might seem overwhelming to an opposing attorney, think about the summary you just read and find the weaknesses: a lot was said, but a lot was also not said. Watch how Boies exploits these weaknesses.

9.4 BOIES CONDUCTS VOIR DIRE OF THE EXPERT

As discussed in chapter 4, in order to testify at trial, an expert must satisfy the Daubert standard, which is a rule of evidence regarding the admissibility of an expert witness's scientific testimony; it is based in part on the U.S. Supreme Court case *Daubert v. Merrell Dow Pharmaceuticals, Inc.*, 509 U.S. 579 (1993). Federal judges and many state judges use this to determine whether an expert's opinion is trustworthy. A judge uses the following criteria: whether a theory or technique can be (and has been) tested, whether it has been subjected to peer review and publication, the known or potential rate of error, and whether the theory or technique is generally accepted.

In a jury trial, judges often hold a Daubert hearing prior to trial if a party intends to challenge an expert's qualifications at trial. In a bench trial, it can easily be done during the witness's testimony, because the trial would not need to be interrupted as it would in a jury trial. In that case, the jury is often excused while the attorney questions the opposing expert to in order to disqualify him from further testimony because he does not meet the Daubert requirements.

> **Practice Tip**
>
> Whether in a deposition or a trial, an expert's claimed expertise can almost always be successfully undercut. Experts have a bad habit of exaggerating their prowess.

If you would like to see Hollywood actors reenacting this trial, go to YouTube and search for Proposition 8 Trial Reenactment. The following testimony can be found on Day 11 Chapter 3 in the video beginning at 7:10 and ending at 20:20. It is also on the book's website.

Here, Boies uses the "C" (*credibility*) of CROSS (see chapter 2) to undermine the witness's testimony on direct.

Q. You got a master's degree, and that degree was in history; is that right?
A. Yes, sir. Comparative labor history.

Q. And you did a thesis for that master's?
A. Yes, sir.

Q. And what was that thesis in?
A. Labor history.

Q. Was it a particular subject?
A. Yes, sir. It was a study of two cabinetmakers' unions in nineteenth century Britain. And it was published in a peer-reviewed academic book several years after I wrote it.

So much for the expert's education helping him. Through just three simple questions, Boies establishes that his master's degree has nothing to do with the issues in the lawsuit. Boies notices from the witness's choice of words—that his thesis was published in a "peer-reviewed" book—that he is getting defensive. Instead of retreating from the expert's answer—as he would have had he not listened carefully—Boies attacks.

Q. Now, "peer-reviewed," you just said. What is your understanding of what a peer-reviewed publication is?
A. It's a publication that prior to being published is reviewed by competent persons to give—to give their views on whether or not—first, whether or not the article should be published. And then, if it should, whether it requires revisions.

Q. Now, other than the thesis that you wrote on cabinetmakers in Britain, have you ever had a peer-reviewed publication?
A. Yes, sir.

Q. And what was that?
A. Well, I co-edited . . . called Black Fathers in Contemporary American Society, that was published by Russell Sage Press. That was a peer-reviewed publication.

Q. Anything else?
A. No, sir. To the best of my memory, that's it. Except it might be of interest to note that in my own organization, where over the past 20 years many of my pieces of work have

been published, we have, to the best of our ability, instituted our **own peer-review process**. And we've been very scrupulous about carrying that out because of our high regard for the entire process. [**Boies never lets the witness take control of the testimony. He fires right back as seen next.**]

Q. *But you do understand that "peer-reviewed," as is normally used—*
A. I am using it as it's normally used.

Q. *"Peer-reviewed," as it is normally used does not refer to something that you do internally. It's done by somebody independent, correct?*
A. All of our peer reviews are done by external people that have no connection to the Institute or the work that we're doing.

Q. *And are you saying that those independent people peer-reviewed your work?*
A. Yes, sir. [**Boies loses some ground here but regroups quickly by reminding the witness in the next question of his previous answer that there were only two peer-reviewed works.**]

Q. *OK. Now, I thought I had two pieces of peer-reviewed publications.*
A. I thought that the import of your question was to exempt from our consideration things that were published by my own organization, for reasons that you're implying. And I'm happy to stipulate that let's bracket that and just say that, apart from anything that was published by my own organization, where you could question, if you wish, the integrity of the peer-review process—although, **I think, if you were familiar with it you would not question it; but as an outsider you may question it**—let's bracket that for a moment and just say everybody else. We're looking at two publications only. [**Here, the witness talks down to Boies, which hurts the witness's credibility because it makes him less likeable.**]

Q. *And those two publications didn't have anything to do with same-sex marriage or the effects of same-sex marriage, correct?*
A. No, sir.

Q. *In other words, I'm correct?*
A. You're correct. They did not.

Boies wins. He has now established that the only two independently peer-reviewed works, as the phrase is commonly used, had nothing to do with the issue before the court. Boies now turns his attention back to the witness's education.

Q. *You have* ***never taught a course*** *in any college or university* ***on marriage****, correct?*
A. No, sir.

Q. *And you have* ***never taught a course*** *in any college or university* ***on fatherhood****, correct?*
A. No, sir.

Q. *And you've* ***never taught a course*** *in any college or university* ***on family structure****?*
A. No, sir.

Q. And do you understand that the fields of psychology and sociology and anthropology are relevant to the subjects of marriage and fatherhood and family structure?
A. That is my understanding, yes, sir.

Q. And you've ***never gotten*** *any kind of* ***degree in psychology****, correct?*
A. No, sir.

Q. Or in psychiatry?
A. No, sir.

Q. Or in sociology?
A. No, sir.

Q. Or in anthropology?
A. I think we could go through the whole list because I've enumerated for you all the degrees I have. [**Although Boies could have combined his three questions, he breaks them down into several questions to emphasize to the judge the witness's lack of relevant education.**]

> **Practice Tip**
>
> Frequency is a great tool to use to help a fact finder remember your point. Never ask a complex question if it can be broken down into several simple ones, so you can repeat the idea you want the fact finder to remember.

Q. And you've ***never taught any course in any college*** *and university—*
A. I have **never been employed by a university** or a college to teach—

Q. In any capacity?
A. —in any way, ever.

After showing that Blankenhorn has no teaching experience, Boies attacks his claim that his testimony in other courts supports his expertise.

Q. And you said you had testified three times. Were any of those three times relating to the effects of same-sex marriage?
A. No, sir.

In this next series of questions, notice how effectively Boies gets the witness to answer his question and how evasive the witness becomes. In the end, it will be obvious that the witness would have had more credibility if he had just answered the questions Boies asked him.

Q. ***In preparation for your testimony, did you undertake any scientific study*** *of what the effects of permitting same-sex marriage had been in any jurisdiction in which same-sex marriage had been permitted?*
A. Specifically in preparation for my testimony, did I undertake such study? The answer to that would be, no, sir, I did not.

Q. OK. ***Independent of the preparation for your testimony,*** *have you conducted any* ***scientific study*** *as to what the effects of permitting same-sex marriage were in any of the jurisdictions where same-sex marriage was permitted?*

A. Well, I have undertaken **a study** of that question in the best way I know how. Whether or not it would meet your definition of "scientific" is probably something we might have to explore. I would be happy to tell you what I did.

Q. *Let me explore it. You are saying that you undertook an attempt to study what the effects were of permitting same-sex marriage in various jurisdictions where same-sex marriage was permitted; is that your—*

A. No, sir. [**Boies has simply summarized the witness's prior answer using the witness's word "study" instead of Boies' phrase "scientific study." But when the witness hears his answer summarized, he knows that he has exaggerated by using the simple word "study" and tries to back off even more.**]

Q. *OK.*

A. I want to say what I did do, though, if I may be permitted.

Q. *Let me be sure I've got answers to my questions first, though, OK, sir.* [**Boies never lets the witness gain control of the examination.**]

A. I thought you were asking me did I undertake independent of this preparation from testimony, I thought your question was: Did I undertake **any effort to understand** the likely consequences of adopting same-sex marriage? And I wish to tell you that I did. [**Now the witness has backed off the word "study" completely and is using the phrase "any effort to understand."**]

Q. *No. I'm sure you would like to answer questions that I'm not asking, sir. (Laughter) And you'll have a chance to do that with your counsel. I would like you to listen to the question I'm asking you, OK, because I think your question kind of* ***slided over a couple of words.*** [**Boies has listened carefully to the expert's answers and notices the witness is trying to wiggle out of the question being asked.**]

Q. *My question was whether you had conducted* ***any study****, in connection with your expert work or otherwise, of the effects of permitting same-sex marriage in the countries where same-sex marriage was permitted? That begins with a yes or no answer.*

A. I don't think I'm able to answer that question yes or no, if those are my only two choices. [**The witness does not want to admit his lack of studies.**]

Q. *Well, the question is whether you have attempted to* ***study*** *the effects of same-sex marriage in the jurisdictions where they have been permitted. You have either attempted to do that or not attempted to do that. It may very well have been that you attempted to do something entirely different or even related to it. But I'm not asking that, do you understand?*

A. May I tell you what I did do?

Q. *I would like you to answer my question, Do you understand what my question is?*

A. No, sir, because—

Q. *If you don't understand my question, anytime you don't understand my question, please let me know.*

A. I'm letting you know now. [**Boies knows that his questions have been clear, but he shows great patience. He will ask his questions as many times as necessary to get the answer he wants.**]

Q. OK. Let me try to be as clear as I can. You are aware that there are some jurisdictions that have permitted same-sex marriage?
A. I am so aware.

Q. OK. Now, have you **studied** *any of those jurisdictions to try to determine what the effect of permitting same-sex marriage in those jurisdictions has been, subsequent to the time that same-sex marriage was adopted?*
A. The answer to your question is: Yes. **[Now, the witness says he has studied.]**

Q. As long as you answered yes, then I can begin to ask more questions.
A. I'm just afraid that you won't accept my definition of "study." And I don't want to try to say something that is—is—that it doesn't meet your definition of a study. **[The witness knows he is in trouble either way. He knows that he has not conducted any scientific studies and his definition of study (see following statements) is not very rigorous.]**

Q. Well, I will explore that. I will explore that. But I would like to do it in an orderly way. And the first thing I'd like to do is, I'd like you to identify which jurisdictions you have, ***in your interpretation of the word "studied," studied****.*
A. I've tried to **pay some attention** to the evolution of the—of this phenomenon of same-sex marriage in the Scandinavian countries. And I have tried to **pay some attention** to the impact of same-sex marriage in Massachusetts. **[Now the witness has backed off the word "study" and is substituting "pay some attention" for it.]**

But what I was trying to say before is that, I have not engaged in a scientific study where I find data and—and write up an article that would be published of that nature. I have not done those things. That's what I was trying to say. I have not done those things.

I have just read articles and had conversations with people, and tried to be an informed person about it. But that is really the extent of it. I haven't developed a methodology or a set of expert, you know, findings about the topic that you're—I have not done that, the topic that you're asking me to address. **[Boies's persistence has paid off. Amazingly, the witness fought answering Boies's questions for several pages of transcript before finally revealing that he only "had conversations with people, and tried to be an informed person about it."]**

MR. BOIES: OK. Your Honor, I would object.
COURT: The objection is that the witness is not qualified to opine on the subject of marriage, fatherhood, and family structure, correct?

MR. BOIES: Yes. And in particular—and in particular, with respect to the effect of same-sex marriage, which is what he is being proffered to do within those general subjects.

***

COURT: OK. Well, the testimony is, of course, governed by the rules of evidence concerning opinion testimony. . . . the Court looks to whether the work that the witness has done meets the standards of intellectual rigor, using criteria much like those that have been developed in the Daubert case. . . .
With respect to Mr. Blankenhorn's qualifications, were this a jury trial, I think the question might be a close one.
But this being a court trial, I'm going to permit the witness to testify....

Even though the judge allowed Blankenhorn to testify as an expert, Boies successfully used the "C" of CROSS to undermine Blankenhorn's *credibility* in important ways. Here is a summary of what he proved.

SUMMARY OF FACTS BOIES PROVED

1. Master's degree was not in subject area of trial expertise.
2. Master's thesis was on unrelated topic: cabinetmakers' union.
3. No peer-reviewed publications regarding marriage.
4. No teaching experience on marriage.
5. No degrees in psychology, sociology, or anthropology.
6. No studies conducted on the effects of same-sex marriage.
7. Witness does not answer simple questions.

9.5 SUMMARY OF BLANKENHORN DIRECT EXAMINATION (PART II)

With that ruling, Cooper continued his direct examination of Blankenhorn. In order to understand Boies's cross of Blankenhorn, let's examine a summary of his testimony on direct.

Blankenhorn explained that the most important thing a marriage regulates is filiation. That is, it establishes who the child's legal and social parents are. It unites the biological, social, and legal dimensions of parenthood. This is true in societies around the world, both now and throughout history.

Also throughout history, marriage has addressed the "need for the child to know and be known by the two people, to make it as likely as we can, that the biological parents are also the social and legal parents." Blankenhorn cited the anthropologist Suzanne Frayser, who said that across cultures, "marriage is a relationship within which a group socially approves and encourages sexual intercourse and the birth of children."

Blankenhorn also referred to the sociologist, Kingsley Davis, who declared that marriage is the "approval of a couple's engaging in sexual intercourse and bearing and rearing offspring." Blankenhorn added, "I don't know how many [sociologists] we've discussed today, five or six. But you could multiply by 10 and you could get 50 or 60 distinguished people saying, in effect, this exact same thing."

Blankenhorn then discussed a competing view of marriage that has recently come forward that supports same-sex marriage. The Law Commission of Canada expressed this view in 2001, when it stated, "The state's objectives under-lying contemporary regulation of marriage relate essentially to the facilitation of private ordering, providing an orderly framework in which people can express their commitment to each other, receive public recognition and support, and voluntarily assume a range of legal rights and obligations."

Support for same-sex marriage also came from Yale Professor William Eskridge, who proclaimed that "in today's society, the importance of marriage is relational and not procreational."

Although Blankenhorn believes that this "relational" or "affective dimension" of marriage is important, it has never been understood to be the heart and soul of marriage. Indeed, in many cultures where marriages are arranged, it has little to do with marriage.

Blankenhorn then discussed the role of religion in marriage. He related to the court that religion did not invent marriage. For example, it does not matter if a society is monotheistic or believes in witchcraft, marriage exists. While it is true that religion and marriage in the U.S. and many countries are interconnected, marriage does not derive from "any ideas about the supernatural. It is what scholars call a natural institution. It derives from facts of our embodiment and reproduction that do not call upon supernatural beliefs for their coherence."

Cooper then asked Blankenhorn to explain why it matters that the child is raised by his own biological parents. Blankenhorn responded that one reason is "kin altruism." That phrase means that "we seem to care a lot about where we came from physically, and we seem to care a lot about the people to whom we are related, particularly closely related." So, humans have organized themselves so that their children can be cared for by their parents.

There is also a large body of literature that supports the proposition that the optimal environment for children is if they are raised from birth by their own natural mother who is married to their natural father. The outcomes of these children, whether it be financial or emotional success, are much better than the outcomes of other children.

Marriage also benefits the mother because it lessens the likelihood of her having to raise the child alone and in isolation. It benefits the father because it connects him to his own child and to the mother of his child in a way that would be unlikely for him to achieve in any other way.

Deinstitutionalization is when an institution such as marriage becomes weaker. For example, when an institution's rules and structures become weaker, the participants will, over time, lose respect for the institution.

Blankenhorn described how marriage over the past 50 years has already been deinstitutionalized. For example, 50 years ago, only a small fraction of U.S. children were born out of wedlock, but now, 38 percent of children are born to unmarried parents.

Also, the United States has the highest divorce rate in the world. So, the weakening of the ideal of marriage permanence "suggests a lessening loyalty to the institution. Other contributing facts that weaken marriage are: the rise of non-marital cohabitation, the increase of third-party participation in procreation and artificial assisted reproductive technologies, and the spread of the idea of same-sex marriage."

Blankenhorn warned that "if we move toward a widespread adoption of same-sex marriage, I believe the effect will be to significantly further and, in some respects, culminate the process of deinstitutionalization of marriage." For example, if you "transfer [marriage] from a child-centered public institution to an adult-centered private institution, a question of private ordering among couples, you have in some ways, you know, completed—that's a culminating trend toward the erasure of marriage's public defined contribution to society."

Blankenhorn testified that his conclusion was supported by many other scholars who believed that same-sex marriage would complete the deinstitutionalization of marriage.

He then discussed the consequences if same-sex marriages were allowed. He believed that there would be higher rates of non-participation in marriage, higher rates of one-parent homes, and a higher rate of divorce, to name but a few.

He also feared that based on his personal experience, he has faced hostility for simply saying that a child needs his father. "And I may sound simplistic, but simply being able to say that children need—a child needs its mother and father, if that becomes just impermissible in any venue, a church, a school, a civic group, a PTA meeting, I think we lose something precious."

Blankenhorn then discussed the changes that have occurred in Canada where same-sex marriages have recently been legalized. For example, Canada struck the term "natural parent" from Canadian law and replaced it with the term "legal parent." This gave the state more power to determine what a "legal parent" was. This increases the likelihood that children will be raised in family forms other than his own two natural parents.

In addition, "there could be the possibility of more public willingness to consider family forms, such as polygamy . . . ." For example, if you dilute the definition of marriage from being solely between a man and a woman, you have increased the possibility of polygamy, which has already challenged society.

Finally, Blankenhorn discussed his support of domestic partnerships as being a "humane compromise" in which society protects marriage but extends protection and recognition to gay and lesbian couples. Although he was originally against it because it might challenge the institution of marriage, he believes it is the fair thing to do for gays and lesbians.

But in the end, Blankenhorn's support for Proposition 8 could be boiled down to three principles: marriage must be between two people of opposite genders, it had to be limited to two people, and sexual intercourse was part of the relationship.

9.6 BOIES'S CROSS-EXAMINATION OF BLANKENHORN

As in previous chapters, when you read the cross-examination below, ask yourself which CROSS category (credibility, restrict the damaging testimony, outrageous statements, prior inconsistent statements, or support your case) Boies is illustrating when he questions the witness. By doing this, you will continue to train yourself to identify when great lawyers do it and then you can use it in your next cross. The answer will be given in the analysis of each section.

If you want to see a reenactment of the entire cross-examination, go to the www.winningatcross.com and view Boies clip 1.

Start Strong

Boies wastes no time. He challenges one of Blankenhorn's strongest assertions in support of marriage: children raised with one biological parent (either born out of wedlock or the result of divorce) are worse off than children that grow up with two married biological parents.

Boies immediately questions him about tab 16 from the exhibit binder, which was a book called *Growing Up with a Single Parent*, by Sara McLanahan. On direct, Blankenhorn stated that McLanahan was "one of the most prominent family sociologists in the country."

Q. *Good afternoon, Mr. Blankenhorn.*
A. Good afternoon.

Q. *Would you turn to tab 16 in your binder? (Witness complied.)*

Q. *And this was one of the documents that you indicated that you had relied on, is that correct?*
A. Yes, sir.

Q. *And Mr. Cooper directed your attention on the first page to a quotation where it said: "Children who grow up in a household with only one biological person are worse off on average than children who grow up in a household with both of their biological parents." Do you recall that?*
A. Yes, sir.

Q. *Now, there are a number of questions that I want to ask you about that, but did you understand the author here to be asserting that the fact that there was only one biological parent was causally related to the fact that the children were less well off?*
A. Yes, sir. That was my understanding—is my understanding.

Q. That is your understanding?
A. Yes, sir.

From the direct and this reaffirmation on cross, Blankenhorn would certainly want you to believe that being raised by only one biological parent would be a major reason why that child would be worse off than a child in a two-parent home. Boies has caught this expert in just the first of many exaggerations. Watch what happens.

Q. Now, did you read this entire chapter?
A. I read the entire book. **[Instead of simply answering the question, the witness gets defensive and will get burned for it.]**

*Q. **Let me see if you remember reading the very next page**, the first full paragraph. "But are single motherhood and [a father's] absence, therefore, the root cause of child poverty, school failure, and juvenile delinquency? Our findings lead us to say no. While living with just one parent increases the risk of each of these negative outcomes, **it is not the only or even the major cause of them.**" Do you recall reading that?*
A. I do. **[It is the only answer the witness can now give.]**

Q. Now, you referred a number of times in your testimony to biological parents; do you recall that?
A. Yes, sir.

Q. And you were not meaning to imply, were you, that biological parents were any better parents than adoptive parents?
A. No, sir.

Notice how in just a few questions Boies has undermined Blankenhorn's contention that it is in the child's best interest to be raised by two biological parents.

Did you notice which category of CROSS Boies used? He undermined the witness's *credibility* (the "C" of CROSS) by showing the judge that Blankenhorn and his attorney cherry-picked quotations to support their position.

> **Practice Tip**
>
> A key to a successful cross-examination is preparation. You must be intimately familiar with the materials the witness has relied on and the witness's prior statements and testimony.

After an exchange with the witness about different types of studies, Boies goes for the kill.

Q. Let me jump right to the bottom line, OK, sir?
A. Good.

Q. Are you aware of any studies showing that children raised from birth by a gay or lesbian couple have worse outcomes than children raised from birth by two biological parents?
A. No, sir. Would it be OK for me to say additional—

Q. It would not be OK for you to volunteer anything. I heard your—the speech that ended, and I'm really trying to move along; OK, sir? You will have a chance to make speeches when your counsel is asking you questions.
A. OK.

Notice that Boies does not follow Younger's commandment or Mauet's advice to ask subtle questions and tie everything up in closing. Instead, what does Boies do? Just like Girardi and Lanier, whom we studied earlier, he tells the witness and the judge exactly what he wants to prove on cross. He confidently proclaims: "Let me jump right to the bottom line, OK?"

Also, Boies never lets the witness get control of the examination. He firmly responds that he heard the witness's speech but points out the need to move forward.

Using a Hostile Witness to Support Your Case

A much-overlooked area of cross-examination techniques is to use the hostile witness to *support* your case by getting him to admit facts that will help you. This is the second "S" of CROSS.

Q. I'm going to try this morning to start with some things that perhaps we can agree on. You agree that marriage is an important public good, as you use that term, correct?
A. Yes, sir.

Q. And could you explain for the record what you mean by a "public good"?
A. I mean that it serves important public purposes, and marriage makes a distinctive contribution to society.

Q. And you believe that marriage is something that benefits both the participants in the marriage, the couple that are married, as well as any children that the couple may raise, correct?
A. Yes, sir.

Q. And you believe that legalizing gay and lesbian marriage would benefit gay and lesbian couples as well as any children they raise, correct?
A. I believe it would be **likely** to do so.

When the witness tries to back away from the proposition by using the word "likely," Boies confronts him. Boies knows that the witness must say "almost certain" because he has used that word in his own writings.

*Q. Well, you believe it would be **almost certain** to do so, correct, sir?*
A. I do believe it is **almost certainly true** that gay and lesbian couples and their children would benefit by having gay marriage.

Q. Now, you have said that, "If adopting same-sex marriage"—and I'm going to refer here to your book The Future of Marriage. And you have got that at tab 13 of the binder that I handed out, and I'm going to be looking at page 20. You can read along with me, if you would like. Tab 13 of the binder, page 20.
A. Yes, sir.

Q. And at the top of the page you write: "If adopting same-sex marriage was likely to be part of a larger societal shift leading to better marriages, less divorce and less unwed childbearing or, more modestly, if it seemed likely that adopting same-sex marriage would not significantly undermine efforts to renew our wider marriage culture, I am confident that most marriage advocates would favor its adoption. I know I would. But if adopting same-sex marriage is likely to impede that larger goal, I would be against it." And that's what you believe, correct, sir?
A. Yes, sir.

Q. And in saying that if adopting same-sex marriage would impede that goal, you would be against it, what you are saying is that you believe that the rights of gays and lesbians should take second place to the needs of an existing social institution, correct?
A. Well, maybe you could point me to the sentence.

Boies is at the ready and has the exact passage necessary if the witness does not answer the question the way he wants. Watch.

Q. Sure. It's actually the very next sentence. You say: "Those who disagree with me can charge that I am proposing a moral metric in which, regardless of the ultimate policy decision on same-sex marriage, the rights of gays and lesbians take second place to the needs of an existing social institution." Do you see that?
A. Yes, sir.

Q. And you say that the charge would be accurate, correct?
A. Yes, sir.

Q. And is it fair
A. I was trying to say that from the point—the answer to your question is yes. I just only might point out that I did say that I was saying I understood and accepted the validity of the argument of those who disagreed with me.

Q. Yes, I appreciate that, sir. Is it fair to summarize, to say that your choice would be to choose marriage as a public good over the rights and needs of gay and lesbian adults and those same-sex couples who are raising children?
A. Well, again, I would like you—I'm not trying to be difficult, but I would just like to see the sentence that you are referring to. **[Watch how Boies does not skip a beat and immediately points the witness to the information that answers his question.]**

Q. Sure. The very bottom of the page, the last sentence. You write: "To the degree that I must choose, with some anguish I will choose children's collective rights and needs. I will choose marriage as a public good over the rights and needs of gay and lesbian adults and those same-sex couples who are raising children." Do you see that?
A. Yes, sir. Mr. Boies, the whole purpose of my book was to argue—

Q. *I'm really not asking for the whole purpose of your book, and—*
A. I would just like to say that the sentences you're—it's an important point. The sentences that you are citing are an argument about what I call goods in conflict. I'm one of those persons who do not believe that this issue is a case of good versus bad. I believe and have gone to great lengths to say that I believe that there are valid arguments on both sides of the issue, and my book is an attempt to explore that. And these sentences you are selecting are examples of me exploring that, what I'm calling goods in conflict.

Here, the witness continues his practice from the proceeding day where he does not answer the question but gives a speech. The judge loses patience.

Judge Warns Witness Not to Be Evasive

Q. *And I thought you—*
A. It just helps to know what I'm trying to argue here.

Q. *And I thought you would be agreeable to what I'm pointing out to you. I just—*
A. I am agreeable. I'm just providing a context so that people can understand, and you can understand, why these sentences are stated as they are.

COURT: All right. Let's have a question and an answer.

Q. *In fact, in your book, The Future of Marriage, you list approximately 20 possible benefits of allowing gay and lesbian marriage, correct?*
A. Yes, sir. Those benefits that I listed in the book were a result of a collaborative discussion that I led and they involved advocates of both sides of the position. And we tried to come up with—over time we tried to come up with a list of the likely or possible benefits of gay marriage, the likely or possible disadvantages. And so I enumerated those in that chapter of my book. **[To answer the question, all the witness needed to say was "yes."]**

Q. *OK. Now, if you turn to page 203 of your book, again behind tab 13, it is the page with the heading "Goods In Conflict," and then the subheading "Positive Consequences."*
A. Yes, sir.

Q. *Now, what I'm going to do is I'm going to ask you just which of these you agree with, if any, because as I understand it, this was sort of a group thought experiment that was going on.*
A. Yes, sir.

Q. *And you put down on a white board a lot of ideas that people had, both for and against gay marriage, correct?*
A. Yes, sir.

Q. *OK. And you did not necessarily agree with any particular idea; you just wrote it down if it was brought up by somebody, correct?*
A. Well, there was a process, but the substance of what you're saying is correct.

Q. *OK. So what I want to know—because you are the witness here, I want to know which, if any, of these positive consequences of gay and lesbian marriage you agree with?*
A. Yes, sir. And I only wish to say that with each of them the issue that we discussed was likely; not definite, but likely.

Q. *Likely?*
A. Yes, sir.

Q. *So—*
A. Because these are all speculative in the sense that they are an attempt to predict something that will happen in the future. It's an important point. And so the issue is likely—

Q. *Mr. Blankenhorn. Mr. Blankenhorn, you may have important points to make.*
A. I think I do actually.

Q. *I know you do. I know you do. But this is not a debate.* **[a great response to use when the witness does not answer a question]**
A. No, sir. I'm trying to have you understand—

Q. *I'm trying to ask you a question.*
A.—the nature of what I wrote in the book.

Q. *I'm trying to ask you a question, sir.*
A. I'm doing my very best to answer your question.

COURT: All right. Let's not interrupt one another.
MR. BOIES: Your Honor, could I ask that the witness be instructed to listen to the question, answer my question and not make a statement that is not responsive to the question, even if he believes it's important.
WITNESS: I don't need such instruction. That's what—my intention is to do exactly that.

After the witness claims he doesn't need an instruction, notice what the court does.

COURT: Mr. Blankenhorn, one of the instructions that the Court gives to the jury when an expert witness testifies is to consider the witness's background, training and experience; the testimony that the witness gives; the reasons that the witness gives for the opinions that he expresses; and all of the other evidence in the case.

And all of that other evidence, of course, includes the demeanor of the witnesses. **And the demeanor of the witnesses is sometimes gauged, importantly, by the responsiveness of the witness to the questions that he's asked. So with that in mind, because I'm sure you would not want your demeanor on the stand to be a negative factor in your testimony, I would urge you to pay close attention to Mr. Boies's questions and to answer them directly, succinctly**. Then to the extent additional elaboration should be brought out, your very able counsel, I'm sure, Mr. Cooper, will be able to do that. So bear that in mind.

WITNESS: Yes, sir, I will.
COURT: All right. Fine.

> **Practice Tip**
>
> Remember the greatest myth of cross-examination is that you can get the witness to confess. As seen here, your goal is simply to prove his testimony is not to be believed.

For a brief period, Blankenhorn followed the judge's admonition, but then he reverted back to being evasive. This undermined his credibility, the "C" of CROSS.

Witness Tries to Evade Questions

Blankenhorn relied on a list of authors to support his opinions. Below, the witness evades directly answering Boies's question by asserting that the authors "stated or suggested" specific things about same-sex marriage. Boies always listens very carefully. He asks the witness to explain those terms, and then proceeds to methodically get Blankenhorn to admit that many experts he relied on did not state that same-sex marriage would be detrimental to heterosexual marriage.

A. I believe that a reason—as you put it, a reasonable reader, reading these materials, would conclude that this author has **stated or suggested** that adopting gay marriage would be likely to weaken marriage as a social institution.

Q. *Now, in that answer you said "stated or suggested." Do you use those terms interchangeably, synonymously or do you mean something different by them?*
A. I mean something different by them.

Q. *What do you mean?*
A. "Stated" would be an unequivocal assertion that is similar to the wording that you have offered in your—you know, an unmistakable, no possible way to doubt the declared intent of the sentence or the paragraph. A "suggestion" would be a way of making an argument, stating it so that a reasonable reader would understand clearly based on the written words that the author has a serious concern or a serious worry or is stating his or her belief that it would be likely that adopting gay marriage would weaken marriage as a social institution.

Q. *Now, with respect to the six items* [**authors' literature**] *that you have identified, let me ask the question separately.*
A. I was afraid that might be where we were going. [**Boies' persistence wears the witness down.**]

Q. *I'm getting predictable. Which of these in your testimony does the author, in this material, state—using "state" the way you have described it—that permitting gay and lesbian marriage would harm heterosexual marriage?*
A. Well, I think you would probably have to take Cherlin off the list. . . . Well, you might have to take Norval Glenn, number 27, off the list . . . but I cannot speak with certainty about [Agacinski] the exact form of words in this one book listed here called Parity of Sexes, so let's take her off the list as well.

If Boies had not been listening carefully, he never would have gotten these admissions. That is the difference between success and failure.

Example of the "O" of CROSS

One goal of cross is to get the witness to make an *outrageous statement*, the "O" of CROSS. If you can get the witness to make an outrageous statement that does not have the ring of truth, the witness will lose credibility and you will win.

On direct, Blankenhorn declared there were three rules of marriage, one of which was that it involved a ceremony between two people—what Blankenhorn called his "rule of two." Watch how Boies backs him into a corner and the witness gives him the "O" of CROSS.

Q. *Now, let me go on to your second rule, your second essential structure of the institution of marriage, which was the rule of two people.*
A. Yes, sir.

Q. *Now, you are obviously aware of a lot of examples of marriages that are inconsistent with that rule, correct?*
A. No, sir.

Q. *You are not? What percentage of marriages over the last 300 years have been limited to two people in your judgment?*
A. **The way that I and many other scholars have looked at this, the answer would be that almost every single marriage has been limited to two people**. . . .

Q. *First of all, you recognize that over the last 300 years there have been more polygamous marriages than there have been marriages that have been limited to two people; would you agree with that?*
A. I don't know, but—my strong suspicion would be that that is erroneous, but I do not know.

***

Q. *Let me ask you some questions about that. What societies are you aware of that prior to the last hundred years had polygamy as a regular course?*
A. The best scholarly estimate I have seen on that is 83 percent.

***

Q. *That's what I'm asking you, OK? And let's take the most populous places, India and China. Is it your judgment that the majority of marriages in those two places prior to the last hundred years have been limited to just two people as opposed to polygamous marriages? (Brief pause.)*

Q. *Do you understand the question?*
A. Completely. And I'm struggling to help you understand my answer which is—my answer to your question is yes. I think I could just save us some time if I would be allowed to say another sentence or two.

Q. Go ahead. But try to keep it brief.
A. I will. I promise you. Even in instances of a man engaging in polygamous marriage, each marriage is separate. He—one man marries one woman. That's the way it works.

***

Blankenhorn's *outrageous statement* (the "O" of CROSS) that a man who marries several women is essentially in a marriage involving only two people, simply defies common sense. He is backed into a corner because his previous claim that marriage is viewed by society as being between two people is undercut by the many polygamous marriages that occurred around the world prior to the last 100 years.

He gets backed further into a corner on this subject in the next section.

Impeachment with Deposition Testimony about Expertise

In this section, Boies wants to show that Blankenhorn is not an expert but only a mouthpiece for other experts: he is just echoing other expert opinions.

Q. Now, it's your testimony that the man with five wives is consistent—that marriage is consistent with what you say is your rule of two; is that correct? That is a yes-or-no answer.
A. Based on the findings of the anthropologists who've actually studied this, yes, the answer to your question is yes.

Q. And when you say based on the scholars that have studied this, that's because you're simply repeating the things that these scholars say?
A. Yes.

Q. You're just a ***transmitter*** *of the findings of these scholars, correct?*
A. Well, **you're putting words in my mouth now**.

Q. No, sir.
A. Yes, sir.

> ### Practice Tip
> Have the exact page and line number of important deposition testimony identified to use for impeachment in case the witness changes his testimony at trial.

Boies is ready to impeach Blankenhorn with the exact word, transmitter, that he used in his sworn deposition.

Q. Well, let's look at your words in your deposition, page 300. Do you have your deposition up there?
A. I don't believe I do. . . . I might be able to save us time by saying that the substance of your comment is correct. I was simply trying to report the view of some scholars. **It's the transmitter thing**. I just was trying to suggest that I was basing my arguments on—on scholarship. I'm not even saying there aren't scholars that have a different point of

view. I'm saying there are scholars, respected scholars, who have made this argument based on ethnographic research. And I've read them. And that's the basis for my assertion. That's all. **[Boies is not going to let Blankenhorn off the hook. He wants him to admit very clearly that he is only a "transmitter" of others' opinions.]**

Q. *I understand. I'm really just addressing whether I was putting words in your mouth. And if you look at page 300, lines 7 through 12. And you can read any other portion of this that you want. But you have said that you are basing your analysis on the work of highly regarded scholars. And then you say—*
A. **Oh, a gotcha moment**. I used the word "I'm a transmitter of findings of eminent scholars." Gotcha. OK.

Q. *That's not a gotcha. I'm just trying to—***[Boies is not going to let the witness take control by characterizing the impeachment as simply a "gotcha moment."]**
A. I said "transmitter" seven months ago in a deposition.

Q. *And what you meant there was that what you were doing was, you weren't making these conclusions on your own. You were simply repeating what these scholars had said. Is that correct?*
A. If I may say it in my own words?

Q. *Well— (simultaneous colloquy)*
A. I was basing—

Q. *Let me look at your own words on page 300, at lines 7 to 12: "I'm simply repeating things that they say. I can assure you, I'm not making any of this up on my own. These are not my own conclusions. I'm—I'm a transmitter here of findings of these eminent scholars." Did you give that testimony at your deposition?*
A. **That's what I said at the deposition.**

The reason Boies wins this battle is two-fold. First, the witness denies the fact that he said he was a transmitter of opinions. He offers explanation after explanation. Second, even when the witness is shown his deposition where he said that he was a transmitter, the witness tries to minimize the impeachment by saying it was a "gotcha moment," as if he had been tricked. Boies does not give in. Instead, he forces him to admit for a second time that he said under oath in his deposition that he was a transmitter.

Boies Impeaches with Deposition About a Rule of Marriage

Blankenhorn's second rule of marriage was that the relationship by definition involved sexual intercourse. Boies challenges him on that contention.

Q. *My question was going to be, and is now, whether you are aware of instances in which marriage—marriages are in— they are inconsistent with your rule of sex?*
A. I'm sorry. You were saying the couple is married and they do not have sexual intercourse, am I aware of such marriages?

Q. That actually wasn't my question, but why don't you answer that question. That's really easy, right? The answer to that is yes, correct?
A. I—I was going to answer no. But maybe I'm misunderstanding the nature of your question.

***

Q. So it's your testimony that you're not aware of any married couples who don't have sex?
A. Well, here we go. Going to make it boring again. There are some married couples in the world today who have never had sexual intercourse? Oh, my gosh, well, I suppose, just thinking **hypothetically**, I'm trying to think.

Q. If you're not aware of them, ***I'm not asking you to hypothesize.***
A. There could be an example, say, of an incarcerated man who marries while he's in incarceration. It could be true that the system he's in is one of the minority of systems that does not produce—allow for conjugal visits, and he will not be able to consummate the sexual relationship with his wife until he is released from prison. And during the time that he is in prison and married, and unable to have a conjugal visit, I guess it's possible or likely that that man will not have had sexual intercourse with his wife, by virtue of incarceration. And he will have to wait until after he is released or he will have to wait until the period of a conjugal visit. That would be an example. . . . **But, hypothetically, could there be such a case? I suppose there could. [At the end of this excerpt, the witness will deny that he used the word hypothetical in this answer.]**

Q. Well, sir, you know perfectly well that these are not sort of just hypothetical cases. Correct, sir?
A. No, sir.

Q. You don't? You don't? Like this example of the incarcerated prisoner, ***you know perfectly well that that's a real example from a real court case; don't you, sir?***
A. **No, sir, I do not.**

Q. You don't?
A. Why would you try to put words in my mouth of that nature?

Q. Well, because it is my understanding that you have previously recognized that—this very specific example of where the United States Supreme Court held that you could not deprive somebody of the right to marry merely because they were incarcerated and could not have sex. . . .

Practice Tip

The power of getting the answer you want on cross lies in choosing a question you can force the witness to answer the way you want or having the witness not answer and being disbelieved by the fact finder.

By now, Boies has trained the judge to realize that if he includes a fact in a question, he has the evidence to back it up. So, Boies impeaches the witness with his deposition.

Q. All right. Let me approach it this way. I'm not asking you to hypothesize. I'm just asking you whether you are aware of any examples of marriages that are inconsistent with your

rule of sex. If you are not aware of them, I don't want you to hypothesize or try to think up what might exist. Just, are you aware of any examples or not?
A. No, sir.

* * *

Q. *Let me approach it this way, because this has gone on long enough. I have found the deposition that I thought existed. Would you turn to page 258 of your deposition. And beginning at line 13: "**But in any society, if a man and woman want to marry and not have sex at all, and neither one seeks divorce, they're free to do that, right?** "ANSWER: Well, you know, the law on this has changed in recent decades. And now, in recent years, **there has been a growing permission on the part of courts to accept married couples who cannot have sexual intercourse. For example, when one spouse is in prison.**" Do you see that, sir?*
A. That's exactly what I told you in my answer.

Q. *This doesn't say it's hypothetical, does it, sir? You're not talking hypothetical—*
A. I did not use—**I don't think I used the word "hypothetical" in my answer**. I said in cases where a prisoner is unable to consummate his marriage, he would have to depend upon getting out of prison to do so, or conjugal visits. I think that's what I said.

The witness, caught in the trap of his deposition, doubles down and now says he did not use the word hypothetical in his earlier trial testimony (see bolded word earlier in this excerpt). Boies has accomplished two things. He has impeached the witness with his prior inconsistent *statement*, the first "S" of CROSS, and he gets the added benefit of the witness making the *outrageous statement* that he never used hypothetical in his previous answer, the "O" of CROSS.

End Strong before a Break

Once you are in trial, the court will tell you (or you will notice) that the court will take a break in the morning, for lunch in the afternoon, and at the end of the day at the same time each day. Be aware of these interruptions, because you always want to end strong before one of these breaks. Why? That way, the fact finder will be thinking about your important point over the break or during the evening until the next day.

In the next example, Boies realizes that it is nearing the end of the day, and he asks some of his best questions at this point. Here, he is using the first "S" of CROSS to show that the witness has made *statements* inconsistent with his trial testimony. These statements are then used for the second "S" of CROSS, to *support* Boies' case.

Q. *Now, in binder number one, we have a copy of your book, Future of Marriage. . . . Would you turn to page two of the book?*
A. Yes, sir.

Q. And the last two sentences. And for context you may want to read earlier in the paragraph. You will see that your writing there on the issue of same-sex marriage is this profound principle of equal dignity, the heart of the matter? "After all, part of the reason why the principle is so revolutionary is that it can grow and deepen over time. Groups that had long been considered effectively outside its moral reach, African-Americans, women, people of certain colors or languages or religions, can over time and often as a result of great struggle, enter into its protective sphere." And then you get to the two sentences that I particularly direct your attention to. You say: "I believe that today the principle of equal human dignity must apply to gay and lesbian persons." Do you see that?
A. Yes, sir.

Q. And you say: "In that sense insofar as we are a nation founded on this principle, we would be more, emphasize more, American on the day we permitted same-sex marriage than we were on the day before." And you wrote those words, did you not, sir?
A. I wrote those words.

Q. And you believed them then, correct?
A. That's correct.

Q. And you believe them now, correct?
A. That's correct.

[Court adjourns.]

Blankenhorn cannot deny what he has written. His *statement* in his book is inconsistent (the first "S" of CROSS) with his trial testimony. It also *supports* (the second "S" of CROSS) the plaintiffs' claims.

Forcing the Witness to Answer the Question

Next, let's look at a great example of how to force a witness to answer your question. What is so incredible is that the witness—after being told to answer the question by the judge—disagrees with the judge when the judge tries to interpret the answer. In exasperation, the judge simply says at the end, "The record is clear on what you said." It is a complete victory for the examiner. Let's watch it unfold.

*Q. And what I'm asking you is, whether any of the scholars that you have relied on have asserted that permitting same-sex marriage would result in a **lower rate of heterosexual marriage?***
A. I—I think the safest answer would, for me, to say **I don't know. [The witness should have stopped right here. But he tries to pretend he knows at his peril.]** But if you'll also permit me, I think—I believe the answer is yes, some of them have.

Q. In that case what I will now do is ask you which ones?
A. Well, I thought you might. That's why I was kind of careful in walking into it, but...

Q. It comes from those discussions.
A. Yes, yes. (laughter)

A. Professor Norval Glenn in his article called the Struggle For Same-Sex Marriage. I have not reread that article in some time, but I know he is a long-time—I have read many things of his and he is a—I know him and I believe that he has voiced reservations about same-sex marriage along the lines of this statement that I read from, in the article; that is, that he is saying that if—

Q. *Sir?* **[Boies does not let the witness get away with a speech when he should be answering a simple question. Boies interrupts him and asks it again below.]**
A. Yes.

Q. *I—I need to have you focus relatively precisely, if I can, on my question. You did read a—or Mr. Cooper read to you a portion from Mr. Glenn's article where he was talking about the deinstitutionalization of marriage, and I do remember that, OK? My question is different, OK?* ***My question is whether Mr. Glenn or any scholar that you relied on has asserted that permitting same-sex marriage will result in a lower rate of heterosexual marriage?*** **[Boies repeats his earlier question.]**
A. The problem here—I'm not trying to be evasive, but you must let me just say my answer, which is that if they are arguing—

Q. *No, no, sir. I don't have to do this. All that's going to happen is you're going to say something, then I'm going to have to follow up. OK? What I'm trying to do is—this is a* ***very simple question****, all right?* **[Boies continues to remind the court that he is asking a simple question.]**
A. It is not simple to me.

Q. *All right. Well, let me try to make it simple.*
A. If you are using—

Q. *Let me try to make it simple.*
A. (Continuing)—the exact form of the words—

Q. *If you are trying to—*

COURT: Let's not argue with one another. Let's just have a question and an answer. (laughter)

Q. *Let me try to make the question as simple as I can. Have any of the scholars that you have said you relied on said* ***in words or in substance****, OK, this permitting same-sex marriage will cause a reduction in heterosexual marriage?* **[Boies now has asked this question three times.]** ***That's "yes," "no," or "I don't know."***
A. I know the answer. I cannot answer you accurately if the only words I'm allowed to choose from is "yes" or "no." **I can give you my answer very briefly in one sentence**.

COURT: If you know the answer, why don't you share it with us?
WITNESS: I would be happy to, but he is only permitting me to give "yes" and "no," and I cannot do that and be accurate.
COURT: He is giving you three choices, "yes," "no," "I don't know."
WITNESS: But I do know. I do know the answer.
COURT: Then is it "yes" or is it "no"?

WITNESS: Your Honor, I can answer the question, but I cannot give an accurate answer if the only two choices I have are "yes" and "no." I—if you give me a sentence, I can answer it. **One sentence is all I'm asking for.**

COURT: All right. Let's take a sentence. One sentence.

A. Can you ask me the question again, please?

The court is becoming exasperated but the witness keeps pushing back. Having persuaded the court to allow him one sentence, Blankenhorn better deliver. Let's see if he does.

Q. Have any of the scholars who you say you relied on asserted, written, that they believe that permitting same-sex marriage will result in a reduction in the heterosexual marriage rate?

A. My answer is that I believe that some of the scholars I have cited have asserted that permitting same-sex marriage would contribute to the deinstitutionalization of marriage, one of the answer—one of the manifestations of which would be a lower marriage rate among heterosexuals.

But I do not have sure knowledge that in the exact form of words you are asking me for they have made the direct assertion that permitting same-sex marriage would directly lower the marriage rate among heterosexuals. [**If you are counting, the witness asked the court for permission to give a one-sentence answer but gives two very long ones instead.**]

Q. Mr. Blankenthorn?

A. Horn.

Q. Mr. Blankenhorn.

A. That wasn't so long.

Q. Questions and answers.

COURT: If I were to take that as an "I don't know" would that be fair?

WITNESS: With respect, your Honor, I would disagree with you. I know exactly my answer to this question, and I have just stated it. And I would be happy to restate it.

COURT: The record is clear on what you said.

This has been a complete victory for Boies. The court asks if it is fair for the witness to admit, "I don't know," which is what he said at the beginning of this excerpt but then started making speeches. After Boies repeats the same simple question several times, the witness has made the detrimental decision to avoid answering the simple question and then arguing with the judge who will decide this case.

But it gets even more incredible. Clearly, the witness does not know the answer to Boies's question. If possible, he digs an even further hole. But let's focus on how well Boies listens, a skill that is a key to cross-examination. By listening intently, Boies catches that the witness has not answered his question and forces the witness to make an *outrageous statement*, the "O" of CROSS.

End Strong

Q. *All right. Mr. Blankenhorn, let me—let me just ask you, hopefully, just two more quick areas. First, would you turn to tab 3 of this binder, the binder that has 15 tabs to it.*
A. I have it, yes, sir.

Q. *And this is the review article that you referred to previously, and published in Developmental and Behavioral Pediatrics; is that correct?*
A. I'm sorry. I'm really sorry, I must be—

Q. *3. Tab 3.*
A. Sorry. "Lesbian Mothers, Gay Fathers, and Their Children."

Q. *Yes.*
A. Yes, sir.

Q. *Are you familiar with this document?*
A. Uhm, I—I don't believe so, sir.

Q. *OK. There's something that's headed the "Abstract." And you know what an abstract is do you not?*
A. Of course.

Q. *And the abstract says: "There is a variety of families headed by a lesbian or gay male parent or same-sex couple. Findings from research suggest that children with lesbian or gay parents are comparable with children with heterosexual parents on key psychosocial developmental outcomes." Do you see that?*
A. Yes, sir.

Q. *And even though you may not be aware of this article, are you aware of other articles in peer-reviewed journals that reach that conclusion?*
A. Yes, sir, I am aware.

Q. *Now, we've talked a lot about the institution of marriage. You would agree that the institution of marriage is constantly evolving, correct?*
A. Yes, sir.

Q. *And always changing, correct?*
A. I wrote those words in my book.

Q. *And no single universally accepted definition of marriage, correct?*
A. I wrote those words, too.

MR. BOIES: Your Honor, I have no more questions.

Not only do you want to end strong before a break in the court proceedings, you want to make sure you end your entire cross-examination on a high note. You want to leave no doubt that you have won. Remember, you get to choose the topics of your questions, so there should be no excuse for not choosing questions you can certainly win on.

Here, Boies uses the second "S" of CROSS to *support* his case. He knows that he will win because he has the power to force the witness to answer the questions he wants through the use of the peer-reviewed article and the witness's own book. That is, the witness cannot deny what the article and his book say.

Epilogue

Two years after the trial, Blankenhorn wrote an op-ed piece for the *New York Times* titled "How My Views on Gay Marriage Changed," where he did not recant his views from the trial but explained that he now supported gay marriage. You can view the article at www.winningatcross.com.

9.7 SUMMARY OF BOIES'S TECHNIQUES

Throughout the examination, the witness did not answer Boies's questions. When this happens, you can do one of two things. As we saw in previous chapters, after the witness fails to answer the question, Mark Lanier often replies, "objection, non-responsive." The judge will then sustain the objection and direct the witness to answer the question. At other times, Lanier will interrupt a rambling witness to make his non-responsive objection. The technique is very effective because it alerts the jury to the witness's unresponsive answer, and Lanier gets an added benefit when the judge sustains the objection and directs the witness to answer the question. The added scolding from the judge shows the jury that the judge agrees with you.

But Boies employs an equally effective technique. Experiment and decide which one works best for you. Unlike Lanier, Boies does not ask for help from the judge; he just repeats his question, over and over if necessary, until he gets the answer from the witness. By doing this, he highlights how unreasonable the witness is each time he does not answer the simple question.

Second, by repeating the question, Boies gets the added benefit of presenting his point to the fact finder multiple times through his questioning, which makes it easier for jurors to remember.

Finally, after the witness fails a second or third time to answer a question, the judge often will intervene and direct the witness to answer it. Consequently, Boies gets the same benefit Lanier achieves through his objection and requests for help from the judge.

Another technique Boies uses is alerting the witness and the fact finder that his question should be easy to answer. He does this by saying, "This is a very simple question." If the question is indeed simple, meaning it contains one proposition to which the witness must answer "yes," "no," or "I don't know," then there are only three possible answers for the witness. When the witness fails to choose an answer, Boies highlights the evasiveness with this response: "Let me try to make it as simple as I can." The fact finder immediately sympathizes with Boies and becomes frustrated with a witness who won't answer the question.

Sometimes, Boies will even direct the witness at the end of his question with the following: *That's "yes," "no," or "I don't know."* As we just saw, even when Boies did this, sometimes the witness still won't choose one of these answers for the question. Such a non-response is a double win for Boies. First, the witness loses credibility, because he fails to answer the question, and second, Boies gets to repeat the question so the fact finder will hear it more than once, maybe even multiple times, which will make the point easier to remember.

9.8 CHAPTER CHECKLIST

1. Boies tells the witness (and in actuality, reveals to the judge or jury) the topic he wants to discuss with the witness before each line of questioning.
2. Whether in a deposition or a trial, an expert's claimed expertise can almost always be successfully challenged. Experts have a bad habit of exaggerating. Boies points out that the expert's "expertise" is not on the narrow subject for which he is testifying.
3. Cross-examine an expert on the degrees and training he has not received to show his untrustworthiness and lack of necessary qualifications to be an expert.
4. To show that a witness lacks qualifications or has not done things he should have, ask a series of questions to emphasize those failures, such as, "You have never taught a course on fatherhood," or "You have never received a degree in . . . ."
5. One technique to use when a witness argues with how a question is phrased is to repeat the question but this time instruct the witness to use the disputed term as it is normally used in English. For example, "But you do understand that 'peer-reviewed' as it is normally used does not refer to something that you do internally?"
6. Start strong. Boies immediately asks the witness about an important proposition that Boies knows he can win.
7. A key to a successful cross-examination is preparation. You must be intimately familiar with the materials the witness has relied on and the witness's prior statements and testimony.
8. Go after the key to your case. Boies says, "Let me jump right to the bottom line, OK, sir?"
9. Don't forget to get helpful information from the witness to *support your case* (the second "S" of CROSS). Boies declares, "I'm going to start with some things that perhaps we can agree on."

10. Remember the greatest myth of cross-examination is that you can get the witness to confess. As seen here, your goal is simply to prove his testimony is not to be believed.
11. Have the exact page and line number identified of important deposition testimony to use for impeachment in case the witness changes his testimony at trial.
12. The power of getting the answer you want on cross lies in choosing a question you can force the witness to answer the way you want, or having the witness not answer and being disbelieved by the fact finder.
13. Listen for instances where the witness cherry-picks a helpful fact from a document on direct. On cross, pounce on this spin and provide the proper context for it to the fact finder. You win twice. Once from the deception and a second time by providing the truth.
14. End strong before each break. Jurors are more likely to remember your points if you make them just before the court adjourns.
15. Assume for a moment this was a jury trial. Be aware that jurors pick up on how the judge views the witness's testimony. When you get the judge on your side in the battle with the witness, you have won the cross-examination.
16. Boies has several different techniques for handling evasive witnesses:
    1) He listens carefully to see if the witness has answered the question.
    2) He asks simple questions that must be answered with "yes," "no," or "I don't know."
    3) He repeats the question until the witness answers it.
    4) When the witness asks if he can explain his answer, Boies responds, "Let me be sure I've got answers to my questions first."
    5) A sterner response he gives is: "No, I'm sure you would like to answer questions that I'm not asking, and you'll have a chance to do that with your counsel."
    6) When the witness gives a rambling answer, Boies replies, "I'm trying to move along. You will have a chance to make speeches when your counsel is asking questions."
    7) When the witness says, "You must let me say my answer," Boies comes back with "No, sir. I don't have to do this," or "This is not a debate."
    8) When the witness does not answer a question, Boies says, "This is a very simple question," and then repeats the question.
    9) At other times, when the witness does not answer a question, Boies repeats the question and instructs the witness by saying, "That's 'yes,' 'no,' or 'I don't know.'"

CHAPTER TEN

The O. J. Simpson and George Zimmerman Trials

"And when you saw these videos, you realized that you had been caught in a lie, didn't you?"—*Barry Scheck*

In this chapter, we will take a close look at significant cross-examinations from two of the most famous trials in the last 50 years. The videos of the cross-examinations can be found on the book's website at www.winningatcross.com under the heading chapter 10.

10.1 Background of People v. O.J. Simpson

Nicole Brown, O.J. Simpson's ex-wife, was stabbed to death near the front steps of her townhome in Los Angeles on the night of June 12, 1994, at 10:15 p.m. Ron Goldman, a friend of Nicole's, was also stabbed and killed. Nicole's home was located at 875 South Bundy Rd. and was referred to at the trial as the Bundy crime scene.

If you weren't a teenager or older during the 1970's, you probably don't realize just how popular O.J. Simpson was back then. Not only was he a Pro Football Hall of Fame running back for the Buffalo Bills, but he also frequently appeared on national TV in widely broadcast Hertz rental car commercials, and he was a movie star in such films as *The Naked Gun*. O.J. was very popular.

O.J. and Nicole had a very troubled relationship. They met when he was a famous 29-year-old pro football star and she was an 18-year-old waitress. They married and had two children. During their marriage, she called 911 many times, including once on New Year's Eve when police went to her home and

CHAPTER ROAD MAP

- Analyze how F. Lee Bailey boxes a witness in so that there is no escape.
- Paint a picture for the jury by using descriptive words in your questions.
- Study the cross-examination of the key prosecution witness that led to the acquittal of George Zimmerman.

found her partially clothed and hiding in the bushes. She told the police that "O.J. was going to kill me." Her face and neck were badly bruised.

On the night of the murders, Nicole went to her children's dance recital. After the recital, she went with friends and family to a restaurant for dinner where her friend Ron Goldman worked. After dinner, she went home. Meanwhile, O.J. had also gone to the dance recital and returned home afterwards to his house located on Rockingham Ave. (His home is referred to as Rockingham throughout the trial.) When Ron Goldman noticed that Nicole's mother had left her eyeglasses at the restaurant, he took them to Nicole's home that night.

Around 11:00 p.m., Nicole's dog was found running loose and covered in blood. A neighbor took the dog to Nicole's house and found two dead bodies. The police were called and when they arrived, they found Ron and Nicole near the front door steps with multiple stab wounds.

The police then went to O.J.'s house to notify him of his ex-wife's death. He was not there, but they found a trail of blood from his car, a white Bronco, to his house. Detective Mark Fuhrman found a bloody glove (an exclusive brand) on Simpson's property that matched a glove found at the crime scene. The blood found inside the Bronco turned out to match Nicole's. There were also two socks found in O.J.'s bedroom that had Nicole's blood on them.

After an 11-month trial, the sequestered jury returned a not guilty verdict in less than four hours.

10.2 Cross-Examination of Mark Fuhrman

F. Lee Bailey's cross-examination of Detective Mark Fuhrman was one of the highlights of the trial, particularly in light of the events that unfolded after the testimony. (See Fuhrman clip 1 at www.winningatcross.com.) He was a key witness at trial because he found a glove at O.J.'s house that matched the one found at the crime scene. But prior to trial, there were allegations that he often used racial slurs (discussed below). At trial, Mark Fuhrman denied using racial slurs in the previous ten years. But after he finished testifying and before the trial was over, the defense learned that Laura McKinney, a screenwriter, had tape recordings of Fuhrman using extensive racial slurs.

Prior to trial, Kathleen Bell, a real estate agent with no connection to the case, wrote a letter to both the prosecution and defense. She said that she had worked as a real estate agent in Redondo Beach for Century 21 and had an office above a Marine recruiting center. Sometimes she would stop in the office to say hello to the two marines who worked there.

Occasionally, she would also see Mark Fuhrman in that office. She claimed that Fuhrman made racial slurs and other derogatory comments about

African-Americans. Those racial comments fit in with the defense theory that the Los Angeles Police Department arrested O.J. in a rush to judgment that was motivated by his race.

To preempt the anticipated cross-examination, one of the prosecutors, Marcia Clark, displayed the letter to the jury and asked Fuhrman if the letter was true on direct examination. He denied its allegations. In the letter, Bell could not remember how the subject was raised, but remembered the following:

> Officer Ferman [sic] said that when he saw a [n-word] driving with a white woman, he would pull them over. I asked would he if he didn't have a reason, and he said he would find one. I looked at the two marines to see if they knew he was joking, but it was obvious to me that he was very serious. Officer Ferman [sic] went on to say that he would like nothing more than to see all the [n-word plural] gathered together and killed. He said something about burning or bombing them, I was too shaken to remember the exact words he used. However, I do remember that what he said was probably the most horrible thing I had ever heard someone say. What frightened me even more was that he was a police officer.

In closing arguments, Johnnie Cochran, O.J.'s lead attorney, would emphasize Bell's letter to prove his claim that the prosecution was motivated by prejudice.

In the following excerpt, Bailey questions Fuhrman about the Bell letter and his preparation for trial with the prosecution. Fuhrman said that the prosecutors had only asked him ten questions.

Q. Were you familiar with the language attributed to you by Ms. Bell in that declaration?
A. Yes.

Q. Was any of that language the subject matter of the questions put to you by [prosecutors in the trial preparation]?
A. They did not use that language. No.

Q. What language did they use instead to help you with the Bell problem?
A. They used the term racial slur.

Bailey cleverly refers to the letter as the "Bell problem." Fuhrman could have answered that he did not consider it a problem because it wasn't true. But he doesn't, and Bailey wins a small battle and will continue to refer to the "Bell problem."

Practice Tip

Use descriptive words in your questions. Bailey refers to Bell's letter as the "Bell problem." The witness does not deny this choice of words, which lets Bailey keep developing this theme for the jury each time he refers to the "Bell problem."

Q. Okay. Now, do you have any memory of even one of these ten questions?
A. No.

Q. Not a single one?
A. No, sir.

Q. And this happened when, Detective Fuhrman?
A. I believe it was two or three weeks ago.

Q. Two or three weeks ago?
A. Yes.

Q. You have been exhibiting a startling memory for details of a crime that was eight months ago, have you not?

MARCIA CLARK: Objection, Your Honor.
COURT: Sustained.

Although Clark does not give the reason for her objection, she makes her objection because she believes the question is argumentative. She implies through her objection that Bailey is using an unfair characterization of Fuhrman's memory when he describes it as "startling." Most judges would have allowed Bailey's question. An argumentative objection is rarely sustained because the whole point of cross-examination is to challenge a witness's credibility. That kind of confrontation will necessarily result in an argument between the lawyer and the witness. It is proper to challenge a witness's memory, and Bailey's use of the word "startling" does not rise to the level of an argumentative question. As we have seen from all the trials examined in this book, judges allow attorneys a lot of latitude on cross-examination. In short, the line between proper confrontation and improper argument is very fuzzy. If a judge sustains an argumentative objection, you are entitled to rephrase the question without the argumentative words. In this example, Bailey just decided to move on. He had made his point to the jury despite the objection.

Q. Did any of the questions require you to say whether or not language of that sort was a part of your vocabulary?
A. I might have offered that.

Q. Tell us please what it was you offered these lawyers in that room about your vocabulary, Detective Fuhrman.

This is an open-ended question. Can you think of an answer that would hurt Bailey? Since the answer is "no," it is safe for Bailey to ask this non-leading question on cross.

A. That I-

MARCIA CLARK: [inaudible 00:01:32]
COURT: Overruled.

Q. *Would you answer?*
A. Yes. That I don't use any type of language to describe people of any race such as what is alleged by Kathleen Bell.

Bailey expects this answer, and it does not undercut his line of cross-examination.

Q. *Did you say, to the lawyers, who were trying to prepare you for the Bell problem, that you never, never used that language?*
A. I wasn't asked, sir.

Q. *Withdrawn. I'll be more specific. Did you tell the lawyers in that room that you never use the word [n-word]?*

MARCIA CLARK [inaudible 00:02:26] objection, Your Honor.
COURT: Overruled.

A. I was never asked.

Q. *I'm asking. Do you?*

MARCIA CLARK: Objection, Your Honor.

A. Do I what?
COURT: That's vague, rephrase the question.

Q. *Do you use the word [n-word] in describing people?*

MARCIA CLARK: Same objection.
COURT: Presently?
F. LEE BAILEY: Yeah.
COURT: Overruled.

A. No, sir.

Q. *Have you used that word in the past 10 years?*
A. Not that I recall, no.

Many attorneys would have stopped with this line of inquiry right here, having gotten Fuhrman to deny he used the "n-word," which lets them bring in Kathleen Bell or others to discredit him. But Bailey wants the issue to be crystal clear for the jury, and he wants to eliminate any wiggle room for Fuhrman. He seizes on the word "recall" and uses common sense in his next series of questions to get either an outrageous answer (Fuhrman confirms he does not remember using the "n-word") or a complete denial.

Q. *You mean, if you called someone a [n-word] you have forgotten it?*
A. I'm not sure I can answer that question the way you phrased it, sir.

Q. *You have difficulty understanding the question? I'll rephrase it.*
A. Yes.

Q. I want you to assume that perhaps at some time, since 1985 or 6, you addressed a member of the African-American race as a [n-word]. Is it possible that you have forgotten that act on your part?
A. No, it's not possible.

> **Practice Tip**
>
> Be precise in your questions and anticipate how a witness could evade your point.

It would have been an outrageous answer if Fuhrman had answered that he could have forgotten. Do you see any wiggle room for Fuhrman? Notice how Bailey asked only if Fuhrman had "addressed" an African-American with the n-word. Fuhrman could have talked to whites about African-Americans and used the "n-word" and still denied the question. In the following exchange, we see how Bailey fixes this problem.

Q. Are you, therefore, saying that you have not used that word in the past 10 years, Detective Fuhrman?
A. Yes, that's what I'm saying.

Q. And you say on your oath, that you have not addressed any black person as a [n-word] or spoken about black people as [n-word]s in the past 10 years, Detective Fuhrman?
A. That's what I'm saying, sir.

This is the air-tight question that provides no escape.

Q. So that anyone who comes to this court and quotes you as using that word, in dealing with African-Americans would be a liar, would they not, Detective Fuhrman?
A. Yes, they would.

Q. All of them, correct?
A. All of them.

Q. All right. Thank you.

As mentioned previously, later in the trial, the defense team would learn that Laura McKinney, a screenwriter, had interviewed Fuhrman between 1985 and 1994 and kept recordings where he had used the "n-word" over 40 times. A portion of those tapes were played for the jury to impeach Fuhrman's testimony above. Fuhrman was recalled as a witness—outside the presence of the jury—and he refused to answer questions about perjury by asserting his rights against self-incrimination under the Fifth Amendment.

When Johnnie Cochran learned of the McKinney tapes, he called it "manna from heaven." Aside from the bungled glove demonstration in court, in which the prosecution asked O.J. to try on the leather glove found at the crime scene and the matching one found outside his home, the McKinney tapes were the second biggest event for the defense at trial.

The McKinney tapes were so devastating that it was the first major topic Clark addressed in her closing argument to the jury. Here is what she said:

Did he lie when he testified in the courtroom saying that he did not use racial epithets in the last ten years? Yes. Is he a racist? Yes. Is he the worst LAPD has to offer? Yes. Do we wish this person was never hired by LAPD? Yes. Should LAPD have ever hired him? No. Should such a person be a police officer? No. In fact, do we wish there was no such person on this planet? Yes.

But the fact that Mark Fuhrman is a racist and lied about it on the witness stand does not mean that we have not proven the defendant guilty beyond a reasonable doubt. And it would be a tragedy, ladies and gentlemen, if with the overwhelming evidence we have presented to you, in spite of all that, you found the defendant not guilty because of the racist attitudes of one police officer.

10.3 Cross-Examination of Officer Dennis Fung

As part of the LAPD investigation, O.J. gave a sample of his blood to the police. Detective Phil Vannatter took the blood sample to Officer Dennis Fung, who was at O.J.'s house conducting a search. In the following excerpt, Barry Scheck, one of O.J.'s lawyers, questions Fung regarding how he carried the sample of O.J.'s blood that Vannatter had given him from the house to the evidence truck. (See Fung Clip 1 at www.winningatcross.com.) Why Vannatter took the blood sample to Fung at O.J.'s house instead of to the LAPD lab or the evidence control unit (as required by the LAPD manual) is a question that was never fully resolved at trial. Note: "SID" mentioned in the excerpt refers to the LAPD's Scientific Investigative Unit.

> **Practice Tip**
>
> Use the theme from your opening statement in your cross and closing argument. Likewise, when your theme is powerful on cross, opposing counsel will need to respond to it in their closing.

Q. Mr. Fung, when we left off we were discussing what you told us about the transfer of the blood vial to you in the foyer of Mr. Simpson's home on the afternoon of June 13th.
A. Yes.

Q. Now, you mentioned to us that you thought that you put the envelope containing the blood vial in a paper bag or what you called a Posse Box.

PROSECUTOR: Objection. Mistates the testimony.
COURT: Sustained.

Although it is impossible to hear, the court transcript reflects that that the prosecutor objected that the question misstated the testimony because Fung had already testified that he did not recall how he carried the blood sample. Despite this objection, Scheck gets Fung to start guessing as to how he carried the vial.

Q. *What is a Posse Box?*
A. A Posse Box is a notepad that's metallic. It has a cover on it that you can store.... It's a box that's shaped like a notepad except it can carry things.

Q. *Did you have one of those with you that day?*
A. I don't recall if we did or not.

Q. *Were you carrying one, to the best of your recollection, that day when you left Mr. Simpson's front door to go back to your crime scene truck on the afternoon of June 13th?*
A. I don't recall if I was or was not carrying a Posse Box.

Q. *Alright. To the best of your recollection, how did you carry this gray envelope containing Mr. Simpson's blood vial when you ... Withdrawn. I take it at some point in time you left the foyer area, and returned to your crime scene truck?*
A. Yes.

Q. *And you were carrying that gray envelope [with the blood vial]?*
A. Either by itself, in a Posse Box, or in a paper bag.

Q. *So, it would be one of those three ways of carrying it. Either out by itself in your hand, in a paper bag, or in a Posse Box.*
A. Yes.

Now, instead of confirming his direct examination testimony that he did not remember how he carried the vial, Fung has now guessed that he must have carried it in one of the three ways. It is a logical guess and makes sense to Fung, but because he doesn't remember, he should not have guessed because the guess becomes sworn testimony that can be attacked. The reason Scheck will win this line of questioning is because he has a video showing what happened. Below is testimony from the next day that begins by referring to the exchange above.

Q. **[Scheck reads the transcript from the previous day that is shown above]** *Question. "I take it at some point in time you left the foyer area and returned to your crime scene truck." Answer, "Yes." Question. "Alright, and were you carrying that gray envelope?" Answer, "Either by itself, in a Posse Box, or in a paper bag." Question. "So, it would be one those three ways of carrying it. Either by itself in your hand, in a paper bag, or in a Posse Box." Answer, "Yes." Were you asked those questions, and did you give those answers yesterday?*
A. Yes I did.

Q. *Now, this morning, did you have an opportunity to look at some video tapes?*
A. Yes.

Q. *And you did that in this court room, outside the presence of the jury, with the judge and counsel present?*
A. Yes.

Q. *Okay. Let's roll it here. Okay, let's stop. Now, the man behind you is a photographer named Mr. Wilson.* **[Scheck plays a video clip showing Fung leaving the foyer area of Simpson's house.]**
A. Yes.

Q. *And he's from SID, correct?* **[SID is the Special Investigations Unit.]**
A. Yes, he is.

Q. *And, as you were walking out that door, if you want to see it again, you have nothing in your hands?*
A. That's correct.

Q. *Alright. You do not have a gray envelope in your hands?*
A. That's correct.

Q. *You do not have a brown paper bag in your hands?*
A. That's correct.

Q. *You do not have a Posse Box in your hand?*
A. That's correct.

Q. *Now, Ms. Mizzola, in her left hand, she has what appears to be a black plastic bag?*
A. Yes.

Q. *And when you saw these series of tapes, Mr. Fung, you realized that you had been caught in a lie, didn't you?*
A. No.

Q. *Well, you had told this jury yesterday that you carried the blood sample either in a brown paper bag, in the Posse Box, or in your hands. Correct?*
A. That's what I stated.

The above example demonstrates how to impeach a witness by using physical evidence. While Scheck calls it a lie, Fung very well could have been mistaken. Nonetheless, the problem is that Fung stated with certainty that *he* carried it one of three ways. In contrast to his testimony, the video showed that Fung did not carry it and that someone else did. Not only that, his assistant is shown carrying it in a different way than Fung said it should have been carried. His assistant carried the blood vial in a large plastic bag that could have led to contamination, and this helped prove the defense's point that the LAPD mishandled important evidence.

When you look at the video, notice that Scheck will often look at the jury when he thinks he is making an important point. Some lawyers do this because they think they can better connect with the jury by making eye contact. Attorneys also think it signals to the jury that they should

Practice Tip

It is fine to look at the jury occasionally, but don't overdo it. It becomes insincere at some point and can backfire when jurors think you are becoming too biased for your side. In addition, jurors don't like their personal space being invaded by attorneys.

really pay attention because the attorney is looking at them. Jurors don't like it and most judges would not even allow it. The reason is that attorneys are only allowed to address the jury during opening statement and closing argument.

In the following excerpt (see the "Fung Clip 2" video at www.winningatcross.com), Scheck questions Fung about collecting socks from O.J.'s bedroom that were on the floor.

Q. Is there any particular reason that there is no time in your evidence collection report for those socks?
A. I collected those socks and did not tell Ms. Mazzola what time I collected them.

Q. You recall that?
A. It's obvious because the time is not written down.

Q. Mr. Fung, I'm asking you about what you remember, not what you're assuming.
A. No, I don't recall then.

Q. So, the answer is, you don't know any reason why the time is not written down?
A. I don't remember why the time is not written down.

Q. All right. What you just said to this jury that what happened was that you did not tell Ms. Mazzola what time you recovered the socks. That's something you're just speculating about, because you think it sounds good. Right?

MARCIA CLARK: Objection.
COURT: Sustained.

Many judges would have allowed the last question and not sustained Clark's objection. Clark objects because she believes it is an argumentative question. In any event, Scheck makes his point to the jury even if the sustained objection prevents an answer because the jury heard Scheck's point.

The reasonable answer based on common sense is that no one could remember several months after the crime why the time was not written down for the collection of one piece of evidence among hundreds of others.

The context for the next part of Fung clip 2 is that there was dirt spread around the steps of Nicole's townhome where the murders occurred. In the following excerpt, Fung refers to this as the "caged-in area" because that is the term the prosecution had used to describe the small fenced-in area where the murders took place, and they emphasized that the victims could not have run away from there once they were attacked.

While we have been looking at different ways to attack a witness, never forget to use the second S (Support Your Case) of CROSS. Scheck wants to show that since there was quite a bit of dirt where the bodies were found, the murderer should have tracked this dirt back to his home. Since there was no dirt found at O.J.'s house, this suggests, according to Scheck, that O.J. must be innocent.

Finally, when you look at the video, notice how Scheck uses his hands to support the meaning of his questions. Note, however, that Scheck makes a mistake similar to the one made in the earlier clip where he tries to look at the jury too much. See if you agree that it is too much.

Q1. Did you consider when you were examining the Bundy crime scene that in a struggle with Mr. Goldman, an assailant might have gotten that area of the shoes, and the socks, and the pants covered with soil from that area?
A. That is a possibility.

Q2. Did you see anything that could be consistent with that?
A. There was a disturbed area in the dirt area.

Q3. What do you mean by disturbed?
A. There was loose dirt in one portion of the caged-in area.

Q4. Loose dirt that could have been kicked up onto Mr. Goldman and an assailant during a struggle?
A. It's possible.

Q5. Now ... Mr. Fung, when you walked up the stairs at Rockingham on the afternoon of June 13, did you see any soil on the carpet of the stairwell?
A. **I did not notice any heavy staining** of the carpet, no.

Q6. Well, did you see any small flecks or flakes of soil on that carpet?
A. No. **[Fung's previous answer that he did not notice any heavy staining becomes very disingenuous when he admits in this answer that he did not even see any small flakes of soil.]**

Q7. In the carpet that covered the entryway to Mr. Simpson's master bedroom, did you see any soil or flecks of soil on that carpet?
A. No.

Q8. In the carpet surrounding the throw rug where you found the socks in Mr. Simpson's master bedroom, did you see any evidence of soil?
A. I did not see any.

Q9. On the throw rug where you found the socks, did you see any evidence of soil?
A. No.

Q10. Or dust?
A. Dust may have been present, but I didn't take a-

Q11. Did you-
A. ... take a note of it.

Q12. I'm sorry. You finished?
A. Yes.

Q13. Did you see on either sock any soil?
A. I didn't notice any.

Scheck employs a strategy worth remembering. In Q5-Q13 he breaks down the specific areas where dirt was not found at O.J.'s home—from the stairway to the bedroom to the socks themselves. By asking multiple questions, Scheck keeps the helpful issue before the jury for a longer period of time. His point would have been easier to forget if he had only asked one question: "No dirt from the crime scene was found at O.J.'s home, was it?"

The last part of the Fung Clip 2 shows the importance of ending the day on a strong point since jurors remember that point better than they remember points made in the middle of a presentation. In addition, the excerpt shows the realities of a lawyer trying to accomplish this goal when confronted by a court with different concerns; namely, getting as much accomplished in one day as possible. We can see this battle play out at the end of the excerpt.

The excerpt also provides another example of how Scheck uses physical evidence to prove his points on cross-examination. This is similar to the approach Lanier uses with emails and other documents in his cross-examinations (see chapter 6-8).

> **Practice Tip**
>
> Use photos or documents in your cross. A witness cannot dispute what they show. The exhibit always wins as long as it speaks for itself, which it usually does.

Here is the context for the following excerpt. The defense contended that the LAPD planted evidence to incriminate O.J. This not only included the glove in O.J.'s backyard that matched the glove found at the crime scene, but also O.J.'s blood that was found in various places, including on the gate of Nicole's yard.

The blood found on the gate had only a 1-in-57 billion chance of not being O.J.'s blood. Consequently, the defense had to show that collection of the blood had been tainted or fabricated. In the following excerpt, Scheck shows Fung some photos taken at two different times. The one on June 13 had less blood than the one taken on July 3, almost three weeks later. The implication was that someone had taken O.J.'s blood from the sample he had given upon his arrest and put it in on Nicole's gate after the earlier photos had been taken on June 13. According to the defense, what else could explain the additional drops found on July 3?

Another fact that supported the defense's theory of fabrication was that the blood taken from the gate in the later photographs on July 3 was almost in perfect condition, despite being out in the elements for such a long period. Indeed, it was in significantly better condition than the blood found right after the crime on the gate. The defense implied, "How could this later discovered blood be in better condition than the blood found much earlier unless it had been planted?"

One answer to the discrepancy is that the photo taken on June 13 was not of sufficient quality to show all the tiny blood drops on the gate. Consequently, the blood discovered on July 3 could have been present at an earlier time. But if the jury were inclined to believe that the LAPD had been sloppy in its evidence collection or planted evidence, then Scheck's line of questioning was persuasive.

Q. *Didn't you tell us on direct examination that you, looking at this picture* [**photo taken on June 13th**], *saw a mark here on the gate, which you thought could correspond to a blood drop that you saw on July 3rd?*
A. Yes.

Q. *That blood drop was designated on July 3rd to be item number 115 in this case. It also bore a photo identification mark of 115?*
A. Yes.

Q. *What you saw on July 3rd was also a blood drop that was marked 116?*
A. Yes.

Q. *Mr. [Hass], can we show that? You see what is marked as 116* [**photo taken on July 3rd**]*?*
A. Yes.

Q. *... as a blood drop on the rear gate?*
A. Yes.

Q. *That's what you saw on July 3rd?*
A. Yes.

Q. *Let's look back at the picture of the gate on June 13th. Where is it, Mr. Fung?*
A. I can't see it in the photograph.

Q. *All right, I think that's the-*
Court: You about to shift gears?

Q. *I really am.*
Court: Well, I mean we've got three minutes.

Q. *You want me to shift gears for three minutes?*
Court: Shift gears.

Q. *I may ask Mr. Blasier for a gear shift in [inaudible 00:06:56].*
Court: All right. Well, I see the lawyer for my 4:30 calendar is here. All right.

Q. *Last question here?*
Court: Last question.

Q. *Do you know of any other pictures taken of that rear gate on June 13th that show anything that could correspond to blood drop number 116?*
A. Are you talking about the photo item, or are you talking about the item number?

Q. *I'm talking about the item number 116, the blood drop that you saw on July 3rd.*
A. A photograph from June 13th?

Q. Yes. This is the best we can do of that gate area?
A. That's the best photograph that I'm aware of.

Q. On July 3rd, you saw blood on the mesh of the gate that you collected that became item number 117?
A. Yes.

Q. Have you seen any pictures taken on June 13th that display anything in the area of what you saw as item 117 on July 3rd?
A. I haven't seen any.

Q. Thank you your Honor.

COURT: All right, ladies and gentlemen, we're going to take our recess for the afternoon. Please remember all of my admonitions to you. Don't discuss the case amongst yourselves. Don't form any opinions about the case. Do not allow anybody to contact or communicate with you. Do not conduct any deliberations until the matter has been submitted to you. As to this matter, we'll stand in recess until tomorrow morning at nine o'clock.

This tug of war between Scheck and Judge Ito shows the difficulty in trying to end on a strong point at the end of the day. You never know how fast an examination will proceed. Even if you time it to within three minutes of a break or the end of court for the day, you might get a judge who won't let you stop. Many judges would, but when Ito pushes back, Scheck gets creative and finds a couple more questions to ask instead of losing his momentum and starting on another topic that he can't finish.

The two sets of clips discussed above show how the defense was able to argue its two main themes during cross-examination to get an acquittal. First, the LAPD was motivated by racial prejudice in a rush to judgment to convict O.J., as evidenced by Mark Fuhrman. Second, the scientific evidence that the prosecution claimed proved O.J.'s guilt was discredited by the LAPD's sloppy evidence collection, an example of which was provided by Fung's testimony.

Now, let's turn our attention to the last trial we will examine in this book, *State v. Zimmerman.*

10.4 BACKGROUND FOR *STATE V. ZIMMERMAN*

The facts of this case were discussed in chapter 1 but are repeated here for your convenience. On Sunday, February 26, 2012, 17-year-old Trayvon Martin and his father, Tracy Martin, visited Tracy Martin's girlfriend Brandy Green and her 12-year-old son, Chad Joseph Green. Green and her son lived in a townhome in a gated complex known as The Retreat at Twin Lakes, in Sanford, Florida.

Around 6:00 p.m., Trayvon left the home and walked to a 7-11 store to buy some Skittles and an Arizona fruit drink. On his way back to Green's house,

George Zimmerman saw him and called the police non-emergency number to report that someone (Trayvon) looked suspicious. Zimmerman lived in The Retreat at Twin Lakes and was the neighborhood watch coordinator.

Zimmerman explained to the non-emergency operator that there had been several break-ins in his neighborhood and "there's a real suspicious guy. . . . This guy looks like he's up to no good, or he's on drugs or something. It's raining and he's just walking around, looking about." Zimmerman further reported that "something's wrong with him. Yup, he's coming to check me out, he's got something in his hands, I don't know what his deal is."

The operator replied that the police were on the way. Zimmerman responded, "These assholes, they always get away." Later in the phone call, Zimmerman said under his breath, "fucking punks."

Meanwhile, Trayvon Martin was talking on his cell phone to his friend, Rachel Jeantel. What happened next was hotly contested at trial. Both sides agreed that before the police arrived, Zimmerman had shot one bullet from his licensed handgun into Trayvon's chest. Trayvon was pronounced dead at the scene.

When police interviewed Zimmerman at the scene, he told them that he shot Trayvon because Trayvon had thrown him to the ground, gotten on top of him, and started hitting him in the face while he was flat on his back on the sidewalk. At trial, the prosecution would argue that Zimmerman profiled Trayvon because he was black, then followed and shot him because he was so frustrated with the numerous burglaries that had occurred in his neighborhood.

George Zimmerman was charged with second degree murder. For second degree murder, the state had to prove that the killing was "done from ill will, hatred, spite or an evil intent." After the close of evidence at trial, the prosecution requested that the jury be given the lesser included offense of manslaughter to consider. The judge agreed. To prove manslaughter, the state had to prove that Zimmerman intentionally committed an act that caused the death of Trayvon Martin.

Zimmerman asserted self-defense to each of these charges. A person is "justified in using deadly force if he reasonably believes that such force is necessary to prevent imminent death or great bodily harm to himself." The danger facing Zimmerman need not have been actual; however, the appearance of danger must have been so real that a reasonably cautious person under the same circumstances would have believed that the danger could be avoided only through the use of that force.

In its opening statement, the prosecution said that evidence of Zimmerman's crime would come from the multiple lies he told to the police after the shooting to cover up the murder. The prosecution highlighted what it claimed were eight lies by Zimmerman:

1. He told the police it was just after his phone call to the police that Trayvon Martin approached him, said a couple of words to him, and punched him and knocked him to the ground. This could not have happened because the defendant hung up at 7:13:43, but Trayvon Martin's call did not end until two minutes later. During that time, the truth is that Zimmerman was looking for Trayvon.
2. The defendant told the police that at one point while he was sitting in his car, Trayvon ran behind some townhomes and then returned, circled his car, and ran away again. This is not true because, if you listen to the non-emergency call, it is physically impossible.
3. He told the police that the reason he got out of his car is because the police operator, Sean Nofke, told him, "We need an address." That did not happen according to the call.
4. Zimmerman told the police that Trayvon was straddled over him and covered his mouth and nose, which was already bleeding from the first blow. But there was no blood on Trayvon Martin's hands or fingernails. Nor was there blood on the cuffs of the sleeves of Trayvon's sweatshirt.
5. The defendant claimed that while Trayvon was on top of him, Trayvon said, "You are going to die tonight." This is a lie because no witness heard this.
6. Zimmerman said that after he shot Trayvon, he got on top of Trayvon's back and spread out his arms. That did not happen, because a neighbor took a photo that showed Trayvon's hands were underneath his chest.
7. Zimmerman said Trayvon went for his gun, but Trayvon's DNA was not found on it.
8. Trayvon's body was found 30 feet away from the spot where Zimmerman claims he was first knocked to the ground by Trayvon.

The prosecution also related that Zimmerman was seen by a physician's assistant the day after the incident. Zimmerman wanted a note from his physician so that he could miss work. She examined his nose. It was not broken and the biggest laceration on the back of his head was 3/4 of an inch.

The prosecution argued that Zimmerman was a wanna-be cop, because he was a criminal justice major, took classes in law of self-defense, wanted to go on police ride-alongs and became a neighborhood watch coordinator. He was told not to be a vigilante in his training. Because of all the crimes in his neighborhood, he profiled Trayvon as a criminal. The prosecution also pointed out that it was unlikely that Zimmerman would have seen Trayvon as a serious threat because Zimmerman had taken a year and a half of martial arts classes.

10.5 CROSS OF JOHN GOOD

John Good was the key prosecution witness at trial. Mark O'Mara conducted the cross-examination for the defense. John Good lived in the apartment complex where Trayvon Martin was killed. Of the few eyewitnesses, he saw the most, but it was not a whole lot. The lighting was bad and the struggle he saw lasted only about eight seconds before shots were fired. Good did not seek the limelight of this famous trial and was very careful with his words on the stand because he did not want the lawyers from either side to twist the description of what he saw to their advantage.

Ironically, although this is a cross-examination, the prosecution should never have called Good as a witness in the first place because Good helped the defense more than the prosecution. Consequently, defense counsel often asks more non-leading questions than normal because he does not fear bad answers and knows that he can elicit helpful ones. O'Mara certainly built his cross on the second S of CROSS to support his case.

Even though Good is a helpful witness for the defense from the outset, we can learn a lot from O'Mara's cross. He clears up confusing points that were made on direct and pushes Good to say things for the defense that he might not have otherwise said.

The cross-examination began with O'Mara briefly discussing with Good his reluctance to become involved in the case and his request for anonymity, which could not be accommodated. O'Mara continues by asking Good about the noise he heard outside his home. O'Mara then asks Good about his use of the words vertical and horizontal during direct examination as he described how the bodies were positioned when he looked out of his apartment. That portion of the direct will be presented first, then we'll look at O'Mara's cross (See John Good Clip at www.winningatcross.com).

Direct Examination of John Good

The prosecutor's questioning picks up after Good explains that he opened the glass door to his back porch because he heard a noise outside.

Q. *What do you see when you look out there at that time?*

A. It looked like a tussle. I could only really see one person. I think I described it as possibly being some type of dog attack because there are a lot of dogs that are in that back area and I could only see an object.

Q. What then did you observe after that?
A. It seemed like a tussle. They were vertical to me just like the blinds were. And then at one point I yelled out, "What's going on?" and "Stop it." I believe. [**The prosecutor tries but never clears up this confusing answer.**]

***

Okay. You mentioned when you put your foot out and you first saw something out there, you mentioned "vertical." Can you elaborate a little bit more on that?
A. If I'm looking at someone in the back yard, they're faced directly onto the ground, they're vertical, they are not horizontal to me.

Q. So, they're vertical the same way you are right now, like this?
A. So, they would be making a "T" with the sidewalk.

Q. Okay, alright. In terms of the sidewalk . . . .

The prosecutor fails to get the witness to accurately describe the position of the "object" he saw when he first looked out from his back porch. It is unclear from the questioning—and even more so as you watch the video—what is happening (this will be cleared up on cross). How can the object look like a dog fight if the object was vertical like a human being standing? If the object was really like an upright "T", it should have looked like an upside down "T" with the sidewalk being the horizontal line of the letter. What the witness means to say—as will be shown on cross—is that the bodies were on the ground but perpendicular to the sidewalk, so that they formed a "T" with the sidewalk.

***

Q. At that point [when the people were horizontal] . . . could you describe the individuals or just clothing descriptions?
A. Well, going back to when they were vertical, I could tell that the person on the bottom had a lighter skin color.

Q. And when you saw them horizontal . . . who was on top and who was on bottom?
A. It was the same position still.

Cross-Examination of John Good

Before you read the following excerpt, ask yourself what is the best way to clear up the confusion that was created by the exchange between the prosecutor and Good regarding the terms vertical and horizontal? It is the same way you should approach any problem on cross-examination.

Demonstrations Are Better Than Words

Q. You used the terms vertical and horizontal and I want to clarify those just so that we are on the same page. I am going to use horizontal as being laying flat on the ground. Okay?

A. Well, that's your perception of it if you are looking at them a different way.

Q. Okay. That's why I want to clear it up. I'm going to suggest, and see if we can agree for this conversation, that horizontal would mean that they are laying on the ground flat. I'm not saying anyone was yet, we'll get to that, but the term horizontal basically means you are laying on the ground flat.
A. They were laying on the ground.

Q. And then vertical would be as I am now standing up vertical. And we'll get to some more of that in a minute. But right now, can we agree that I am standing up vertically?
A. Correct.

***

Q. Tell me now, using the terms we have agreed to [horizontal and vertical] what was it you remember seeing? **[A non-leading question that can be used if the witness is friendly, which this one is.]**
A. They were laying on the ground. And if you fell back vertically, that is how I would be looking at them.

Q. So, if I was on my back, vertically, that was one of the people? **[This is a confusing question but O'Mara will soon fix it.]**
A. That was how I could see it.

Q. Okay. . . .the person you could see from the back, was he like this? **[O'Mara goes to the well of the courtroom, turns his back to Good and kneels down.]**
A. At the beginning, no.

Q. Okay. How was he and just sort of point me how he was when you first saw him?
A. You would have to go all the way to the ground.

Q. Over more, like that **[O'Mara leans over but is still on his knees]***?*
A. No, it was more just flat on flat.

Q. So it was one person horizontal on top of the other?
A. Correct.

Q. And when did that change?
A. When it moved up to the sidewalk.

Q. So as we now move closer to the sidewalk, what is the positioning of the two, of what you see?
A. It happened very quick.

Q. Okay.
A. But that is when it was more of a straddle position once it got on the sidewalk.

Q. And when you say straddle, can you explain that in more detail.
A. Can we get another visual?

Q. If you wish . . . .
A. No. It was more of just the person on top legs were over the person on the bottom who was laying flat on the ground.

Q. So, the person on top is like this **[O'Mara gets on his knees and spreads them a little wider than shoulder width]** *over the person on bottom?*
A. I would say that is accurate.

Q. Okay. And the person on bottom was laying flat.
A. Correct.

Q. Could you tell if he was on his back or not?
A. He was on his back.

Q. At this point, what is the person . . . on the top wearing?
A. It was the same person that was on top when they were T-shaped to the sidewalk.

Q. They did not change positions, did they?
A. No.

Q. Except the one on top wearing black, instead of laying down on the guy on the bottom was now straddling him, correct?
A. Correct. **[O'Mara returns to the podium.]**

Q. Now they are closer to the cement pathway, correct?
A. They would be on the cement at that point.

> **Practice Tip**
>
> Use visual aids or demonstrations whenever possible to make your point on.

O'Mara gets Good to paint a much better picture for the jury about the positioning of Trayvon and Zimmerman than the prosecutor did. He does this by using his body as a visual aid so that Good can direct him to certain positions so the jury can see what Good saw. When the prosecutor had the witness describe the positions using words, everyone was lost. When O'Mara conducted a demonstration with his body, the picture was crystal clear. To prove my point, look at the video clip and see how much better you understand what happened after viewing it.

Clear Up Confusing Testimony on Direct

Q. From the time that you first stepped out to watch them until the time you turned back around, was about eight to ten seconds?
A. I would say because it was very quick.

Q. Eight to ten seconds?
A. Yeah, it wasn't a long time.

Q. Okay. Mr. de la Rionda [the prosecutor] asked you if it could have been as little as two, and I thought you said, "yes." But it was a lot more than two wasn't it?
A. I didn't say the entire thing was two seconds.

Q. Ah, let's do that then. The entire time that you were actually watching what was going on?
A. Eight to ten seconds.

Q. And that's when you had your focus specifically on what turned out to be as we now know, George Zimmerman and Trayvon Martin.

On direct, Good had testified a couple of different ways on this issue. He certainly said at one point that he only saw the struggle for two to three seconds. On cross, O'Mara makes certain that he clears up this confusion. This example shows you the importance of listening carefully when opposing counsel is asking questions. You may need to add a topic to your outline for cross that you did not intend to discuss, as was done here by O'Mara.

Q. And, uhm, even in your initial statement when you first had an opportunity to talk to an officer about this the very first time, you were explaining as best you can recall what you saw?
A. Correct.

Q. And, uhm, what you saw was the person on top in an MMA style straddle position?
A. Correct.

Q. That was further described, was it not, as being ground and pound?
A. Correct.

Q. What is ground and pound?
A. That is usually what takes place in that type of position.

Q. Sure. So, MMA . . . is mixed martial arts?
A. Correct.

Q. You knew it enough to start giving terminology like ground and pound to what you saw, right?
A. It was the first thing that came to my mind, yes.

Q. That the person on top was grounding and pounding the person on the bottom?
A. That is what it looked like, yes. [**This question and answer is devastating to the prosecution. It supports the defense theory that Zimmerman was in reasonable fear of serious bodily harm and had the right to shoot Trayvon in self-defense.**]

Q. So, explain what ground and pound is in your mind?
A. Uh, the person on top being able to punch the person on the bottom, but the person on the bottom also has a chance to get out or punch the person on top. [**Good wants to be careful with his words and explains in this answer that the person on bottom is not defenseless. But O'Mara prods Good in the next questions to help the defense.**]

Q. Which is the dominant position?
A. The top position.

Q. Because why?
A. For most people that would be the dominant position.

***

Q. The person you now know to be Trayvon Martin was on top, correct?
A. Correct.

Q. And he was the one who was raining blows down on the person on the bottom, George Zimmerman, right?
A. That's what it looked like. [**Another devastating answer to the prosecution's case.**]

***

Q. That's when you saw him striking down?
A. That's when it looked like, yes, arm movement going downward.

Q. How many times do you think?
A. I have no idea. As soon as I saw all the movement going downward, that's when I turned around and went back inside.

Q. That's when you knew ***it was very serious****?*
A. Yes. It looked like it was getting serious and not just someone playing around.

Q. And that's when you can hear George Zimmerman screaming for help, right?
A. Incorrect.

Q. When was it?
A. That was in the beginning when I finally saw someone under the person on top.

***

Q. They are now in the true ground and pound position. And Mr. de la Rionda I think made some histrionics about what you heard [**O'Mara knocks on podium**] *so, I now have to do it as well, okay? Did you hear something like this?* [**O'Mara bends down and pounds fist on the floor.**]
A. No.

Q. Could something like that might have happened without you being able to hear it?

DE LA RIONDA: Objection, speculation.
COURT: Sustained.

Q. Were you paying attention to the noise of the ground and pound you were watching?
A. Probably not. I was just seeing to make sure if it was serious or not and that's when I went back inside.

Q. Have you ever heard the sound of a skull being smacked against concrete?
A. I can't remember.

Q. Have you heard the sound of a fist driving into a nose or a head or a face?
A. I can't remember.

Q. So, while it wasn't the histrionics that Mr. de la Rionda suggested, it certainly could be, it could have occurred that Mr. Trayvon Martin was hitting Mr. Zimmerman but you just don't remember today the sound of that?

DE LA RIONDA: Objection, speculation.
COURT: Sustained. Rephrase your question.

Q. *Sure, I'll rephrase it. . . . You're certainly not telling this jury that you know that Mr. Martin was not striking George Zimmerman in the face?*
A. I can't 100 percent confirm that that was happening.

***

Q. *You of course have testified at your deposition and at other times regarding what you heard . . . and the seeming disparity between what you remember hearing and what the 911 seems to indicate, right?* **[In Florida, depositions are allowed in criminal cases.]**
A. If you're referring to the call that was played at my deposition, yes.

Q. *Yes. It just doesn't seem like the same screams to you, does it?*
A. Well, one's coming from an audio [the tape] and one I was hearing in person [the night of the incident]. It did not sound the same to me.

Q. *So you perceived them differently than what you heard on the 911 call?*
A. Yes.

Q. *You are certainly not suggesting to this jury that they are not the same screams from different perspectives are you?*
A. I could not say.

Q. *You are aware that Ms. Lauer's call to 911 was timed perfectly with the screams that she heard and the gunshot that you heard?*
A. What do you mean?

Q. *You heard the gunshot, correct?*
A. Correct.

Q. *And you've also heard that gunshot on Ms. Lauer's tape?*
A. Correct.

Q. *So, going back in time from the gunshot backwards on Ms. Lauer's tape, there was probably 40 seconds worth of screaming [before the gunshot] . . . ?*

DE LA RIONDA: Objection, speculation . . . .
COURT: He can testify if he knows.

A. Can you repeat the question?

Q. *. . . We're going to listen to Ms. Lauer's call again, and as you're listening to it, I want you to think through . . . and I want you to testify what you remember seeing in the timeline with you hearing the gunshot?*
A. I won't be able to tell you.

Q. *I'm going to let you hear the tape and then we will go from there.* **[O'Mara is persistent and is determined to get the information he needs from the witness even if the witness is reluctant.]**
. . . .**[O'Mara plays Lauer's 911 call for jury]** . . . .

Q. *I know from different perspectives, but with your knowledge of the information in this case, that was the same gunshot you heard from inside your house?*

A. It did not sound the same. It sounded like a rock hitting my window because I was inside.

***

Q. It was only a few seconds before that gunshot that you were outside looking at the two individuals in the ground and pound positioning?
A. Correct.

***

Q. The yells, the "helps" that you heard were always the same voice, correct?
A. That I personally heard?

Q. Yes.
A. Yes.

Q. There is no second voice yelling anything was there?
A. Not that I heard.

Through his persistence, O'Mara gets Good to say that he was outside just before the gunshot and that he only heard one person screaming (Good will later say that person was Zimmerman). This is consistent with the 911 recording where there is only one person screaming. Consequently, unlike the suggestion during direct testimony, the voice screaming on the 911 call had to be the same person who Good heard screaming.

A Good Theme

Q. When you went outside that time out to your porch you actually told him to "stop," right?
A. I said, "Cut it out, stop," something like that.

Q. And the person who we now know to be Trayvon Martin on top didn't stop, did he?
A. No one stopped.

Q. He didn't even acknowledge that you were there?
A. I don't remember seeing anyone turn around.

Q. Did he even look at you?
A. No.

Q. He just kept doing what he was doing?
A. Yes.

Q. Even though you asked him to stop?
A. I guess I asked him, yes.

O'Mara paints the picture with several layers. Instead of just asking one question, "Did you tell him to stop?", he asks the same question with slight variations to keep the issue in front of the jury longer. Not only does the jury hear what

Good said, but the jury now knows that Trayvon ignored the request and "kept doing what he was doing."

Ending Memorably

Q. *And, uh, the voice screaming for help, however many times that you heard it, was just one person's voice?*
A. When I heard it outside? Yeah, I believe it was just one person's voice.

Q. *And you now believe that was George Zimmerman's voice, correct?*
A. I never said that. I said it could have been his, but I was not 100 percent sure.

Q. *I'm not asking for 100 percent certainty, I'm asking you to use your common sense and to tell us if you think that was George Zimmerman's voice screaming for help, the person on the bottom?*
A. That's just my opinion.

Q. *Nothing further, your honor.*

O'Mara ends on a memorable note. There would be several witnesses later in the trial who would identify the screams on the 911 call as being either Trayvon or Zimmerman (depending on if they were prosecution or defense witnesses). But Good is the only neutral eyewitness who could say that the screams came from Zimmerman.

To highlight what a mistake it was for the prosecution to sponsor this witness on direct, let's look at the facts that O'Mara was able to establish through his cross of Good (the second S of CROSS) because the prosecution had sponsored him. First, Trayvon was straddling Zimmerman in a mixed martial arts position while Zimmerman was lying on his back on the sidewalk. Second, Trayvon was grounding and pounding Zimmerman, which means it appeared he was punching him while Zimmerman was on his back. Third, it looked like Trayvon was "raining blows" down on Zimmerman. Fourth, there was only one person screaming for help. Fifth, the voice screaming for help was Zimmerman's. Sixth, Good told Trayvon to "stop," but he didn't. Seventh, Trayvon's assault on Zimmerman was so serious that Good called 911.

10.6 CHAPTER CHECKLIST

Cross-examinations in the Simpson Trial

1. Be precise in your questions and anticipate how a witness could evade your point. Bailey pins Fuhrman down on his claim that he never used racial slurs.

2. Use descriptive words in your questions. Bailey refers to Bell's letter as the "Bell problem." The witness does not deny this choice of words, which lets Bailey keep his theme before the jury each time he refers to the "Bell problem."
3. Use your theme from your opening statement in your cross and closing argument. Likewise, when your theme is powerful on cross, opposing counsel will need to respond to it in their closing as Clark did when she apologized for Fuhrman's conduct.
4. Bailey boxes Fuhrman into a corner from which he cannot escape when he asks, very precisely, "And you say on your oath, that you have not addressed any black person as a [n-word] or spoken about black people as [n-word]s in the past 10 years, Detective Fuhrman?"
5. It is fine to look rarely at the jury, but don't overdo it. It becomes insincere at some point and can backfire when jurors think you are becoming too biased for your side. In addition, jurors don't like their personal space being invaded by attorneys.
6. While cross-examiners focus on ways to attack a witness, never forget to use the second S of CROSS to support your case. Scheck wanted to show that since there was quite a bit of dirt where the bodies were found, the murderer should have tracked this dirt back to his home. Since no dirt was found at O.J.'s house, he must be innocent.
7. By asking multiple questions about areas that did not have any dirt, Scheck keeps the helpful issue before the jury longer. His point would have been easier to forget if he had only asked one question: "No dirt from the crime scene was found at O.J.'s home, was it?"
8. Use photos or documents in your cross. A witness cannot dispute what they show. The exhibit always wins as long as it speaks for itself, which it usually does.
9. End the day on a strong point. Jurors will remember it more easily and are likely to continue thinking about it until the trial starts the next day.

Cross-examination in the Zimmerman Trial

1. Clear up misstatements made on direct. O'Mara makes sure the witness explains that he saw the struggle for longer than the two seconds which he suggested on direct.
2. When the witness uses confusing terms on direct, such as horizontal and vertical, use a demonstration or visual aid to get the witness to explain the terms so that the jury understands your point.
3. O'Mara paints the picture of what Good saw with several layers. Instead of just asking one question, "Did you tell him [Trayvon] to stop?", he asks the same question with slight variations to keep the issue in front of the jury lon-

ger. Not only does the jury hear what Good said, but the jury now knows that Trayvon ignored the request and "kept doing what he was doing."

4. O'Mara is always in control. When the witness gives an unclear answer, O'Mara asks the right question until the witness gives a correct explanation.
5. O'Mara listens to the witness's answer as if he were on the jury. He senses when the jury is confused and clears up the confusion immediately.

ENDNOTES

Chapter 1

[1.] This is widely considered Daniel Webster's most famous speech, which was given in response to South Carolina Senator Hayne's speech that had widely gone off topic on the issue the Senate was considering—whether the sale of public lands should be curtailed and whether some land offices should be closed. Haynes had given a very emotional speech that further urged the rights of states to ignore federal laws. Webster's reply, which argued for the need to preserve the Union, was given in the U.S. Senate in January 1830, and at one time, its conclusion was required memorization in schools. For the complete speech, go to http://www.senate.gov/artandhistory/history/resources/pdf/WebsterReply.pdf.

[2] "The Lanyard" from *The Trouble with Poetry and Other Poems* by Billy Collins, copyright © 2005 by Billy Collins. Used by permission of Random House, an imprint and division of Penguin Random House LLC. All rights reserved.

Chapter 2

[1] Throughout this book, transcripts have been edited for length and clarity.

Chapter 4

[1] Since this was not a jury trial, the judge accepted a written statement of the expert as direct testimony that was submitted earlier in the proceedings. At trial, the witness swore that the statement was truthful, and it was admitted as evidence. Then, the cross-examination began.

Chapter 6

[1] As with the transcripts in all the chapters, they have been edited for length and clarity.

ACKNOWLEDGEMENTS

There are so many people that made this book a success. First, I want to thank Tom Girardi and Mark Lanier for their participation. Their generosity in sharing their time with me—and ultimately their skills with you—make this book what it is.

The book also benefitted from many reviewers. Among them are Carter Morris, who was a constant source of feedback and needed enthusiasm when writing got tough. He has observed virtually all of the DePuy hip implant bellwether trials. His wise counsel and wit made the Lanier chapters much better than they ever would have been without his participation. Also Kevin Keller, a fantastic prosecutor, who provided encouragement and sound guidance for the entire book. I also benefitted from the invaluable insights from my longtime friend and colleague, Quentin Brogdon. I was also fortunate to benefit from the wise advice from Sean Gallagher.

I am very lucky to have Tim Johnson for an editor. His expertise, encouragement, and steady hand improved everything about the book from the mundane punctuation to more significant issues of writing clearly and persuasively.

I am also grateful to Jason Bloom for his generosity and wise advice. Gloria Pennell, as always, provided unfailing support for my writing and vision for this book.

Finally, I want to thank my wife, Linda, who continues to support my passion to share with others what I have learned from my own trials and observing great lawyers. She has unending patience and belief in me and what I do.

ABOUT THE AUTHOR[1]

Shane Read is a nationally recognized expert who has helped thousands of attorneys throughout the USA and Europe transform their deposition, trial, and oral advocacy skills through his consultations, training programs, and keynote speeches.

He is the author of bestselling litigation textbooks that include *Turning Points at Trial, Winning at Cross-Examination, Winning at Persuasion for Lawyers,* and *Winning at Deposition.* Two of his textbooks have won the Association of Continuing Legal Education's top honor for Professional Excellence. He is the only author to win this award twice. His textbooks have been adopted in law schools across the country and critically acclaimed by publications such as Bar Journals and Kirkus Reviews. In addition, his textbooks have been endorsed by judges, professors, a former U.S. Attorney General, a former U.S. Solicitor General, and past presidents of city, state and national trial lawyers' organizations such as IATL and ABOTA.

He has been an adjunct professor in trial advocacy since 1999 at Southern Methodist University's Dedman School of Law. He has also taught new and experienced lawyers throughout the United States, including training programs at national law firms, the National Institute of Trial Advocacy's headquarters, the Department of Justice's National Advocacy Center, and state bars around the country.

He is a graduate of Yale University and the University of Texas School of Law. He began his legal career in 1989 at Akin Gump in Dallas, before joining the U.S. Attorney's Office in Washington, D.C., from 1992 to 1998. Since 1998, he has worked at the U.S. Attorney's Office in Dallas in both the civil and criminal sections. He has tried over 100 trials to verdict over the past 30 years and has served as lead counsel for 22 oral arguments before appellate courts.

For more information go to www.shaneread.com.

[1]The views expressed in this book are solely those of the author and do not reflect the views of the Department of Justice.

INDEX

A

C

E

F

G

H

I

J

N

O

P

Q

U

V

W

Y

Z

Made in the USA
Monee, IL
13 September 2026

62979541R10208